I decided to become a manga artist when I was in second grade, but before that, I supposedly claimed I would grow up to be a fire truck. There's always a turning point in life. Here's *World Trigger* volume 3.

—Daisuke Ashihara, 2013

Daisuke Ashihara began his manga career at the age of 27 when his manga *Room 303* won second place in the 75th Tezuka Awards. His first series, *Super Dog Rilienthal*, began serialization in *Weekly Shonen Jump* in 2009. *World Trigger* is his second serialized work in *Weekly Shonen Jump*. He is also the author of several shorter works, including the one-shots *Super Dog Rilienthal*, *Trigger Keeper* and *Elite Agent Jin*.

WORLD TRIGGER VOL. 3
SHONEN JUMP Manga Edition

STORY AND ART BY DAISUKE ASHIHARA

Translation/Lillian Olsen
Touch-Up Art & Lettering/Annaliese Christman
Design/Sam Elzway
Editor/Hope Donovan

WORLD TRIGGER © 2013 by Daisuke Ashihara/SHUEISHA Inc.
All rights reserved.
First published in Japan in 2013 by SHUEISHA Inc., Tokyo.
English translation rights arranged by SHUEISHA Inc.

The stories, characters and incidents mentioned
in this publication are entirely fictional.

Printed in the U.S.A.

Published by VIZ Media, LLC
P.O. Box 77010
San Francisco, CA 94107

10 9 8 7 6 5 4 3 2 1
First printing, December 2014

SHONEN JUMP MANGA EDITION

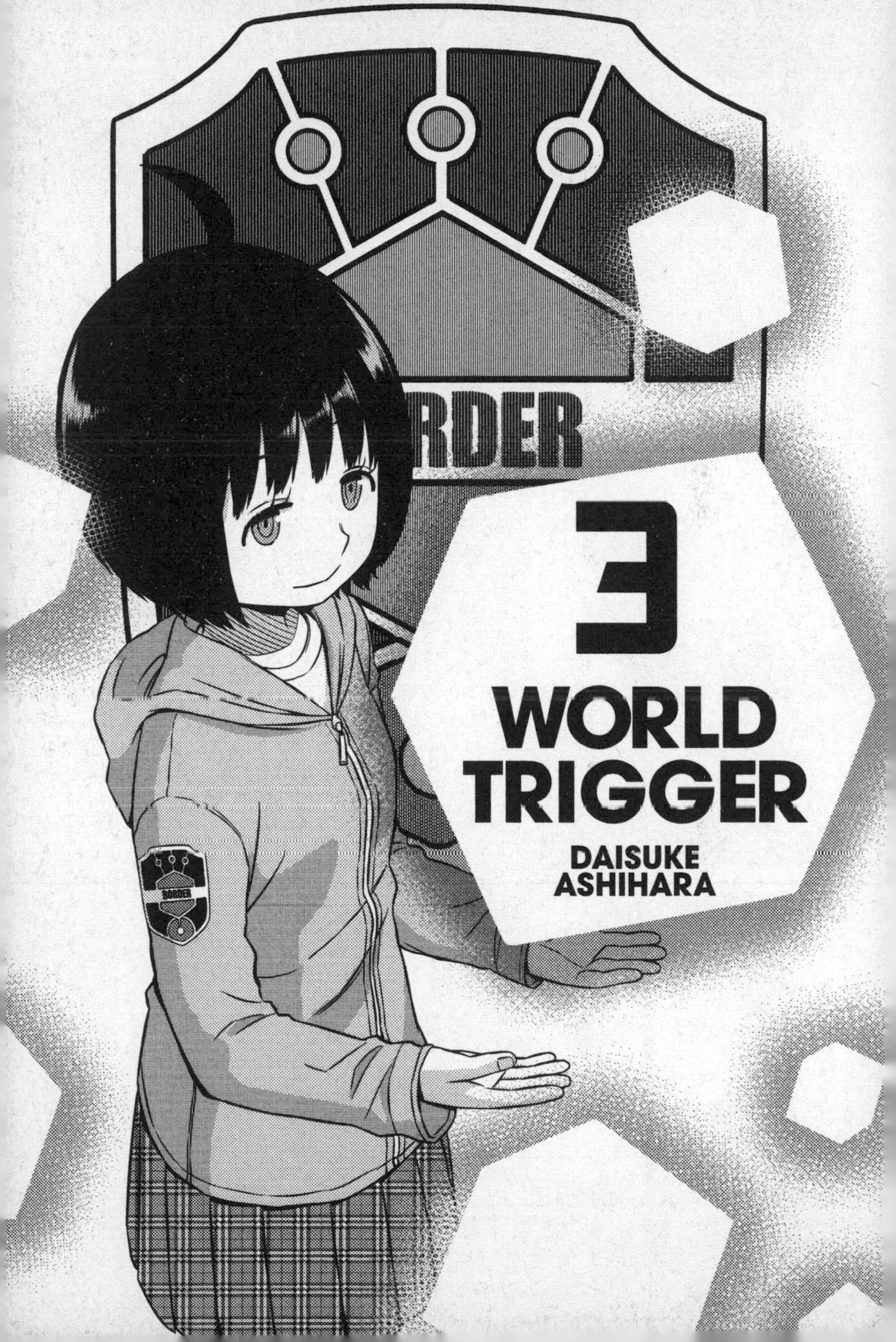

3

WORLD TRIGGER

DAISUKE ASHIHARA

WORLD TRIGGER CHARACTERS

REPLICA

Yuma's chaperone.

OSAMU MIKUMO

Ninth-grader who's compelled to help those in trouble. Border agent.

YUMA KUGA

Since he's a Neighbor, he lacks common sense. Has a Black Trigger.

YUICHI JIN

S-Rank Border agent. Can see the future with his Side Effect. Has a Black Trigger?

CHIKA AMATORI

Targeted by Neighbors because of her high Trion levels.

ARASHIYAMA SQUAD

HQ's A-Rank #5 squad. As the face of Border, they're celebrities in Mikado City.

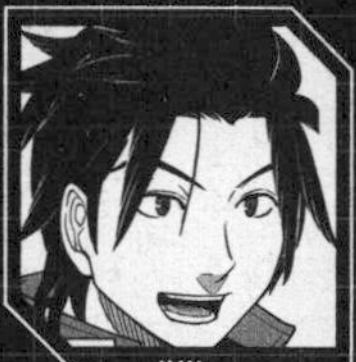
JUN ARASHIYAMA

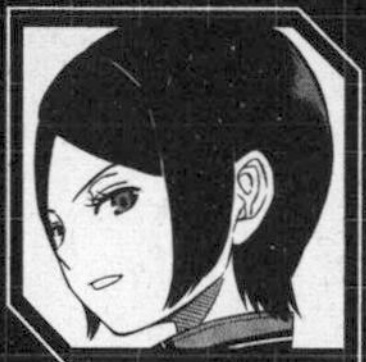
AI KITORA

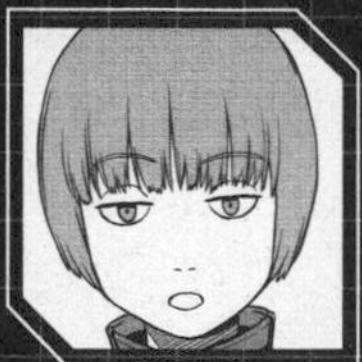
MITSURU TOKIEDA

MIWA SQUAD

HQ's A-Rank #7 squad. Captain Miwa blames Neighbors for the death of his older sister.

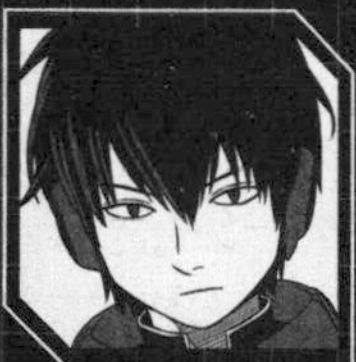
SHUJI MIWA

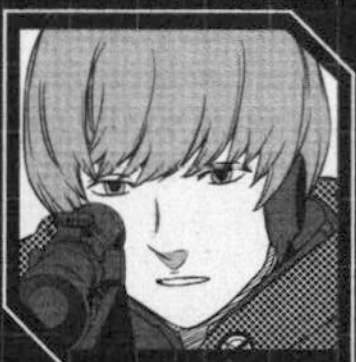
TORU NARASAKA

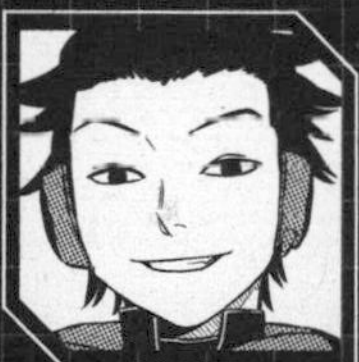
YOSUKE YONEYA

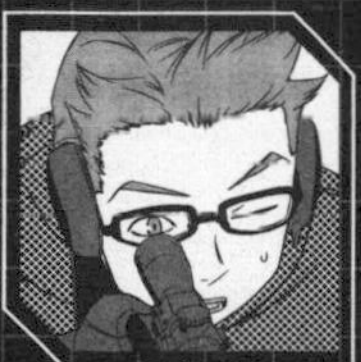
SHOHEI KODERA

BORDER SENIOR OFFICERS

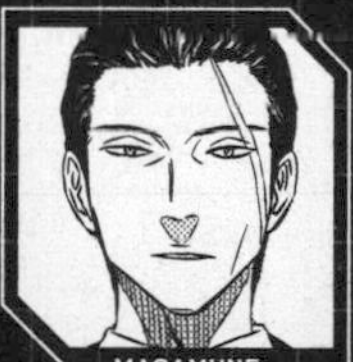
MASAMUNE KIDO

HQ Commander

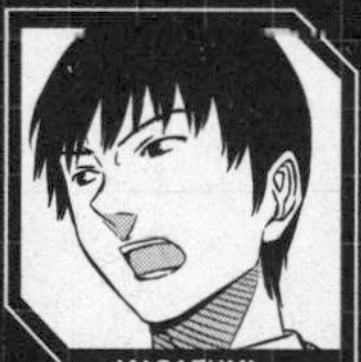
MASAFUMI SHINODA

HQ Director, Defense Force Commander

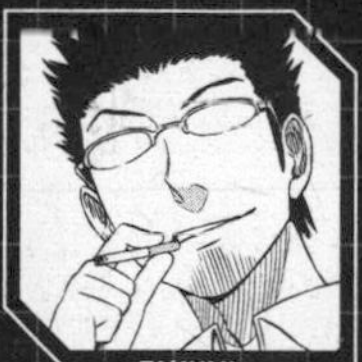
TAKUMI RINDO

Tamakoma Branch Director

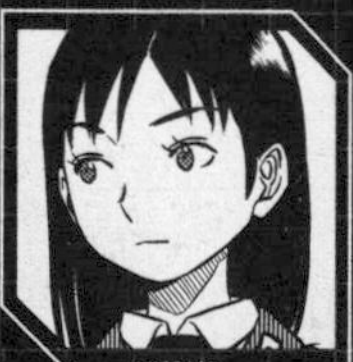
KYOKO SAWAMURA

HQ Assistant Director

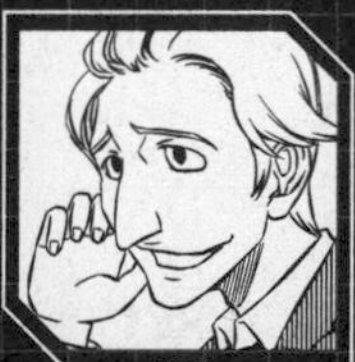
EIZO NETSUKI

PR Director

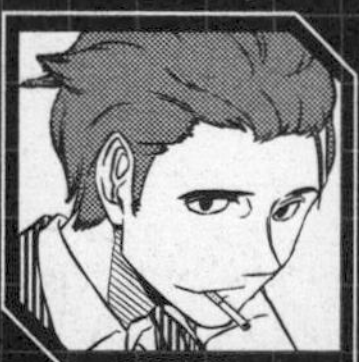
KATSUMI KARASAWA

Business Director

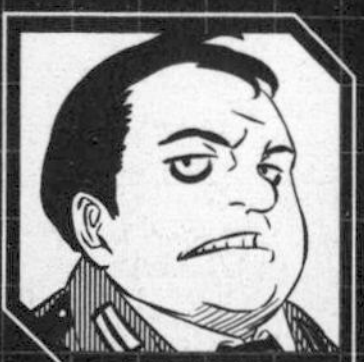
MOTOKICHI KINUTA

R&D Director

WORLD TRIGGER DATA BASE

Neighbors

Invaders from another world appearing in Mikado City through Gates. Most of the "Neighbors" are Trion soldiers built for war. The Neighbors who actually live on the other side of the Gates are human, like Yuma.

▼ Trion solider built for war

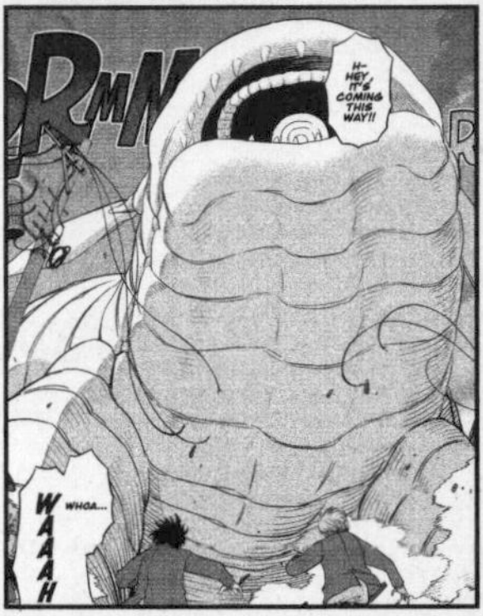
H-HEY, IT'S COMING THIS WAY!!
WHOA...
WAAAAH

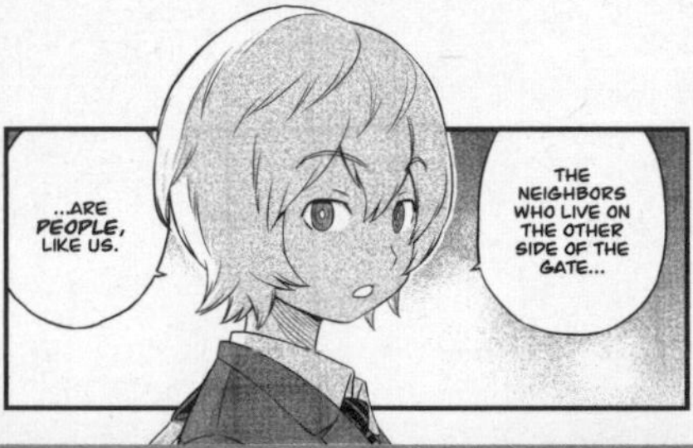
THE NEIGHBORS WHO LIVE ON THE OTHER SIDE OF THE GATE...
...ARE PEOPLE, LIKE US.

Invasion ▽ △ Resistance

Border

Its official name is the Border Defense Agency, or "Border" for short. Its purpose is to research Neighbor technology and protect the city from Neighbors. Agents are classified as follows: C-Rank for trainees, B-Rank for main forces and A-Rank for elites.

A-Rank (elite) About 30 people

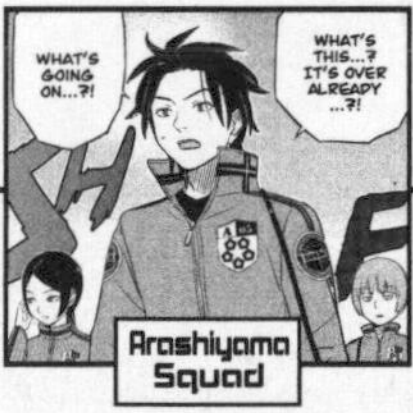
WHAT'S THIS...?! IT'S OVER ALREADY ...?!
WHAT'S GOING ON...?!
Arashiyama Squad

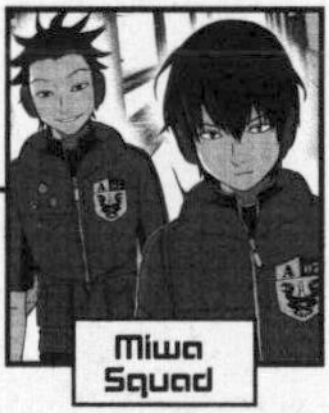
Miwa Squad

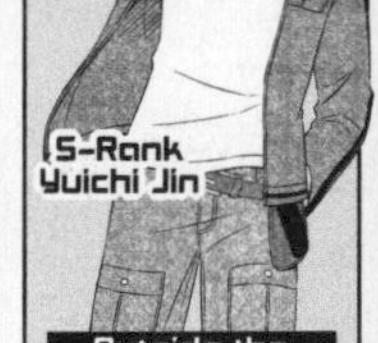
YO!
S-Rank Yuichi Jin

Outside the rankings

B-Rank (main force) About 100 people

Osamu is here!!

C-Rank (trainees) About 400 people

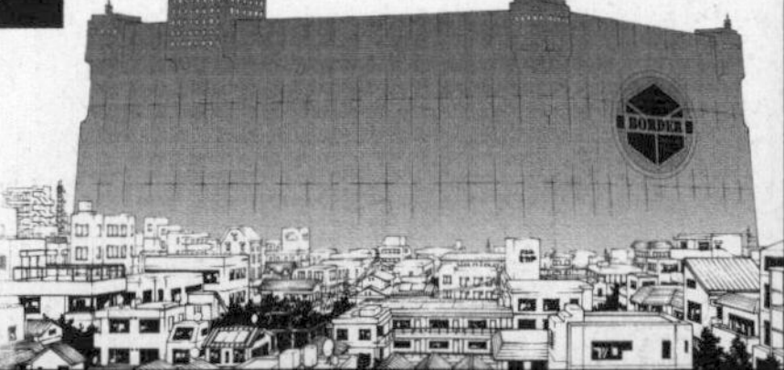
BORDER

Trigger

Technology created by Neighbors to manipulate Trion. Used mainly as weapons, there are various types.

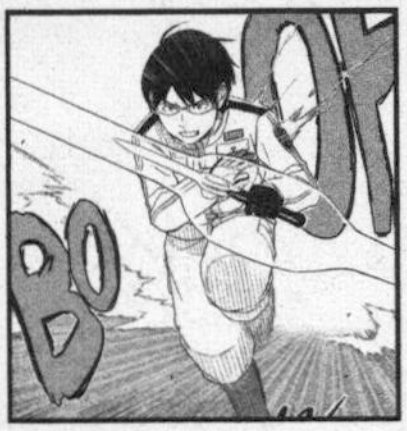

▲ Trainee Trigger

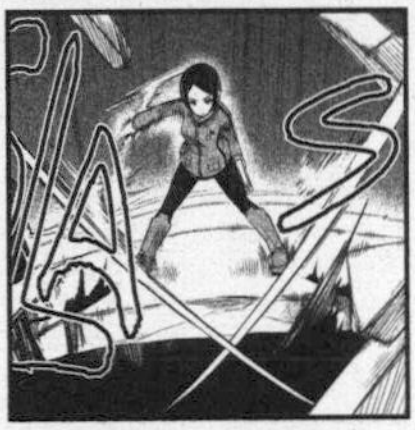

▲ Border Agent Trigger

▼ Black Trigger

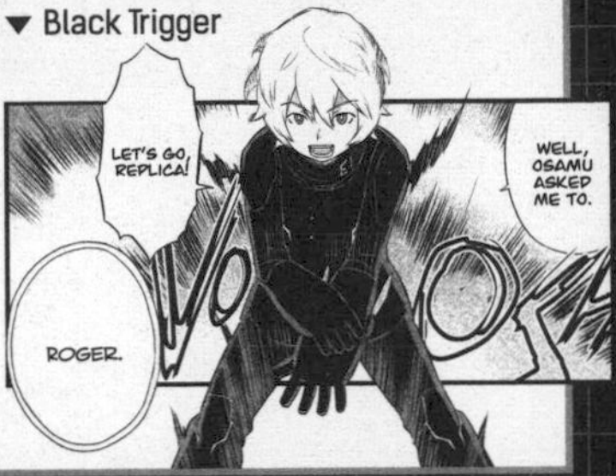
WELL, OSAMU ASKED ME TO.
LET'S GO, REPLICA!
ROGER.

Trion

A Trigger's energy source. Everyone has a Trion gland, but they're not all equal. Two people using the same Trigger may get different results.

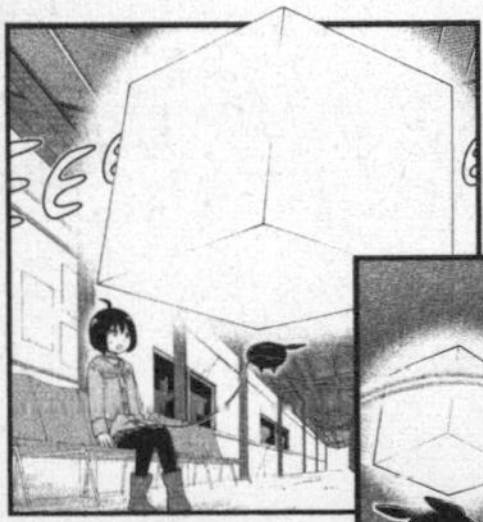

◀ Chika's Trion level

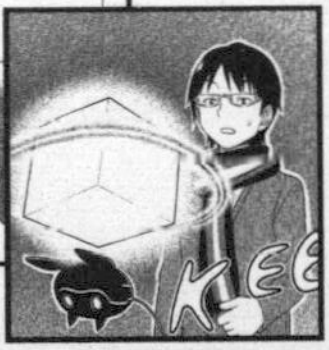

▶ Osamu's Trion level

Side Effect

Term for extrasensory perception abilities manifested by rare individuals with high Trion levels. A Side Effect is not a supernatural ability; rather, it is an extension of a human ability.

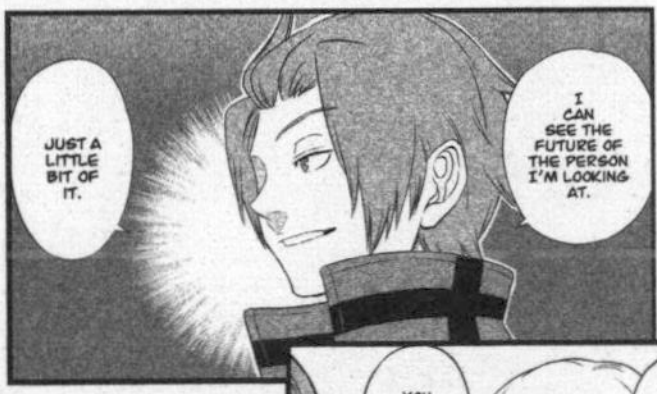
I CAN SEE THE FUTURE OF THE PERSON I'M LOOKING AT.
JUST A LITTLE BIT OF IT.

▲ Jin sees the future

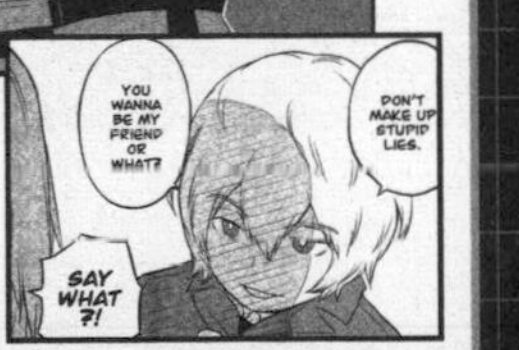
DON'T MAKE UP STUPID LIES.
YOU WANNA BE MY FRIEND OR WHAT?
SAY WHAT ?!

▶ Yuma detects lies

STORY

About four years ago, a Gate connecting to another dimension opened in Mikado City, leading to the appearance of invaders called Neighbors. After the establishment of the Border Defense Agency, people were able to return to their normal lives.

Osamu Mikumo is a C-Rank Border trainee and junior high student who finds out that transfer student Yuma Kuga is a Neighbor. Osamu gets drawn into Neighbor attacks, and is threatened with being expelled from Border. With S-Rank agent Yuichi Jin's help, he ends up promoted to B-Rank instead. Meanwhile, Yuma meets Chika Amatori, a girl targeted by Neighbors who is, by chance, also Osamu's friend. Just then, Miwa Squad, suspicious that Yuma's a Neighbor, attacks him. Yuma beats them back, but Border HQ finds out that he's a Neighbor with a Black Trigger. Commander Kido orders Yuma's capture!

WORLD TRIGGER
CONTENTS

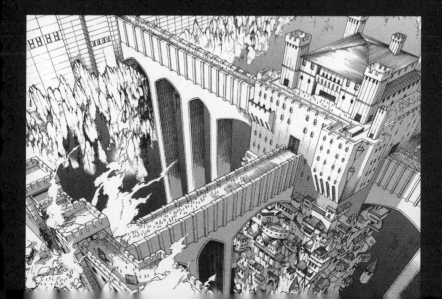

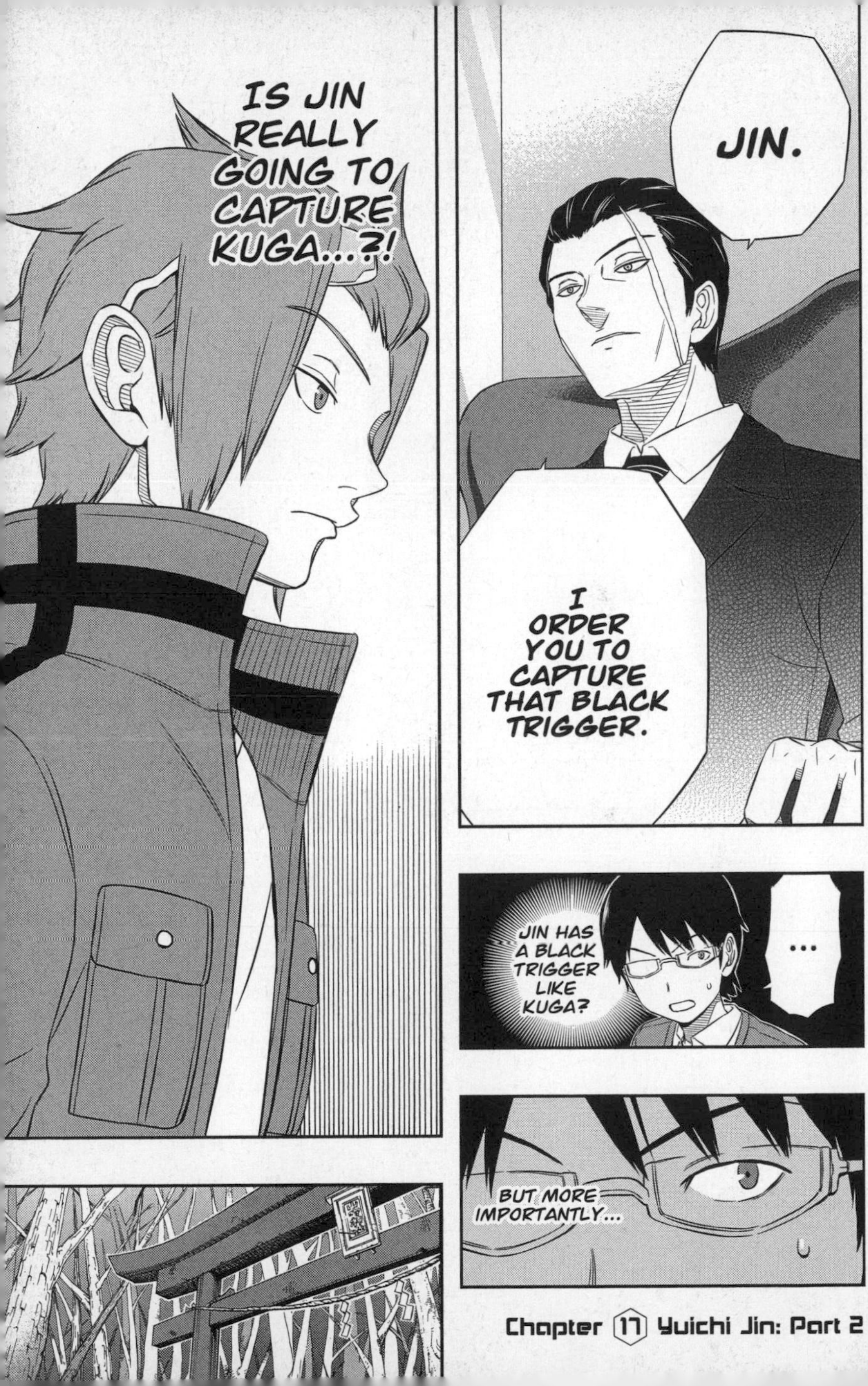
JIN.
I ORDER YOU TO CAPTURE THAT BLACK TRIGGER.
IS JIN REALLY GOING TO CAPTURE KUGA...?!
...
JIN HAS A BLACK TRIGGER LIKE KUGA?
BUT MORE IMPORTANTLY...

Chapter 17 Yuichi Jin: Part 2

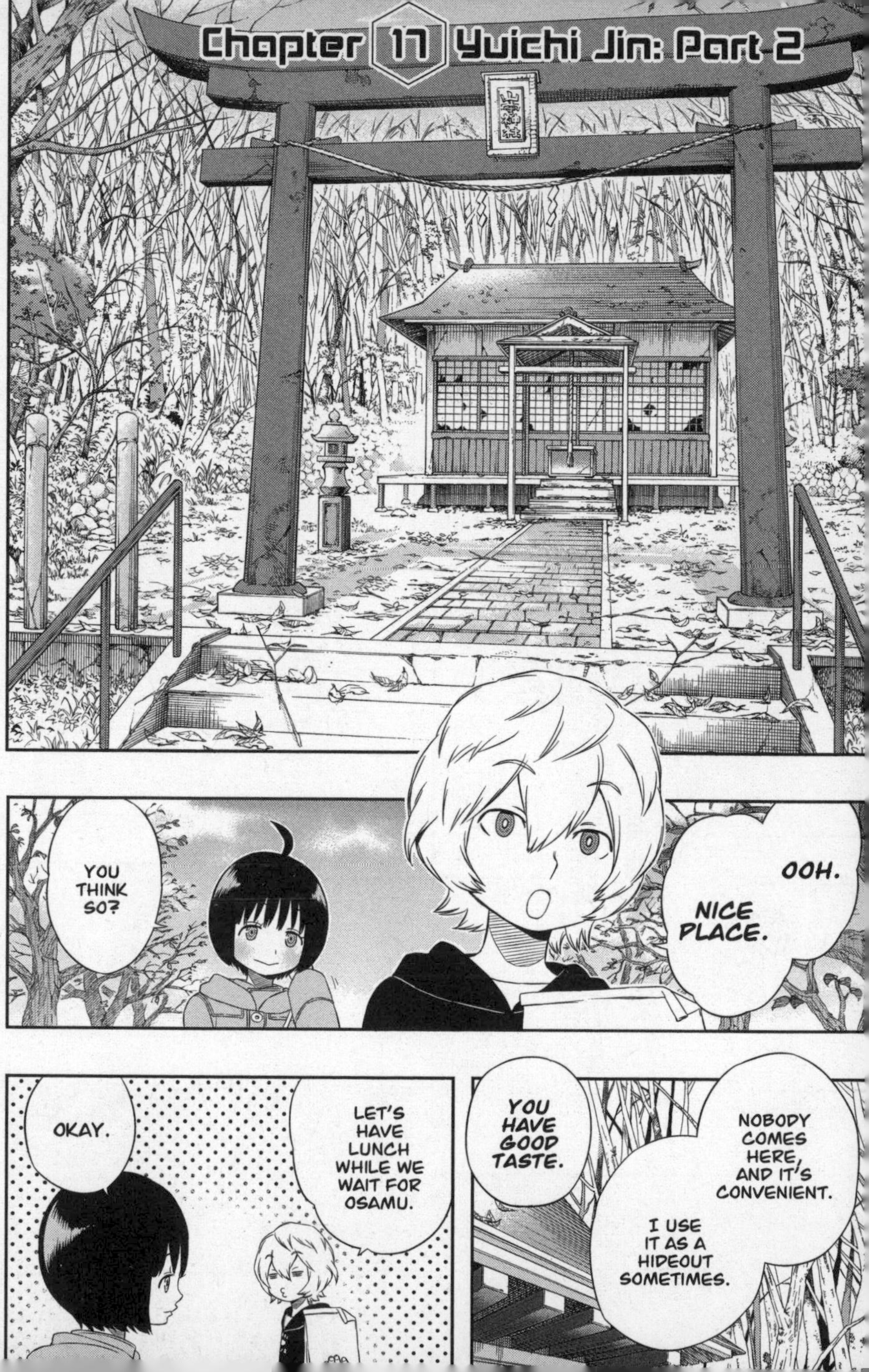
Chapter 17 Yuichi Jin: Part 2
OOH.
NICE PLACE.
YOU THINK SO?
NOBODY COMES HERE, AND IT'S CONVENIENT.
I USE IT AS A HIDEOUT SOMETIMES.
YOU HAVE GOOD TASTE.
LET'S HAVE LUNCH WHILE WE WAIT FOR OSAMU.
OKAY.

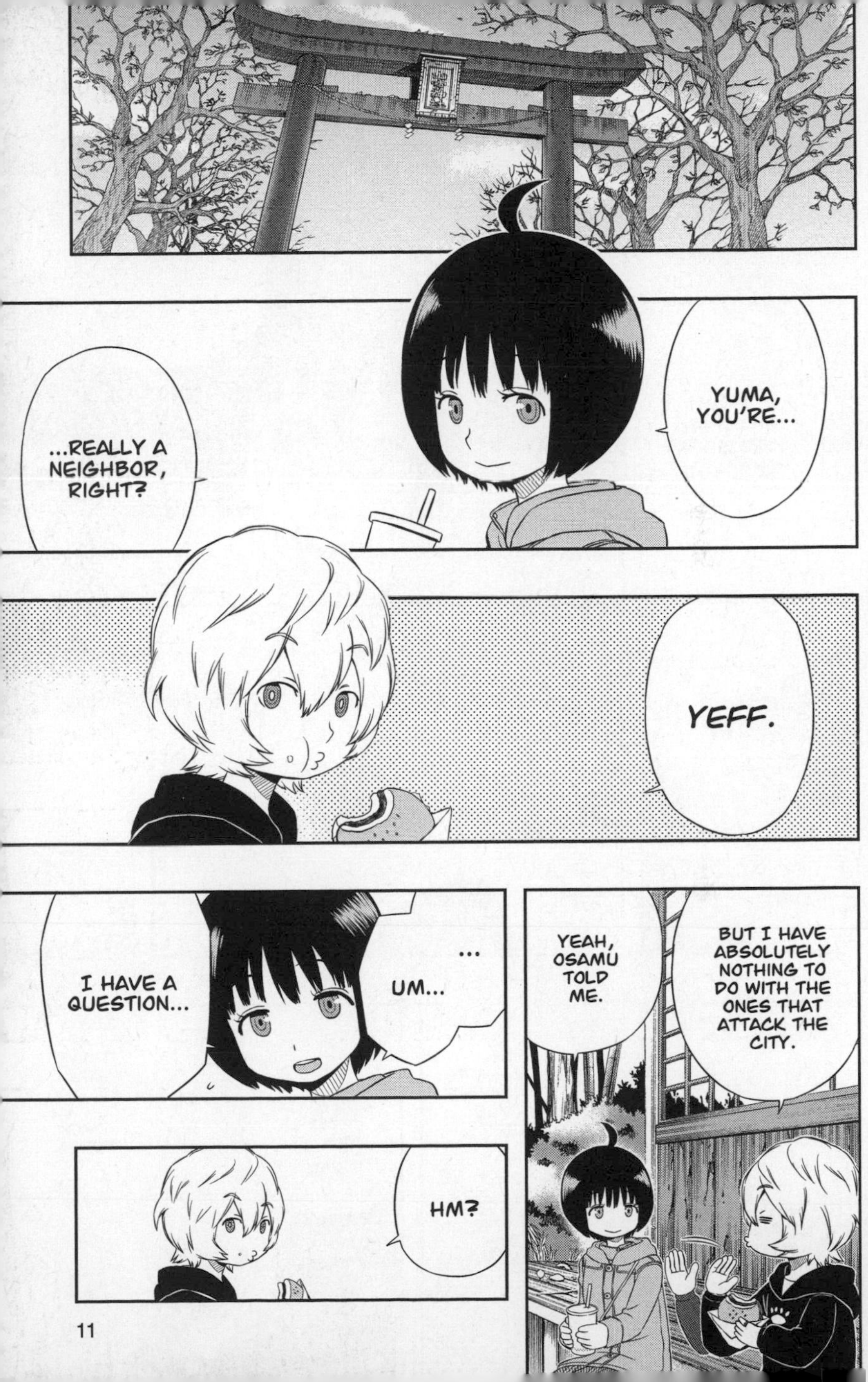
YUMA, YOU'RE...
...REALLY A NEIGHBOR, RIGHT?
YEFF.
BUT I HAVE ABSOLUTELY NOTHING TO DO WITH THE ONES THAT ATTACK THE CITY.
YEAH, OSAMU TOLD ME.
...
UM...
I HAVE A QUESTION...
HM?

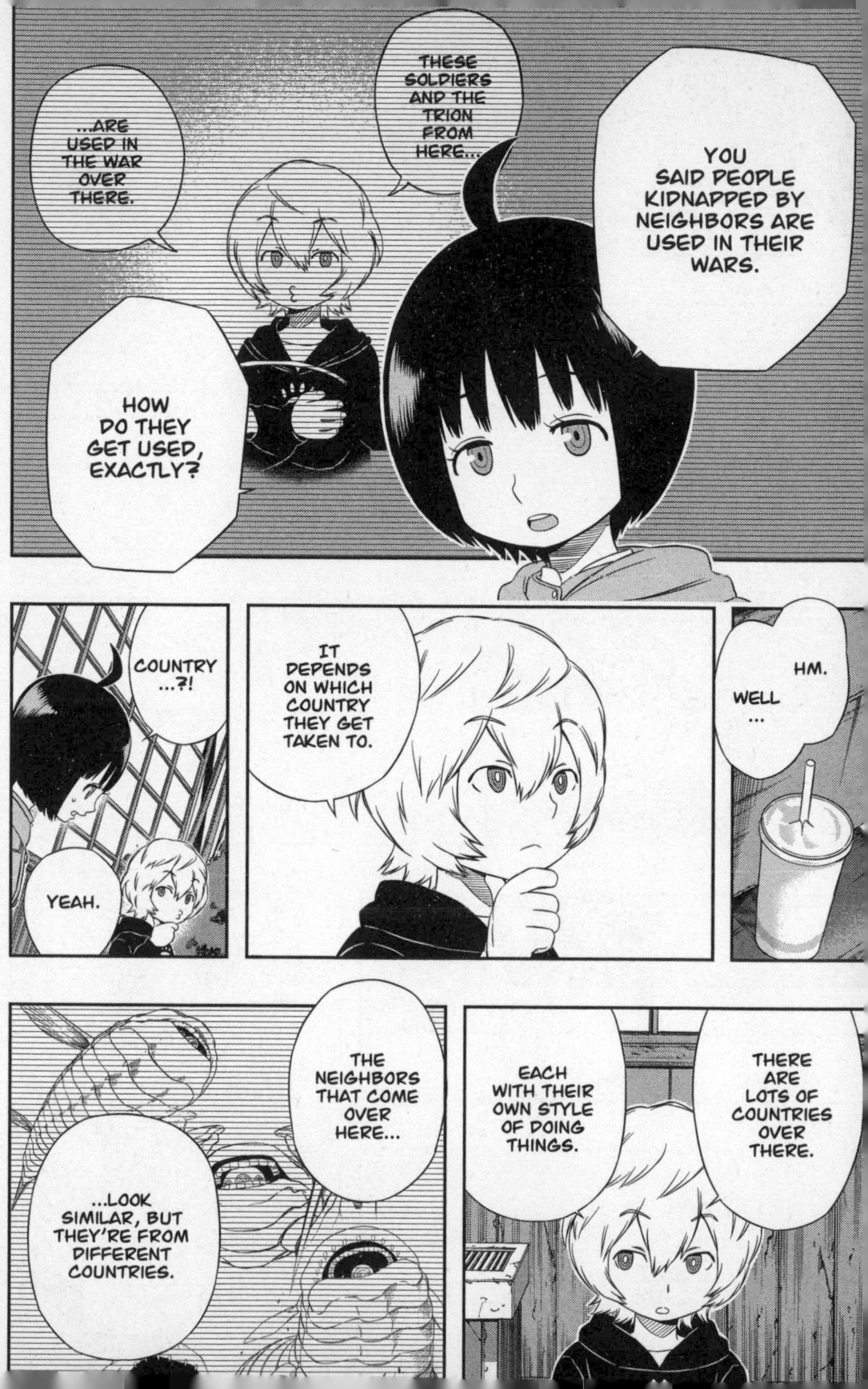
YOU SAID PEOPLE KIDNAPPED BY NEIGHBORS ARE USED IN THEIR WARS.
THESE SOLDIERS AND THE TRION FROM HERE...
...ARE USED IN THE WAR OVER THERE.
HOW DO THEY GET USED, EXACTLY?
HM.
WELL...
IT DEPENDS ON WHICH COUNTRY THEY GET TAKEN TO.
COUNTRY...?!
YEAH.
THERE ARE LOTS OF COUNTRIES OVER THERE.
EACH WITH THEIR OWN STYLE OF DOING THINGS.
THE NEIGHBORS THAT COME OVER HERE...
...LOOK SIMILAR, BUT THEY'RE FROM DIFFERENT COUNTRIES.

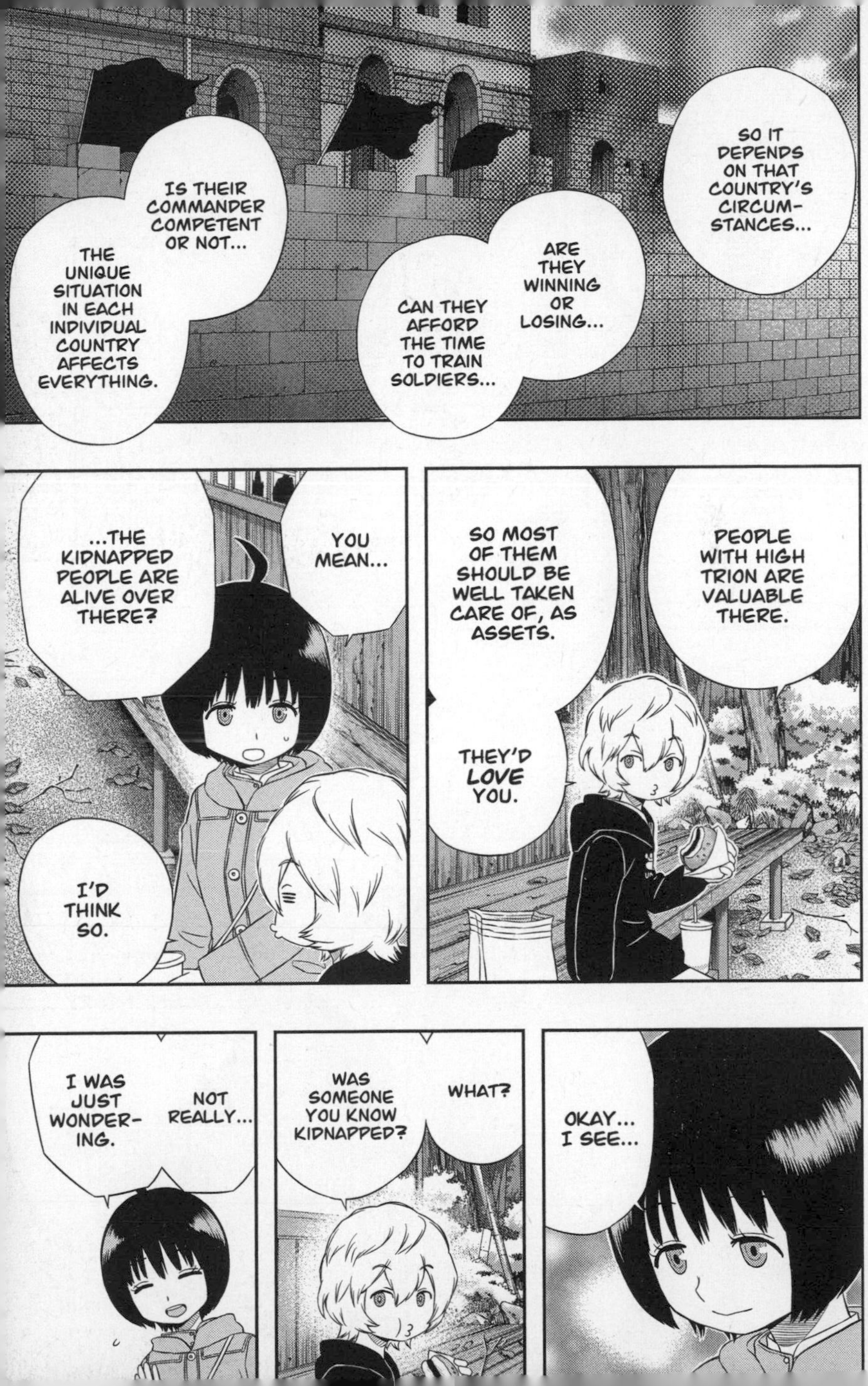
SO IT DEPENDS ON THAT COUNTRY'S CIRCUM-STANCES...
ARE THEY WINNING OR LOSING...
CAN THEY AFFORD THE TIME TO TRAIN SOLDIERS...
IS THEIR COMMANDER COMPETENT OR NOT...
THE UNIQUE SITUATION IN EACH INDIVIDUAL COUNTRY AFFECTS EVERYTHING.
PEOPLE WITH HIGH TRION ARE VALUABLE THERE.
SO MOST OF THEM SHOULD BE WELL TAKEN CARE OF, AS ASSETS.
THEY'D *LOVE* YOU.
YOU MEAN...
...THE KIDNAPPED PEOPLE ARE ALIVE OVER THERE?
I'D THINK SO.
OKAY... I SEE...
WHAT?
WAS SOMEONE YOU KNOW KIDNAPPED?
NOT REALLY...
I WAS JUST WONDER-ING.

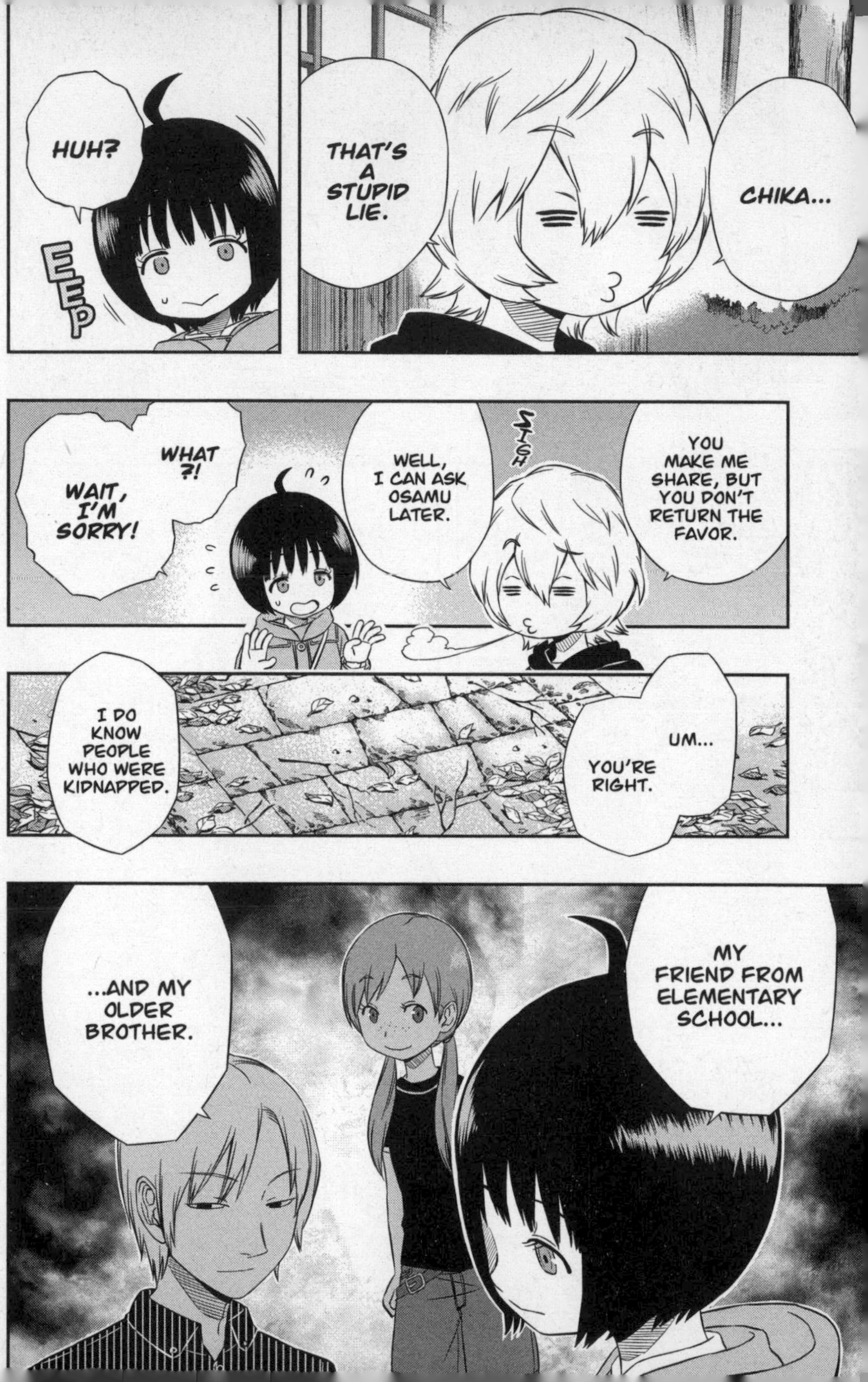
CHIKA...
THAT'S A STUPID LIE.
HUH?
EEP
YOU MAKE ME SHARE, BUT YOU DON'T RETURN THE FAVOR.
SIGH
WELL, I CAN ASK OSAMU LATER.
WHAT?!
WAIT, I'M SORRY!
UM...
YOU'RE RIGHT.
I DO KNOW PEOPLE WHO WERE KIDNAPPED.
MY FRIEND FROM ELEMENTARY SCHOOL...
...AND MY OLDER BROTHER.

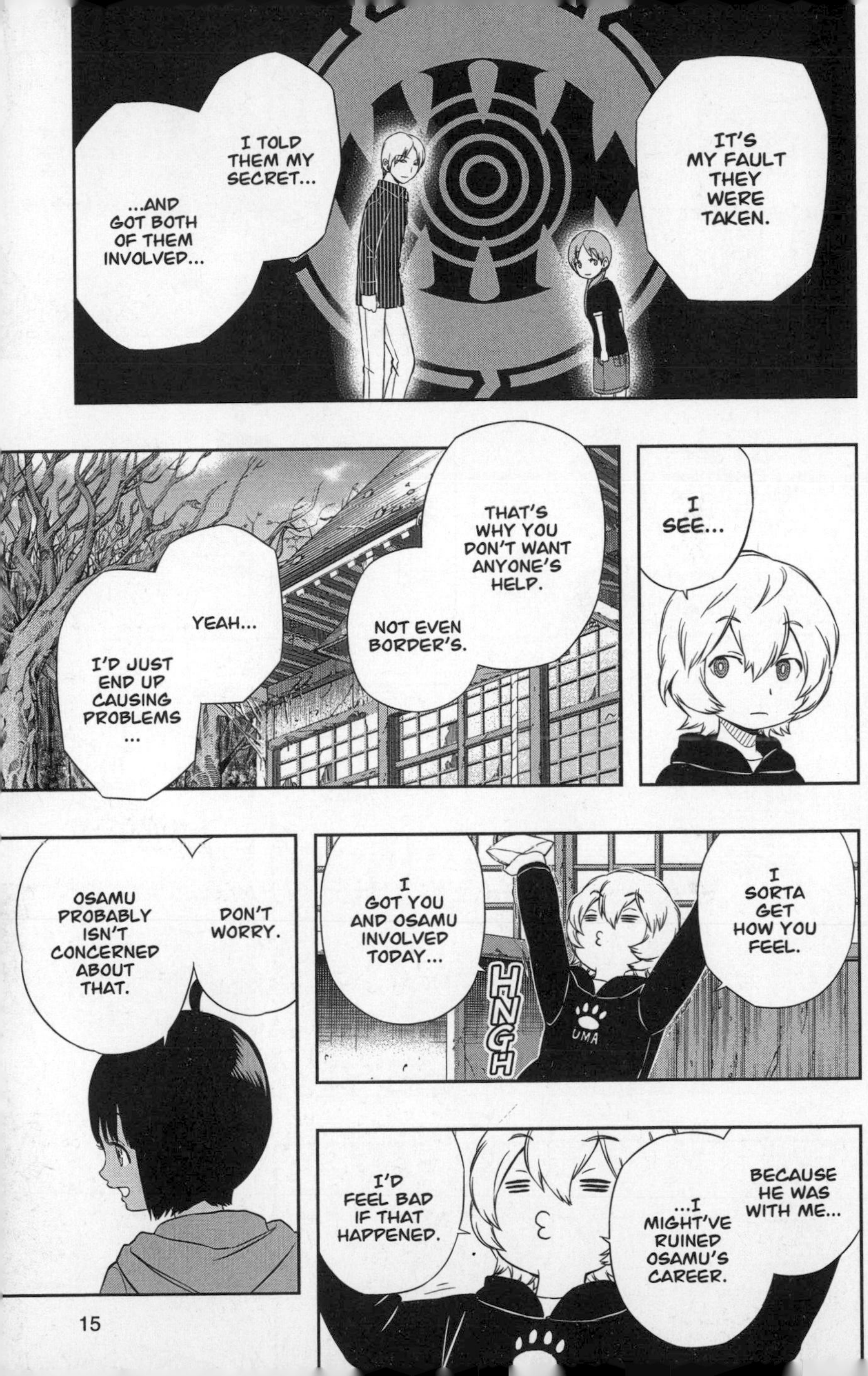
IT'S MY FAULT THEY WERE TAKEN.
I TOLD THEM MY SECRET...
...AND GOT BOTH OF THEM INVOLVED...
I SEE...
THAT'S WHY YOU DON'T WANT ANYONE'S HELP.
NOT EVEN BORDER'S.
YEAH...
I'D JUST END UP CAUSING PROBLEMS...
I SORTA GET HOW YOU FEEL.
I GOT YOU AND OSAMU INVOLVED TODAY...
HNGH
UMA
BECAUSE HE WAS WITH ME...
...I MIGHT'VE RUINED OSAMU'S CAREER.
I'D FEEL BAD IF THAT HAPPENED.
DON'T WORRY.
OSAMU PROBABLY ISN'T CONCERNED ABOUT THAT.

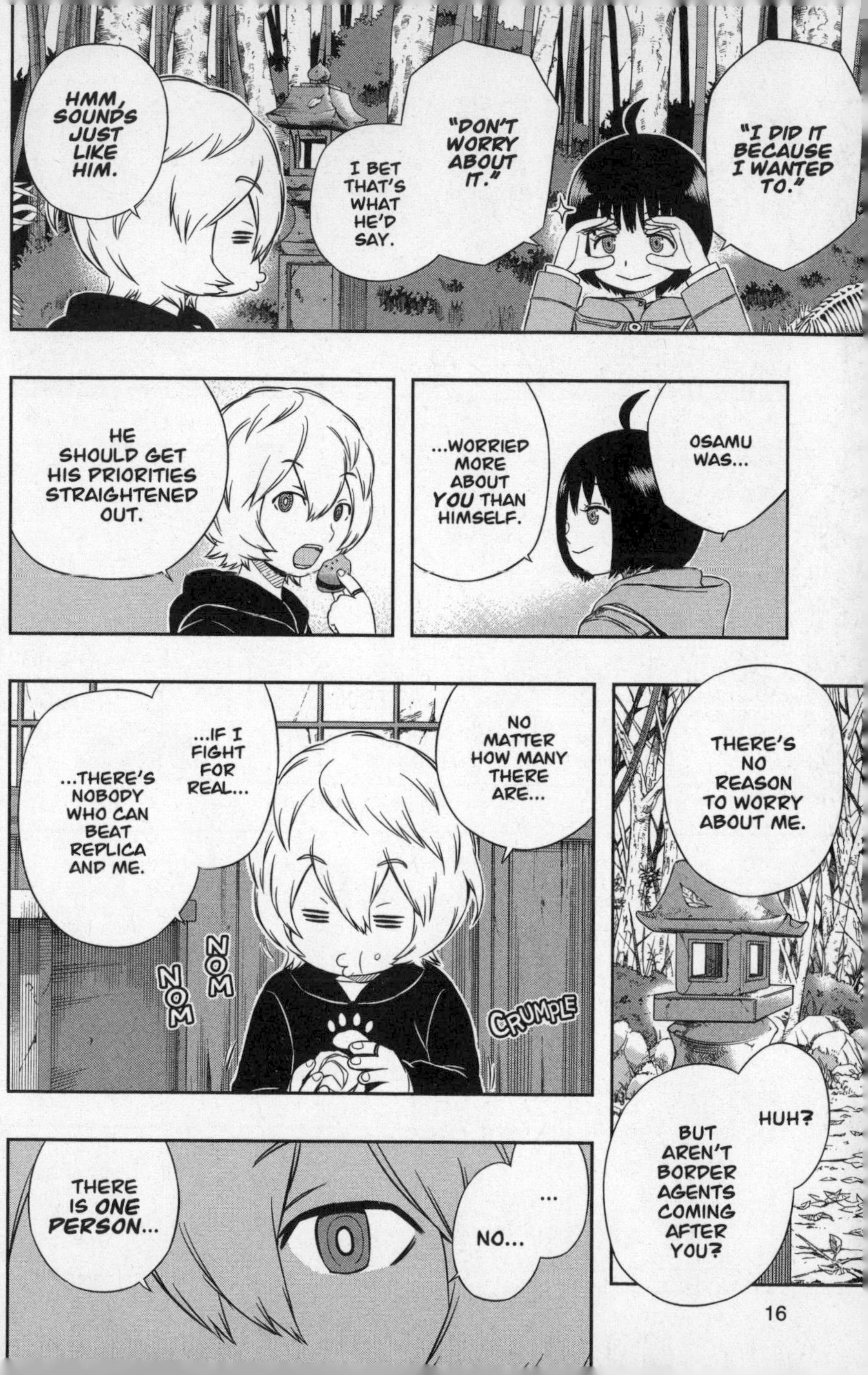
"I DID IT BECAUSE I WANTED TO."
"DON'T WORRY ABOUT IT."
I BET THAT'S WHAT HE'D SAY.
HMM, SOUNDS JUST LIKE HIM.
OSAMU WAS...
...WORRIED MORE ABOUT YOU THAN HIMSELF.
HE SHOULD GET HIS PRIORITIES STRAIGHTENED OUT.
THERE'S NO REASON TO WORRY ABOUT ME.
HUH?
BUT AREN'T BORDER AGENTS COMING AFTER YOU?
NO MATTER HOW MANY THERE ARE...
...IF I FIGHT FOR REAL...
...THERE'S NOBODY WHO CAN BEAT REPLICA AND ME.
NOM
NOM
CRUMPLE
...
NO...
THERE IS ONE PERSON...

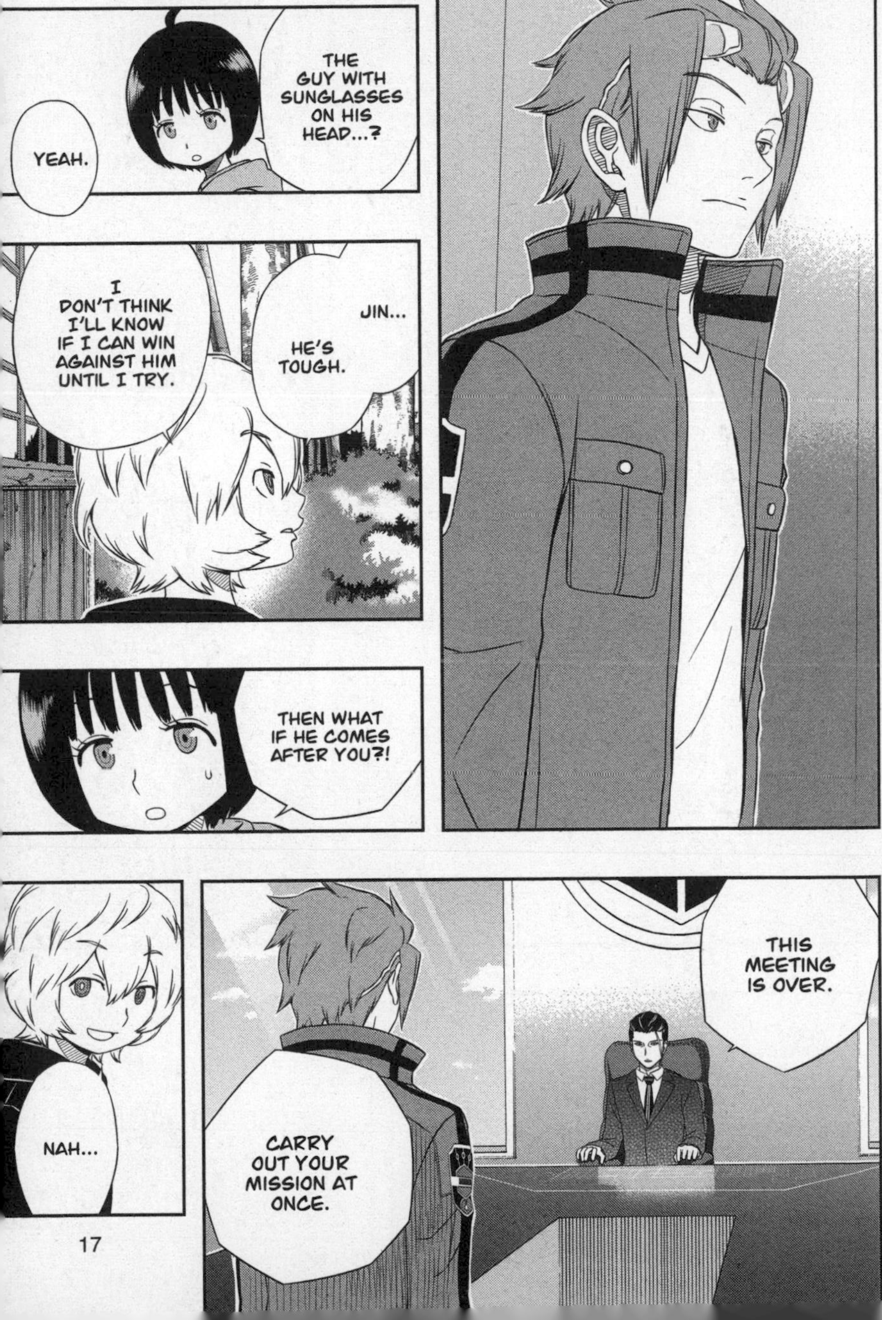
THE GUY WITH SUNGLASSES ON HIS HEAD...?
YEAH.
JIN... HE'S TOUGH.
I DON'T THINK I'LL KNOW IF I CAN WIN AGAINST HIM UNTIL I TRY.
THEN WHAT IF HE COMES AFTER YOU?!
THIS MEETING IS OVER.
CARRY OUT YOUR MISSION AT ONCE.
NAH...

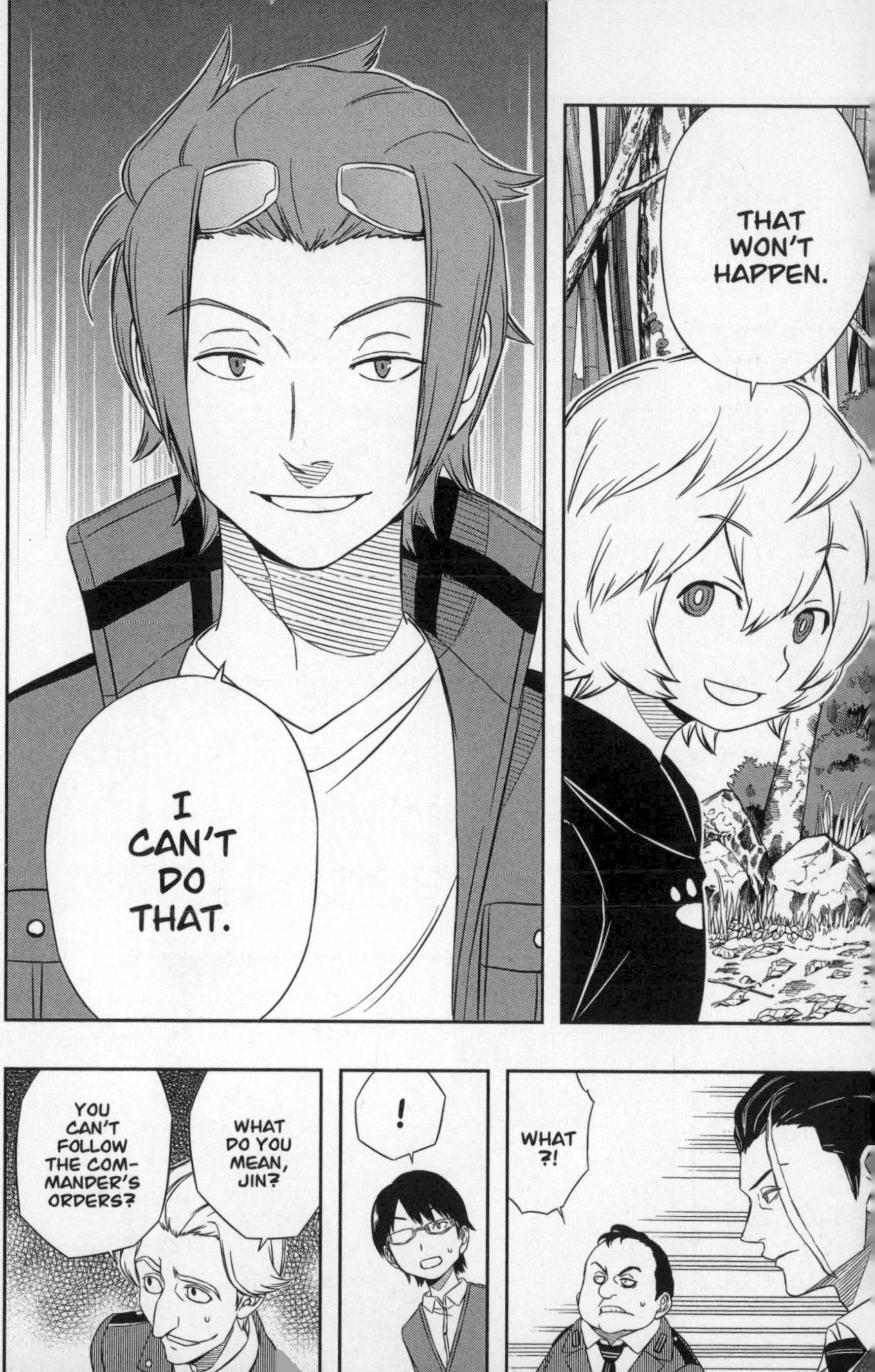
THAT WON'T HAPPEN.
I CAN'T DO THAT.
WHAT?!
!
WHAT DO YOU MEAN, JIN?
YOU CAN'T FOLLOW THE COM-MANDER'S ORDERS?

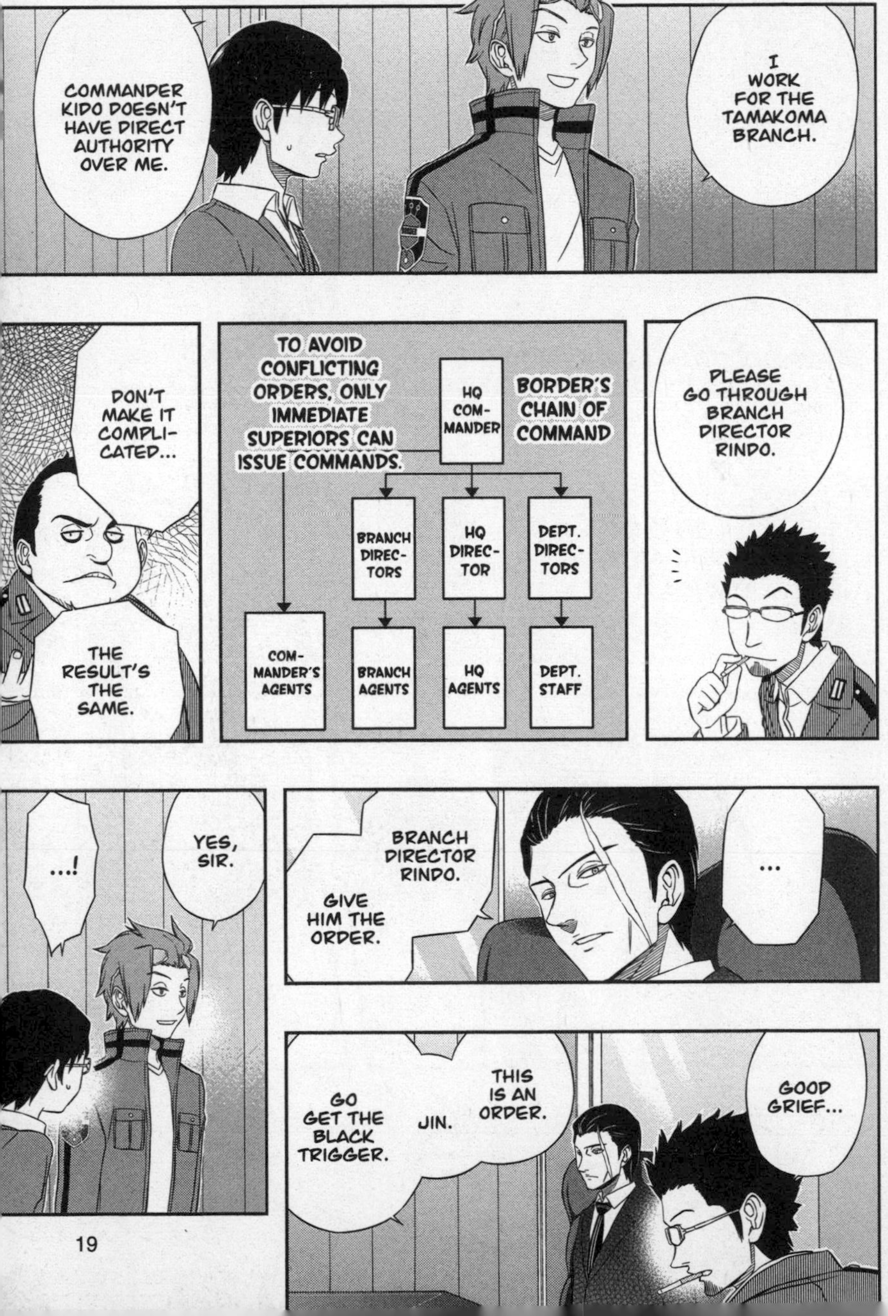
I WORK FOR THE TAMAKOMA BRANCH.
COMMANDER KIDO DOESN'T HAVE DIRECT AUTHORITY OVER ME.
PLEASE GO THROUGH BRANCH DIRECTOR RINDO.
BORDER'S CHAIN OF COMMAND
HQ COMMANDER
BRANCH DIRECTORS
HQ DIRECTOR
DEPT. DIRECTORS
COMMANDER'S AGENTS
BRANCH AGENTS
HQ AGENTS
DEPT. STAFF
TO AVOID CONFLICTING ORDERS, ONLY IMMEDIATE SUPERIORS CAN ISSUE COMMANDS.
DON'T MAKE IT COMPLICATED...
THE RESULT'S THE SAME.
...
BRANCH DIRECTOR RINDO.
GIVE HIM THE ORDER.
GOOD GRIEF...
THIS IS AN ORDER.
JIN.
GO GET THE BLACK TRIGGER.
YES, SIR.
...!

HOWEVER...

...YOU CAN DECIDE **HOW** TO DO IT.

...?!

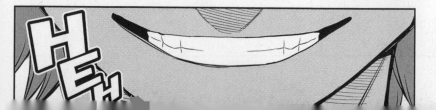

HEH...

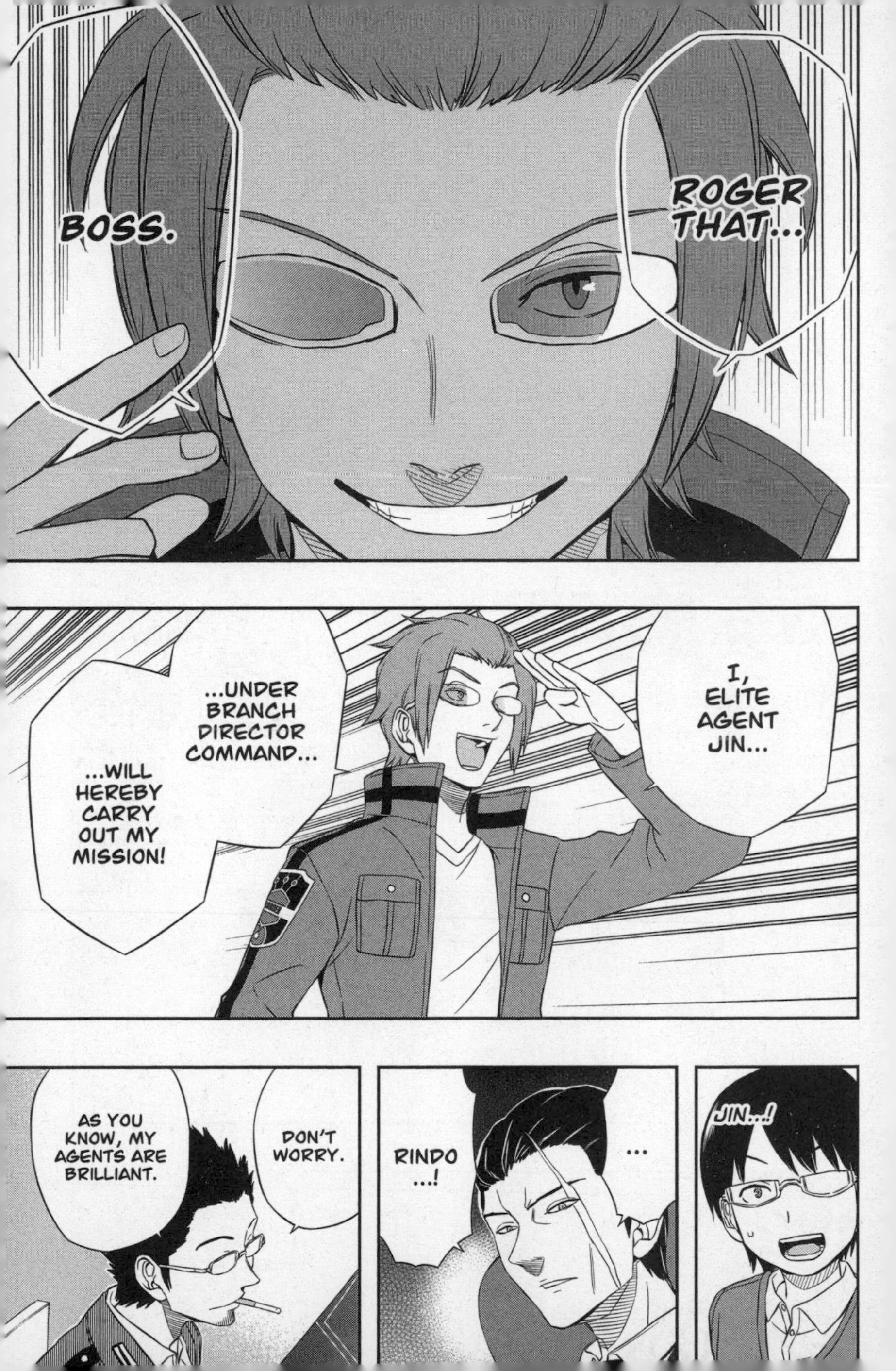
ROGER THAT...
BOSS.
I, ELITE AGENT JIN...
...UNDER BRANCH DIRECTOR COMMAND...
...WILL HEREBY CARRY OUT MY MISSION!
JIN...!
...
RINDO ...!
DON'T WORRY.
AS YOU KNOW, MY AGENTS ARE BRILLIANT.

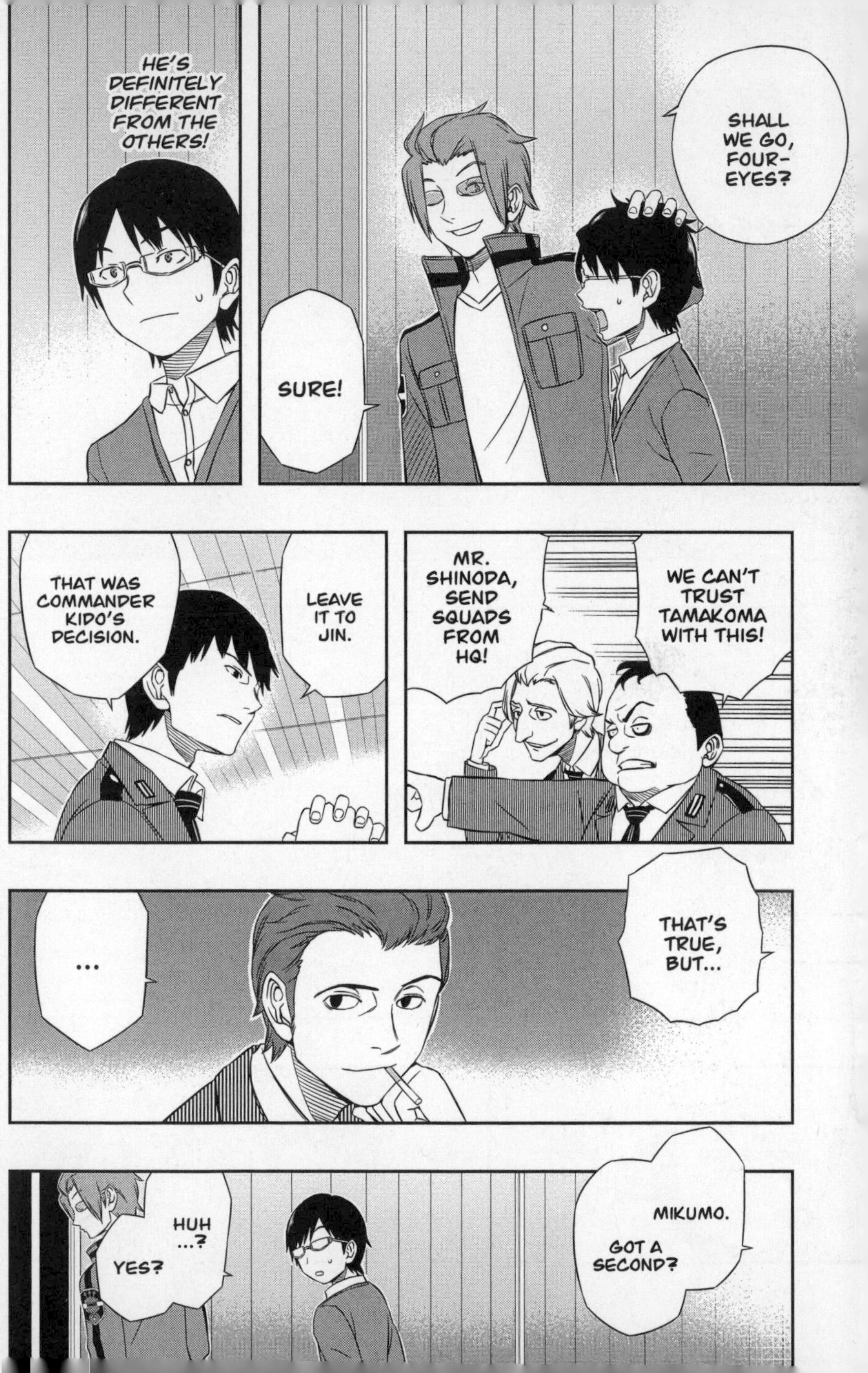

SHALL WE GO, FOUR-EYES?
SURE!
HE'S DEFINITELY DIFFERENT FROM THE OTHERS!
WE CAN'T TRUST TAMAKOMA WITH THIS!
MR. SHINODA, SEND SQUADS FROM HQ!
LEAVE IT TO JIN.
THAT WAS COMMANDER KIDO'S DECISION.
THAT'S TRUE, BUT...
...
MIKUMO.
GOT A SECOND?
HUH ...?
YES?

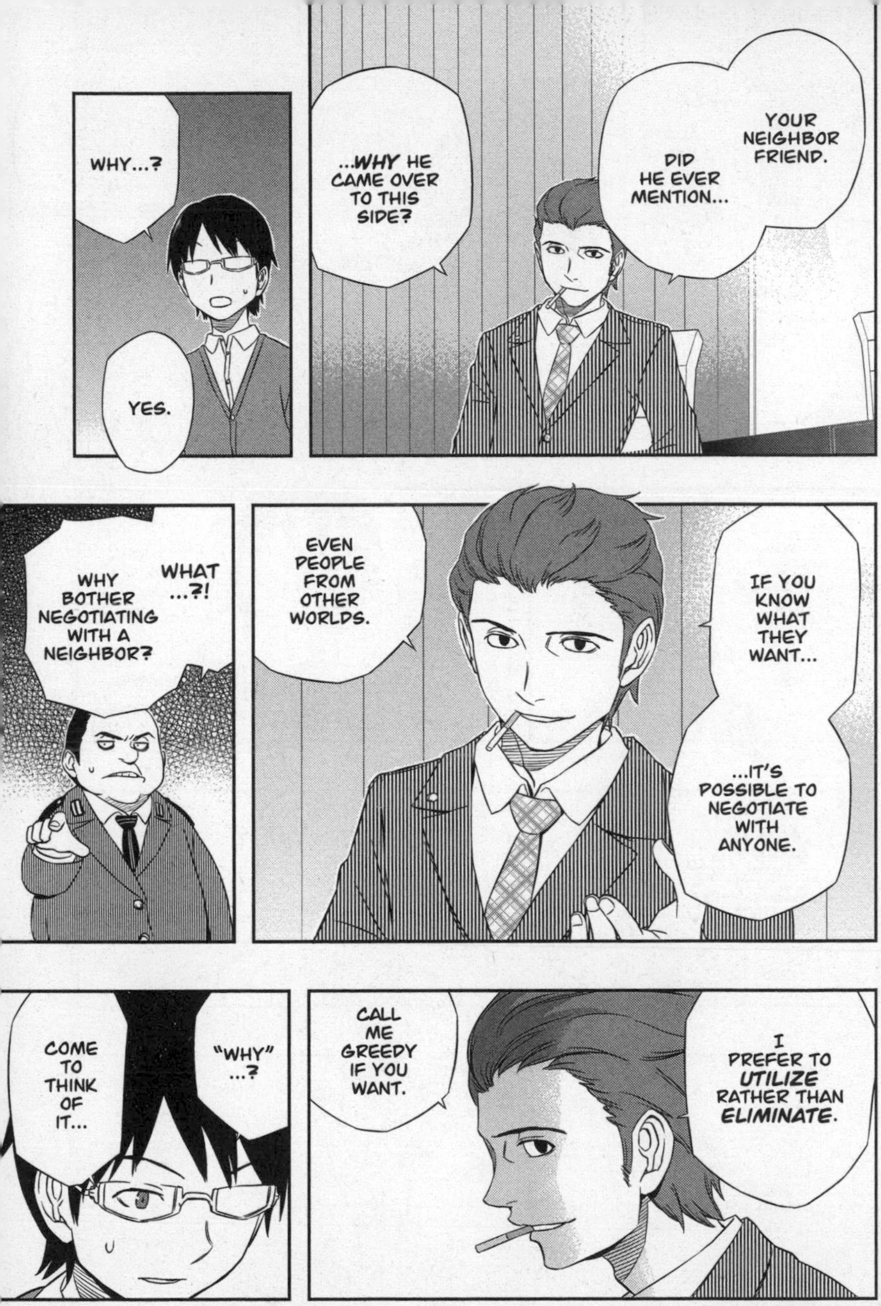
YOUR NEIGHBOR FRIEND.
DID HE EVER MENTION...
...WHY HE CAME OVER TO THIS SIDE?
WHY...?
YES.
IF YOU KNOW WHAT THEY WANT...
...IT'S POSSIBLE TO NEGOTIATE WITH ANYONE.
EVEN PEOPLE FROM OTHER WORLDS.
WHAT ...?!
WHY BOTHER NEGOTIATING WITH A NEIGHBOR?
I PREFER TO UTILIZE RATHER THAN ELIMINATE.
CALL ME GREEDY IF YOU WANT.
"WHY" ...?
COME TO THINK OF IT...

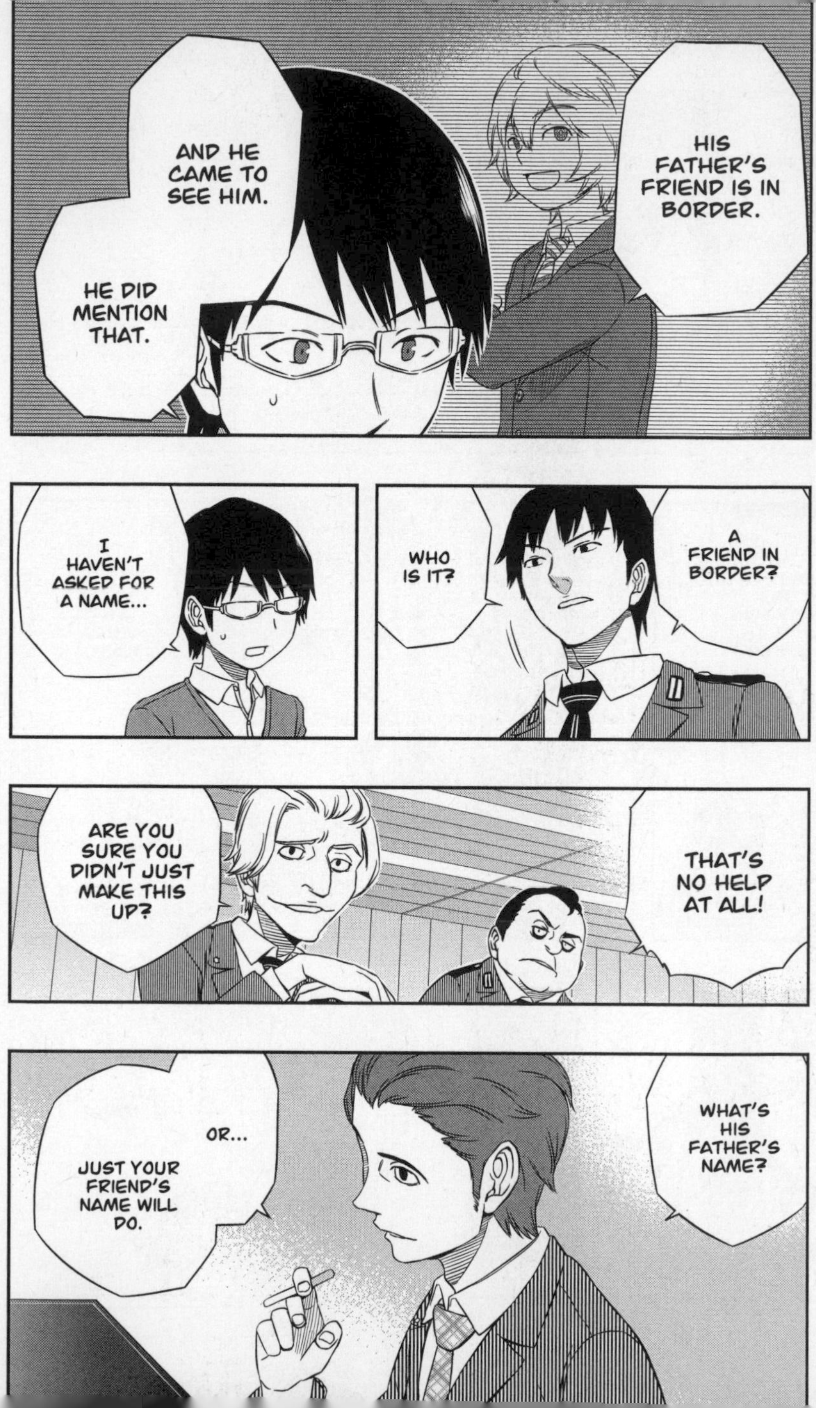
HIS FATHER'S FRIEND IS IN BORDER.
AND HE CAME TO SEE HIM.
HE DID MENTION THAT.
A FRIEND IN BORDER?
WHO IS IT?
I HAVEN'T ASKED FOR A NAME...
THAT'S NO HELP AT ALL!
ARE YOU SURE YOU DIDN'T JUST MAKE THIS UP?
WHAT'S HIS FATHER'S NAME?
OR...
JUST YOUR FRIEND'S NAME WILL DO.

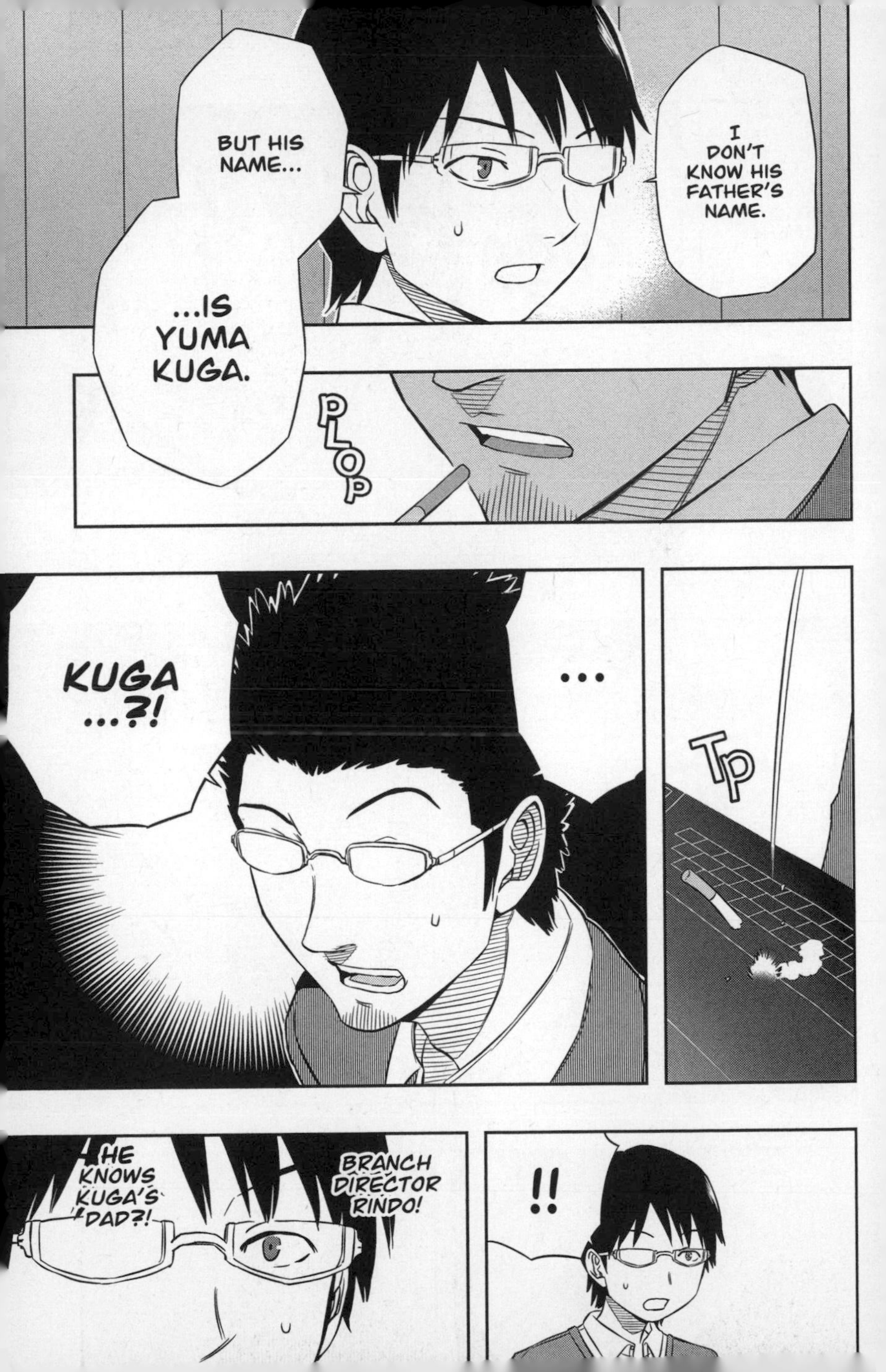
I DON'T KNOW HIS FATHER'S NAME.
BUT HIS NAME...
...IS YUMA KUGA.
PLOP
Tp
...
KUGA ...?!
!!
BRANCH DIRECTOR RINDO!
HE KNOWS KUGA'S DAD?!

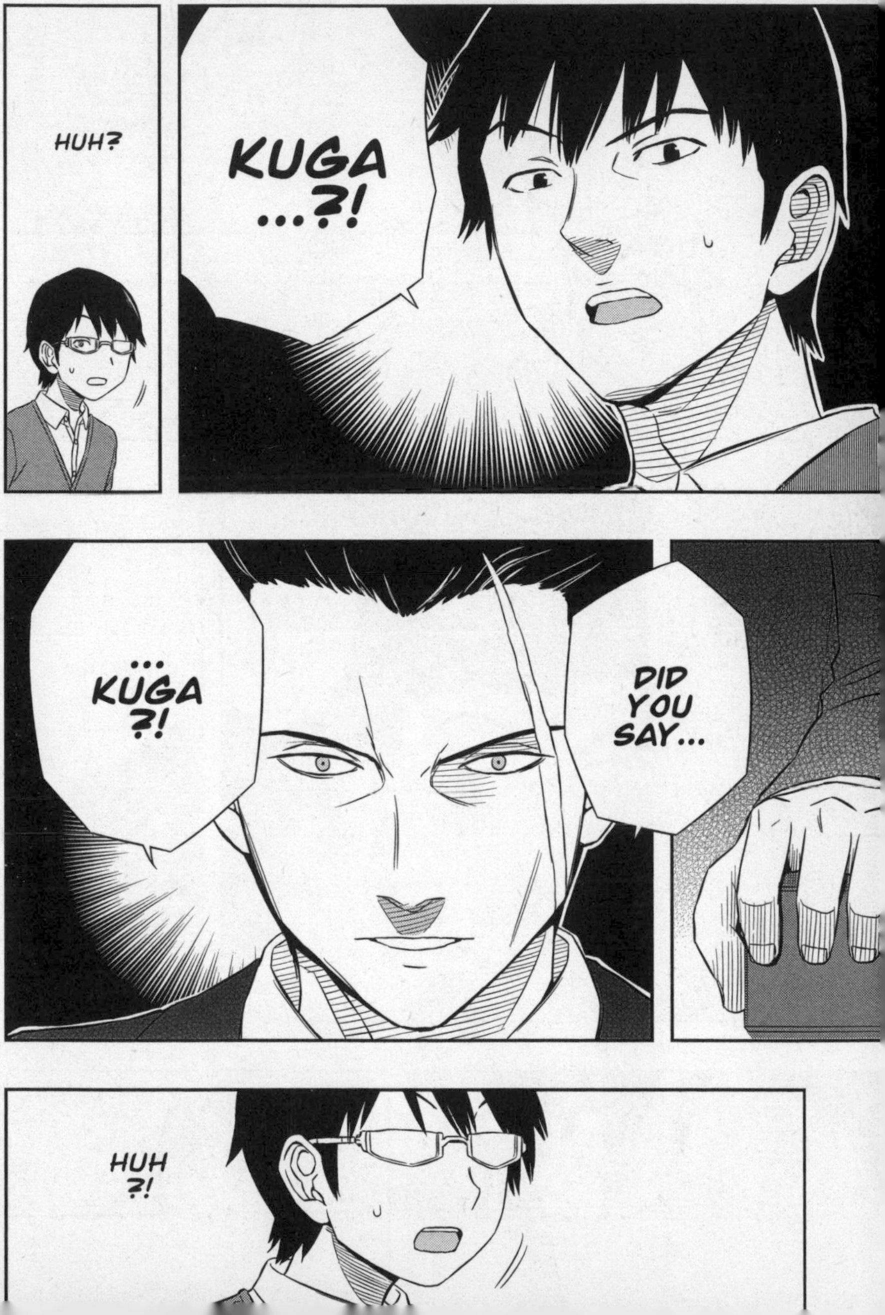
KUGA ...?!
HUH?
DID YOU SAY...
...KUGA ?!
HUH ?!

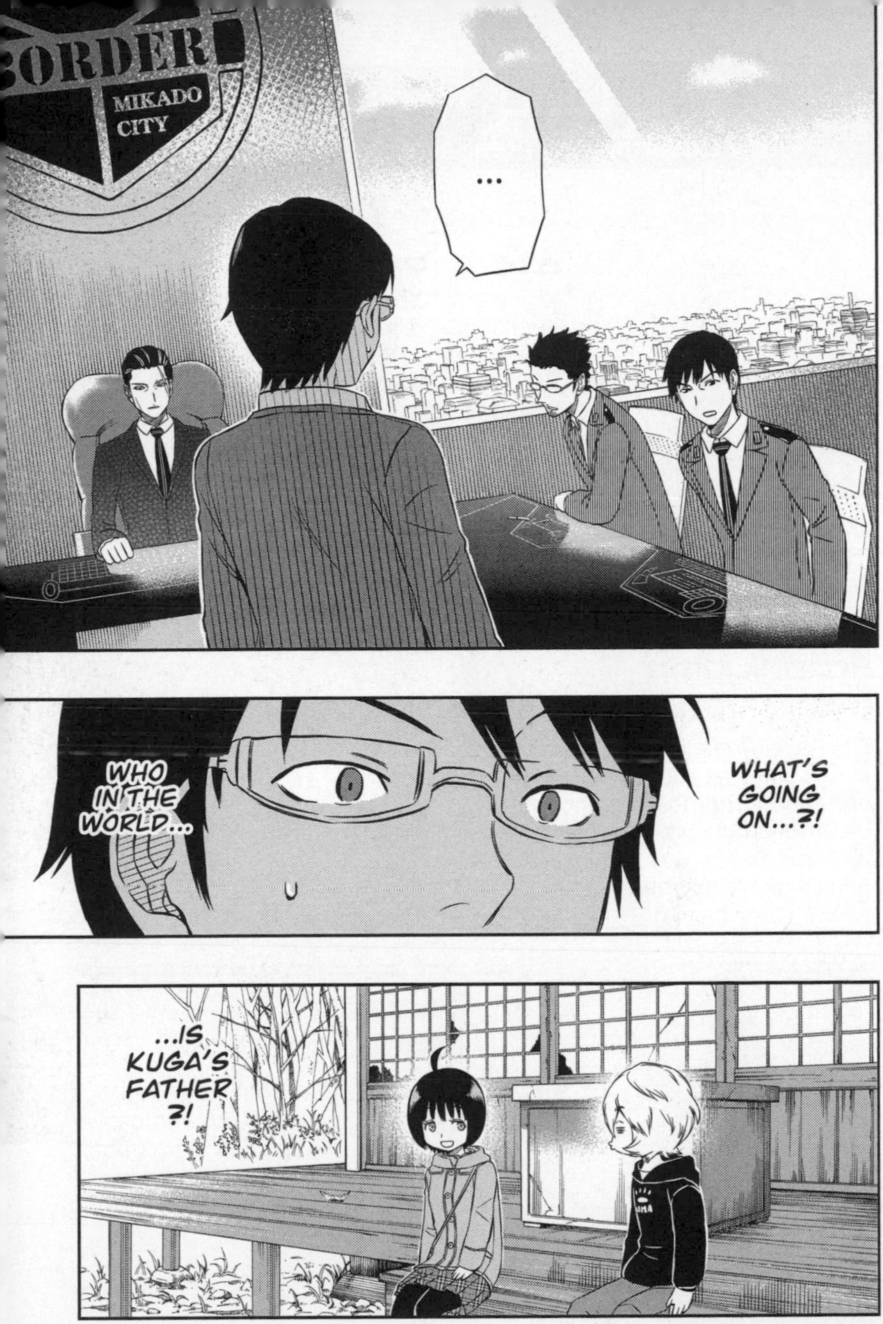
BORDER
MIKADO CITY
...
WHAT'S GOING ON...?!
WHO IN THE WORLD...
...IS KUGA'S FATHER ?!

The Way They Were

or, I Unearthed My Pre-Serialization Sketchbook

A-Rank #5
Ai Kitora (15)
9th grade

Kitora (early version)

Not very different from now. Just the part in her hair and the barrettes? I must've had a clear image of what she should look like. Her personality was more deadly serious than arrogant at this point. I was probably going to have her do a "seriousness face-off" with Osamu.

Arashiyama (early version)

Who is this? Arashiyama Squad at this point was about a group of competent members supporting an incompetent captain, so he looks a bit weak. But he was supposed to be good when it mattered.

A-Rank #5
Jun Arashiyama (18)
12th grade

A-Rank #5
Mitsuru Tokieda (16)
10th grade

Tokieda (early version)

And who is that? Mitsuru looked more foreign. And he was probably more expressive. I don't remember how he became so poker-faced, with that bowl cut. Maybe he was too normal before.

Chapter 18 Yugo Kuga

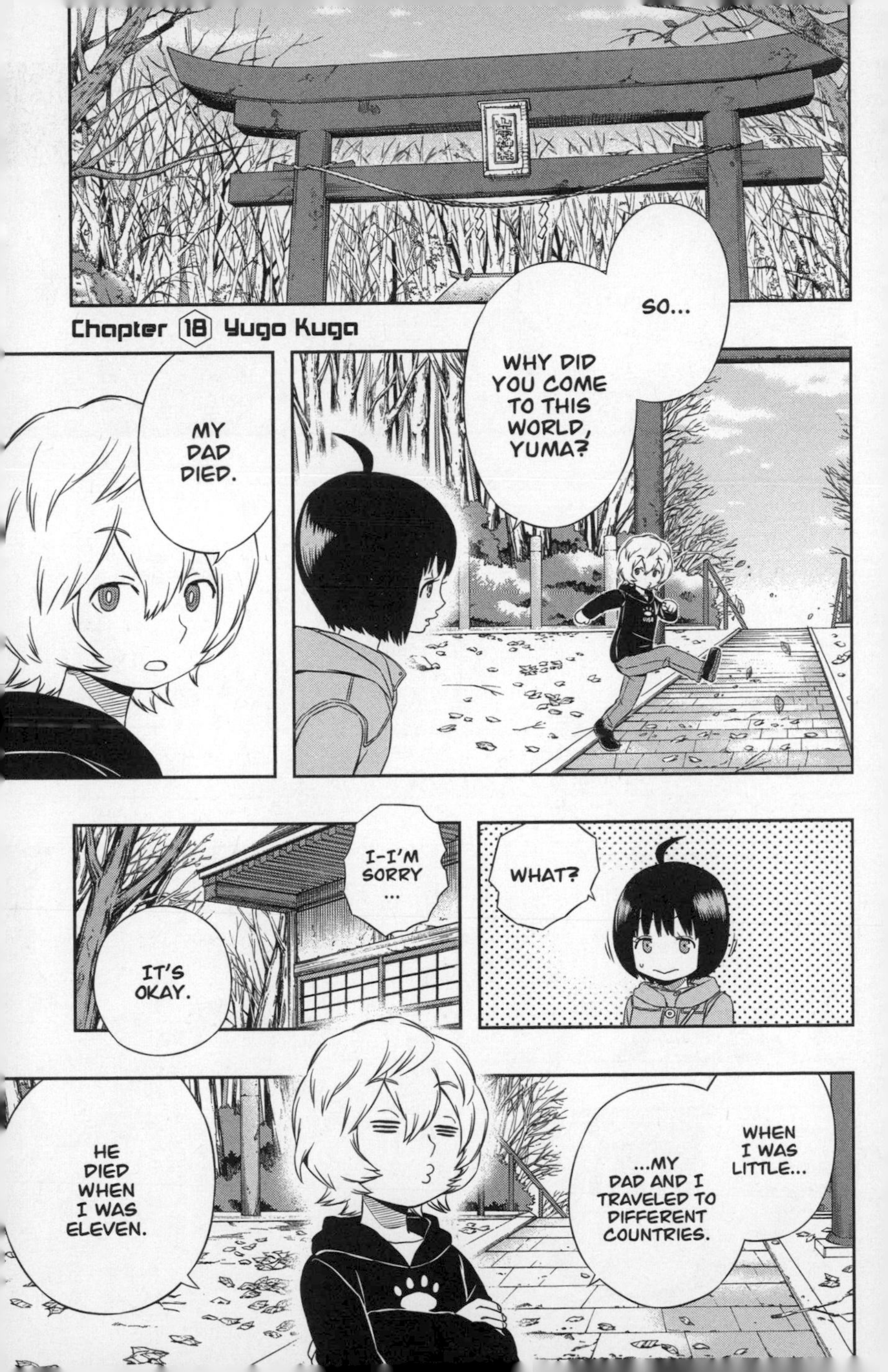
SO...
WHY DID YOU COME TO THIS WORLD, YUMA?
MY DAD DIED.
WHAT?
I-I'M SORRY ...
IT'S OKAY.
WHEN I WAS LITTLE...
...MY DAD AND I TRAVELED TO DIFFERENT COUNTRIES.
HE DIED WHEN I WAS ELEVEN.

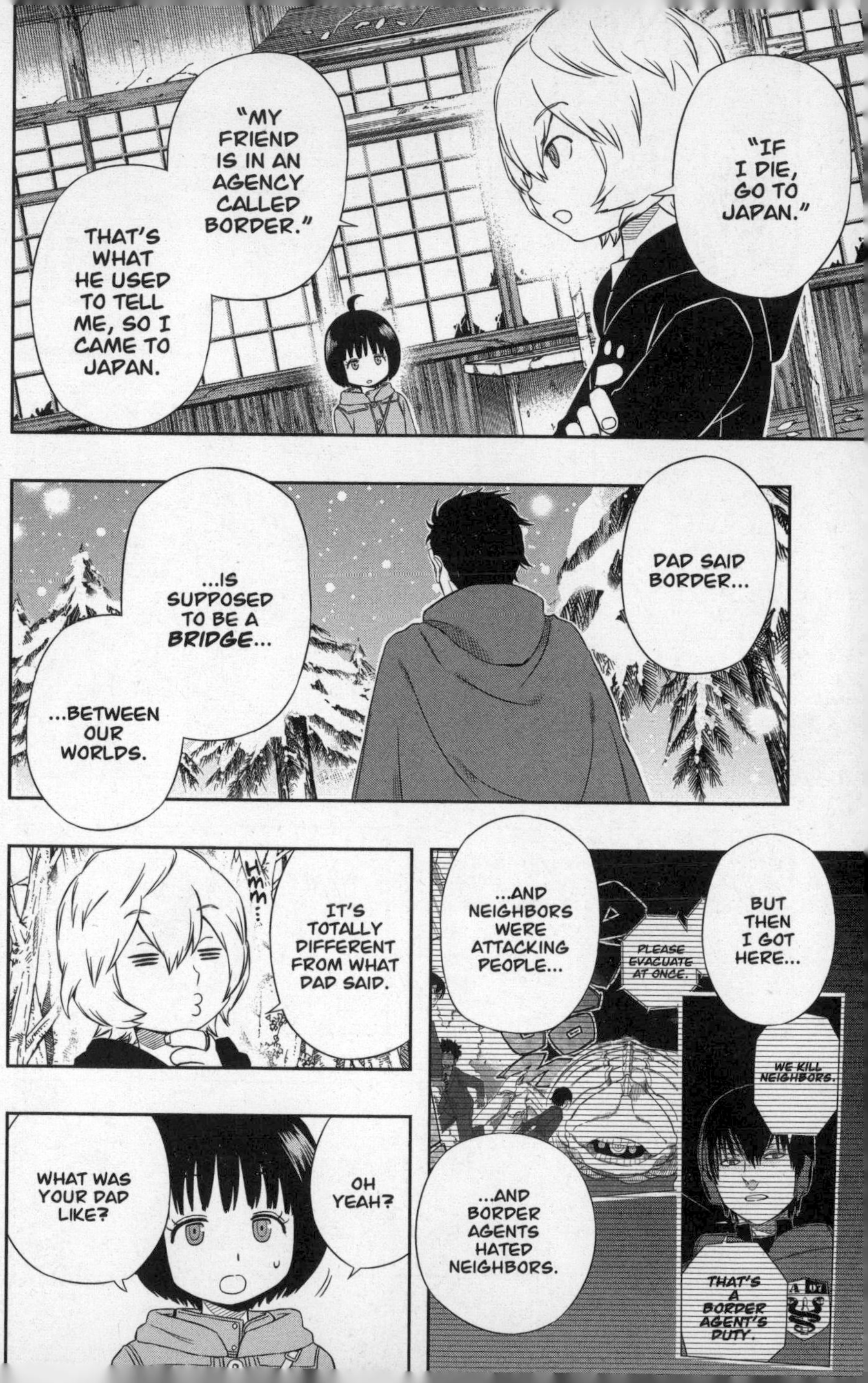
"IF I DIE, GO TO JAPAN."
"MY FRIEND IS IN AN AGENCY CALLED BORDER."
THAT'S WHAT HE USED TO TELL ME, SO I CAME TO JAPAN.
DAD SAID BORDER...
...IS SUPPOSED TO BE A BRIDGE...
...BETWEEN OUR WORLDS.
BUT THEN I GOT HERE...
PLEASE EVACUATE AT ONCE.
...AND NEIGHBORS WERE ATTACKING PEOPLE...
WE KILL NEIGHBORS.
THAT'S A BORDER AGENT'S DUTY.
...AND BORDER AGENTS HATED NEIGHBORS.
HMM...
IT'S TOTALLY DIFFERENT FROM WHAT DAD SAID.
OH YEAH?
WHAT WAS YOUR DAD LIKE?

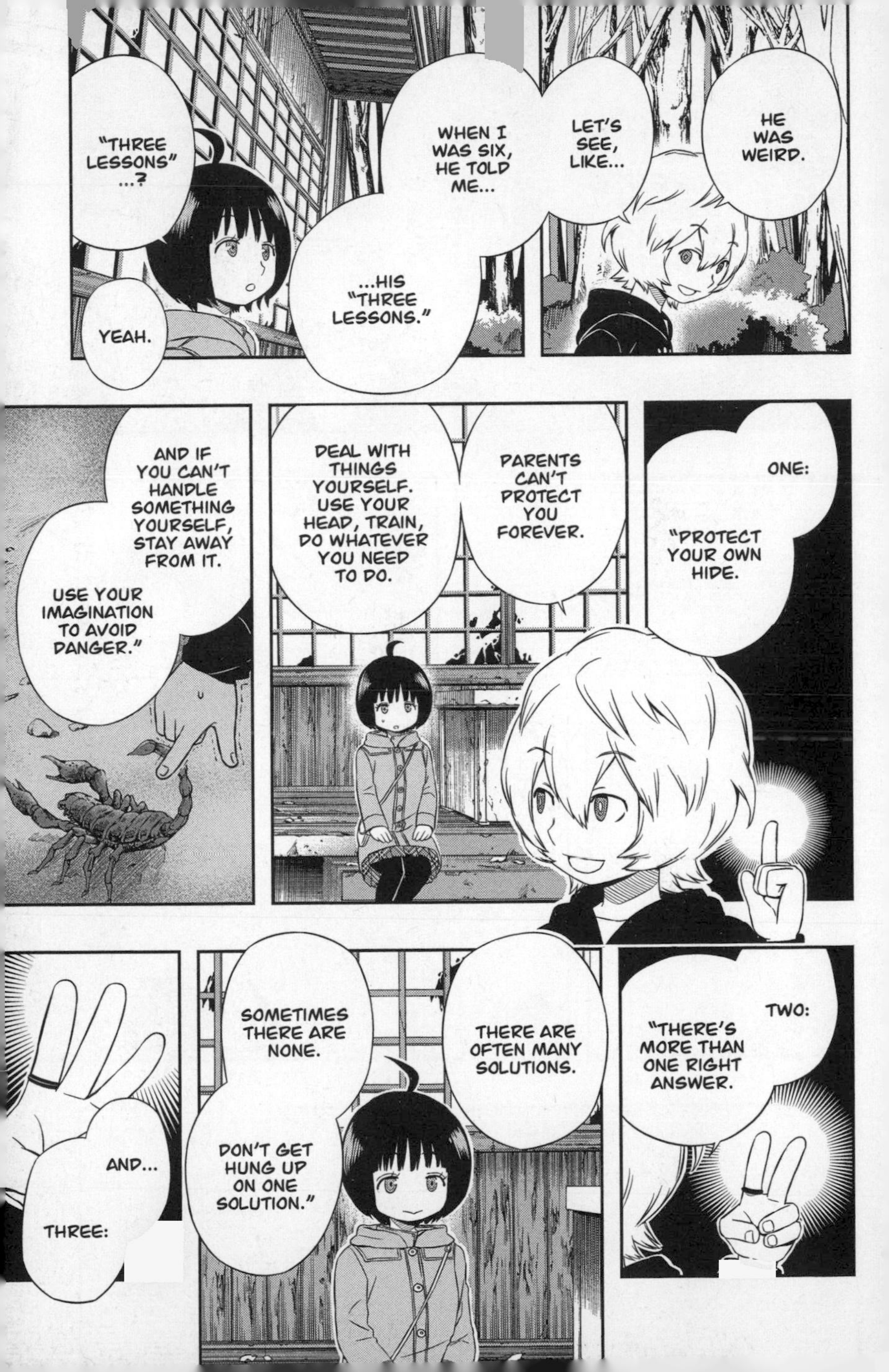
HE WAS WEIRD.
LET'S SEE, LIKE...
WHEN I WAS SIX, HE TOLD ME...
...HIS "THREE LESSONS."
"THREE LESSONS"...?
YEAH.
ONE:
"PROTECT YOUR OWN HIDE.
PARENTS CAN'T PROTECT YOU FOREVER.
DEAL WITH THINGS YOURSELF. USE YOUR HEAD, TRAIN, DO WHATEVER YOU NEED TO DO.
AND IF YOU CAN'T HANDLE SOMETHING YOURSELF, STAY AWAY FROM IT.
USE YOUR IMAGINATION TO AVOID DANGER."
TWO:
"THERE'S MORE THAN ONE RIGHT ANSWER.
THERE ARE OFTEN MANY SOLUTIONS.
SOMETIMES THERE ARE NONE.
DON'T GET HUNG UP ON ONE SOLUTION."
AND...
THREE:

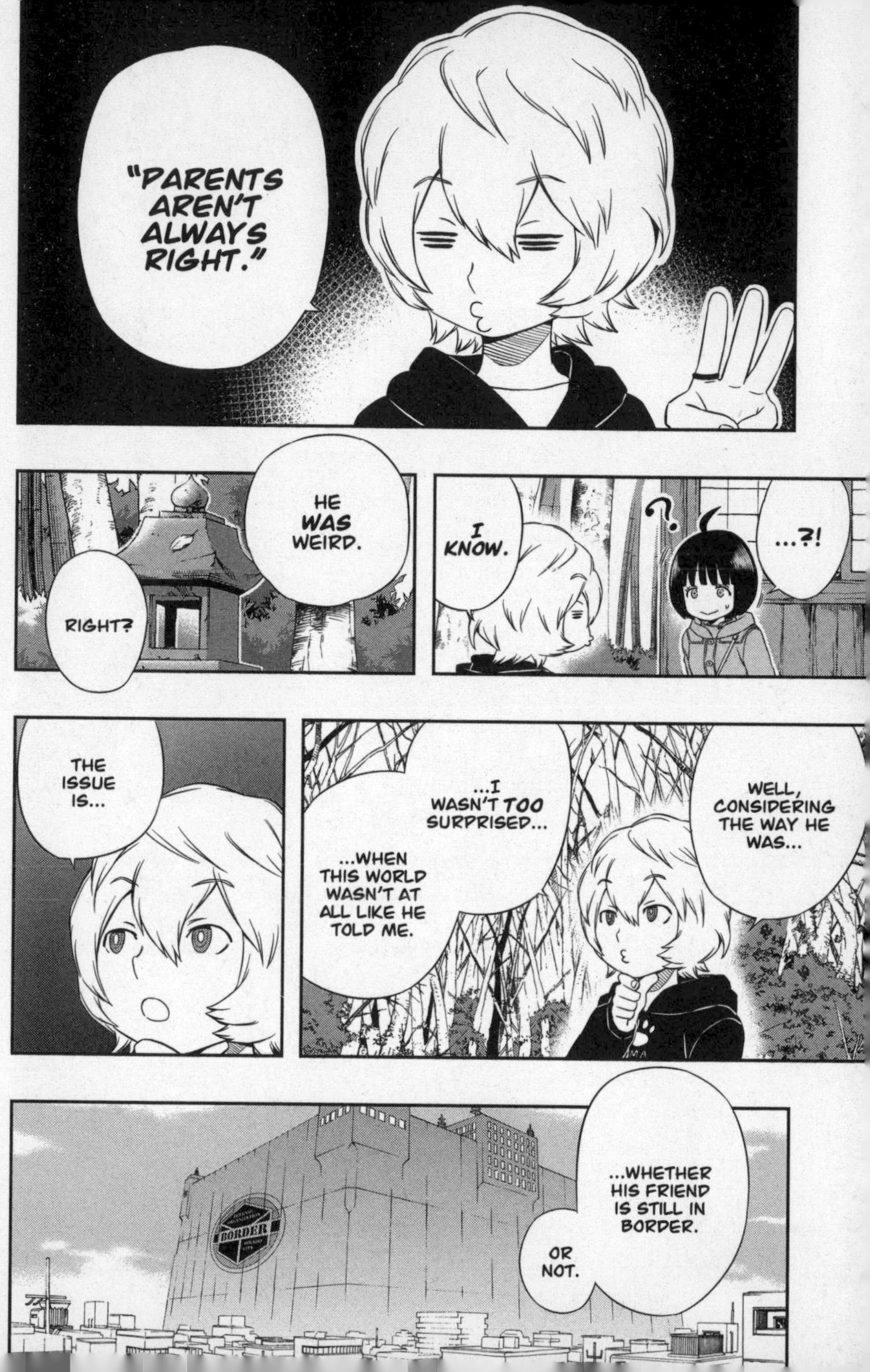
"PARENTS AREN'T ALWAYS RIGHT."
...?!
I KNOW.
HE WAS WEIRD.
RIGHT?
WELL, CONSIDERING THE WAY HE WAS...
...I WASN'T TOO SURPRISED...
...WHEN THIS WORLD WASN'T AT ALL LIKE HE TOLD ME.
THE ISSUE IS...
...WHETHER HIS FRIEND IS STILL IN BORDER.
OR NOT.
BORDER

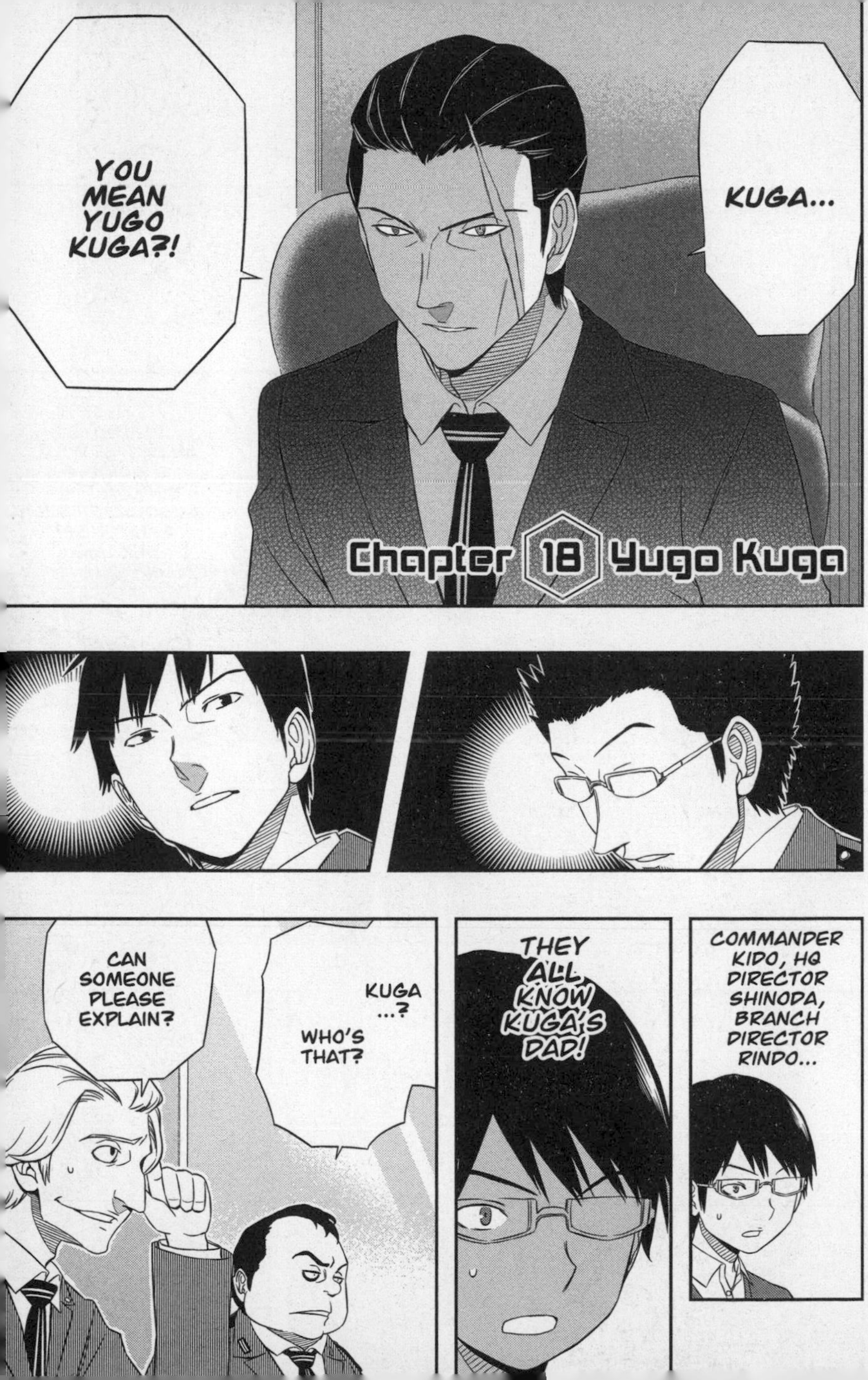
KUGA...
YOU MEAN YUGO KUGA?!
Chapter 18 Yugo Kuga
COMMANDER KIDO, HQ DIRECTOR SHINODA, BRANCH DIRECTOR RINDO...
THEY ALL KNOW KUGA'S DAD!
KUGA ...?
WHO'S THAT?
CAN SOMEONE PLEASE EXPLAIN?

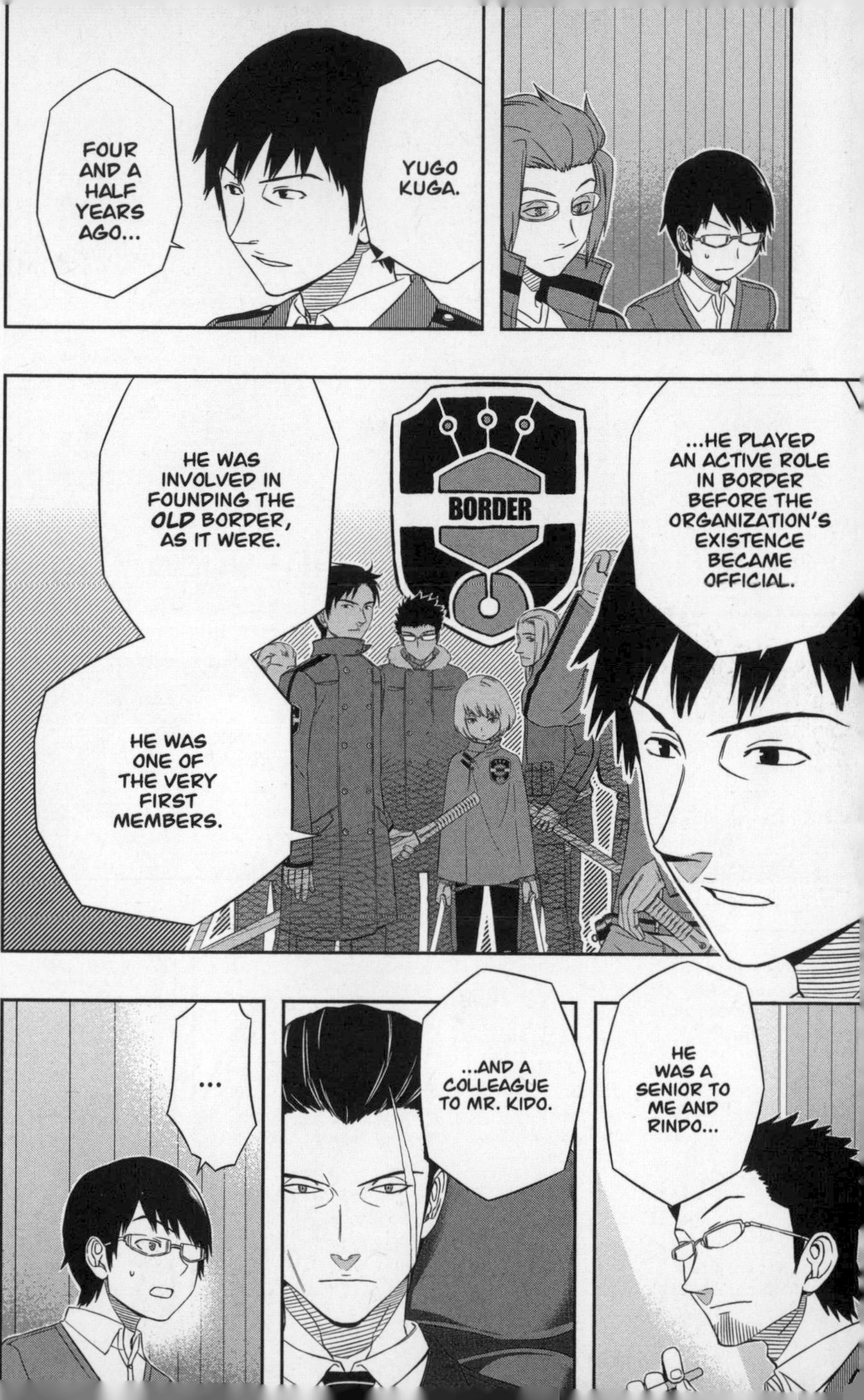
YUGO KUGA.
FOUR AND A HALF YEARS AGO...
...HE PLAYED AN ACTIVE ROLE IN BORDER BEFORE THE ORGANIZATION'S EXISTENCE BECAME OFFICIAL.
BORDER
HE WAS INVOLVED IN FOUNDING THE *OLD* BORDER, AS IT WERE.
HE WAS ONE OF THE VERY FIRST MEMBERS.
HE WAS A SENIOR TO ME AND RINDO...
...AND A COLLEAGUE TO MR. KIDO.
...

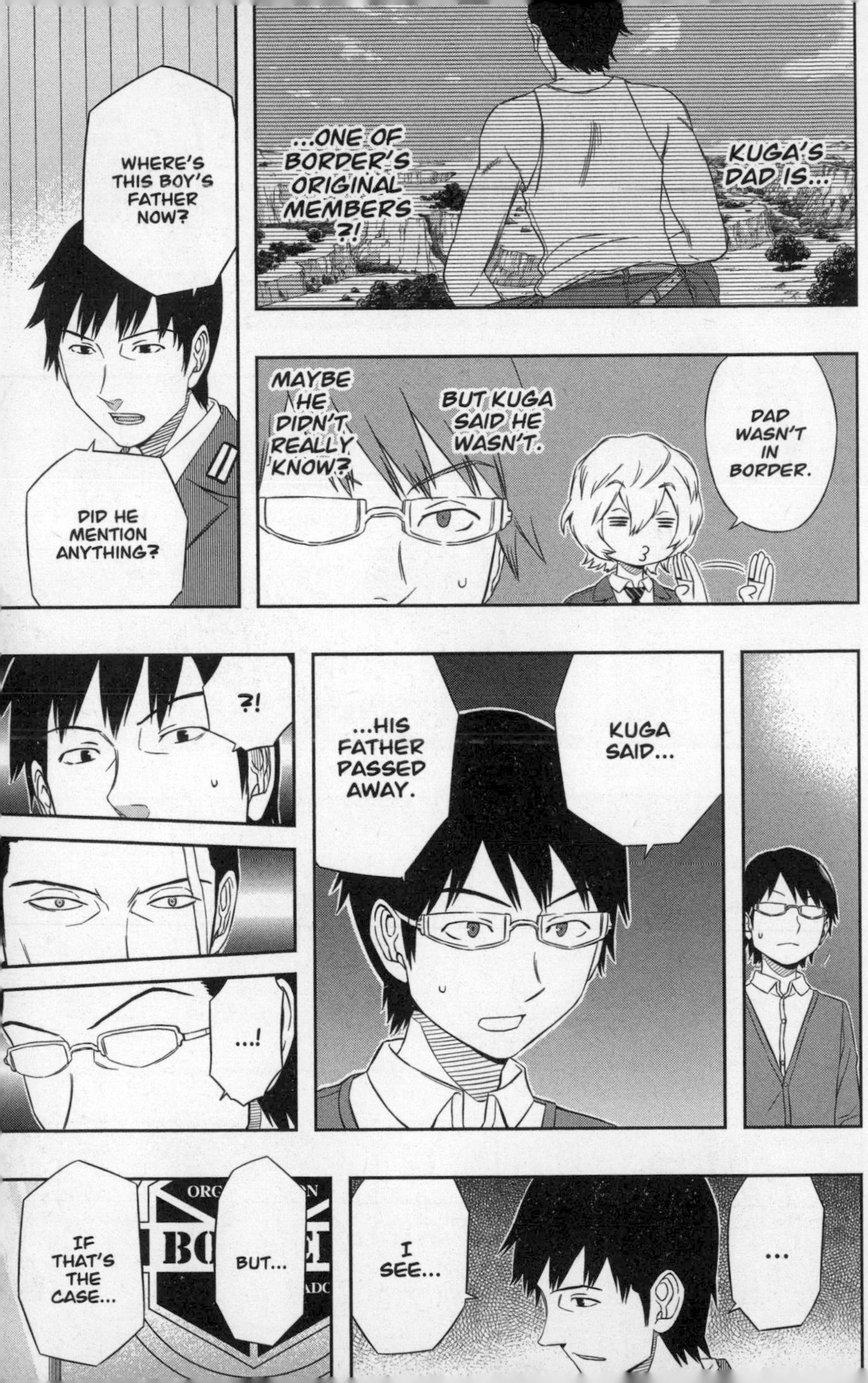
KUGA'S DAD IS...
...ONE OF BORDER'S ORIGINAL MEMBERS ?!
DAD WASN'T IN BORDER.
BUT KUGA SAID HE WASN'T.
MAYBE HE DIDN'T REALLY KNOW?
WHERE'S THIS BOY'S FATHER NOW?
DID HE MENTION ANYTHING?
KUGA SAID...
...HIS FATHER PASSED AWAY.
?!
...!
...
I SEE...
BUT...
IF THAT'S THE CASE...

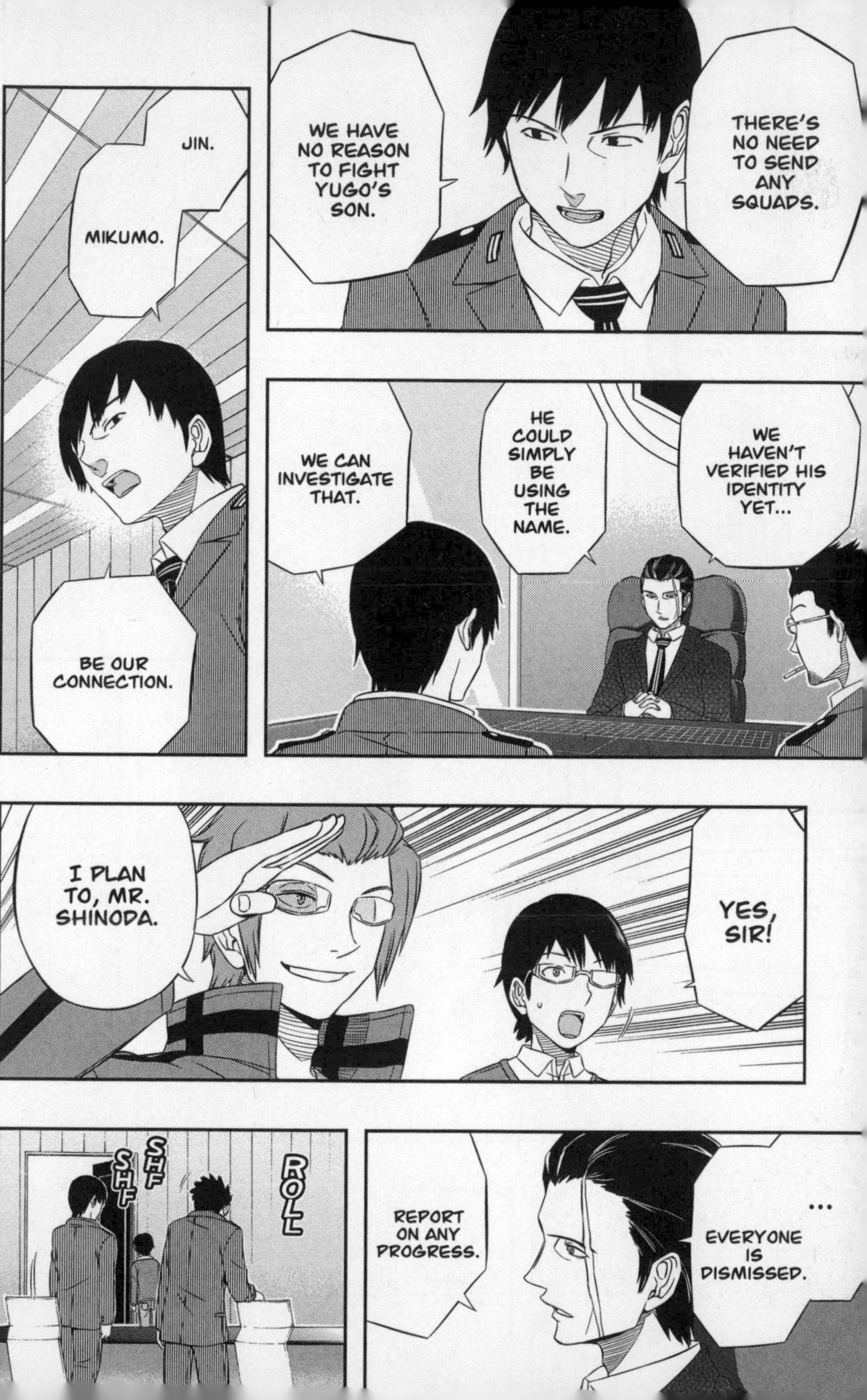
THERE'S NO NEED TO SEND ANY SQUADS.
WE HAVE NO REASON TO FIGHT YUGO'S SON.
WE HAVEN'T VERIFIED HIS IDENTITY YET...
HE COULD SIMPLY BE USING THE NAME.
WE CAN INVESTIGATE THAT.
JIN.
MIKUMO.
BE OUR CONNECTION.
YES, SIR!
I PLAN TO, MR. SHINODA.
...
EVERYONE IS DISMISSED.
REPORT ON ANY PROGRESS.
ROLL
SHF SHF

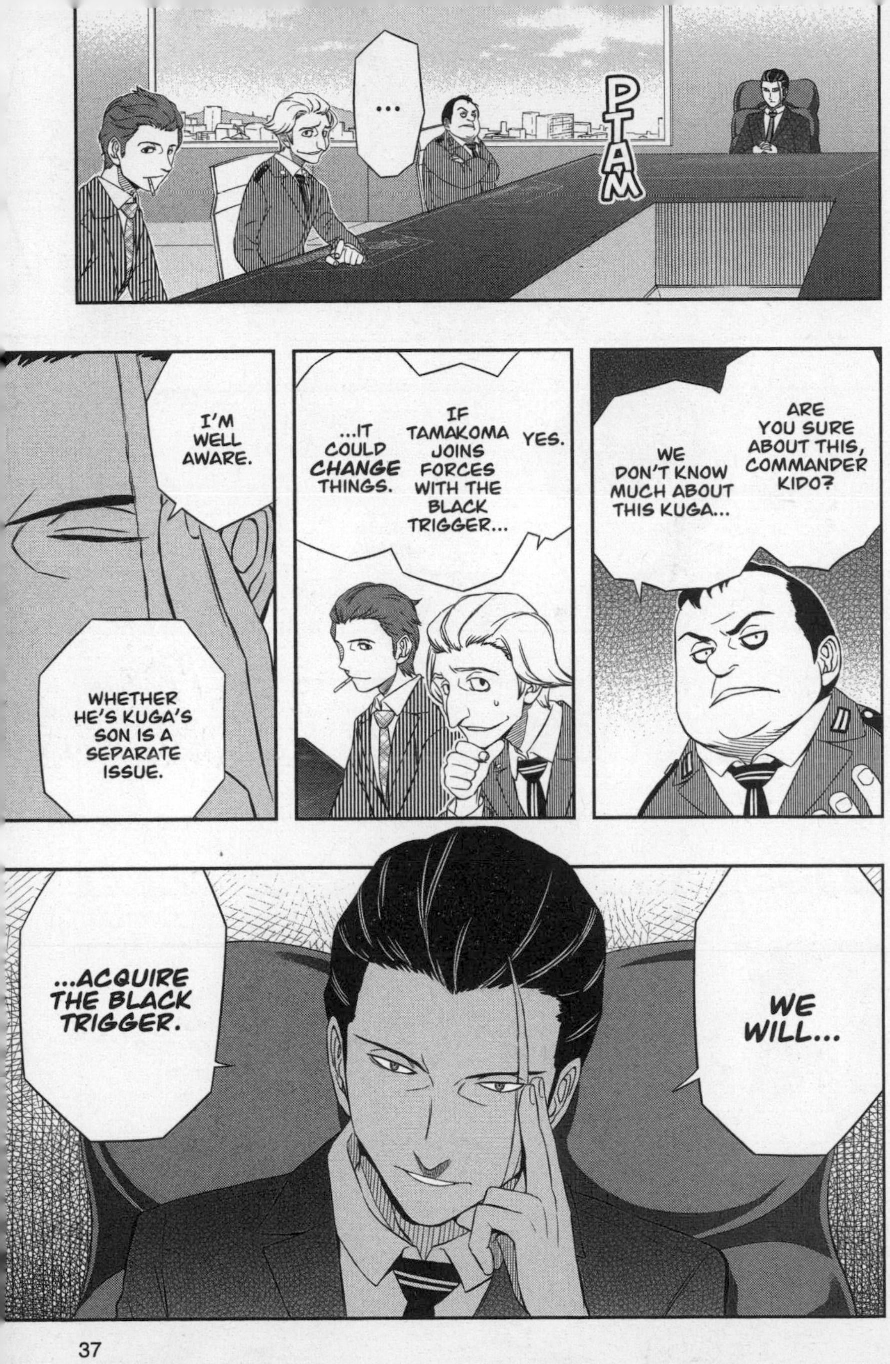
PTAM
...
ARE YOU SURE ABOUT THIS, COMMANDER KIDO?
WE DON'T KNOW MUCH ABOUT THIS KUGA...
YES.
IF TAMAKOMA JOINS FORCES WITH THE BLACK TRIGGER...
...IT COULD CHANGE THINGS.
I'M WELL AWARE.
WHETHER HE'S KUGA'S SON IS A SEPARATE ISSUE.
WE WILL...
...ACQUIRE THE BLACK TRIGGER.

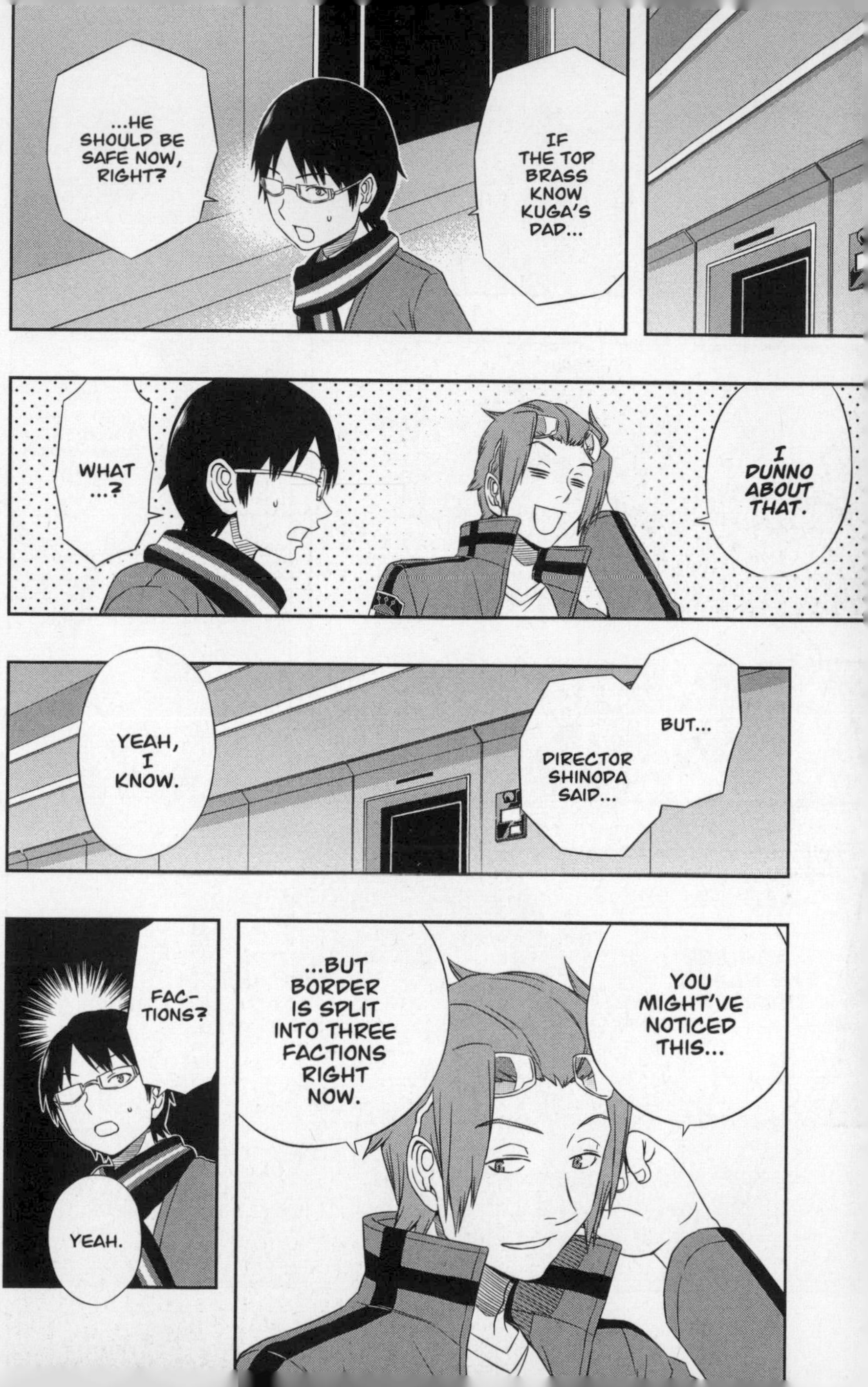
IF THE TOP BRASS KNOW KUGA'S DAD...
...HE SHOULD BE SAFE NOW, RIGHT?
I DUNNO ABOUT THAT.
WHAT...?
BUT... DIRECTOR SHINODA SAID...
YEAH, I KNOW.
YOU MIGHT'VE NOTICED THIS...
...BUT BORDER IS SPLIT INTO THREE FACTIONS RIGHT NOW.
FAC-TIONS?
YEAH.

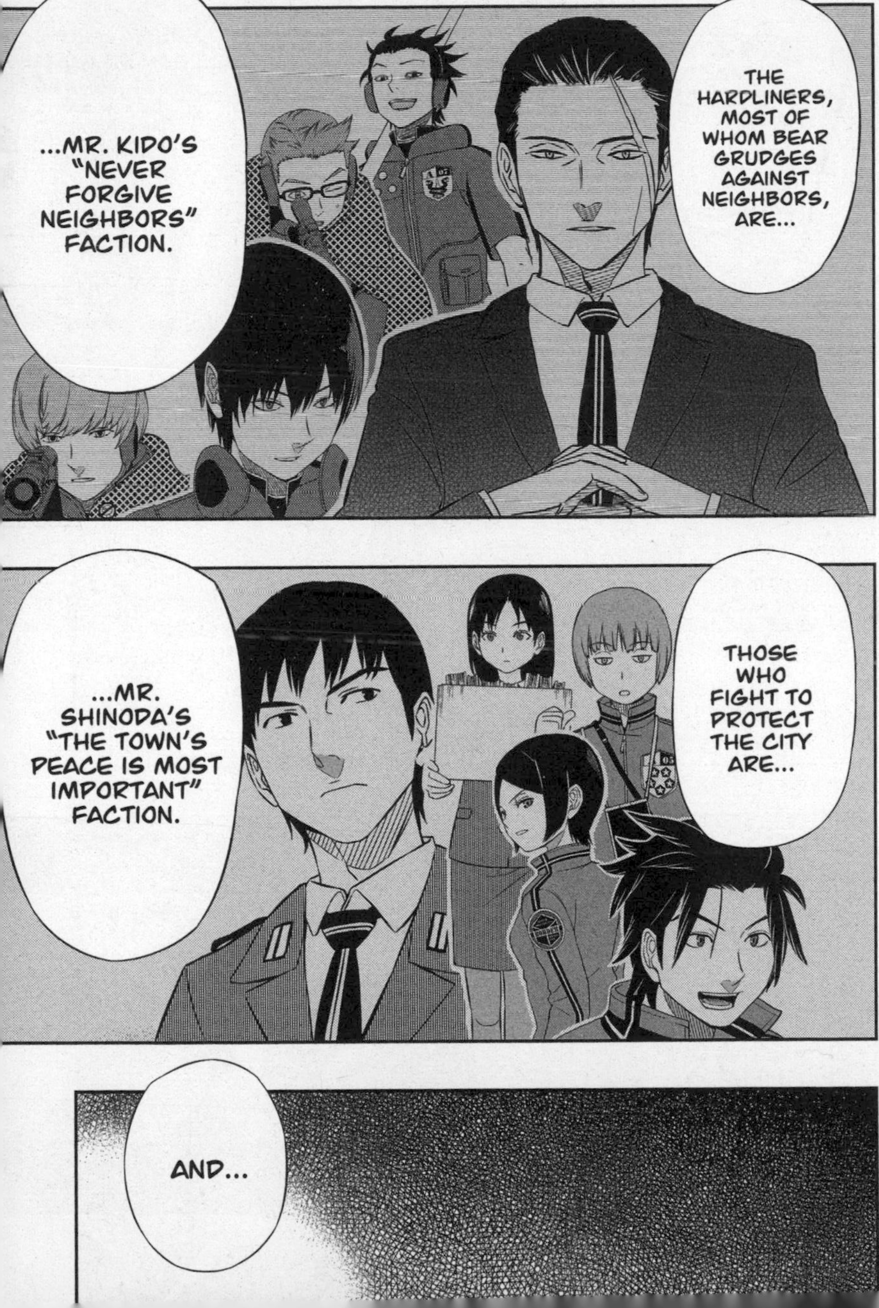
THE HARDLINERS, MOST OF WHOM BEAR GRUDGES AGAINST NEIGHBORS, ARE...
...MR. KIDO'S "NEVER FORGIVE NEIGHBORS" FACTION.
THOSE WHO FIGHT TO PROTECT THE CITY ARE...
...MR. SHINODA'S "THE TOWN'S PEACE IS MOST IMPORTANT" FACTION.
AND...

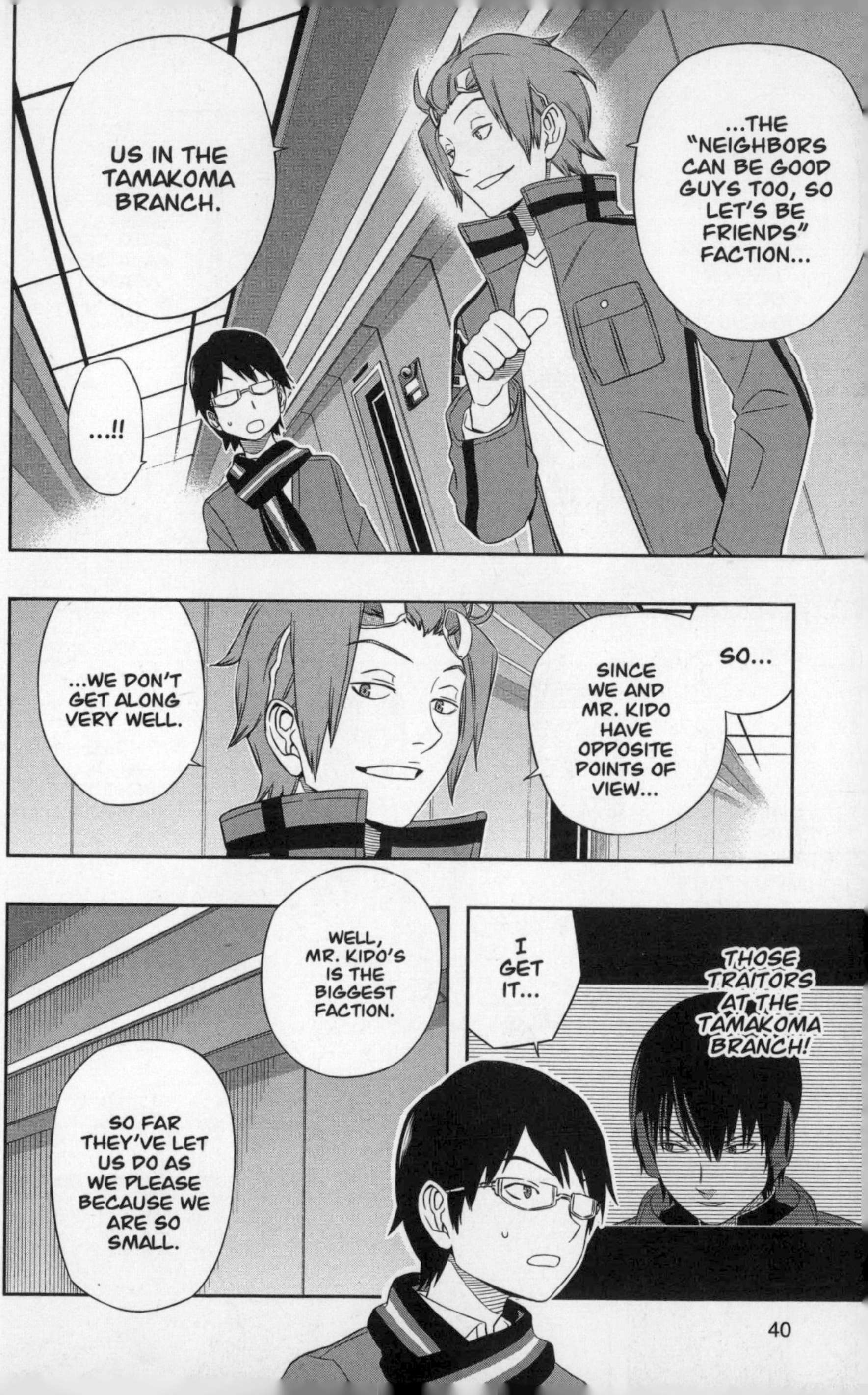
...THE "NEIGHBORS CAN BE GOOD GUYS TOO, SO LET'S BE FRIENDS" FACTION...
US IN THE TAMAKOMA BRANCH.
...!!
SO...
SINCE WE AND MR. KIDO HAVE OPPOSITE POINTS OF VIEW...
...WE DON'T GET ALONG VERY WELL.
I GET IT...
THOSE TRAITORS AT THE TAMAKOMA BRANCH!
WELL, MR. KIDO'S IS THE BIGGEST FACTION.
SO FAR THEY'VE LET US DO AS WE PLEASE BECAUSE WE ARE SO SMALL.

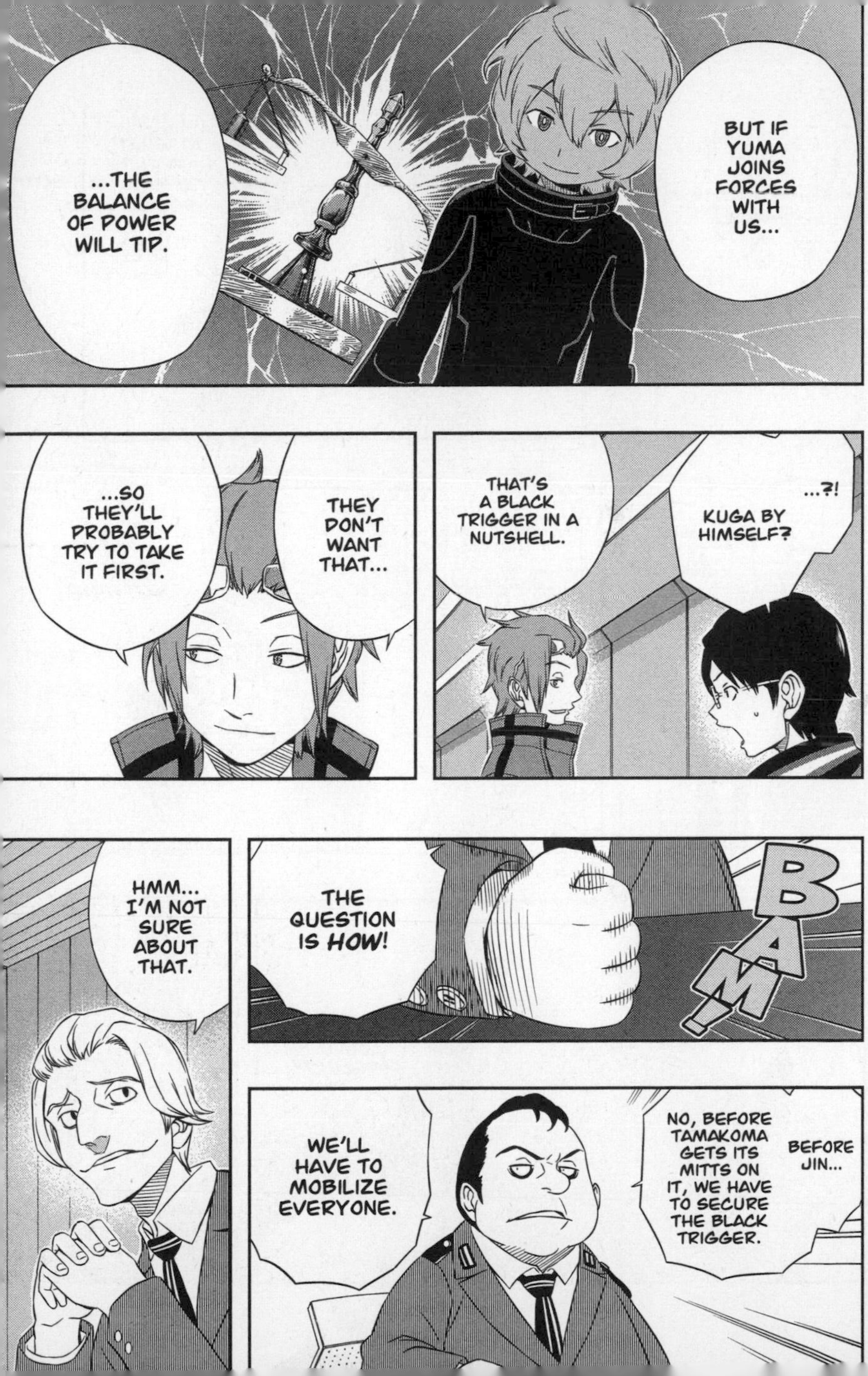
BUT IF YUMA JOINS FORCES WITH US...
...THE BALANCE OF POWER WILL TIP.
...?!
KUGA BY HIMSELF?
THAT'S A BLACK TRIGGER IN A NUTSHELL.
THEY DON'T WANT THAT...
...SO THEY'LL PROBABLY TRY TO TAKE IT FIRST.
BAM!
THE QUESTION IS *HOW*!
BEFORE JIN...
NO, BEFORE TAMAKOMA GETS ITS MITTS ON IT, WE HAVE TO SECURE THE BLACK TRIGGER.
WE'LL HAVE TO MOBILIZE EVERYONE.
HMM... I'M NOT SURE ABOUT THAT.

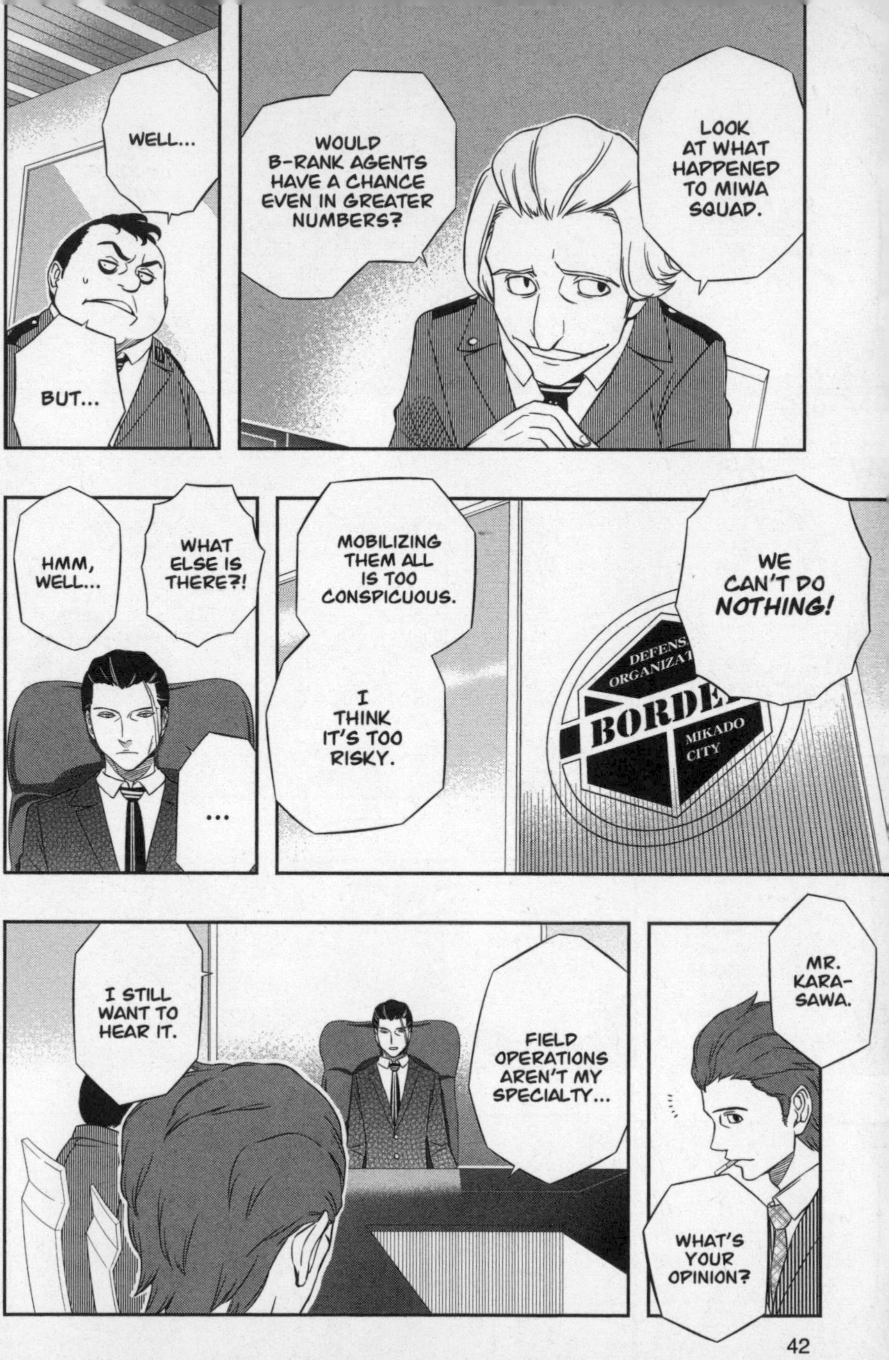
LOOK AT WHAT HAPPENED TO MIWA SQUAD.
WOULD B-RANK AGENTS HAVE A CHANCE EVEN IN GREATER NUMBERS?
WELL...
BUT...
WE CAN'T DO NOTHING!
MOBILIZING THEM ALL IS TOO CONSPICUOUS.
I THINK IT'S TOO RISKY.
WHAT ELSE IS THERE?!
HMM, WELL...
...
MR. KARA-SAWA.
WHAT'S YOUR OPINION?
FIELD OPERATIONS AREN'T MY SPECIALTY...
I STILL WANT TO HEAR IT.

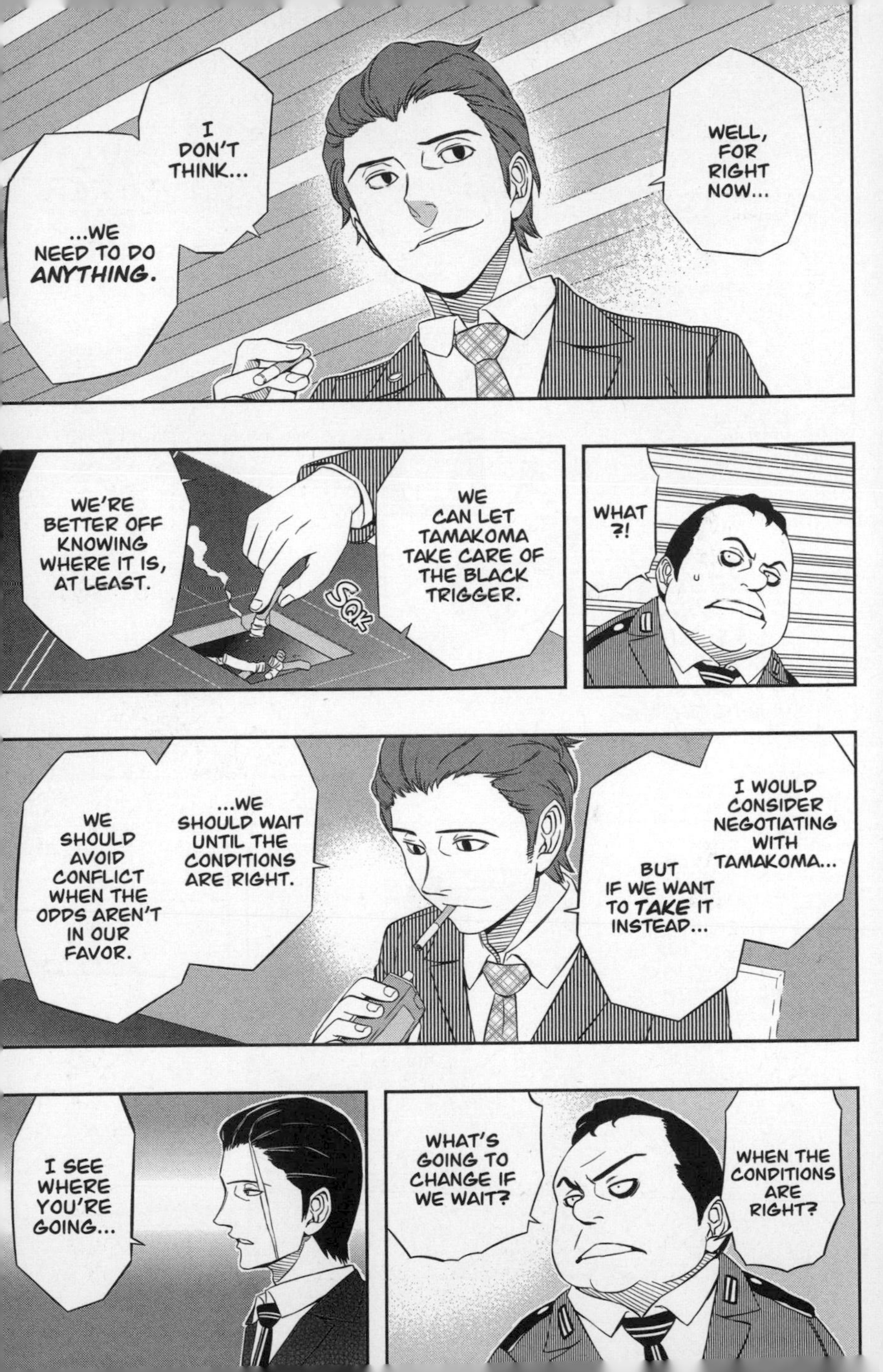
WELL, FOR RIGHT NOW...
I DON'T THINK...
...WE NEED TO DO ANYTHING.
WHAT?!
WE CAN LET TAMAKOMA TAKE CARE OF THE BLACK TRIGGER.
SQK
WE'RE BETTER OFF KNOWING WHERE IT IS, AT LEAST.
I WOULD CONSIDER NEGOTIATING WITH TAMAKOMA...
BUT IF WE WANT TO TAKE IT INSTEAD...
...WE SHOULD WAIT UNTIL THE CONDITIONS ARE RIGHT.
WE SHOULD AVOID CONFLICT WHEN THE ODDS AREN'T IN OUR FAVOR.
WHEN THE CONDITIONS ARE RIGHT?
WHAT'S GOING TO CHANGE IF WE WAIT?
I SEE WHERE YOU'RE GOING...

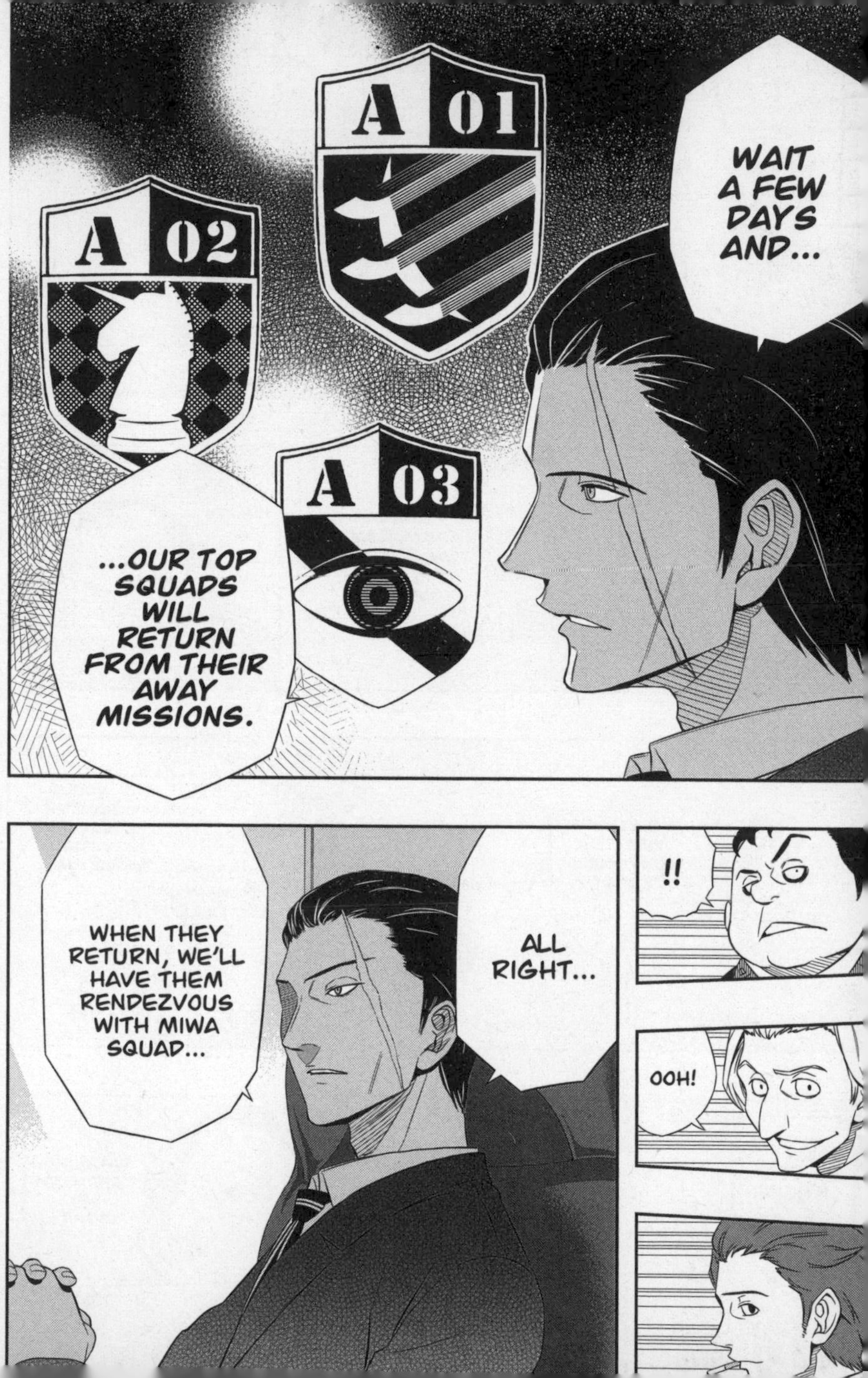
WAIT A FEW DAYS AND...
A 01
A 02
A 03
...OUR TOP SQUADS WILL RETURN FROM THEIR AWAY MISSIONS.
!!
OOH!
ALL RIGHT...
WHEN THEY RETURN, WE'LL HAVE THEM RENDEZVOUS WITH MIWA SQUAD...

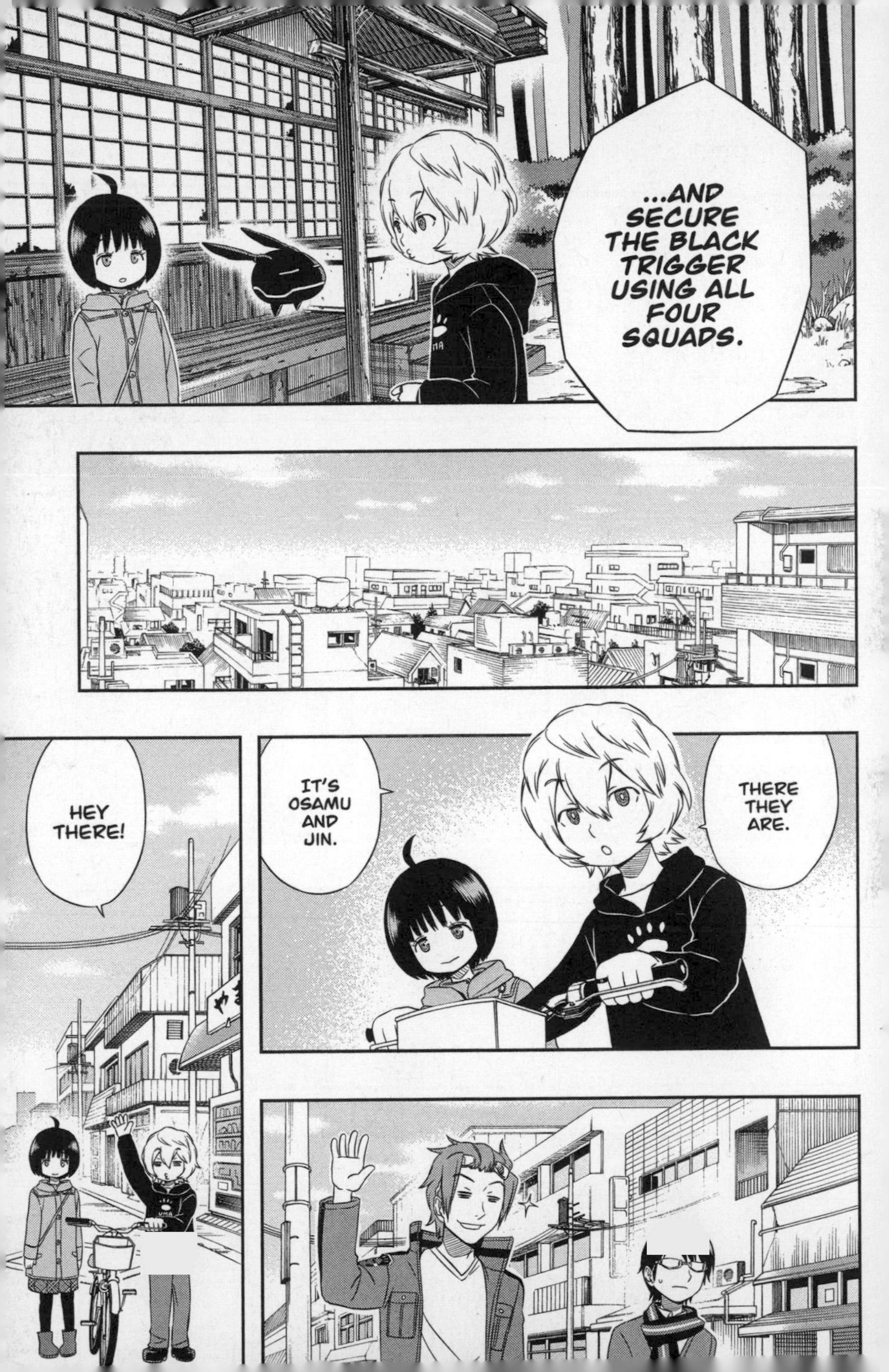
...AND SECURE THE BLACK TRIGGER USING ALL FOUR SQUADS.
THERE THEY ARE.
IT'S OSAMU AND JIN.
HEY THERE!

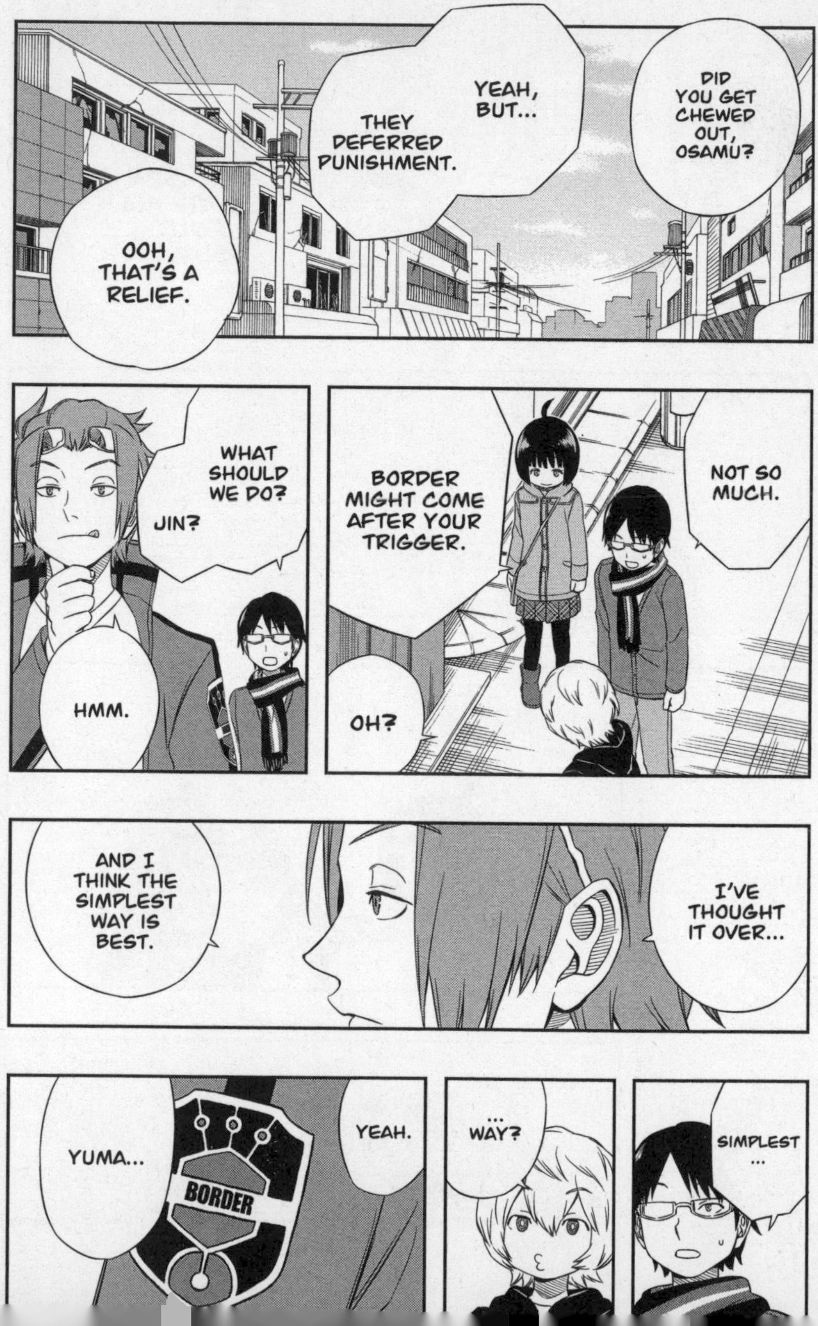
DID YOU GET CHEWED OUT, OSAMU?
YEAH, BUT...
THEY DEFERRED PUNISHMENT.
OOH, THAT'S A RELIEF.
NOT SO MUCH.
BORDER MIGHT COME AFTER YOUR TRIGGER.
OH?
WHAT SHOULD WE DO? JIN?
HMM.
I'VE THOUGHT IT OVER...
AND I THINK THE SIMPLEST WAY IS BEST.
SIMPLEST...
...WAY?
YEAH.
YUMA...
BORDER

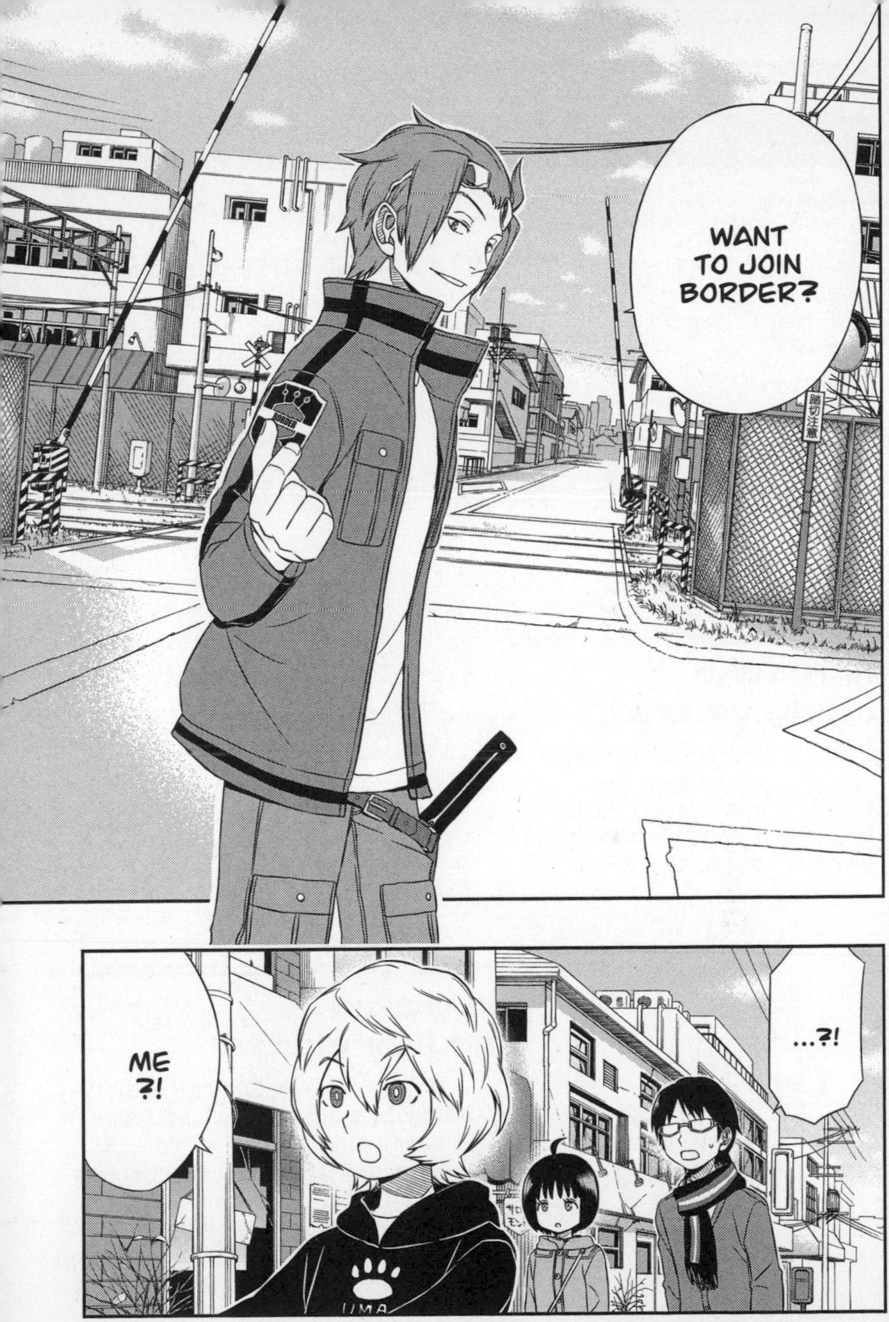
WANT TO JOIN BORDER?
...?!
ME?!

The Way They Were: Part 2

A record of the changes

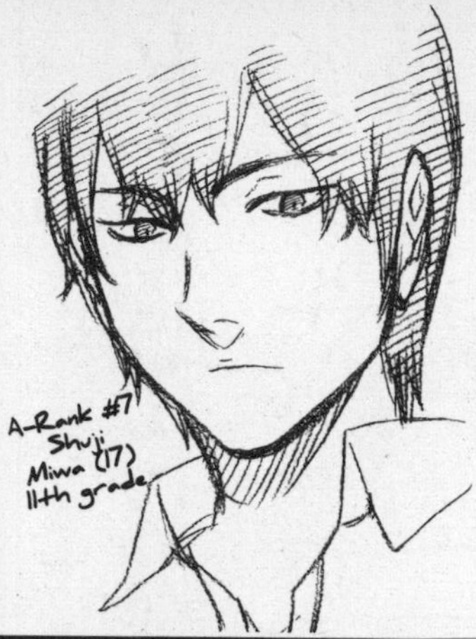
A-Rank #7
Shuji
Miwa (17)
11th grade

Miwa [early version]

Rather mature for 17. He didn't have a sister complex at this point. He looks like a mix between Karasuma and Kazama (a character who appears later in this volume). His concept became totally different, but the points "the first A-Rank Border agent who battles Yuma" and "uses bullets that become weights" never changed.

Narasaka [early version]

Didn't change much. He was always a good sniper. The handsome, artsy type. He looks like he'd be at home playing the piano or bass guitar.

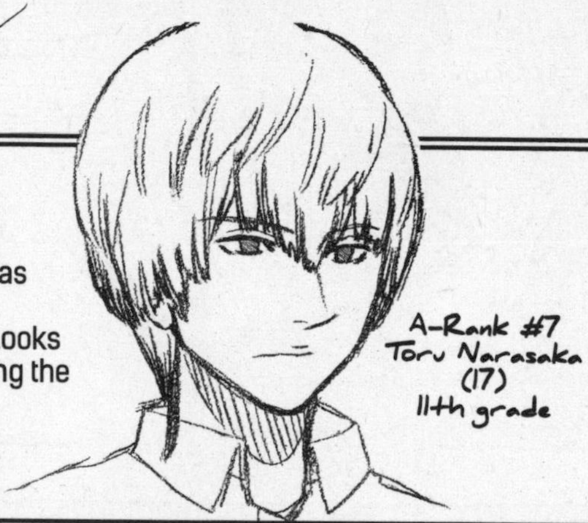
A-Rank #7
Toru Narasaka
(17)
11th grade

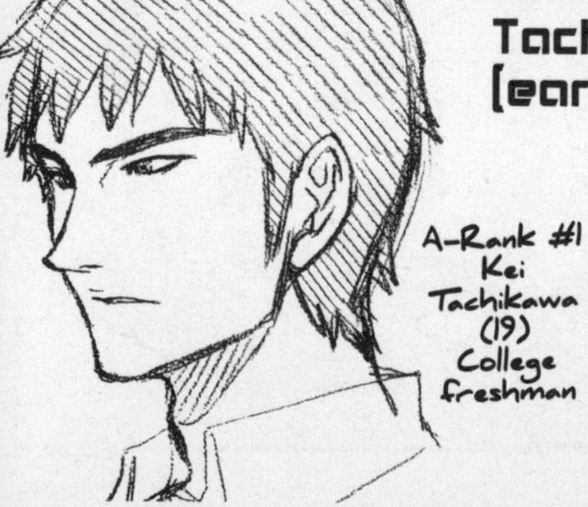
A-Rank #1
Kei
Tachikawa
(19)
College
freshman

Tachikawa [early version]

He looks like Mr. Shinoda, with maybe a little Reiji, who appears later in this volume, mixed in. A reticent master, the total opposite of Jin. He becomes a character after this volume, so if you're a reader of the graphic novels instead of the weekly serialization, then you can see for yourself how he's changed from this initial design as you keep reading.

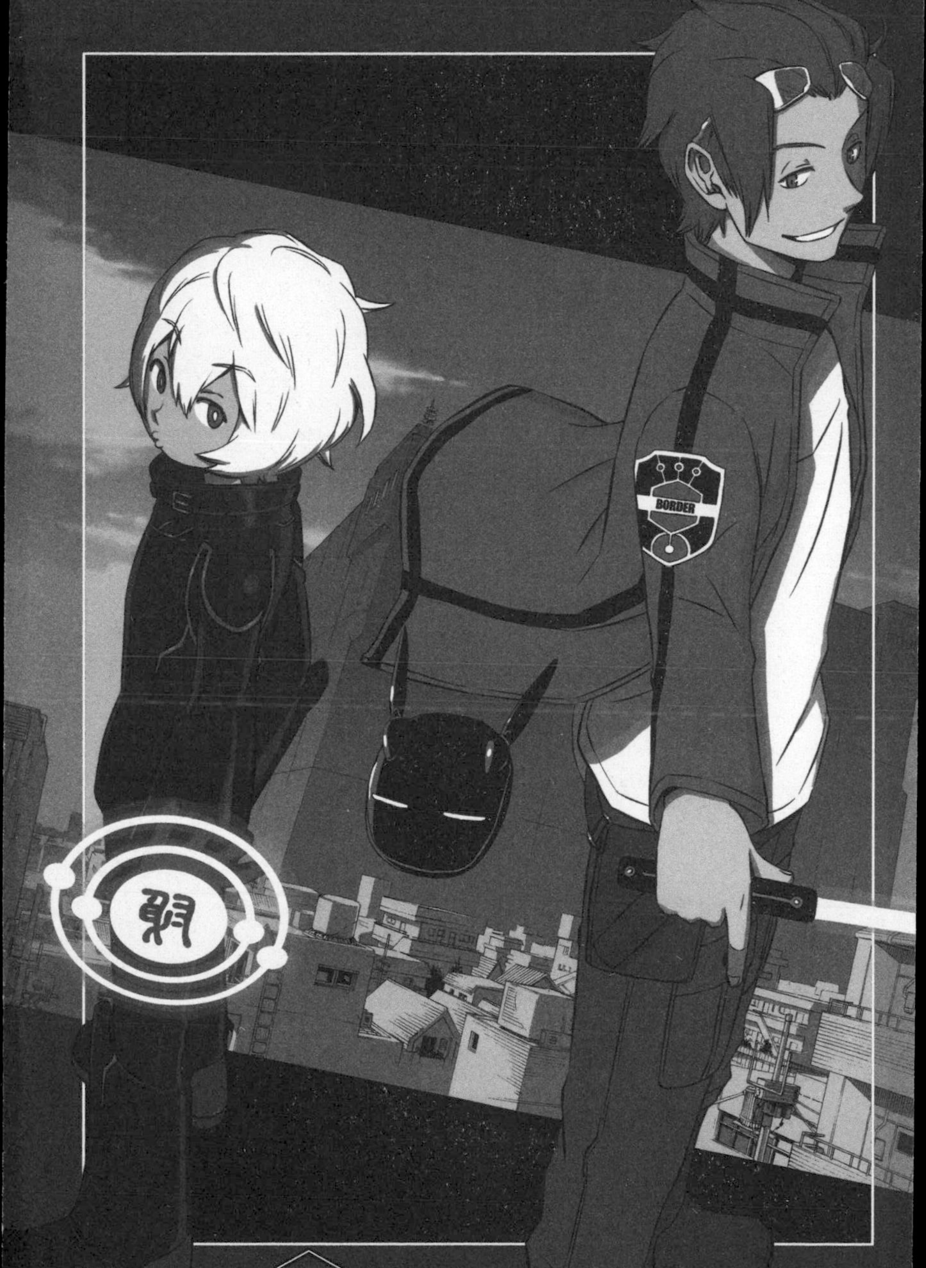
BORDER

Chapter 19 Tamakoma Branch

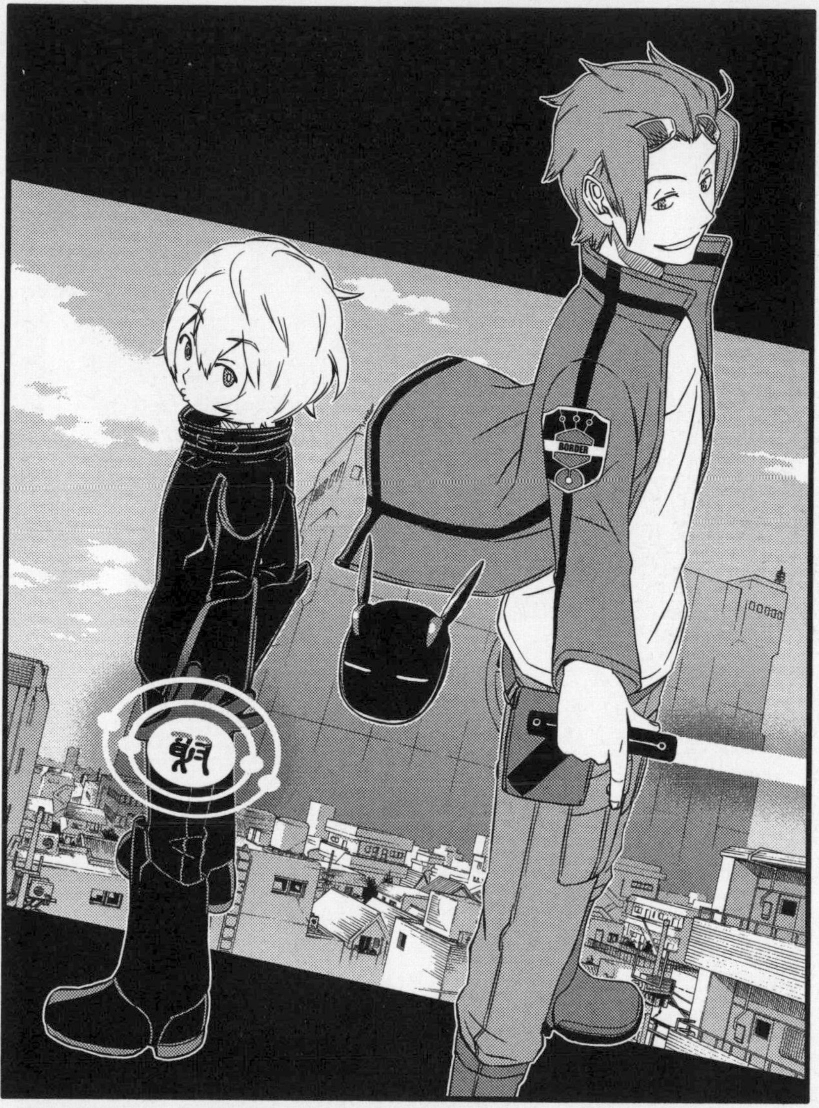
BORDER

■ 2013 *Weekly Shonen Jump* issue 30, center color page (fourth one)

I left Jin's jacket open to express the billowing breeze. Yuma and Osamu don't have that kind of design. I just realized that Jin's weapon belt is reversed left to right.

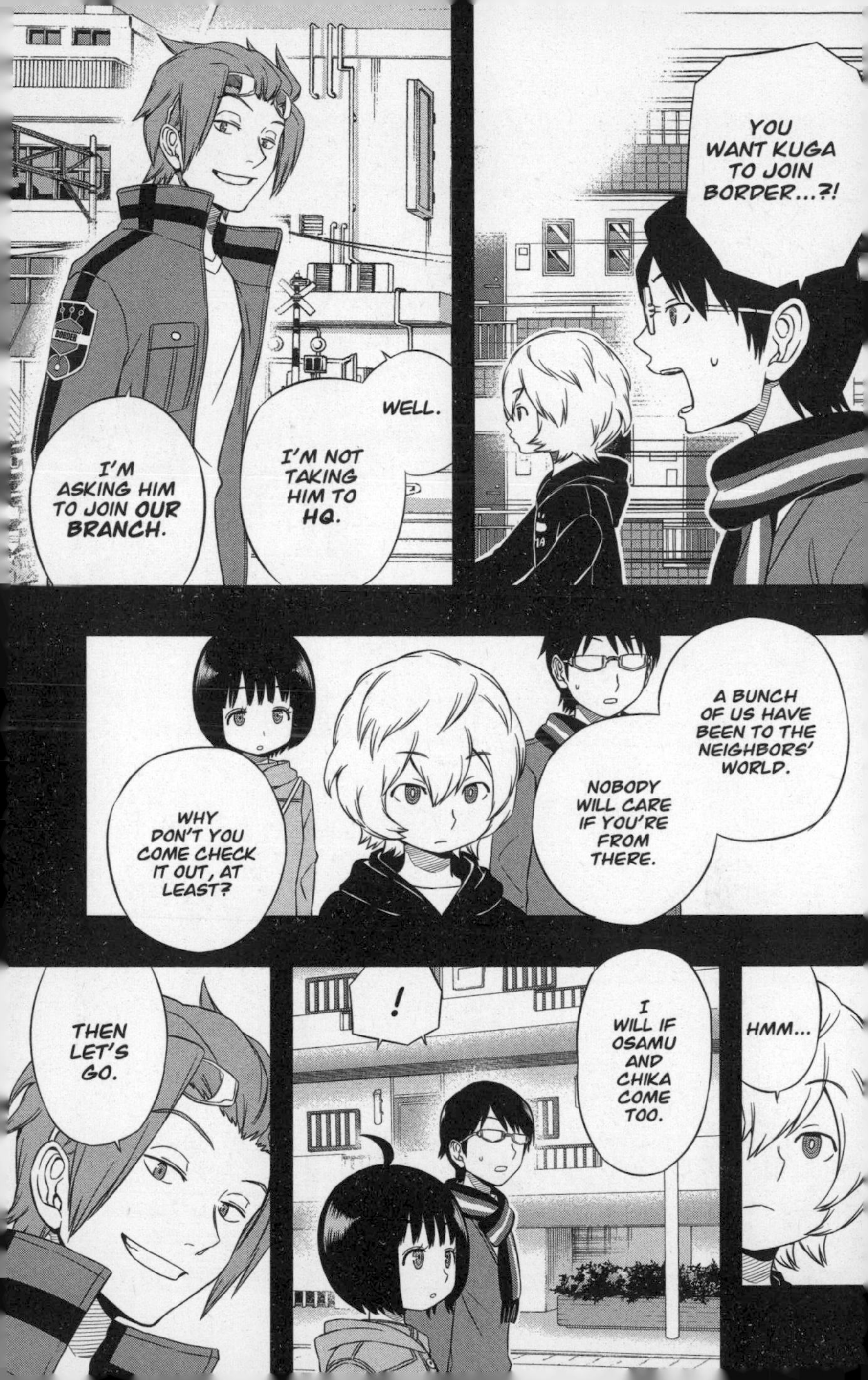
YOU WANT KUGA TO JOIN BORDER...?!
WELL.
I'M NOT TAKING HIM TO HQ.
I'M ASKING HIM TO JOIN OUR BRANCH.
A BUNCH OF US HAVE BEEN TO THE NEIGHBORS' WORLD.
NOBODY WILL CARE IF YOU'RE FROM THERE.
WHY DON'T YOU COME CHECK IT OUT, AT LEAST?
HMM...
I WILL IF OSAMU AND CHIKA COME TOO.
!
THEN LET'S GO.

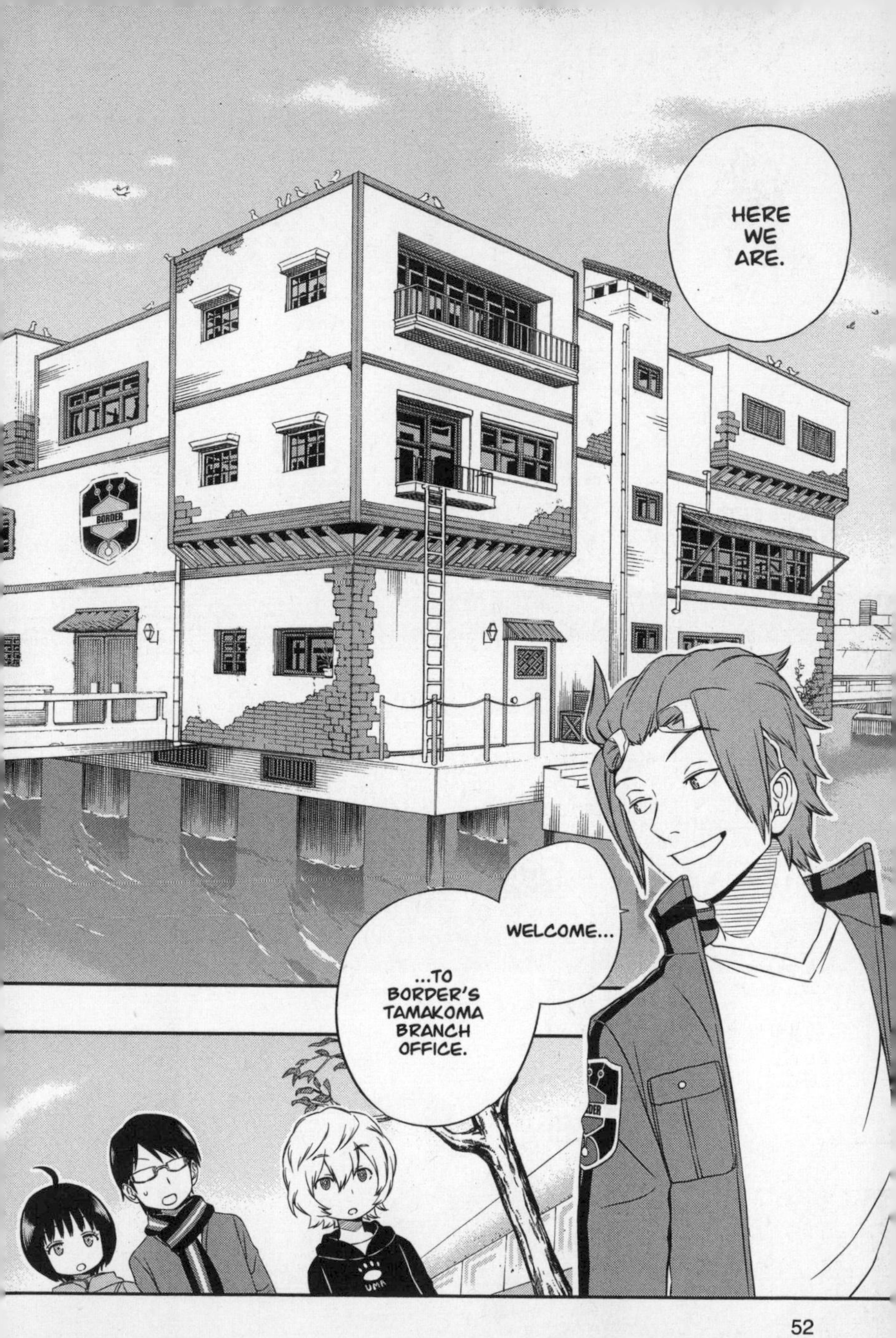
HERE WE ARE.
WELCOME...
...TO BORDER'S TAMAKOMA BRANCH OFFICE.

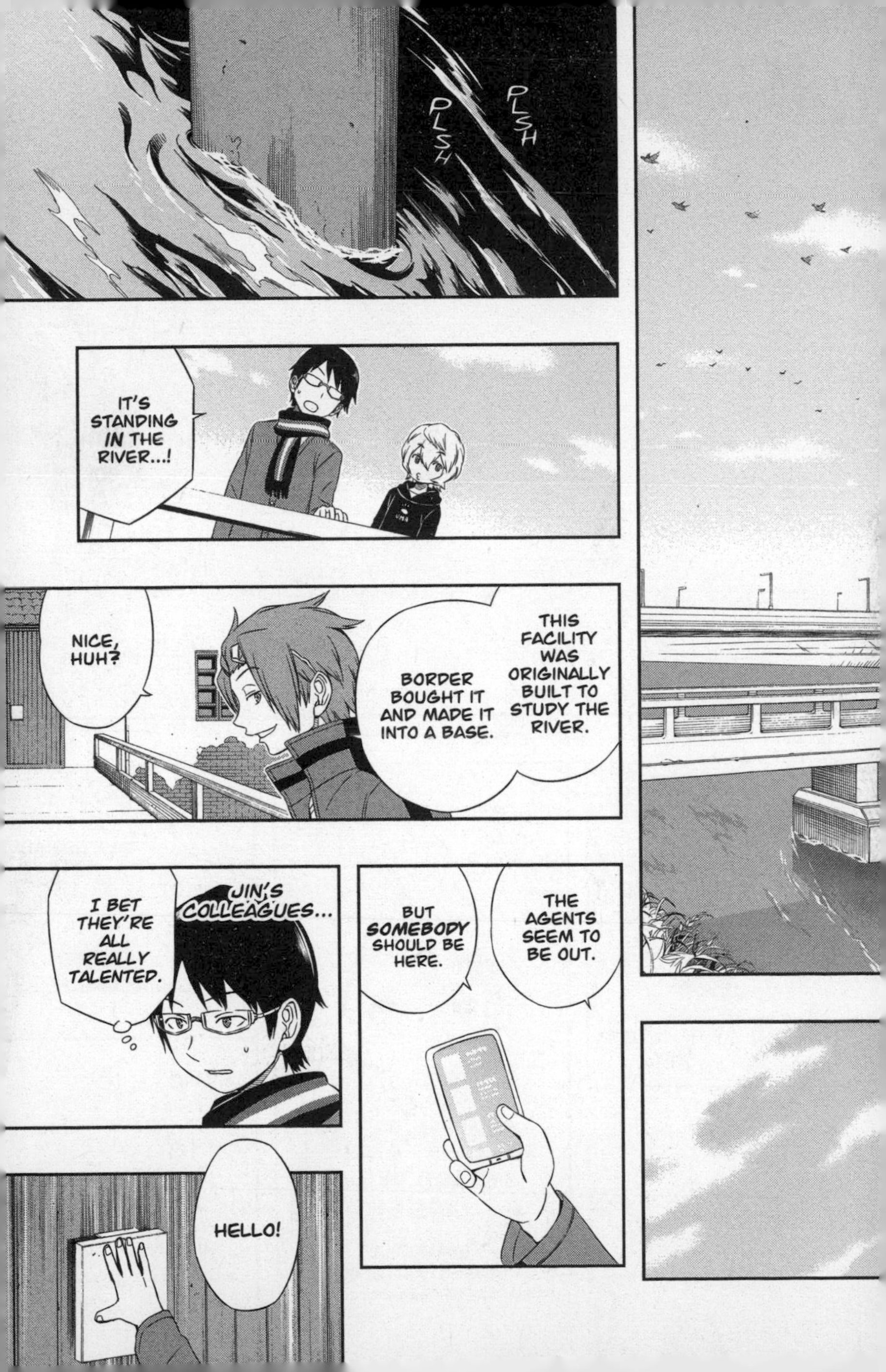
PLSH
PLSH
IT'S STANDING IN THE RIVER...!
THIS FACILITY WAS ORIGINALLY BUILT TO STUDY THE RIVER.
BORDER BOUGHT IT AND MADE IT INTO A BASE.
NICE, HUH?
THE AGENTS SEEM TO BE OUT.
BUT SOMEBODY SHOULD BE HERE.
JIN'S COLLEAGUES...
I BET THEY'RE ALL REALLY TALENTED.
HELLO!

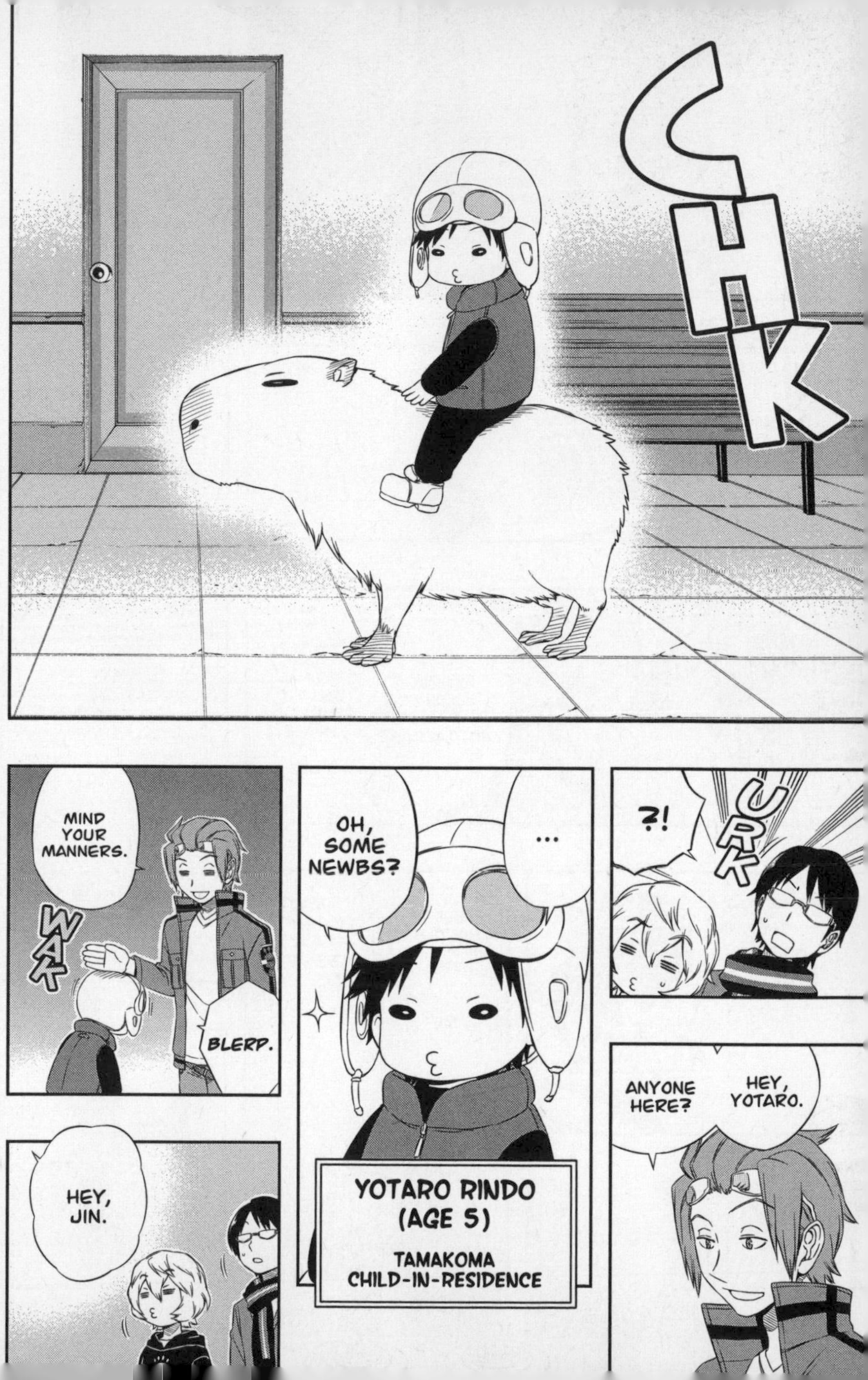
CHK
URK
?!
HEY, YOTARO.
ANYONE HERE?
...
OH, SOME NEWBS?
YOTARO RINDO (AGE 5)
TAMAKOMA CHILD-IN-RESIDENCE
MIND YOUR MANNERS.
WAK
BLERP.
HEY, JIN.

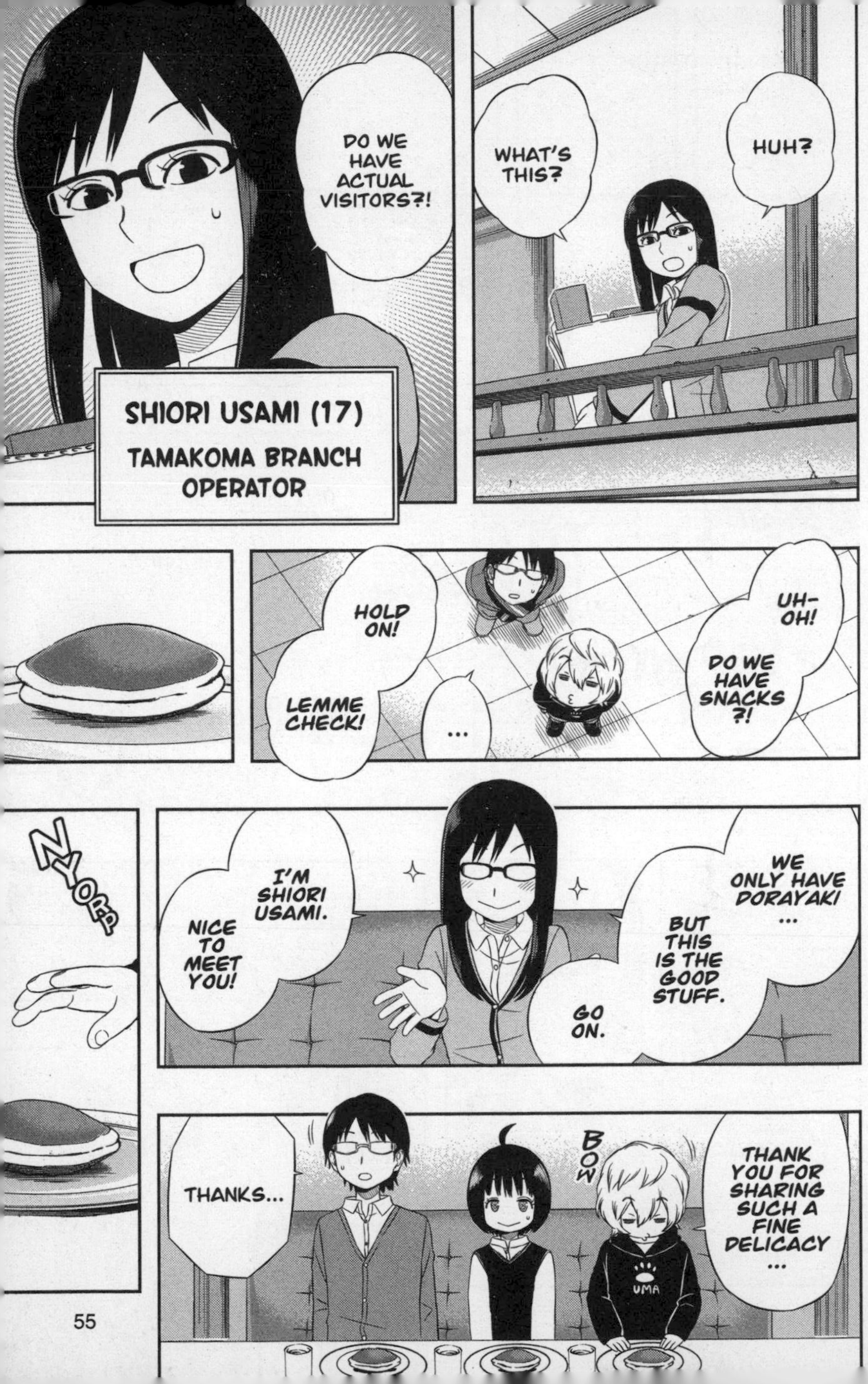
HUH?
WHAT'S THIS?
DO WE HAVE ACTUAL VISITORS?!
SHIORI USAMI (17)
TAMAKOMA BRANCH OPERATOR
UH-OH!
DO WE HAVE SNACKS?!
...
HOLD ON!
LEMME CHECK!
WE ONLY HAVE DORAYAKI...
BUT THIS IS THE GOOD STUFF.
GO ON.
I'M SHIORI USAMI.
NICE TO MEET YOU!
NYORP
BOW
THANK YOU FOR SHARING SUCH A FINE DELICACY...
THANKS...
UMA

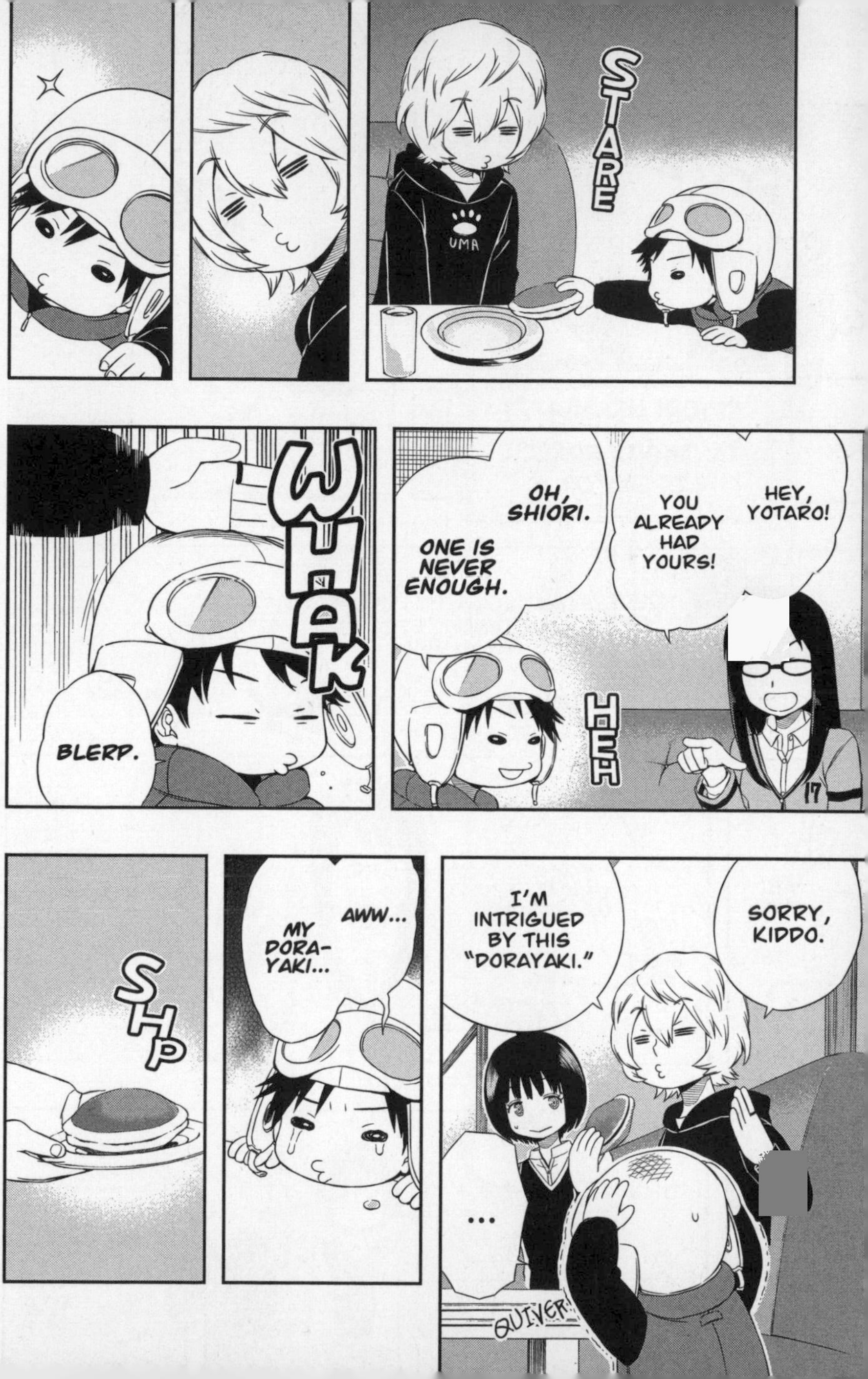
STARE
HEY, YOTARO!
YOU ALREADY HAD YOURS!
OH, SHIORI.
ONE IS NEVER ENOUGH.
HEH
WHAK
BLERP.
SORRY, KIDDO.
I'M INTRIGUED BY THIS "DORAYAKI."
...
QUIVER
AWW...
MY DORA-YAKI...
SHP

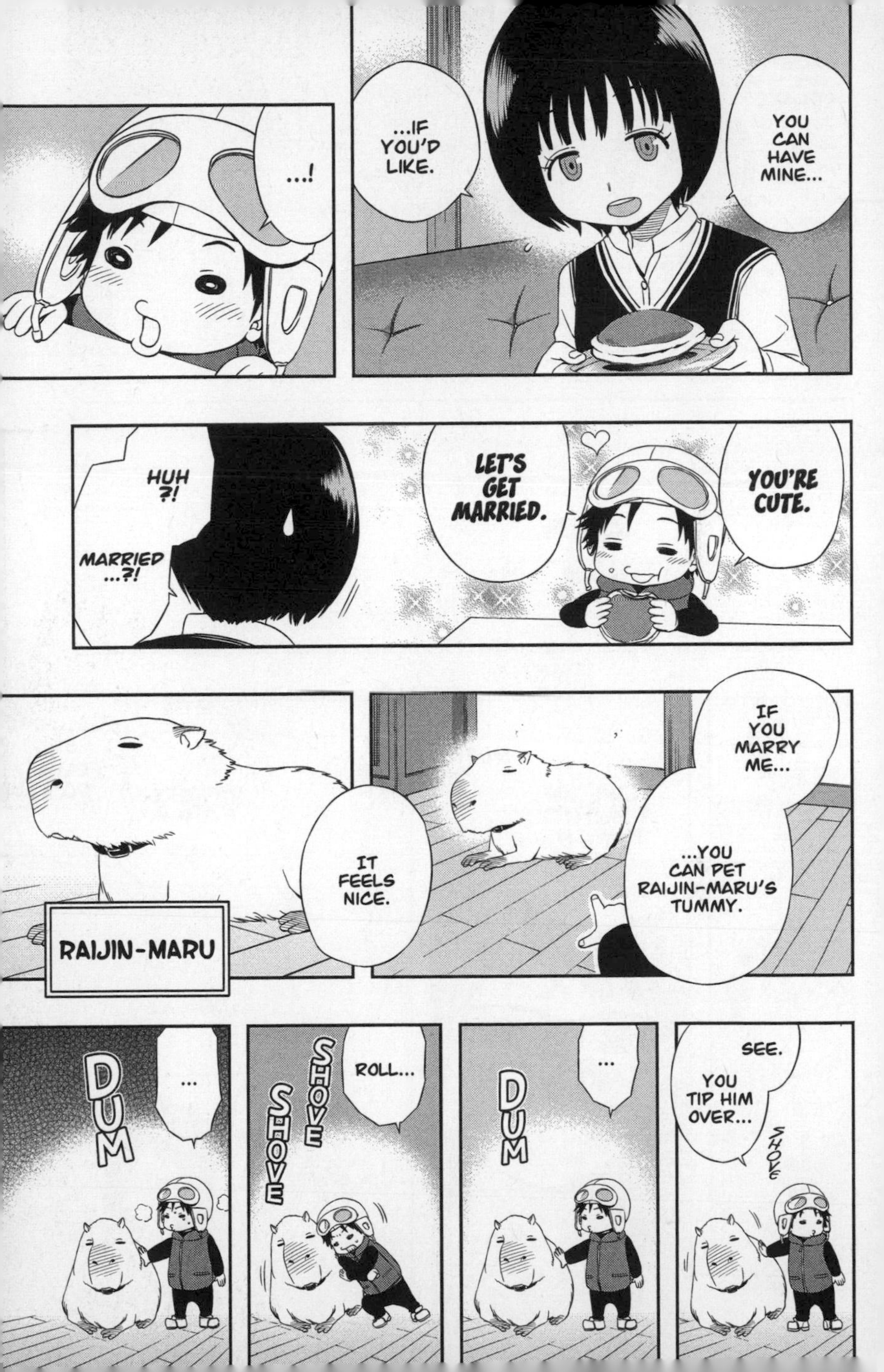
YOU CAN HAVE MINE...
...IF YOU'D LIKE.
...!
YOU'RE CUTE.
LET'S GET MARRIED.
HUH ?!
MARRIED ...?!
IF YOU MARRY ME...
...YOU CAN PET RAIJIN-MARU'S TUMMY.
IT FEELS NICE.
RAIJIN-MARU
SEE.
YOU TIP HIM OVER...
SHOVE
...
DUM
ROLL...
SHOVE
SHOVE
...
DUM

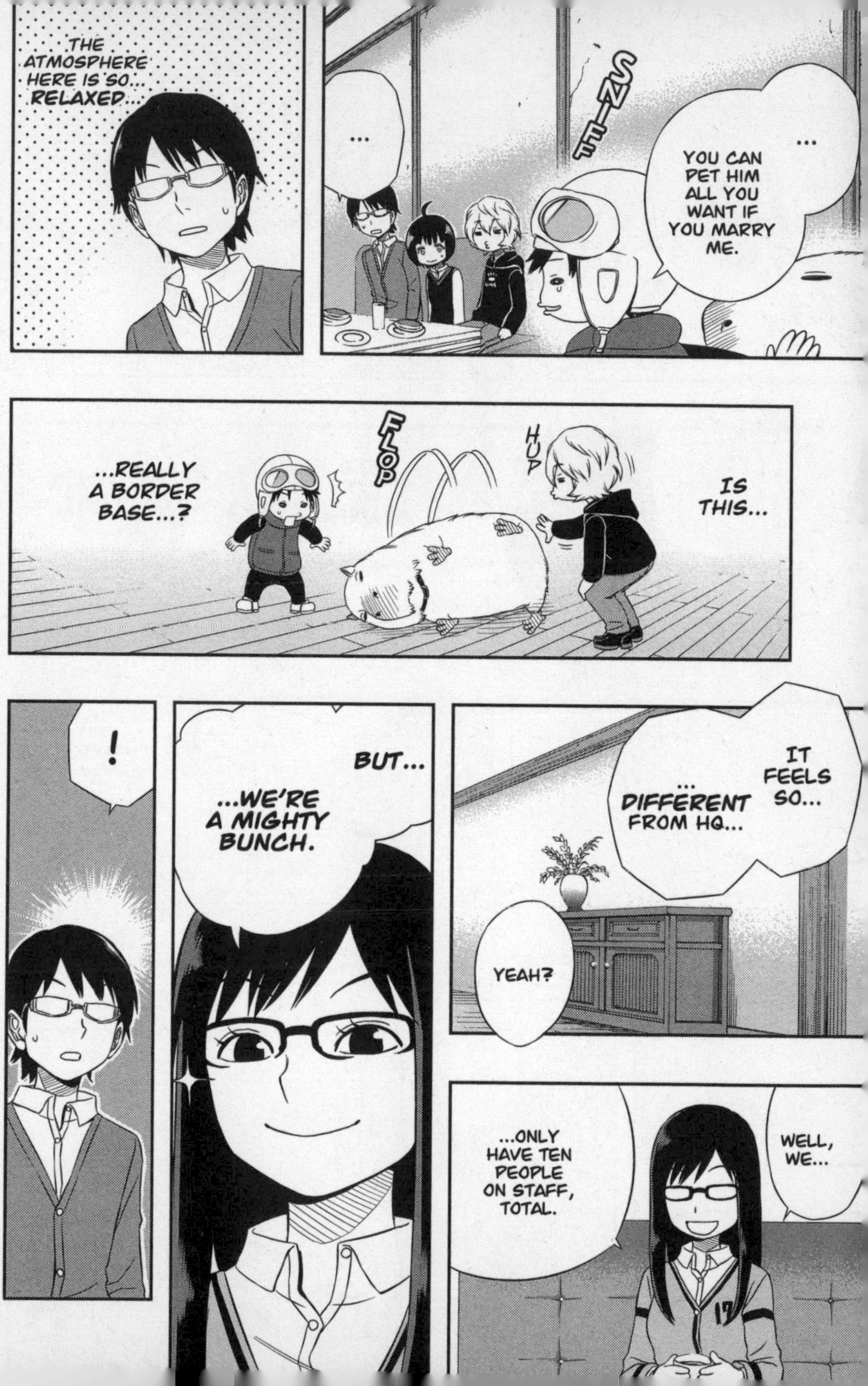
...
YOU CAN PET HIM ALL YOU WANT IF YOU MARRY ME.
SNIFF
...
THE ATMOSPHERE HERE IS SO... RELAXED...
IS THIS...
HUP
FLOP
...REALLY A BORDER BASE...?
IT FEELS SO...
...DIFFERENT FROM HQ...
YEAH?
WELL, WE...
...ONLY HAVE TEN PEOPLE ON STAFF, TOTAL.
BUT...
...WE'RE A MIGHTY BUNCH.
!

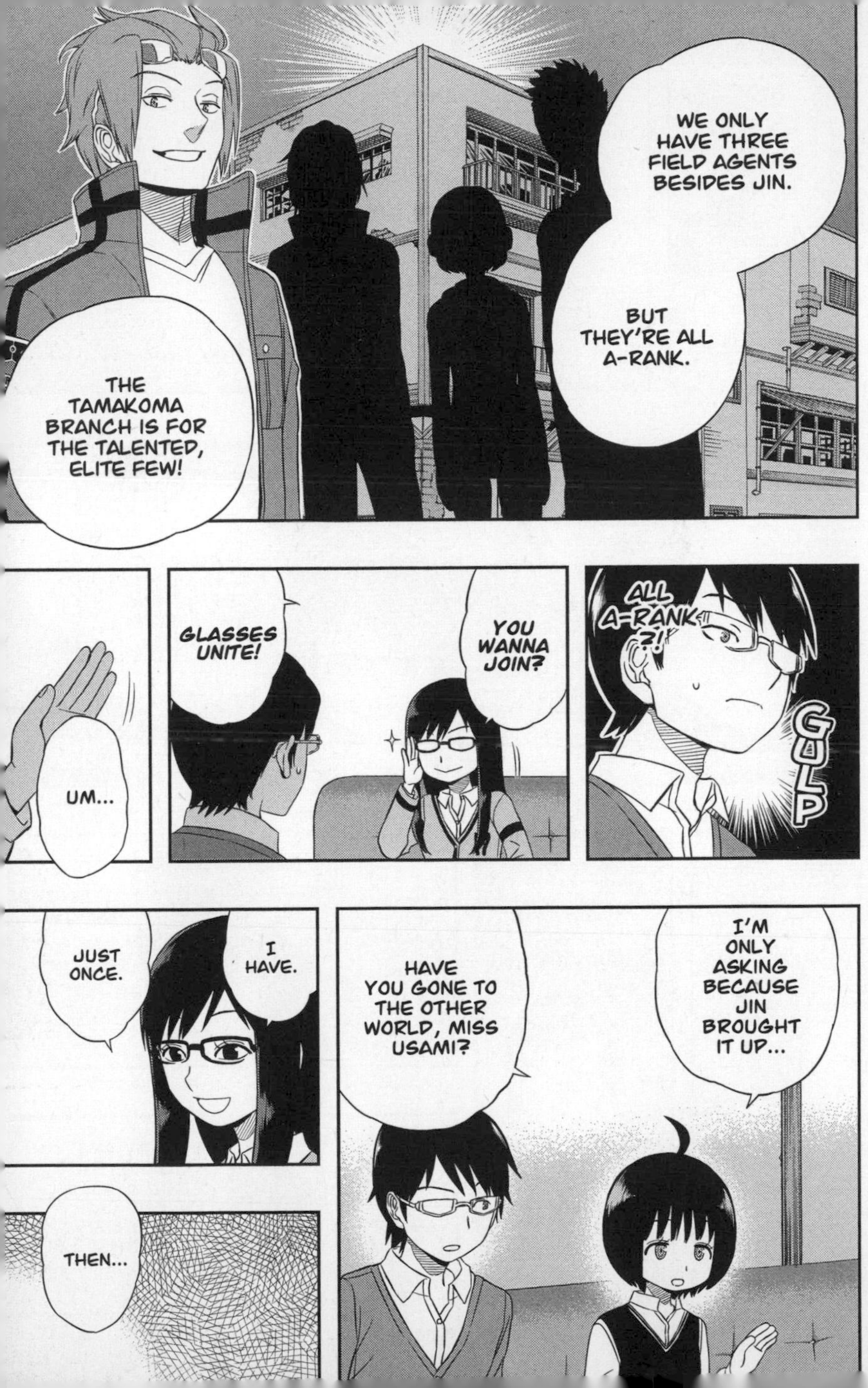
WE ONLY HAVE THREE FIELD AGENTS BESIDES JIN.
BUT THEY'RE ALL A-RANK.
THE TAMAKOMA BRANCH IS FOR THE TALENTED, ELITE FEW!
ALL A-RANK?!
GULP
YOU WANNA JOIN?
GLASSES UNITE!
UM...
I'M ONLY ASKING BECAUSE JIN BROUGHT IT UP...
HAVE YOU GONE TO THE OTHER WORLD, MISS USAMI?
I HAVE.
JUST ONCE.
THEN...

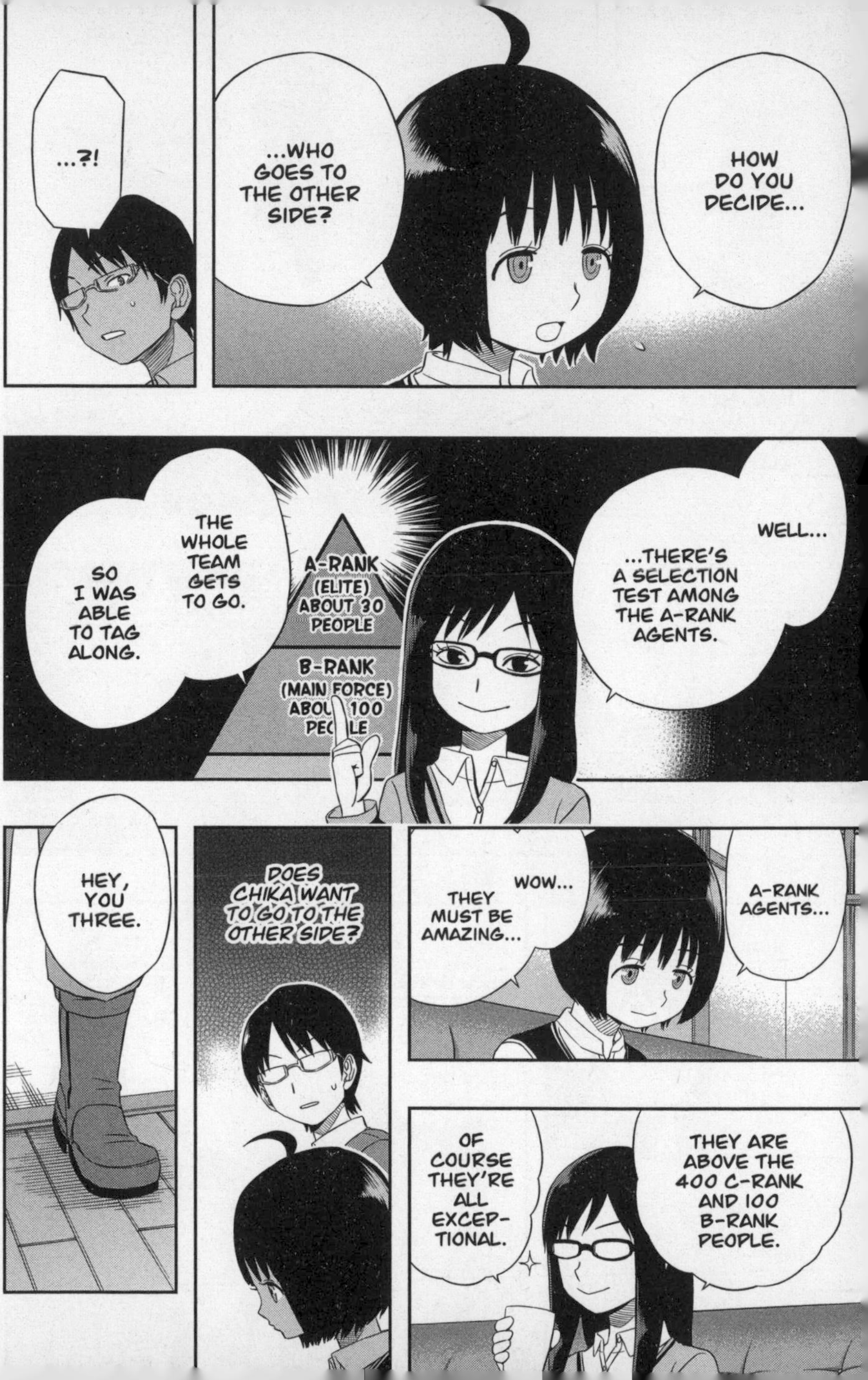
HOW DO YOU DECIDE...
...WHO GOES TO THE OTHER SIDE?
...?!
WELL...
...THERE'S A SELECTION TEST AMONG THE A-RANK AGENTS.
A-RANK (ELITE) ABOUT 30 PEOPLE
B-RANK (MAIN FORCE)
THE WHOLE TEAM GETS TO GO.
SO I WAS ABLE TO TAG ALONG.
A-RANK AGENTS...
WOW... THEY MUST BE AMAZING...
THEY ARE ABOVE THE 400 C-RANK AND 100 B-RANK PEOPLE.
OF COURSE THEY'RE ALL EXCEP-TIONAL.
DOES CHIKA WANT TO GO TO THE OTHER SIDE?
HEY, YOU THREE.

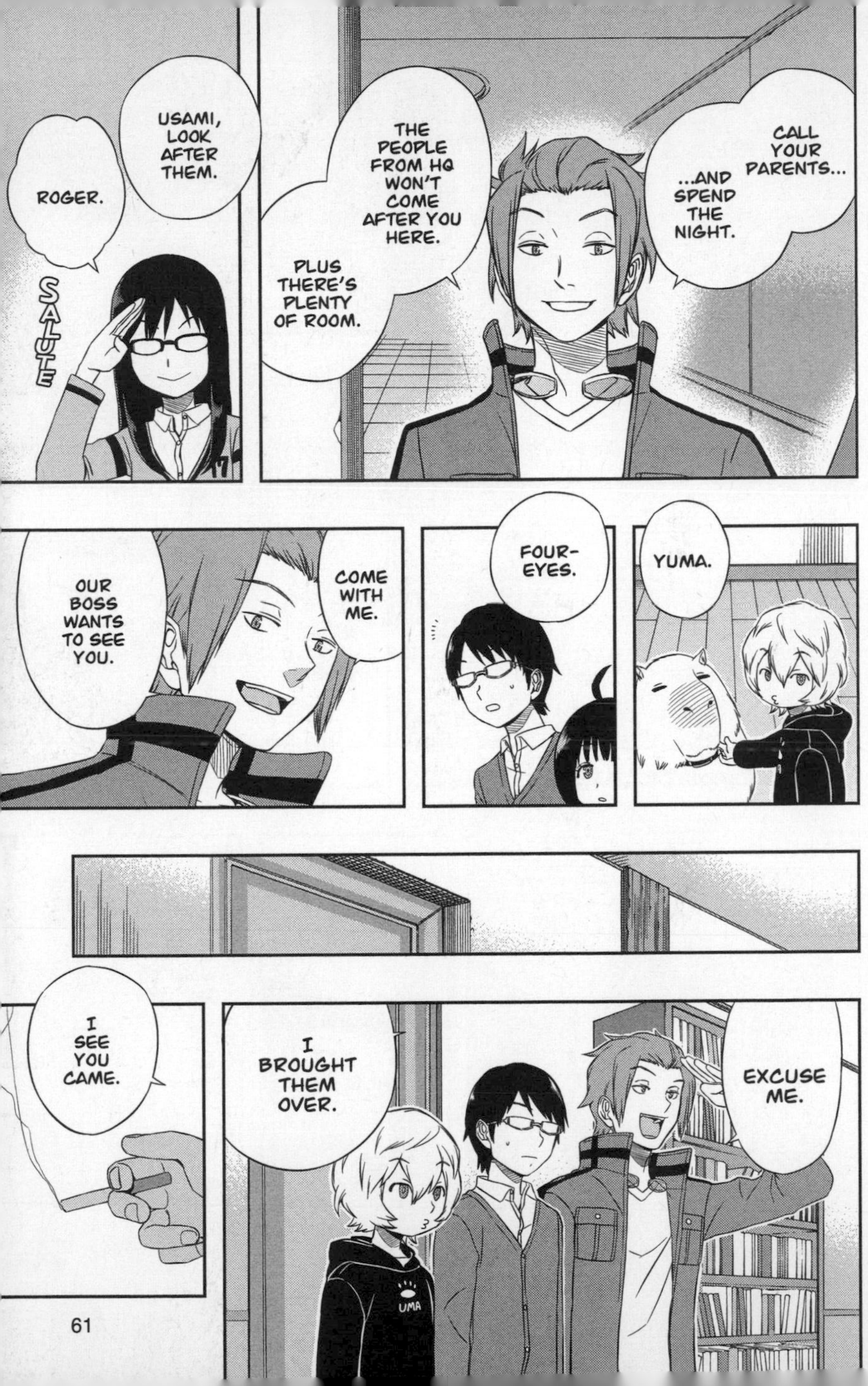
CALL YOUR PARENTS...
...AND SPEND THE NIGHT.
THE PEOPLE FROM HQ WON'T COME AFTER YOU HERE.
PLUS THERE'S PLENTY OF ROOM.
USAMI, LOOK AFTER THEM.
ROGER.
SALUTE
YUMA.
FOUR-EYES.
COME WITH ME.
OUR BOSS WANTS TO SEE YOU.
EXCUSE ME.
I BROUGHT THEM OVER.
I SEE YOU CAME.

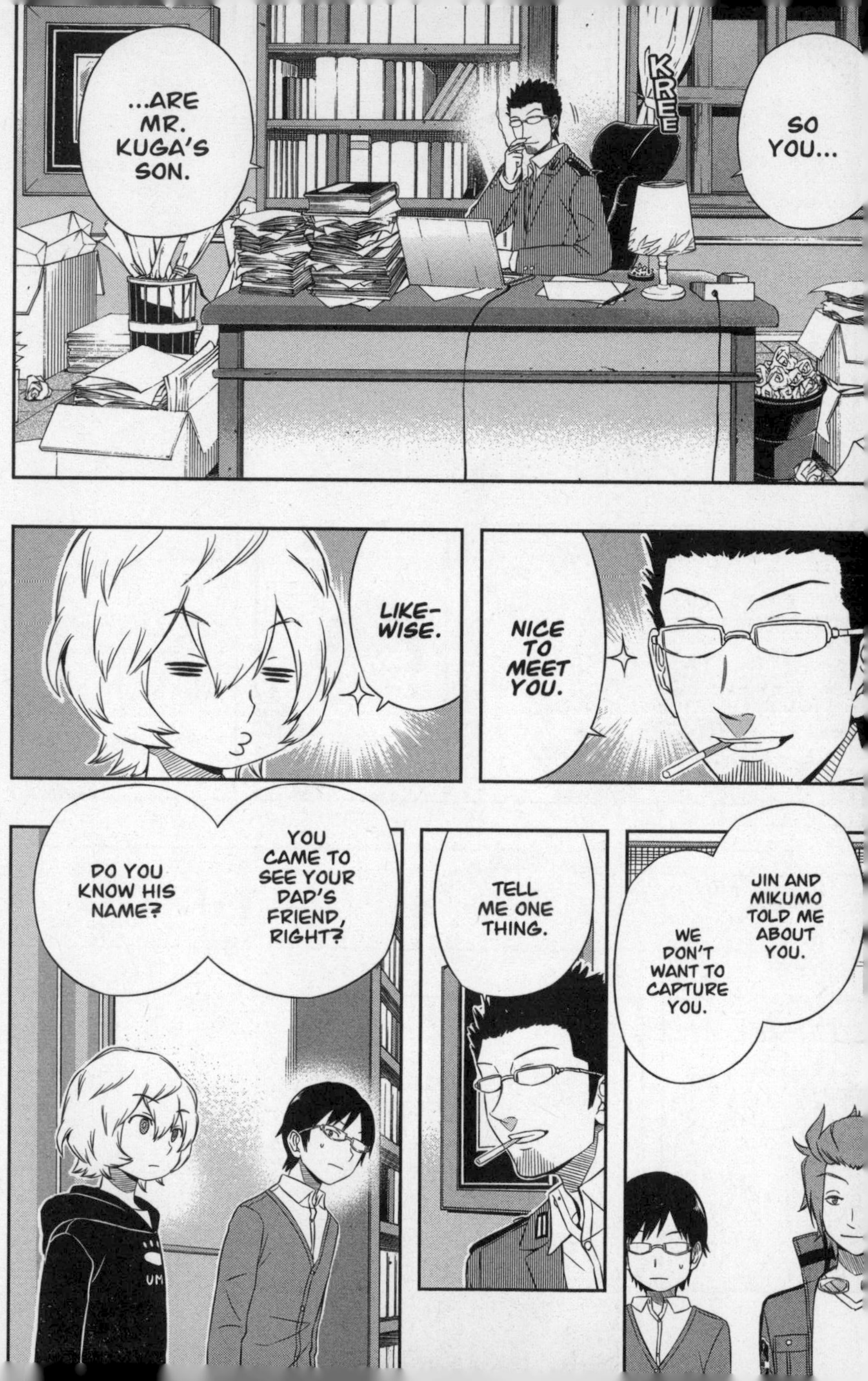
SO YOU...
KREE
...ARE MR. KUGA'S SON.
NICE TO MEET YOU.
LIKE-WISE.
JIN AND MIKUMO TOLD ME ABOUT YOU.
WE DON'T WANT TO CAPTURE YOU.
TELL ME ONE THING.
YOU CAME TO SEE YOUR DAD'S FRIEND, RIGHT?
DO YOU KNOW HIS NAME?

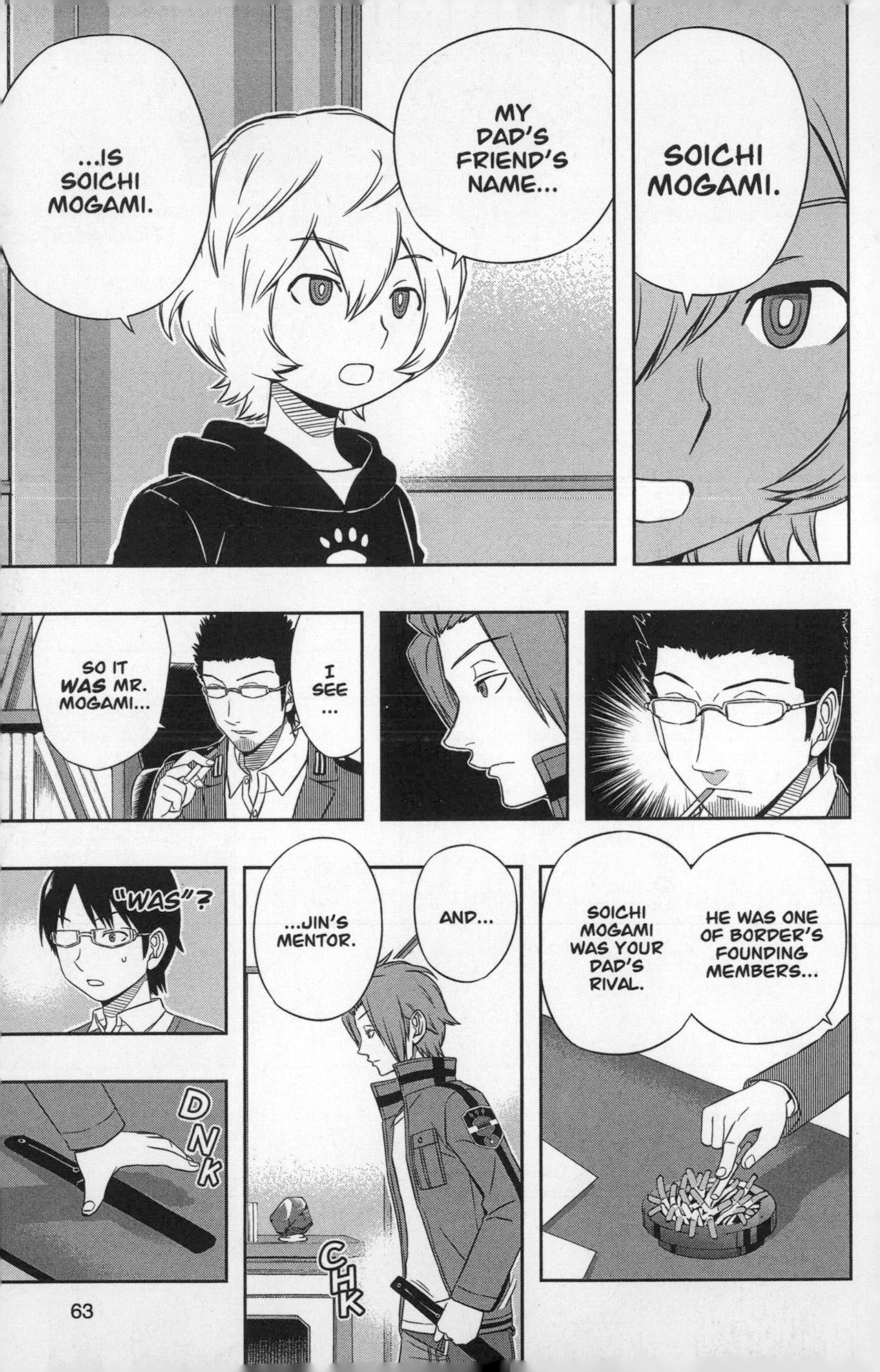
SOICHI MOGAMI.
MY DAD'S FRIEND'S NAME...
...IS SOICHI MOGAMI.
I SEE ...
SO IT WAS MR. MOGAMI...
HE WAS ONE OF BORDER'S FOUNDING MEMBERS...
SOICHI MOGAMI WAS YOUR DAD'S RIVAL.
AND...
...JIN'S MENTOR.
CHK
"WAS"?
DNK

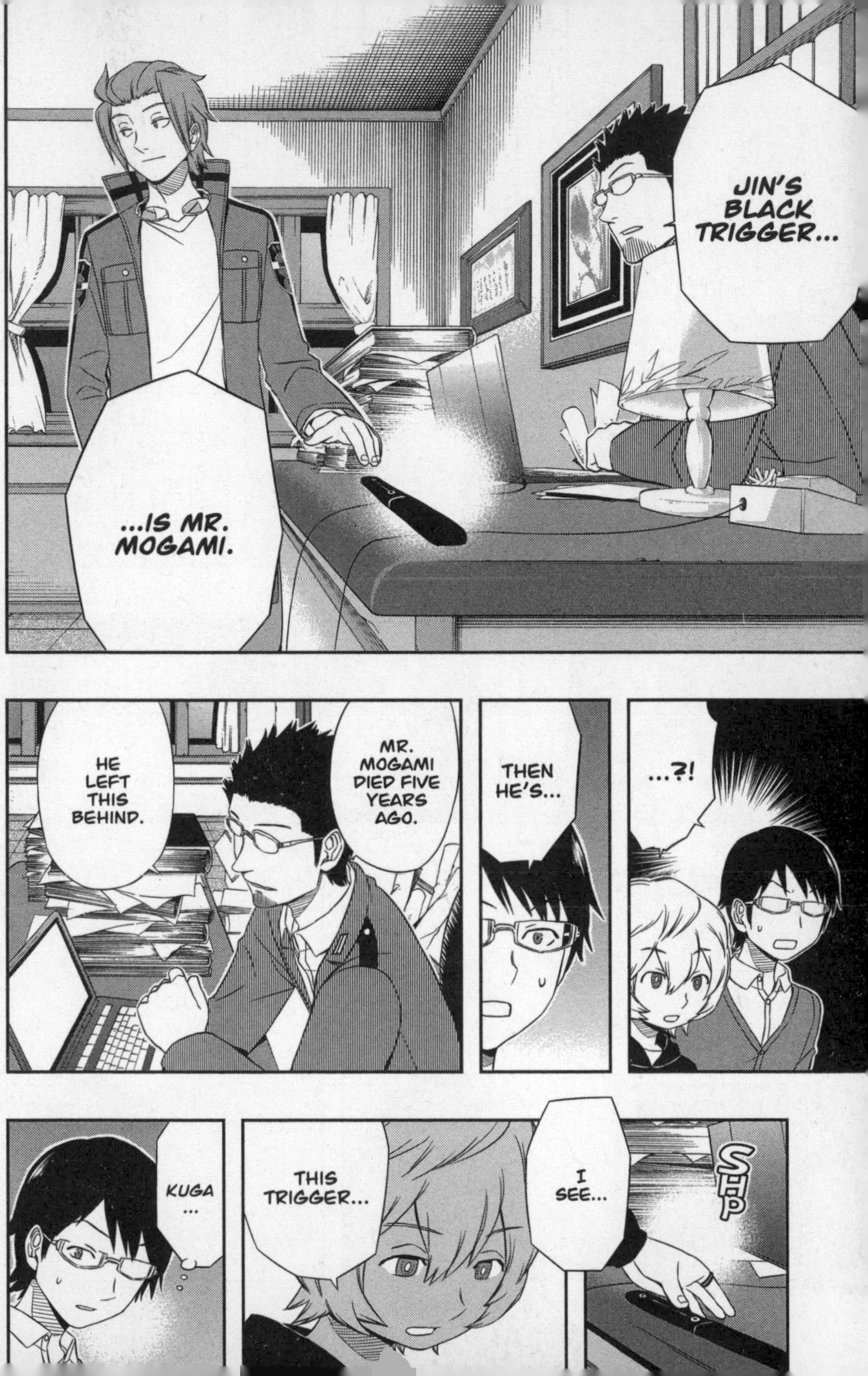
JIN'S BLACK TRIGGER...
...IS MR. MOGAMI.
...?!
THEN HE'S...
MR. MOGAMI DIED FIVE YEARS AGO.
HE LEFT THIS BEHIND.
SHP
I SEE...
THIS TRIGGER...
KUGA ...

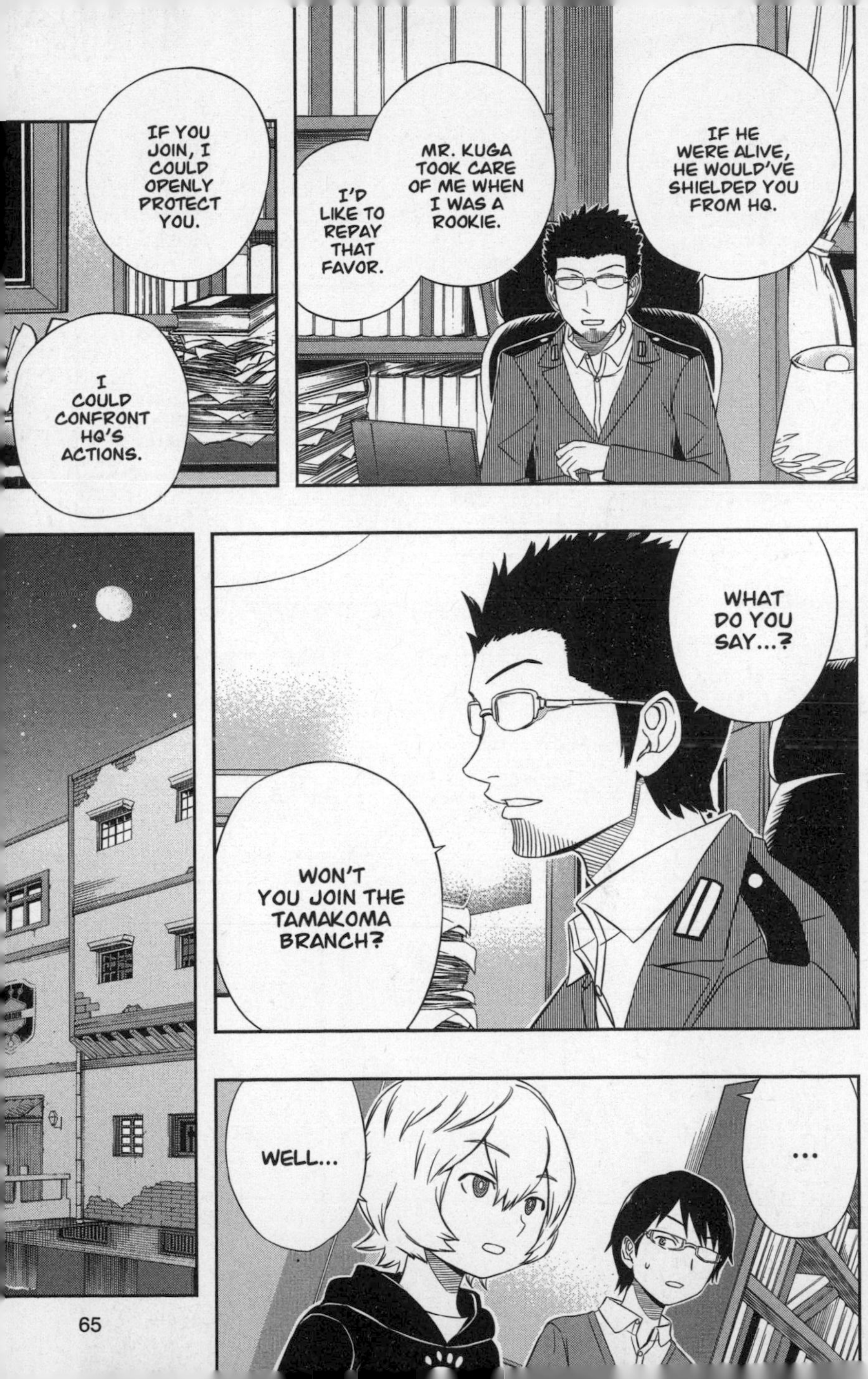
IF HE WERE ALIVE, HE WOULD'VE SHIELDED YOU FROM HQ.
MR. KUGA TOOK CARE OF ME WHEN I WAS A ROOKIE.
I'D LIKE TO REPAY THAT FAVOR.
IF YOU JOIN, I COULD OPENLY PROTECT YOU.
I COULD CONFRONT HQ'S ACTIONS.
WHAT DO YOU SAY...?
WON'T YOU JOIN THE TAMAKOMA BRANCH?
...
WELL...

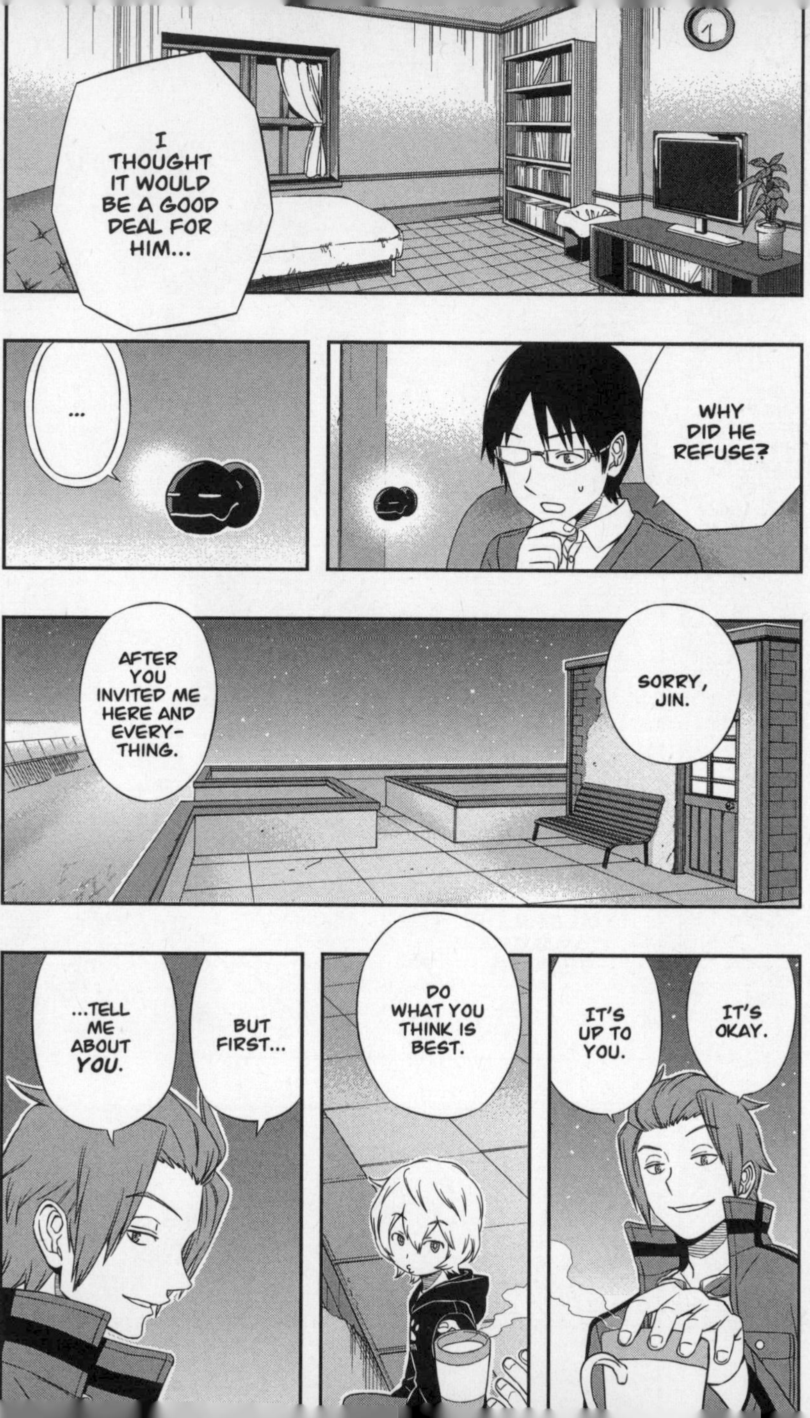
I THOUGHT IT WOULD BE A GOOD DEAL FOR HIM...
WHY DID HE REFUSE?
...
SORRY, JIN.
AFTER YOU INVITED ME HERE AND EVERYTHING.
IT'S OKAY.
IT'S UP TO YOU.
DO WHAT YOU THINK IS BEST.
BUT FIRST...
...TELL ME ABOUT YOU.

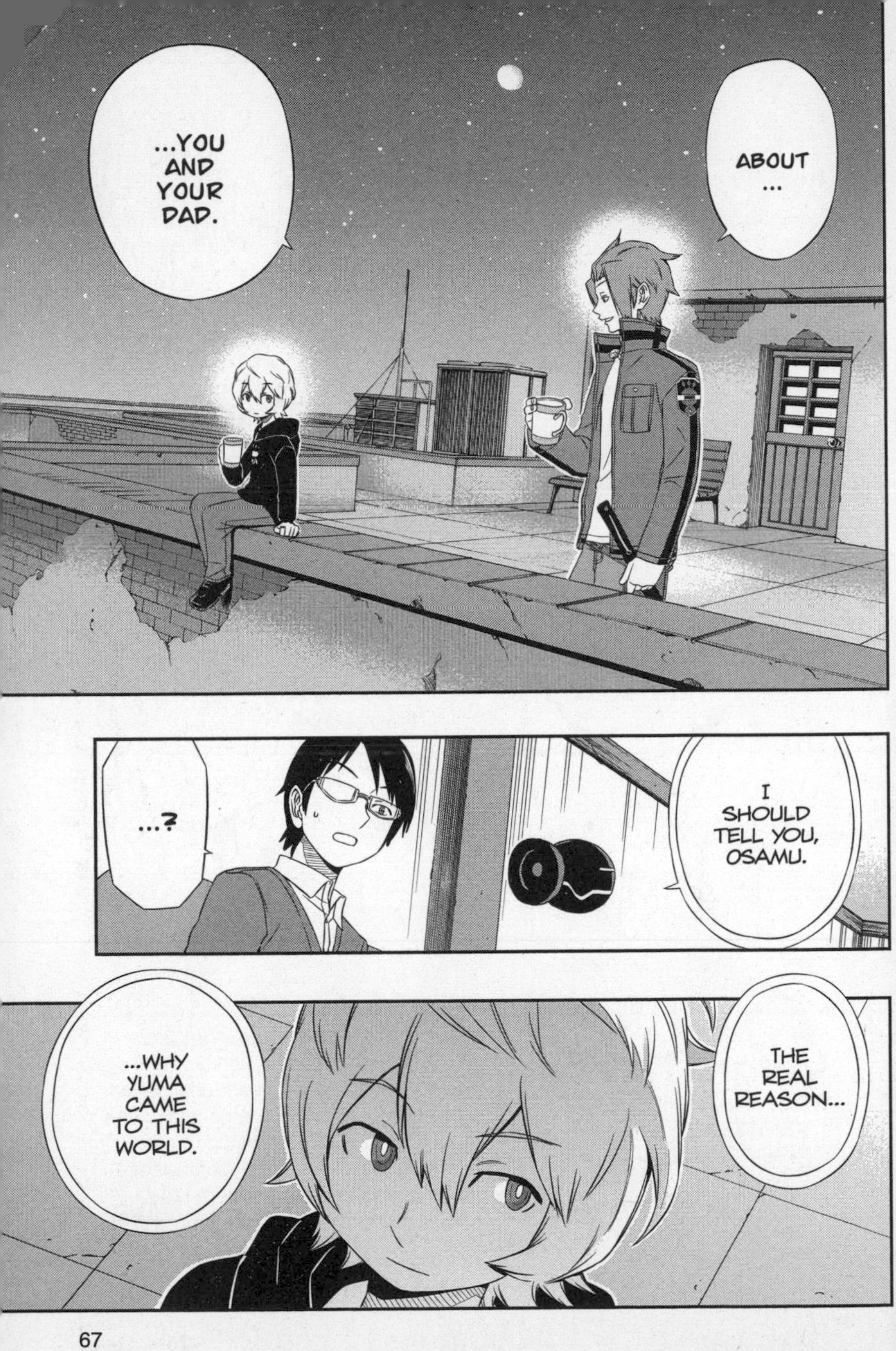
ABOUT ...
...YOU AND YOUR DAD.
I SHOULD TELL YOU, OSAMU.
...?
THE REAL REASON...
...WHY YUMA CAME TO THIS WORLD.

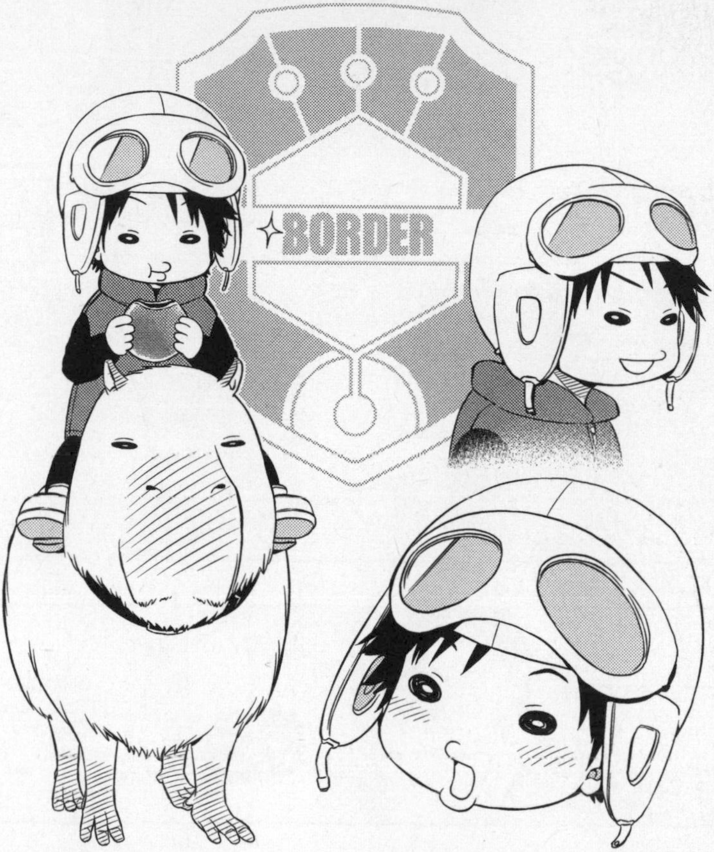
BORDER

Yotaro Rindo

- 5 years old (kindergartner)
- Born Sept. 22
- Falco, Blood type AB
- Height: 3'3"
- Likes: Snacks that other people are eating, girls, riding Raijin-maru

Yotaro also appeared in the one-shot. There, he had an older sister, but we'll see... When I was little, I went through a period where I wanted to ride a large dog or lion around, so I've always wanted to draw a character who rides a dog-like creature. I'm glad I got the chance. (Gomuzo from a previous title was also conceived along the same line.)

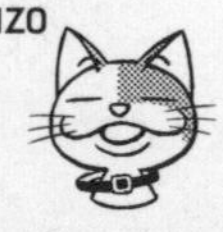

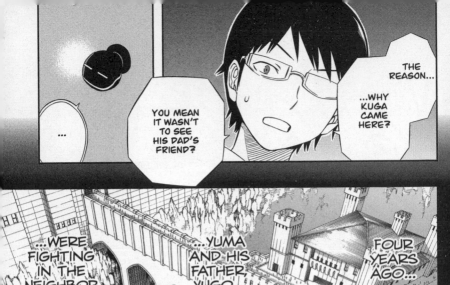

THE REASON...
...WHY KUGA CAME HERE?
YOU MEAN IT WASN'T TO SEE HIS DAD'S FRIEND?
...
FOUR YEARS AGO...
...YUMA AND HIS FATHER, YUGO...
...WERE FIGHTING IN THE NEIGHBOR WARS.
Chapter 20 Yuma Kuga: Part 4
ENEMY CLOSING IN!
WE DON'T HAVE MANY BULLETS LEFT!
TRION SOLDIERS!! I SEE BANDERS!

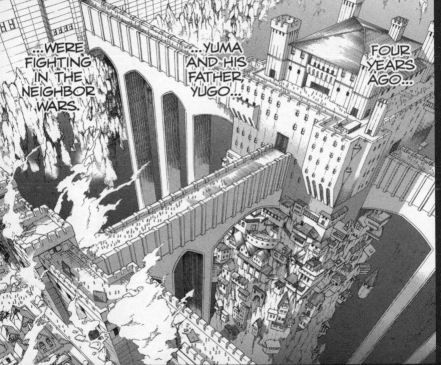

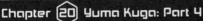

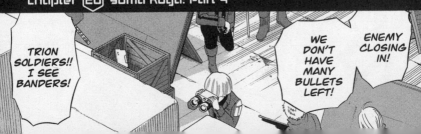

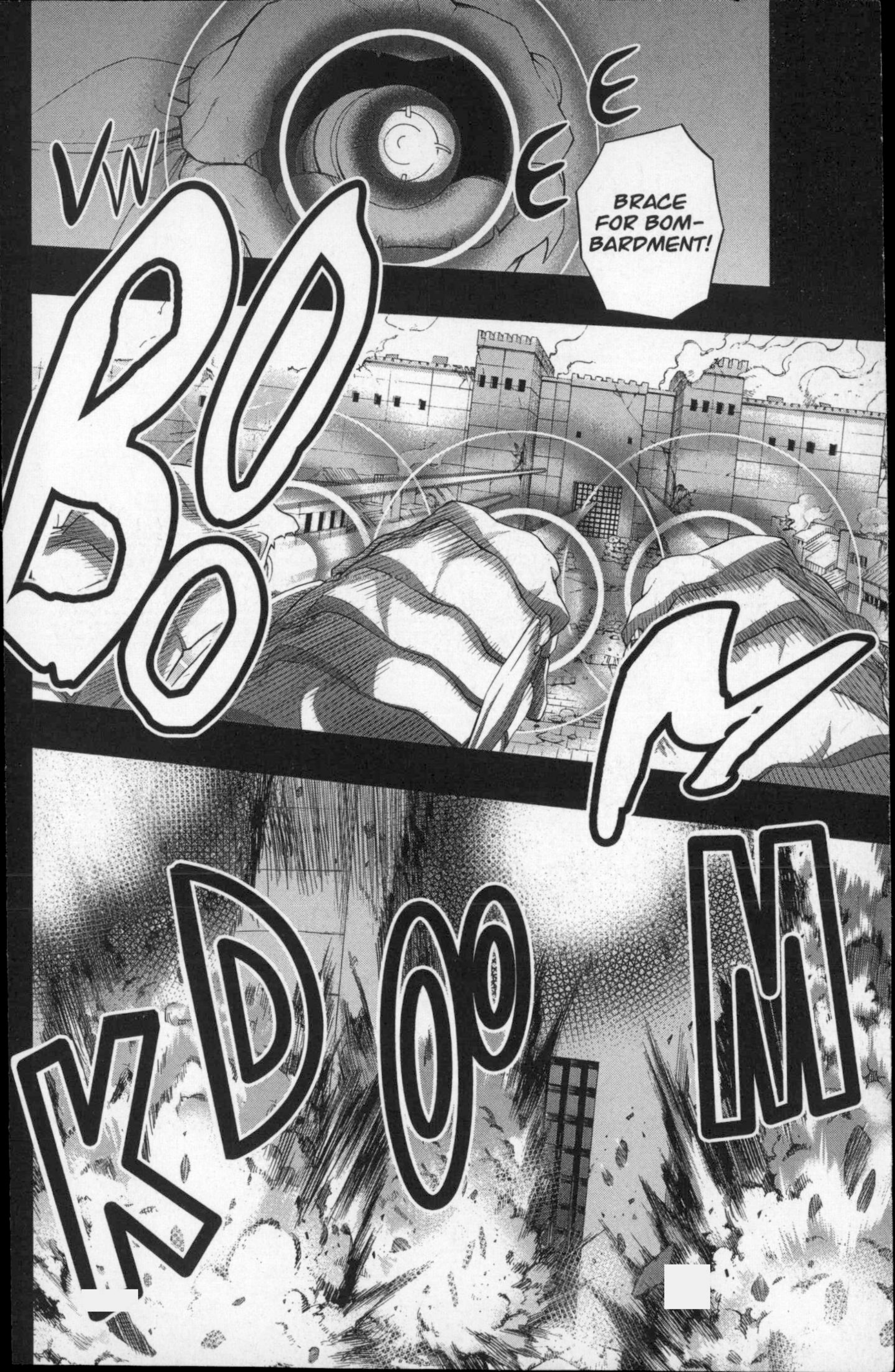
BRACE FOR BOM-
BARDMENT!
VWEEE
BOOM
KDOOM

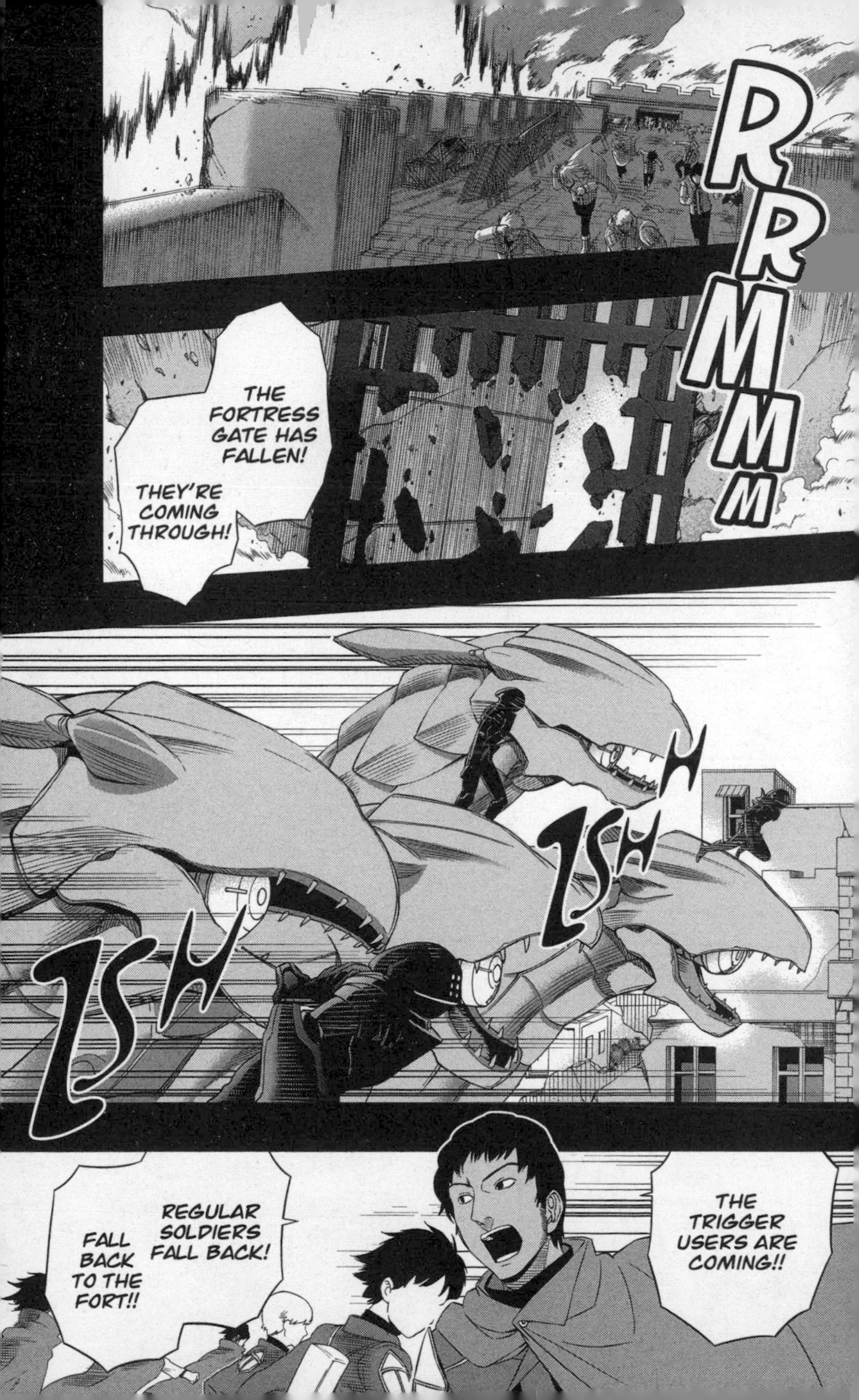
RRMMM
THE FORTRESS GATE HAS FALLEN!
THEY'RE COMING THROUGH!
ZSHH
ZSH
ZSH
THE TRIGGER USERS ARE COMING!!
REGULAR SOLDIERS FALL BACK!
FALL BACK TO THE FORT!!

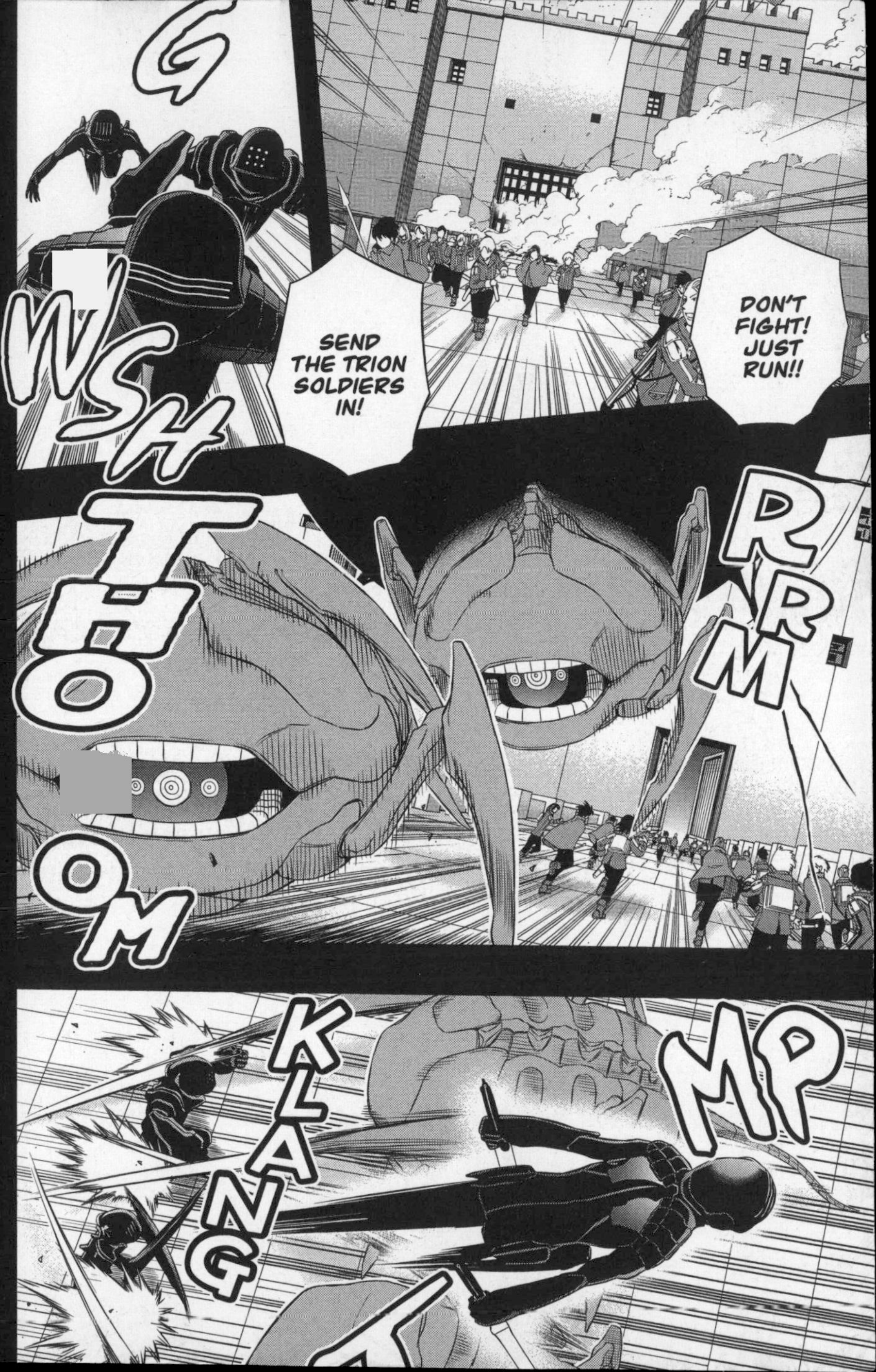
DON'T FIGHT! JUST RUN!!
SEND THE TRION SOLDIERS IN!
G
WSH
RRM
THOOM
MP
KLANG

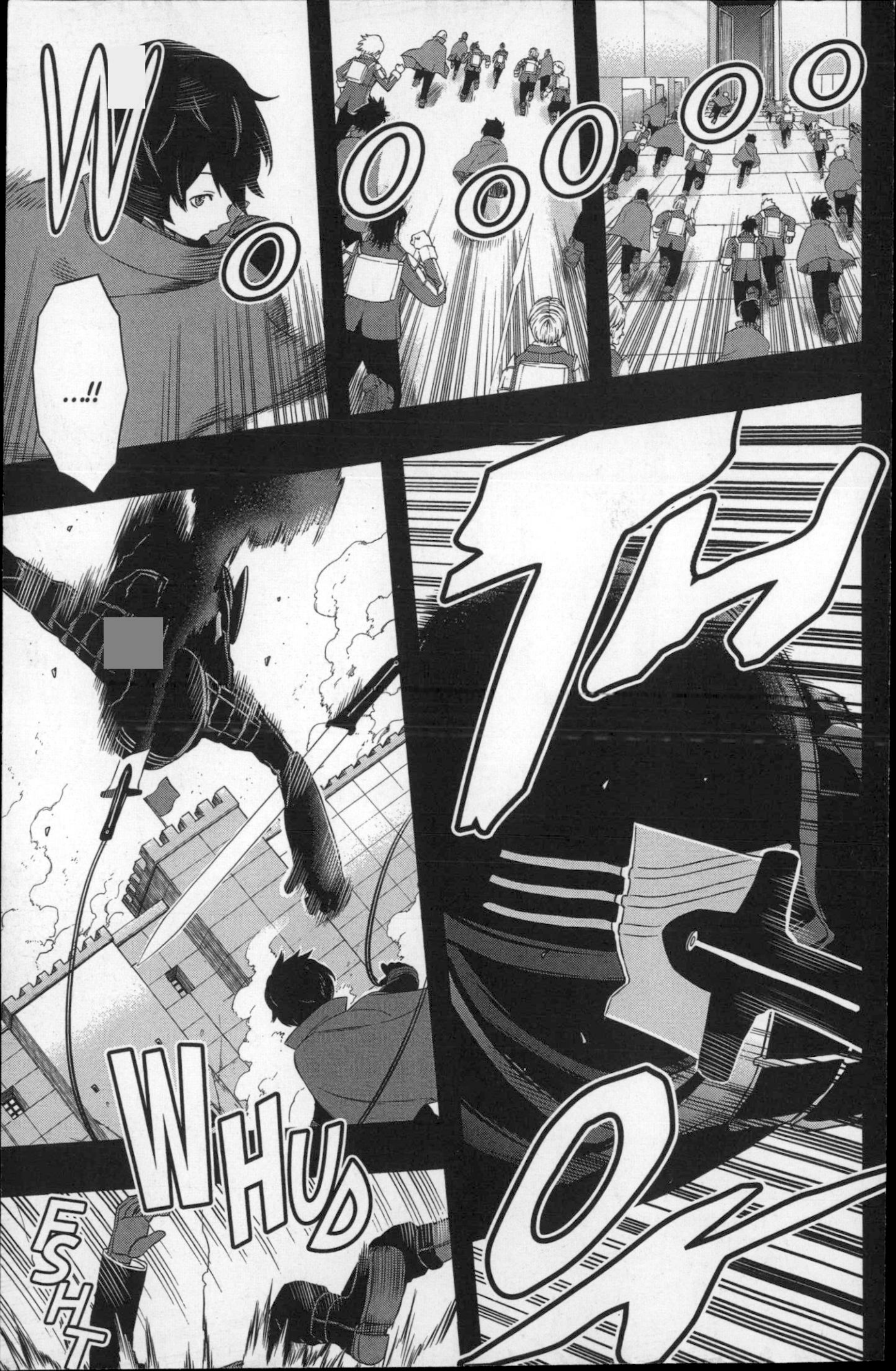

WOOOOOOO
...!!
WHUD
FSHT

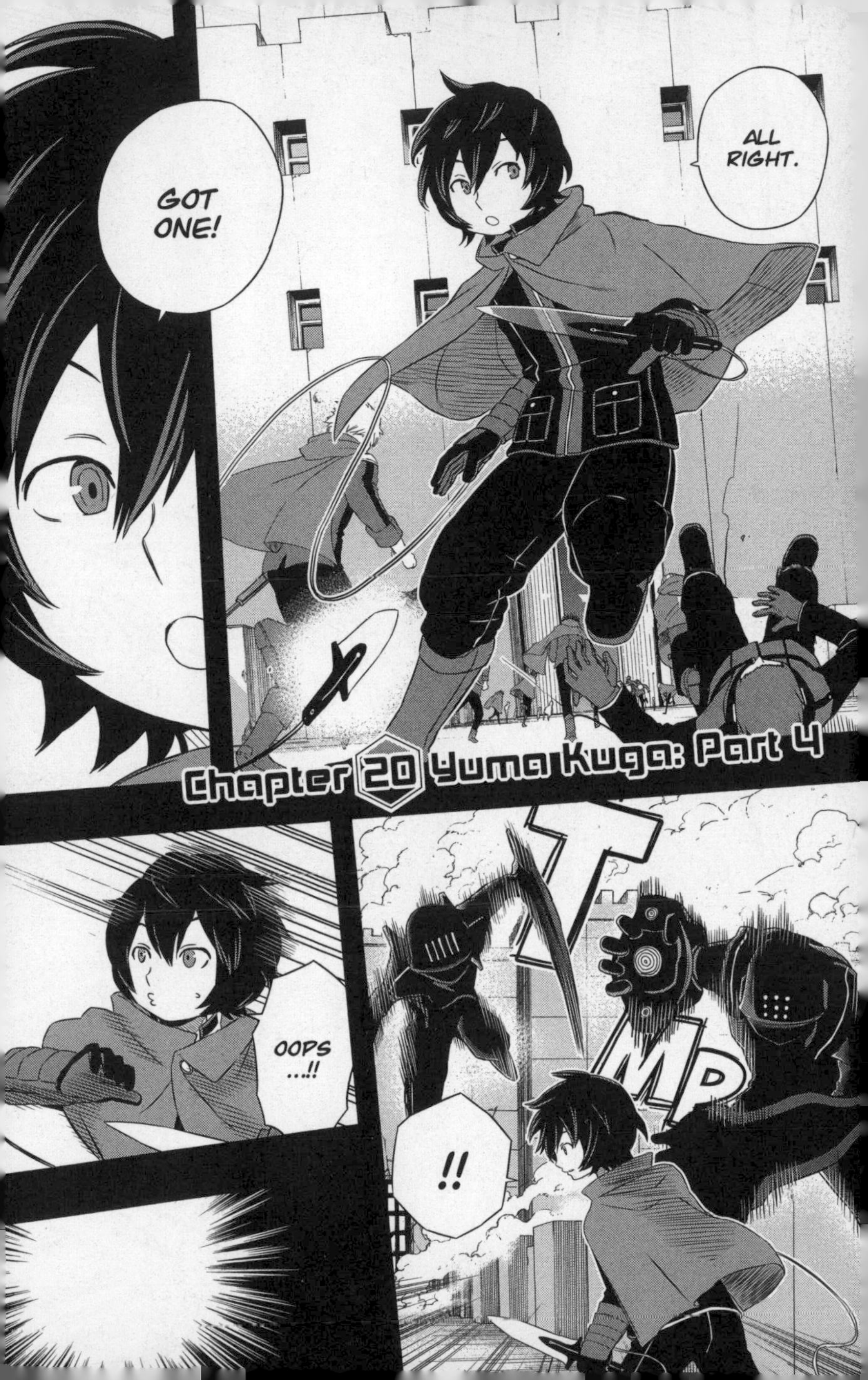
ALL RIGHT.
GOT ONE!
Chapter 20 Yuma Kuga: Part 4
!!
OOPS ...!!

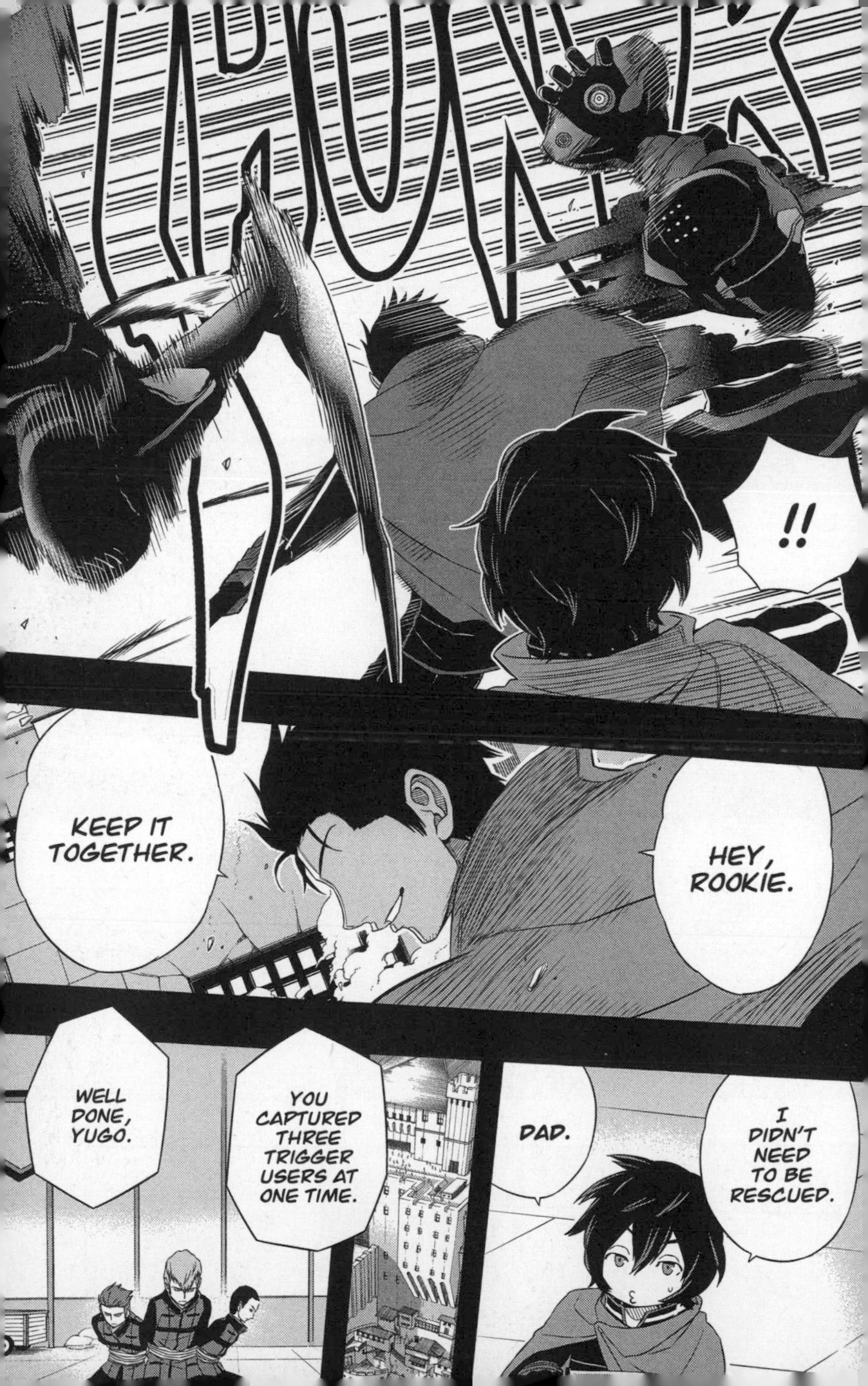
!!
HEY, ROOKIE.
KEEP IT TOGETHER.
I DIDN'T NEED TO BE RESCUED.
DAD.
YOU CAPTURED THREE TRIGGER USERS AT ONE TIME.
WELL DONE, YUGO.

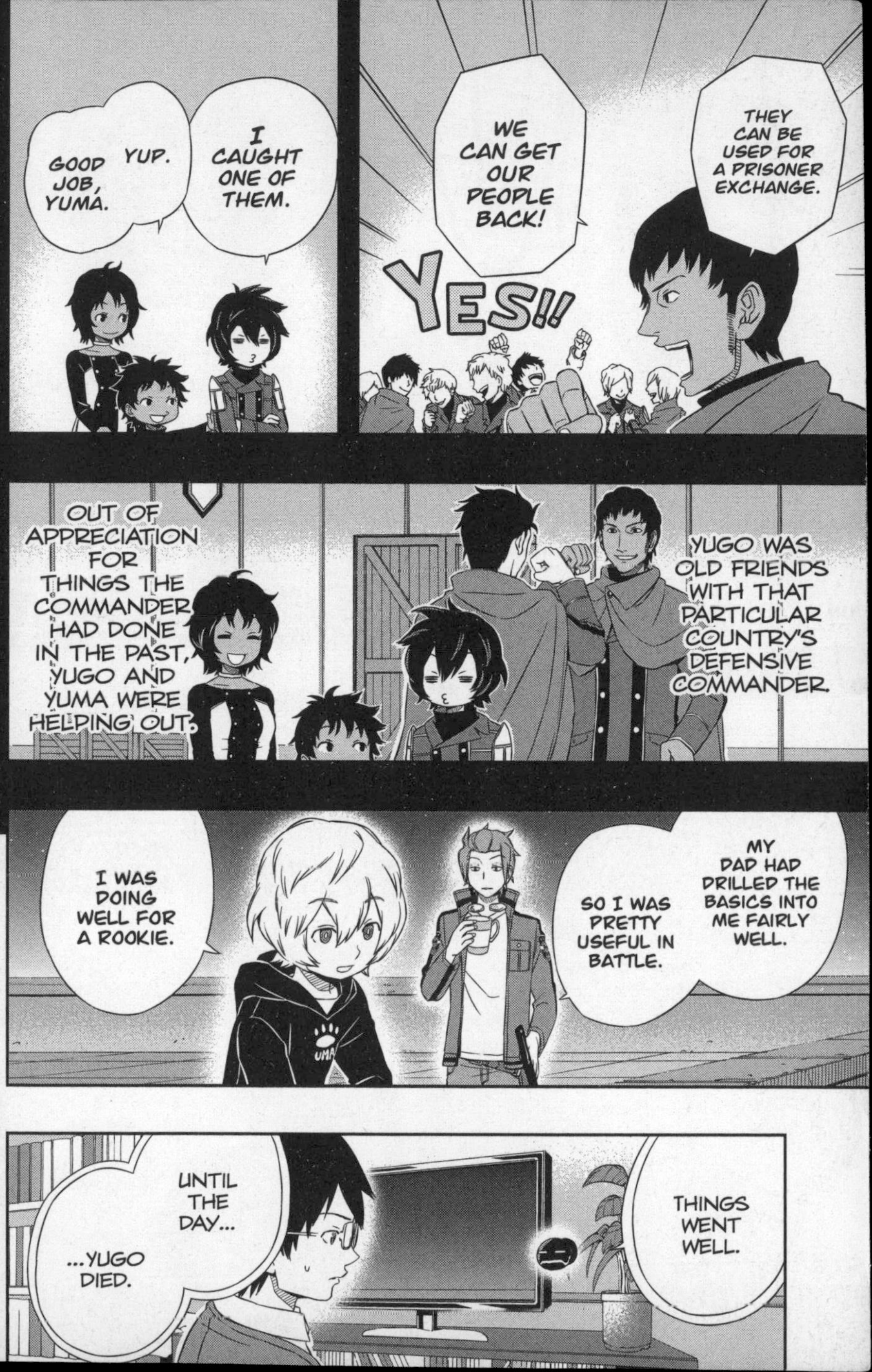
THEY CAN BE USED FOR A PRISONER EXCHANGE.
WE CAN GET OUR PEOPLE BACK!
YES!!
I CAUGHT ONE OF THEM.
GOOD JOB, YUMA.
YUP.
YUGO WAS OLD FRIENDS WITH THAT PARTICULAR COUNTRY'S DEFENSIVE COMMANDER.
OUT OF APPRECIATION FOR THINGS THE COMMANDER HAD DONE IN THE PAST, YUGO AND YUMA WERE HELPING OUT.
MY DAD HAD DRILLED THE BASICS INTO ME FAIRLY WELL.
SO I WAS PRETTY USEFUL IN BATTLE.
I WAS DOING WELL FOR A ROOKIE.
THINGS WENT WELL.
UNTIL THE DAY...
...YUGO DIED.

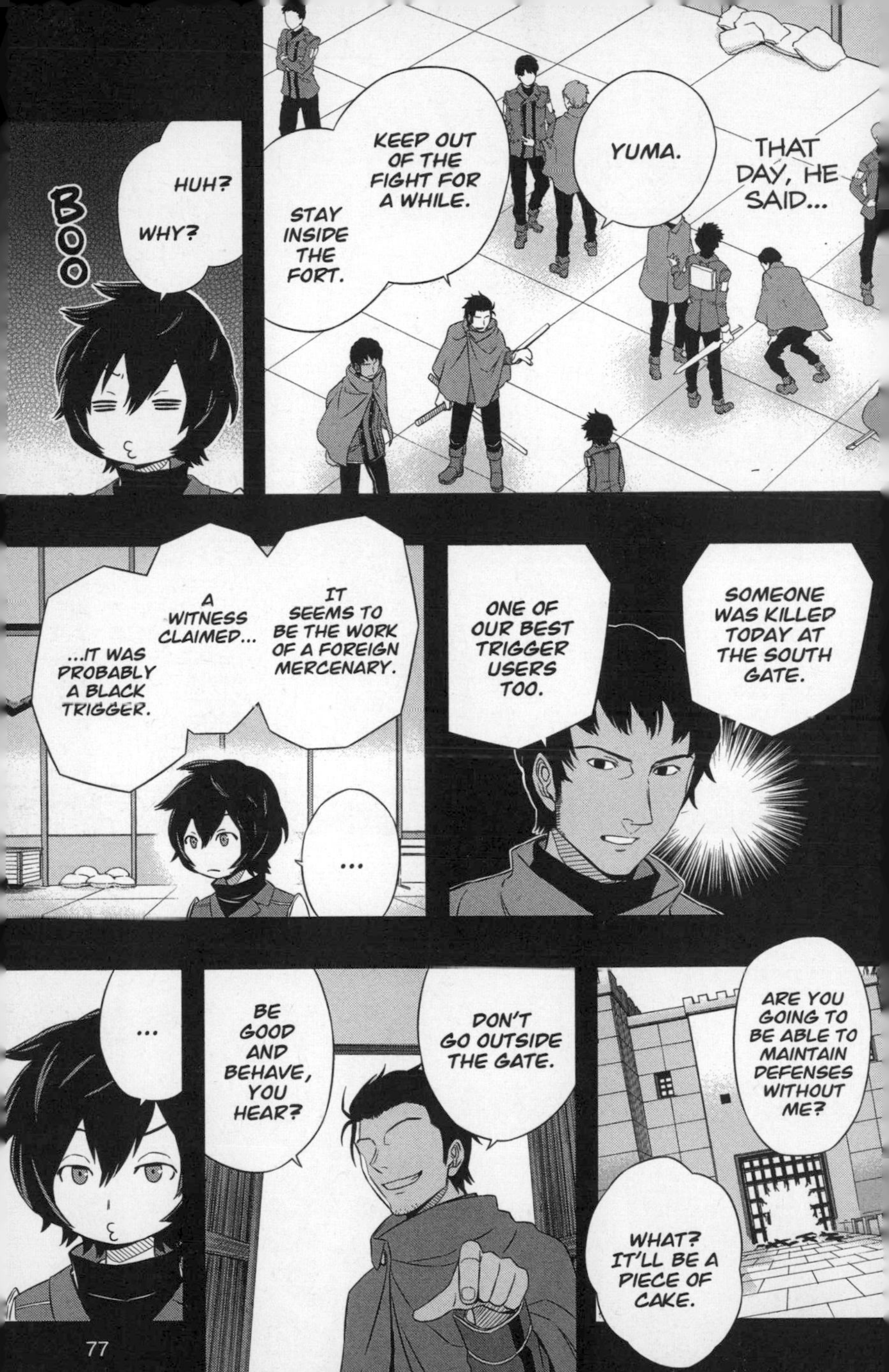
THAT DAY, HE SAID...
YUMA.
KEEP OUT OF THE FIGHT FOR A WHILE.
STAY INSIDE THE FORT.
HUH? WHY?
BOO
SOMEONE WAS KILLED TODAY AT THE SOUTH GATE.
ONE OF OUR BEST TRIGGER USERS TOO.
IT SEEMS TO BE THE WORK OF A FOREIGN MERCENARY.
A WITNESS CLAIMED...
...IT WAS PROBABLY A BLACK TRIGGER.
...
ARE YOU GOING TO BE ABLE TO MAINTAIN DEFENSES WITHOUT ME?
WHAT? IT'LL BE A PIECE OF CAKE.
DON'T GO OUTSIDE THE GATE.
BE GOOD AND BEHAVE, YOU HEAR?
...

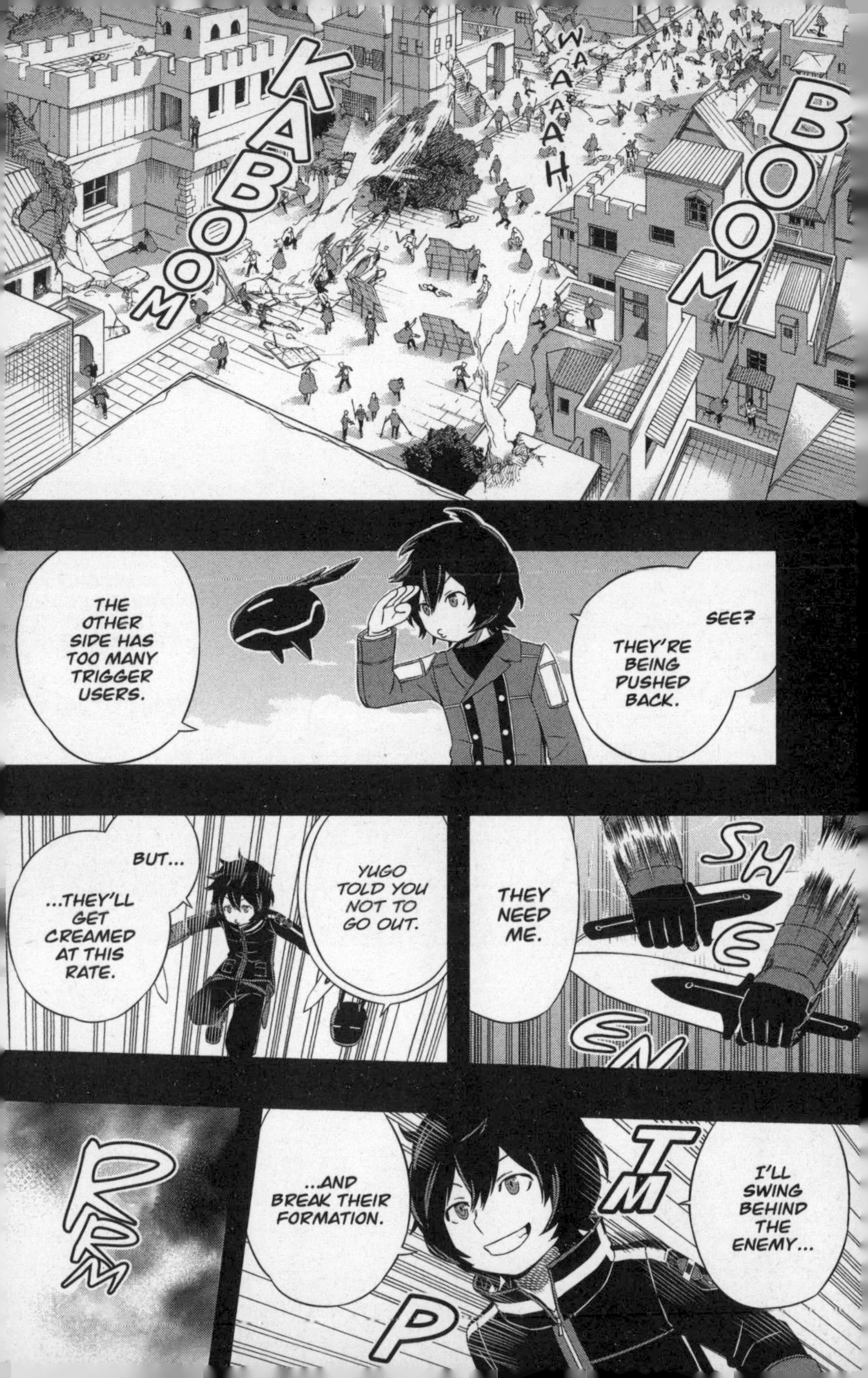
BOOM
WAAAAAH
KABOOM
SEE?
THEY'RE BEING PUSHED BACK.
THE OTHER SIDE HAS TOO MANY TRIGGER USERS.
SHEEN
THEY NEED ME.
YUGO TOLD YOU NOT TO GO OUT.
BUT...
...THEY'LL GET CREAMED AT THIS RATE.
I'LL SWING BEHIND THE ENEMY...
TMP
...AND BREAK THEIR FORMATION.
RRM

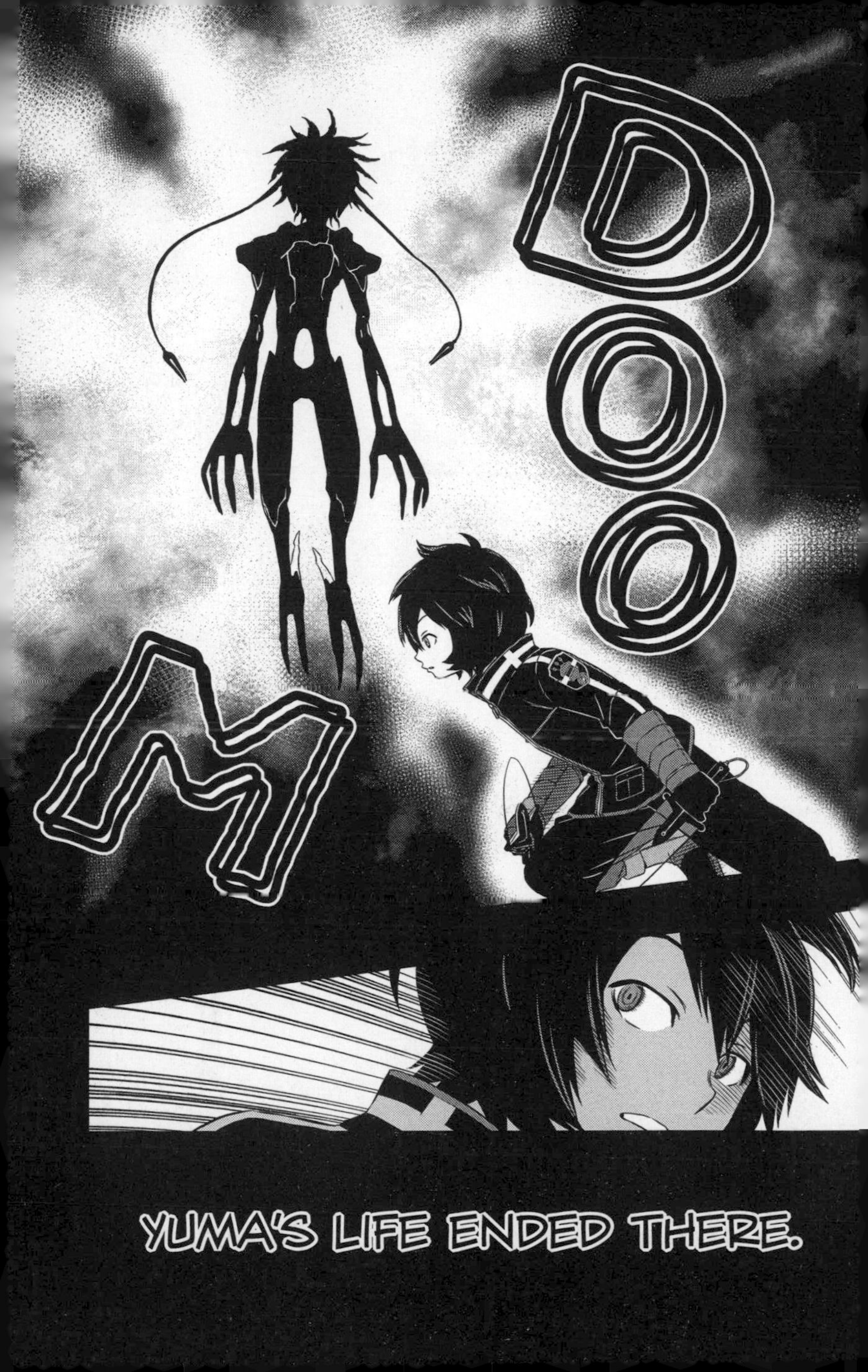
DOOOM
YUMA'S LIFE ENDED THERE.

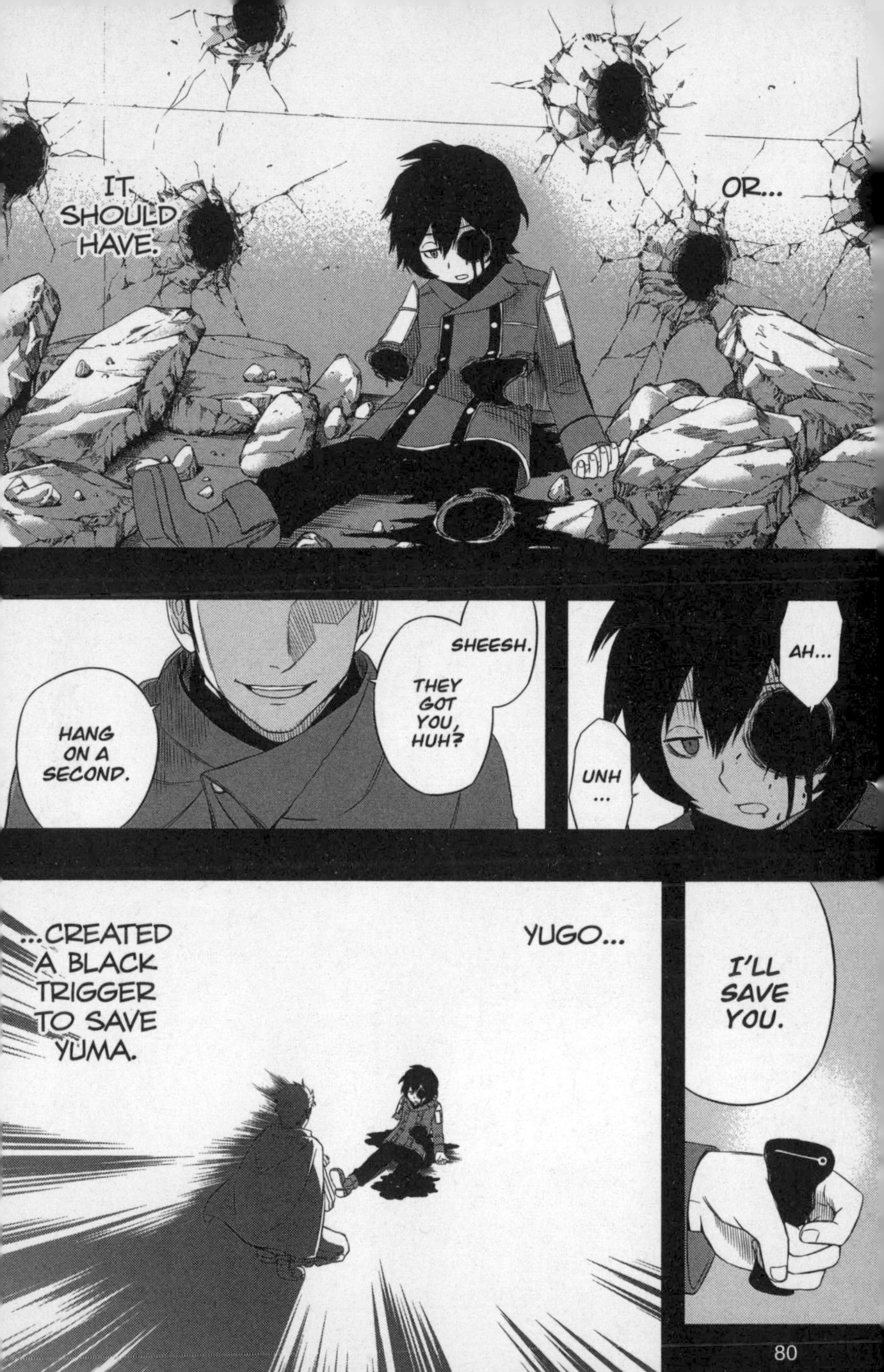

OR...
IT SHOULD HAVE.
AH...
UNH ...
SHEESH.
THEY GOT YOU, HUH?
HANG ON A SECOND.
I'LL SAVE YOU.
YUGO...
...CREATED A BLACK TRIGGER TO SAVE YUMA.

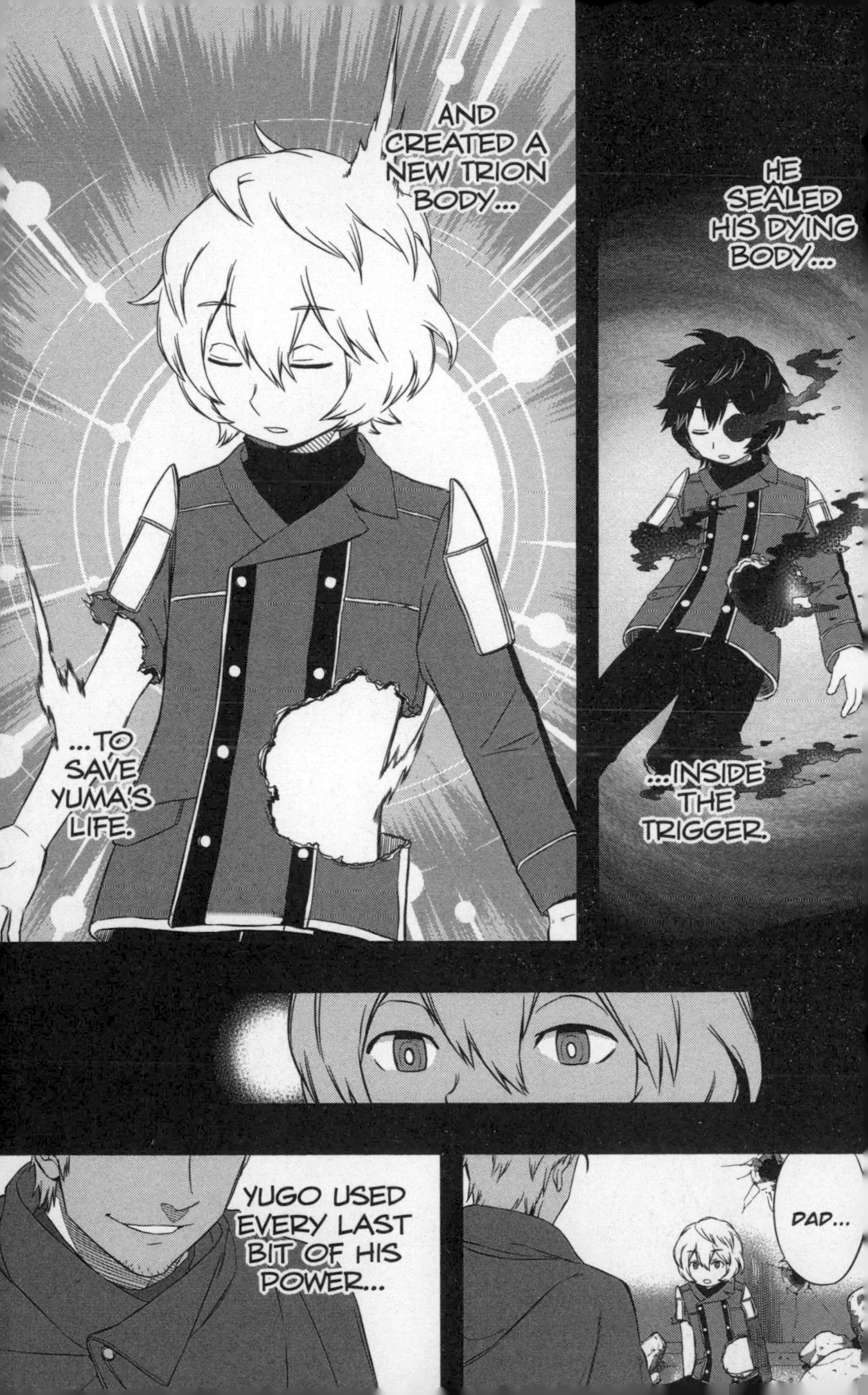
HE SEALED HIS DYING BODY...
...INSIDE THE TRIGGER.
AND CREATED A NEW TRION BODY...
...TO SAVE YUMA'S LIFE.
DAD...
YUGO USED EVERY LAST BIT OF HIS POWER...

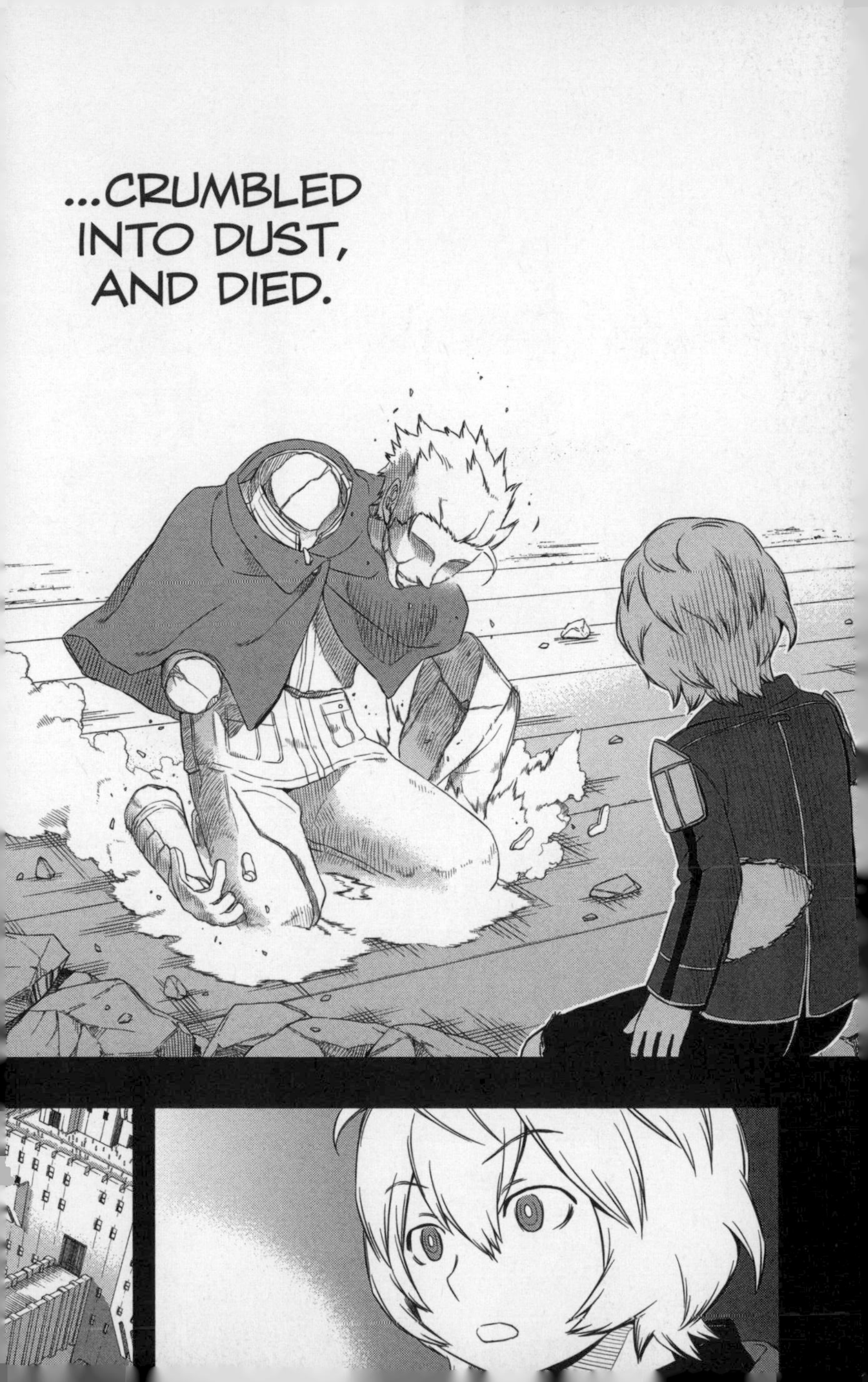
...CRUMBLED INTO DUST, AND DIED.

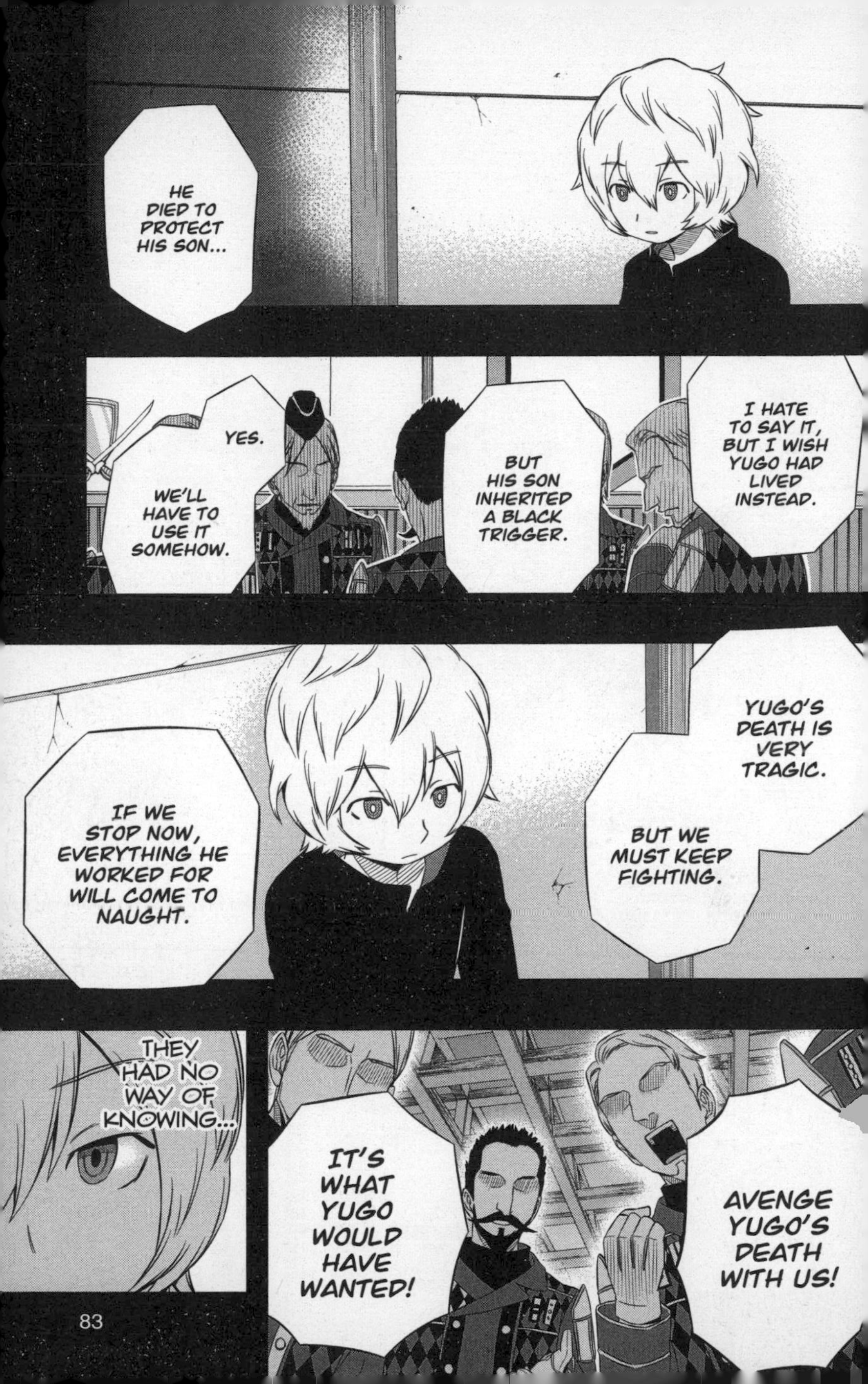
HE DIED TO PROTECT HIS SON...
I HATE TO SAY IT, BUT I WISH YUGO HAD LIVED INSTEAD.
BUT HIS SON INHERITED A BLACK TRIGGER.
YES.
WE'LL HAVE TO USE IT SOMEHOW.
YUGO'S DEATH IS VERY TRAGIC.
BUT WE MUST KEEP FIGHTING.
IF WE STOP NOW, EVERYTHING HE WORKED FOR WILL COME TO NAUGHT.
AVENGE YUGO'S DEATH WITH US!
IT'S WHAT YUGO WOULD HAVE WANTED!
THEY HAD NO WAY OF KNOWING...

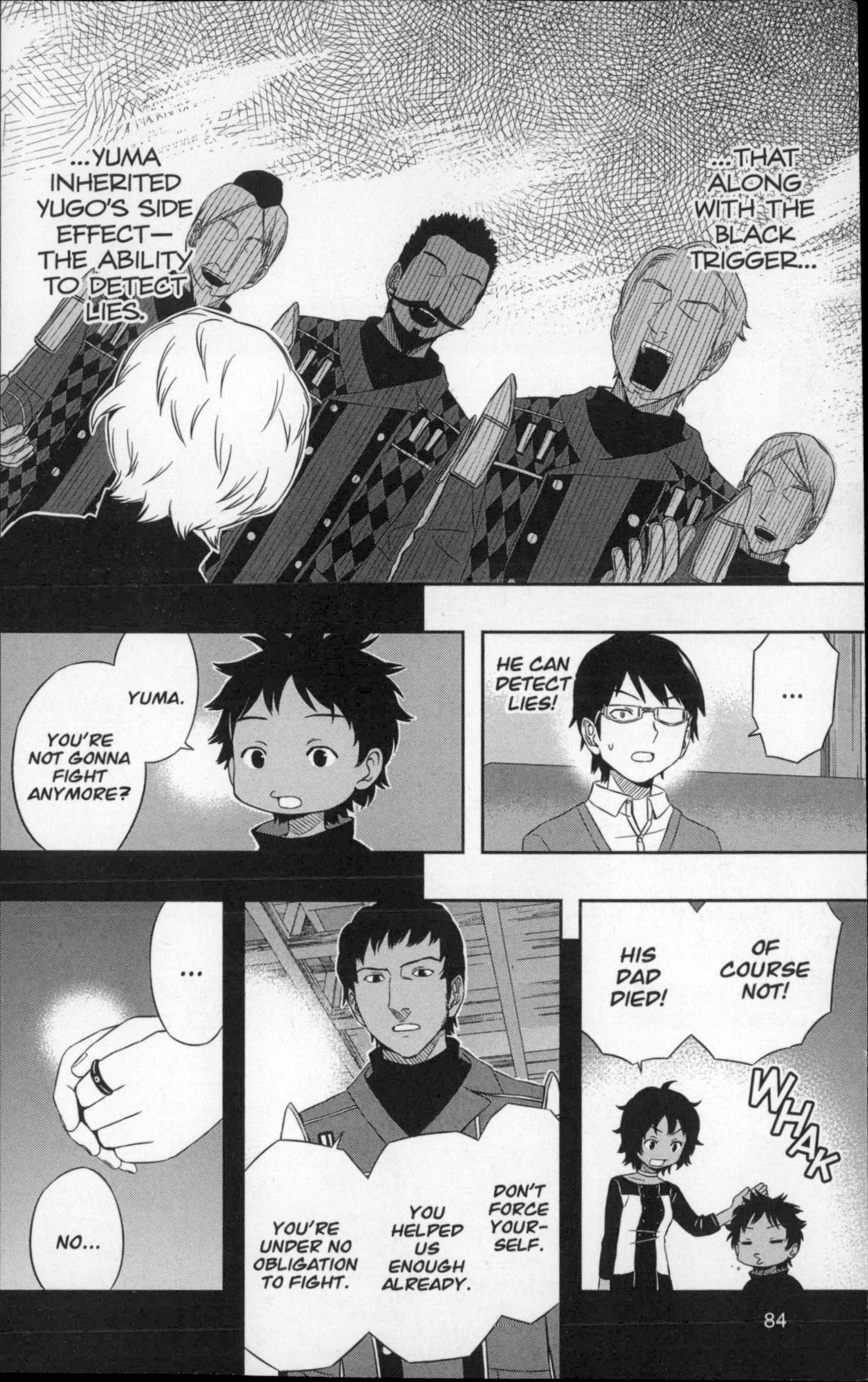
...THAT ALONG WITH THE BLACK TRIGGER...
...YUMA INHERITED YUGO'S SIDE EFFECT—THE ABILITY TO DETECT LIES.
...
HE CAN DETECT LIES!
YUMA.
YOU'RE NOT GONNA FIGHT ANYMORE?
OF COURSE NOT!
HIS DAD DIED!
WHAK
DON'T FORCE YOUR-SELF.
YOU HELPED US ENOUGH ALREADY.
YOU'RE UNDER NO OBLIGATION TO FIGHT.
...
NO...

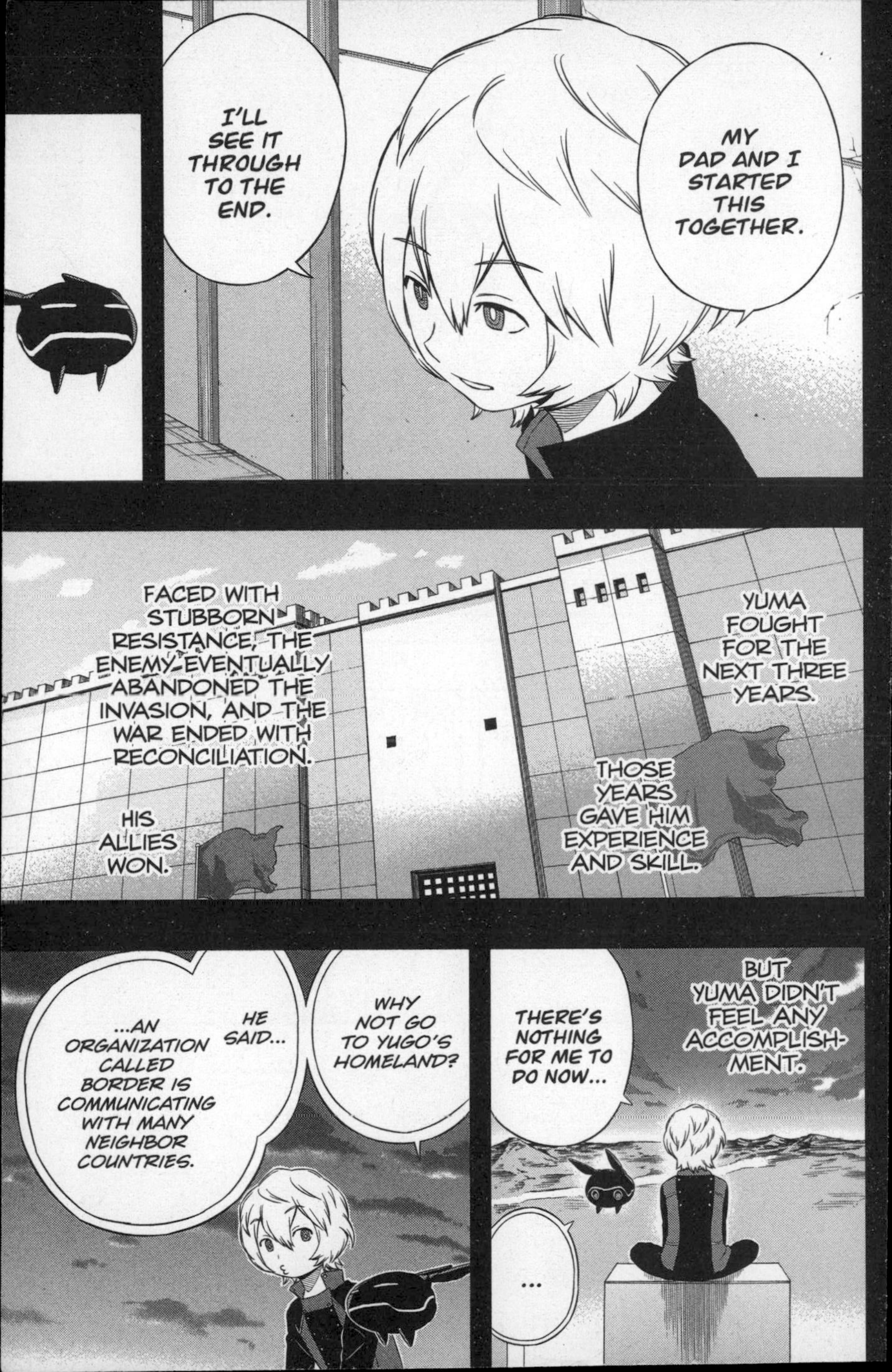
MY DAD AND I STARTED THIS TOGETHER.
I'LL SEE IT THROUGH TO THE END.
YUMA FOUGHT FOR THE NEXT THREE YEARS.
FACED WITH STUBBORN RESISTANCE, THE ENEMY EVENTUALLY ABANDONED THE INVASION, AND THE WAR ENDED WITH RECONCILIATION.
HIS ALLIES WON.
THOSE YEARS GAVE HIM EXPERIENCE AND SKILL.
BUT YUMA DIDN'T FEEL ANY ACCOMPLISH-MENT.
THERE'S NOTHING FOR ME TO DO NOW...
...
WHY NOT GO TO YUGO'S HOMELAND?
HE SAID...
...AN ORGANIZATION CALLED BORDER IS COMMUNICATING WITH MANY NEIGHBOR COUNTRIES.

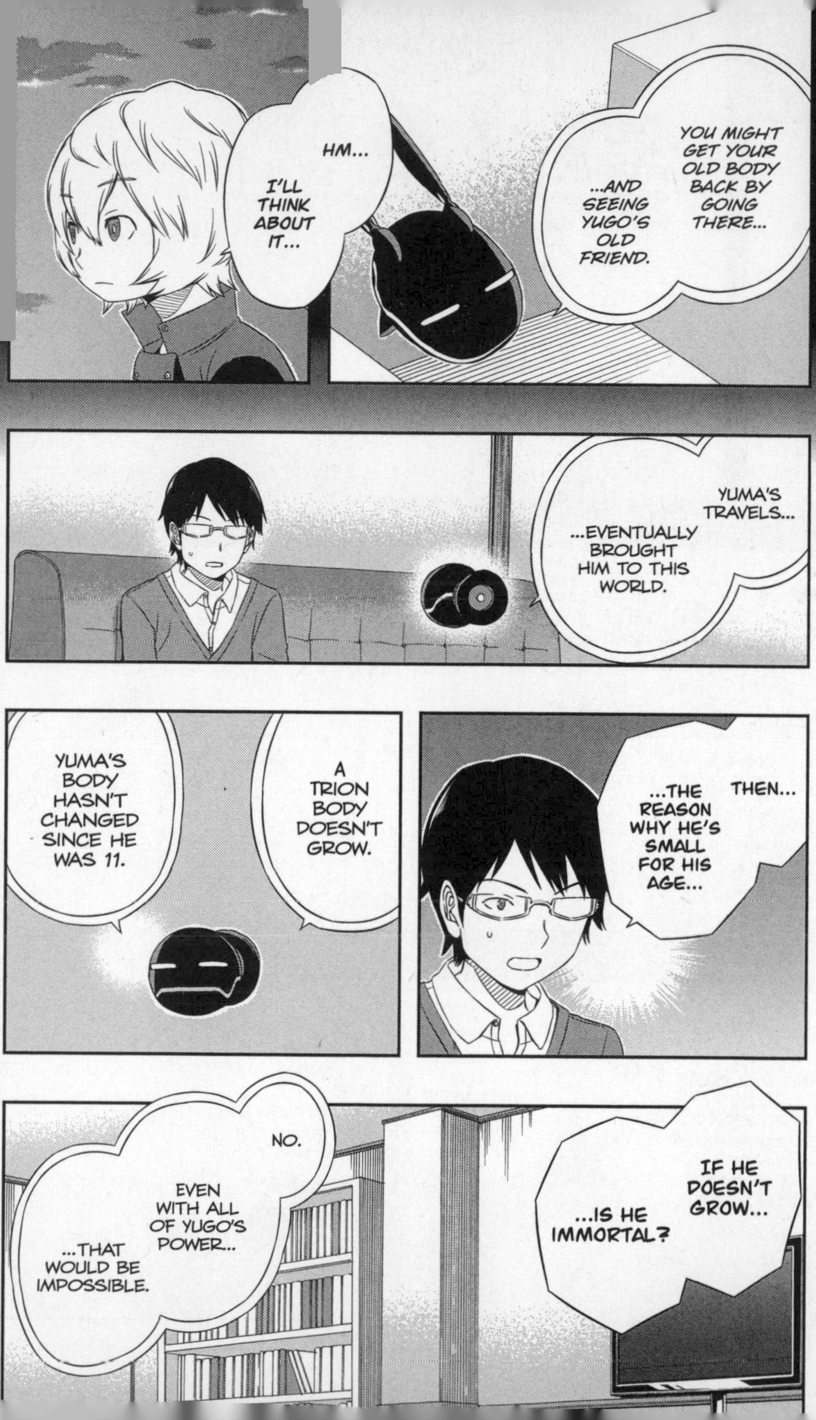
YOU MIGHT GET YOUR OLD BODY BACK BY GOING THERE...
...AND SEEING YUGO'S OLD FRIEND.
HM...
I'LL THINK ABOUT IT...
YUMA'S TRAVELS...
...EVENTUALLY BROUGHT HIM TO THIS WORLD.
THEN...
...THE REASON WHY HE'S SMALL FOR HIS AGE...
A TRION BODY DOESN'T GROW.
YUMA'S BODY HASN'T CHANGED SINCE HE WAS 11.
IF HE DOESN'T GROW...
...IS HE IMMORTAL?
NO.
EVEN WITH ALL OF YUGO'S POWER...
...THAT WOULD BE IMPOSSIBLE.

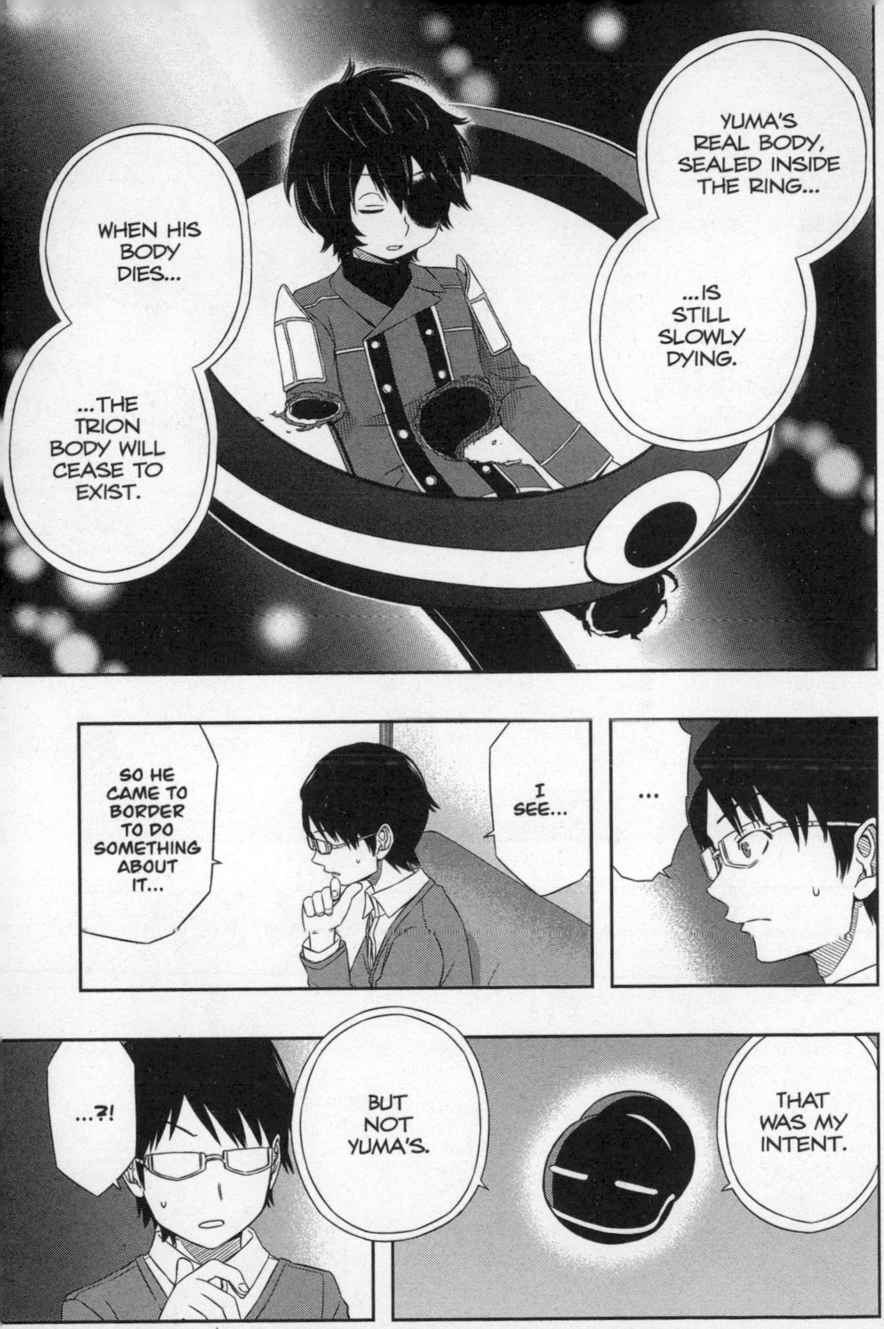
YUMA'S REAL BODY, SEALED INSIDE THE RING...
...IS STILL SLOWLY DYING.
WHEN HIS BODY DIES...
...THE TRION BODY WILL CEASE TO EXIST.
...
I SEE...
SO HE CAME TO BORDER TO DO SOMETHING ABOUT IT...
THAT WAS MY INTENT.
BUT NOT YUMA'S.
...?!

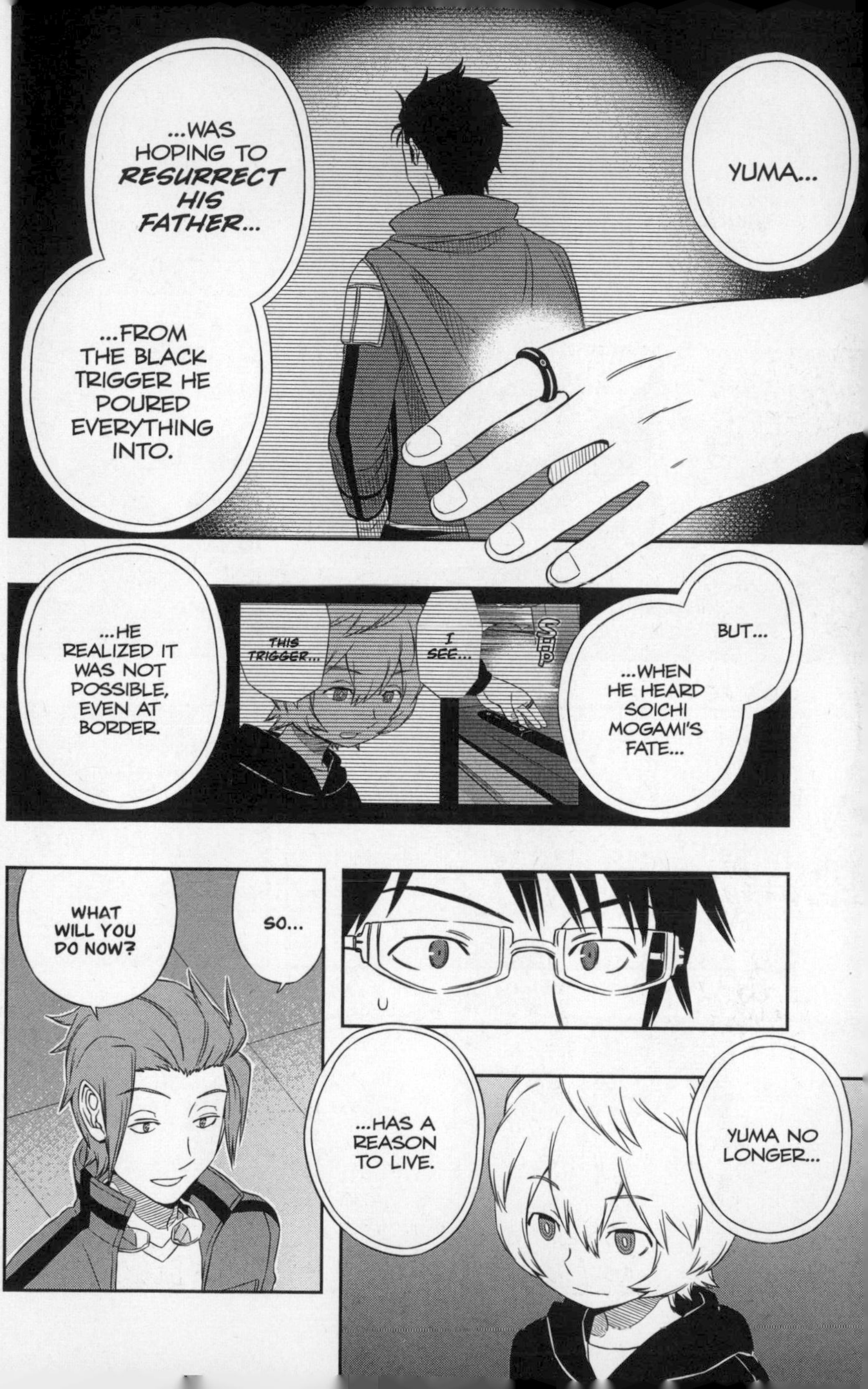
YUMA...
...WAS HOPING TO *RESURRECT HIS FATHER...*
...FROM THE BLACK TRIGGER HE POURED EVERYTHING INTO.
BUT...
...WHEN HE HEARD SOICHI MOGAMI'S FATE...
SHP
I SEE...
THIS TRIGGER...
...HE REALIZED IT WAS NOT POSSIBLE, EVEN AT BORDER.
YUMA NO LONGER...
...HAS A REASON TO LIVE.
SO...
WHAT WILL YOU DO NOW?

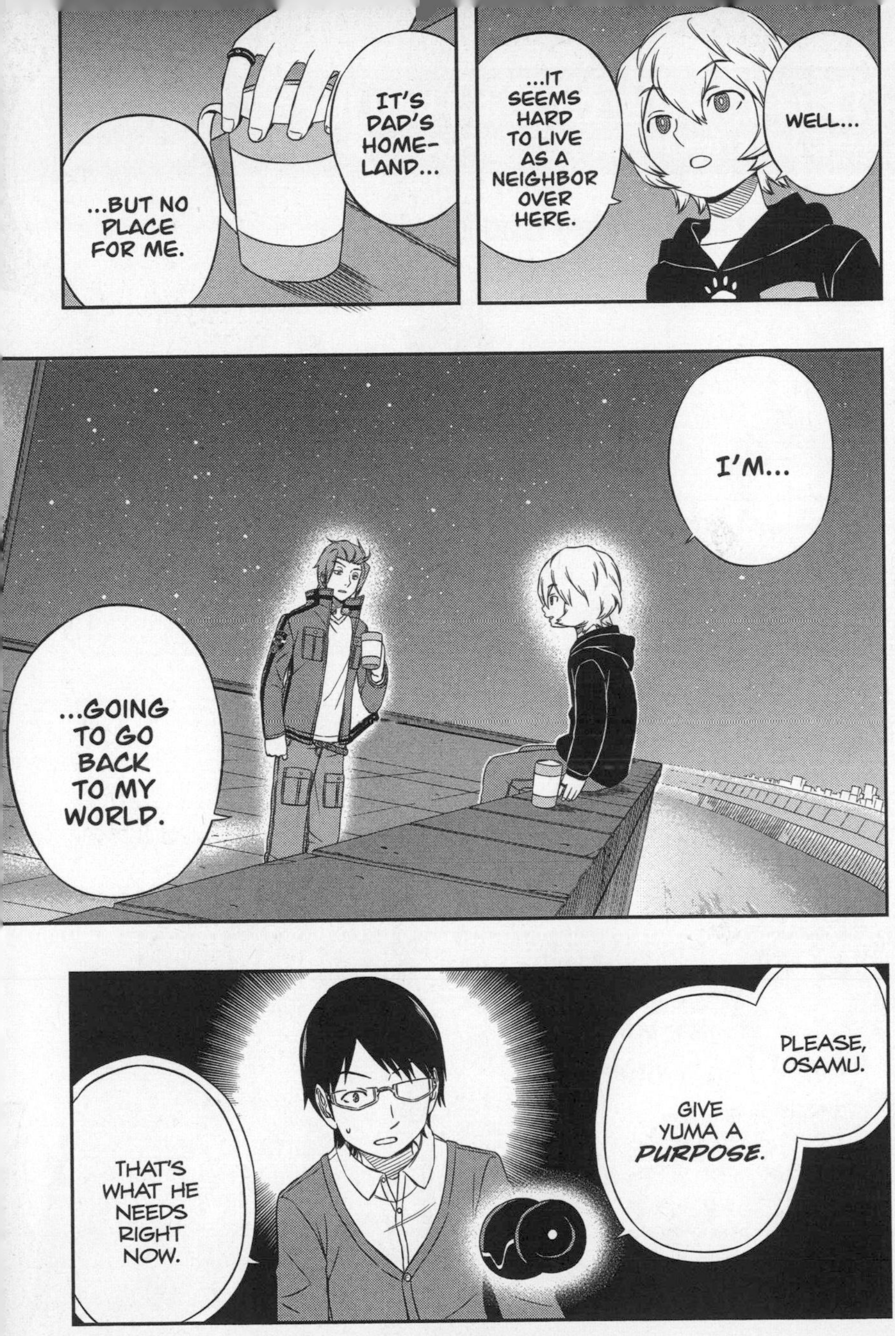
WELL...
...IT SEEMS HARD TO LIVE AS A NEIGHBOR OVER HERE.
IT'S DAD'S HOME-LAND...
...BUT NO PLACE FOR ME.
I'M...
...GOING TO GO BACK TO MY WORLD.
PLEASE, OSAMU.
GIVE YUMA A *PURPOSE*.
THAT'S WHAT HE NEEDS RIGHT NOW.

The Lives of Bit Players: Part 3

By the time they reappear, you've forgotten who they are, and then you forget again.

■Neighbor friends (Chapter 20~)

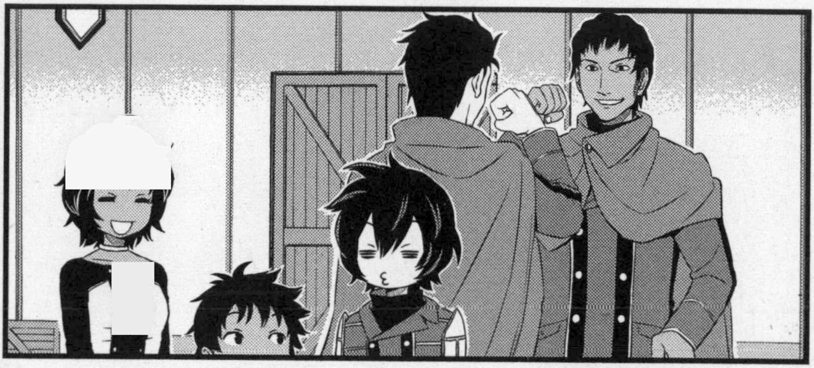

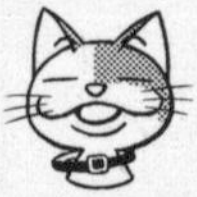

Will Yuma ever see them again? These three are a family. Where's the mother?

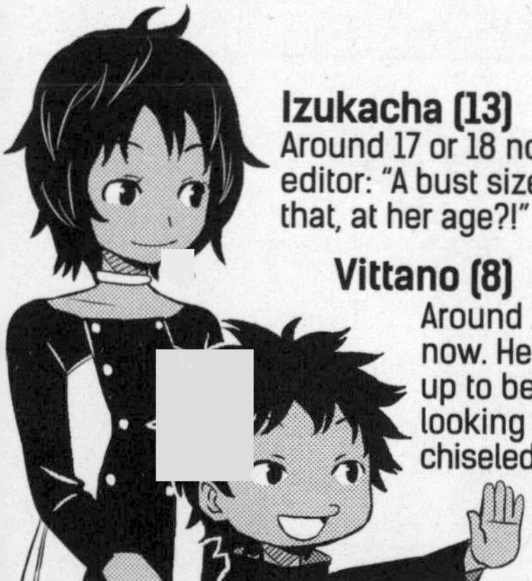

Izukacha (13)
Around 17 or 18 now. My editor: "A bust size like that, at her age?!"

Vittano (8)
Around 12 or 13 now. He'll grow up to be good-looking with chiseled features.

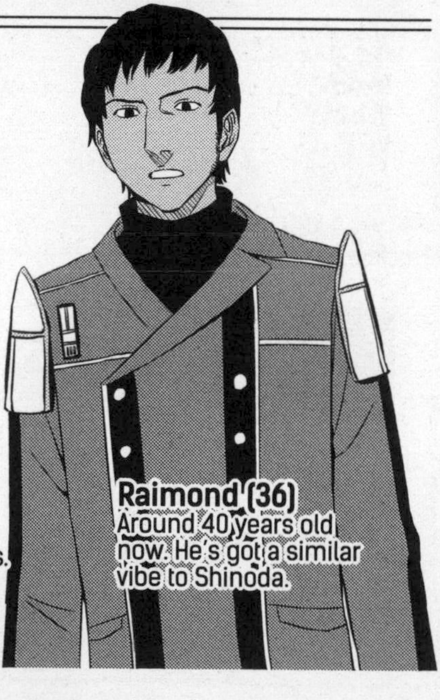

Raimond (36)
Around 40 years old now. He's got a similar vibe to Shinoda.

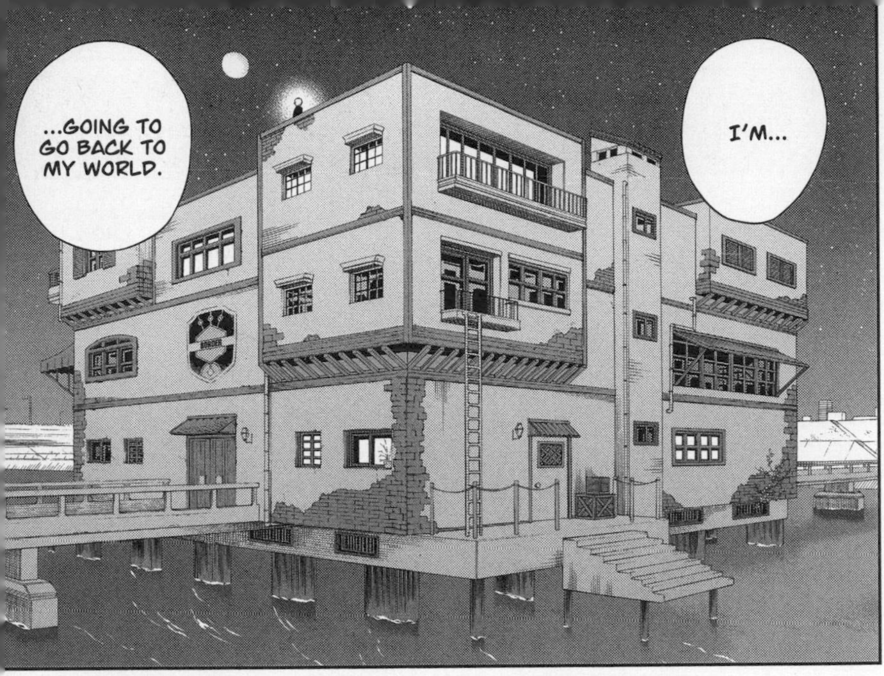
I'M...
...GOING TO GO BACK TO MY WORLD.

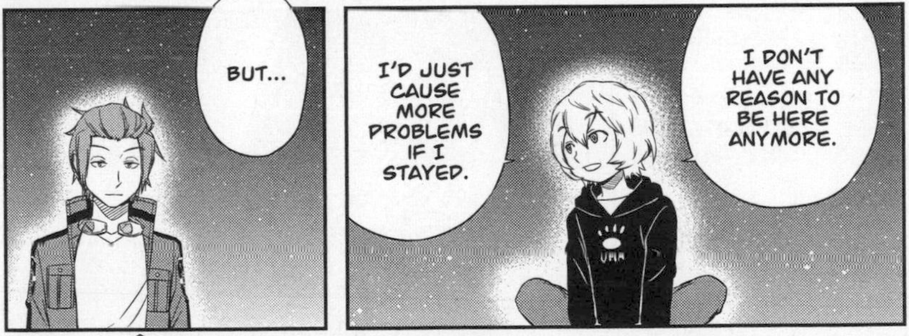
I DON'T HAVE ANY REASON TO BE HERE ANYMORE.
I'D JUST CAUSE MORE PROBLEMS IF I STAYED.
BUT...

Chapter 21 Osamu Mikumo: Part 3

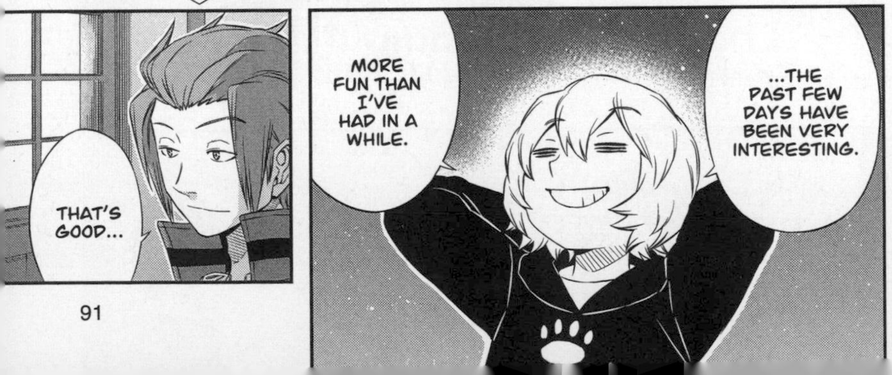
...THE PAST FEW DAYS HAVE BEEN VERY INTERESTING.
MORE FUN THAN I'VE HAD IN A WHILE.
THAT'S GOOD...

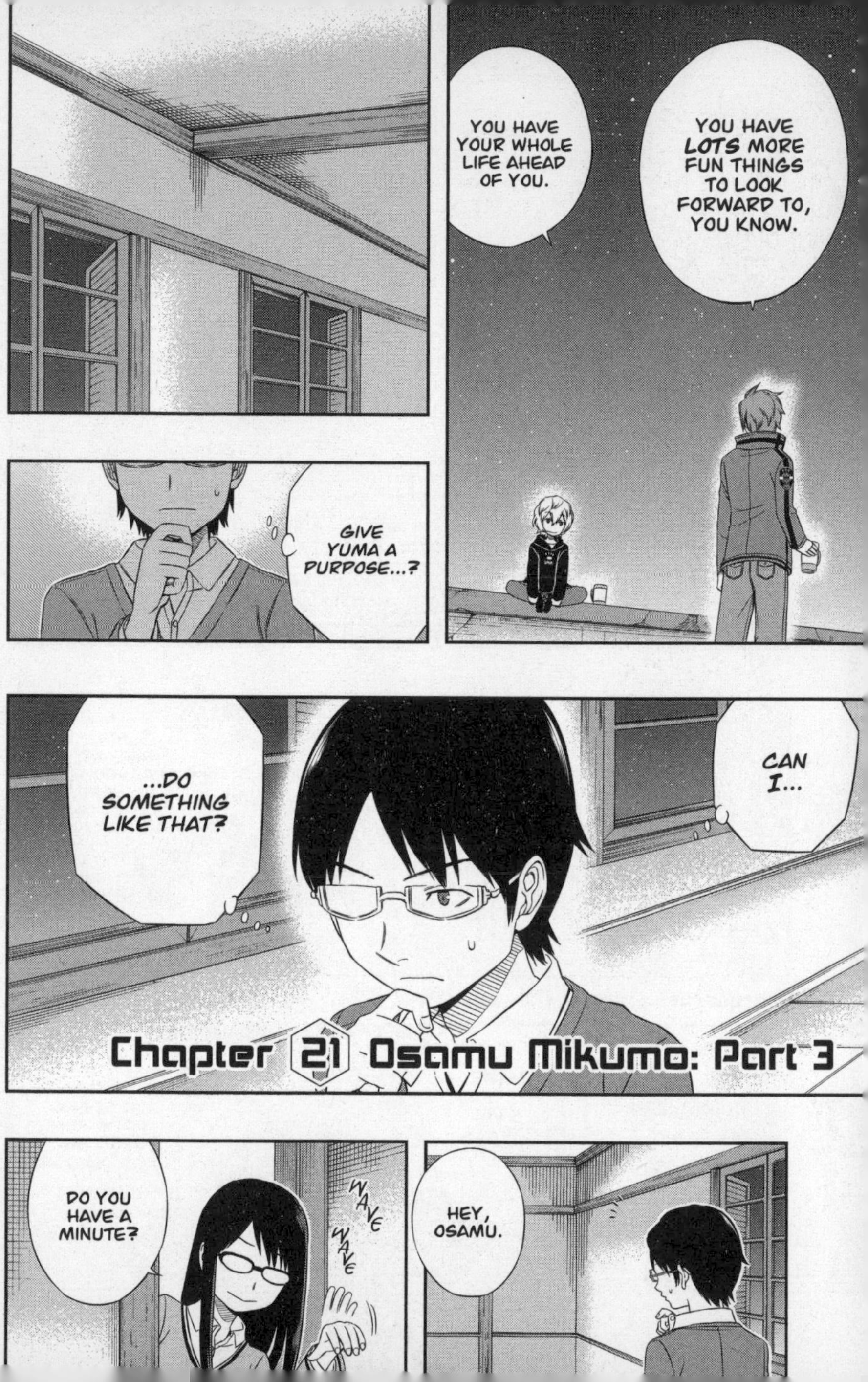
YOU HAVE LOTS MORE FUN THINGS TO LOOK FORWARD TO, YOU KNOW.
YOU HAVE YOUR WHOLE LIFE AHEAD OF YOU.
GIVE YUMA A PURPOSE...?
CAN I...
...DO SOMETHING LIKE THAT?
Chapter 21 Osamu Mikumo: Part 3
HEY, OSAMU.
WAVE
WAVE
DO YOU HAVE A MINUTE?

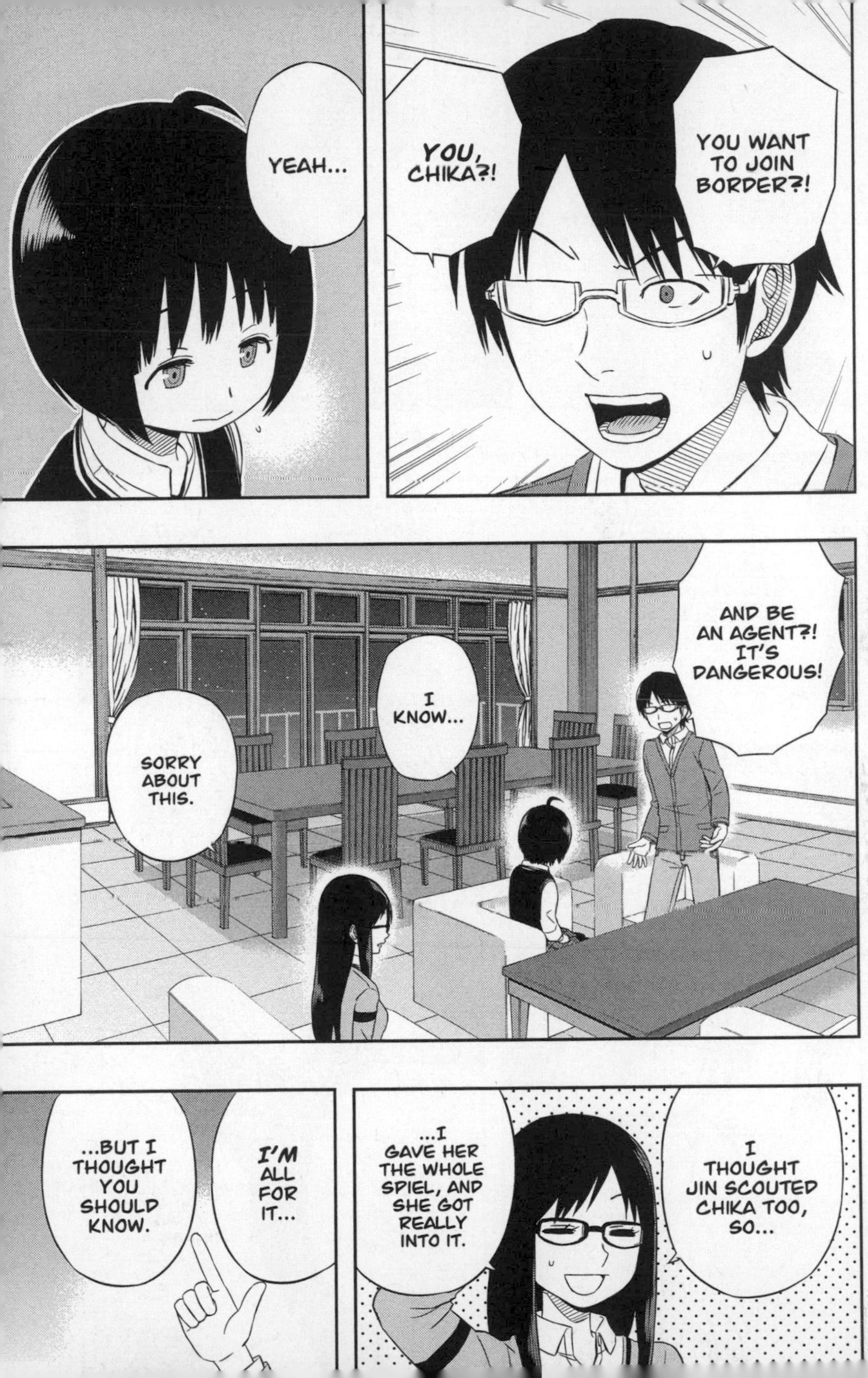
YOU WANT TO JOIN BORDER?!
YOU, CHIKA?!
YEAH...
AND BE AN AGENT?! IT'S DANGEROUS!
I KNOW...
SORRY ABOUT THIS.
I THOUGHT JIN SCOUTED CHIKA TOO, SO...
...I GAVE HER THE WHOLE SPIEL, AND SHE GOT REALLY INTO IT.
I'M ALL FOR IT...
...BUT I THOUGHT YOU SHOULD KNOW.

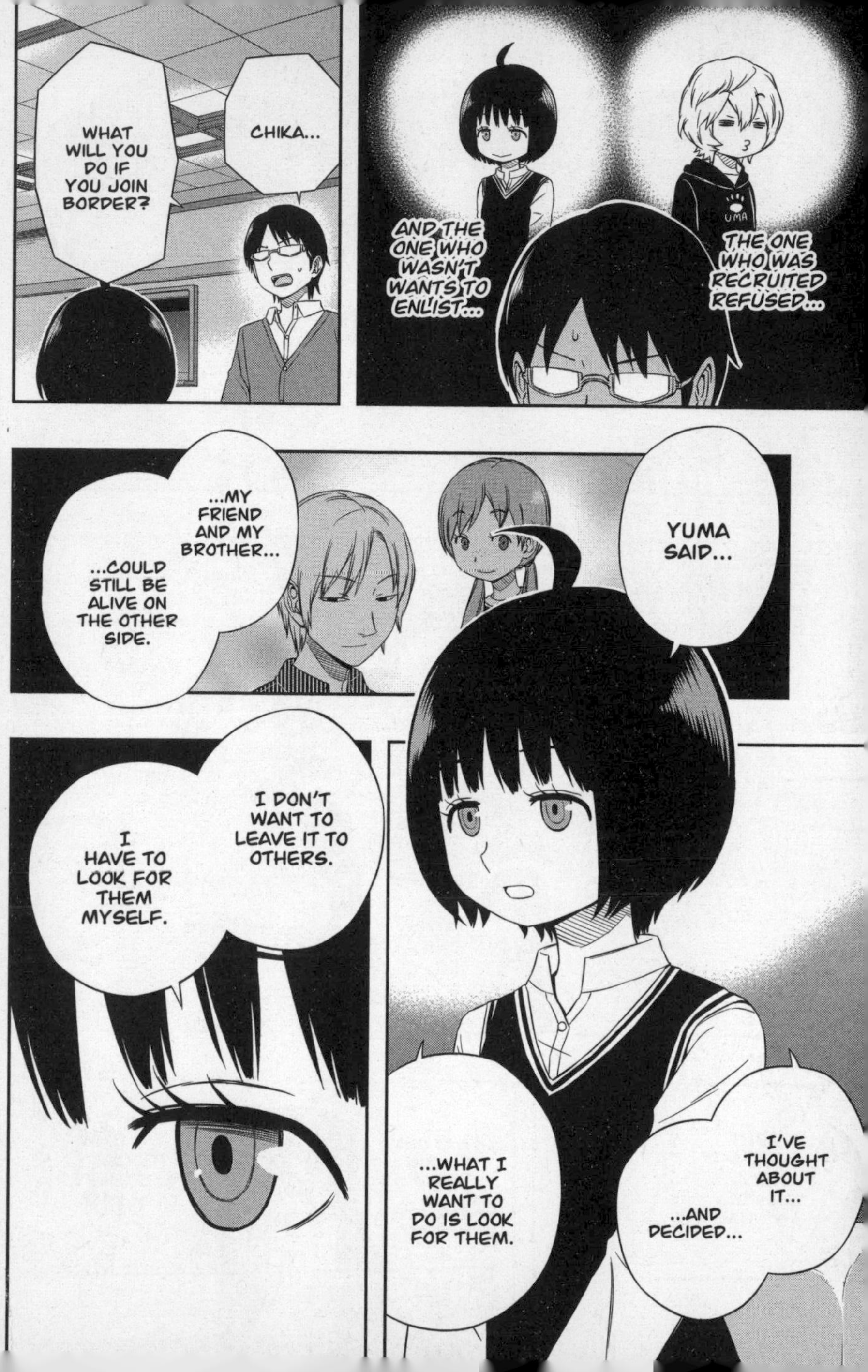
THE ONE WHO WAS RECRUITED REFUSED...
AND THE ONE WHO WASN'T WANTS TO ENLIST...
CHIKA...
WHAT WILL YOU DO IF YOU JOIN BORDER?
YUMA SAID...
...MY FRIEND AND MY BROTHER...
...COULD STILL BE ALIVE ON THE OTHER SIDE.
I'VE THOUGHT ABOUT IT...
...AND DECIDED...
...WHAT I REALLY WANT TO DO IS LOOK FOR THEM.
I DON'T WANT TO LEAVE IT TO OTHERS.
I HAVE TO LOOK FOR THEM MYSELF.

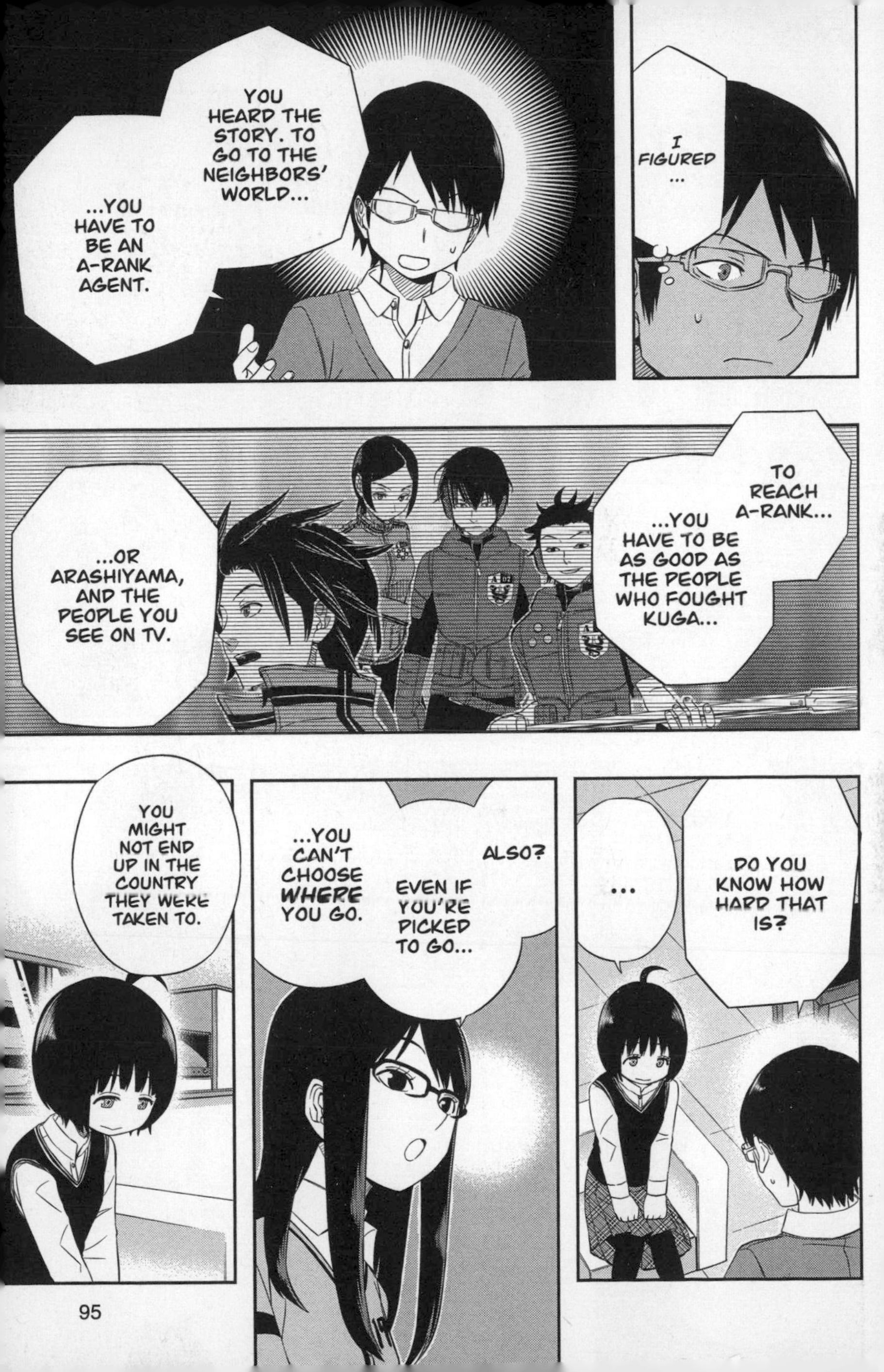
I FIGURED ...
YOU HEARD THE STORY. TO GO TO THE NEIGHBORS' WORLD...
...YOU HAVE TO BE AN A-RANK AGENT.
TO REACH A-RANK...
...YOU HAVE TO BE AS GOOD AS THE PEOPLE WHO FOUGHT KUGA...
...OR ARASHIYAMA, AND THE PEOPLE YOU SEE ON TV.
DO YOU KNOW HOW HARD THAT IS?
...
ALSO?
EVEN IF YOU'RE PICKED TO GO...
...YOU CAN'T CHOOSE **WHERE** YOU GO.
YOU MIGHT NOT END UP IN THE COUNTRY THEY WERE TAKEN TO.

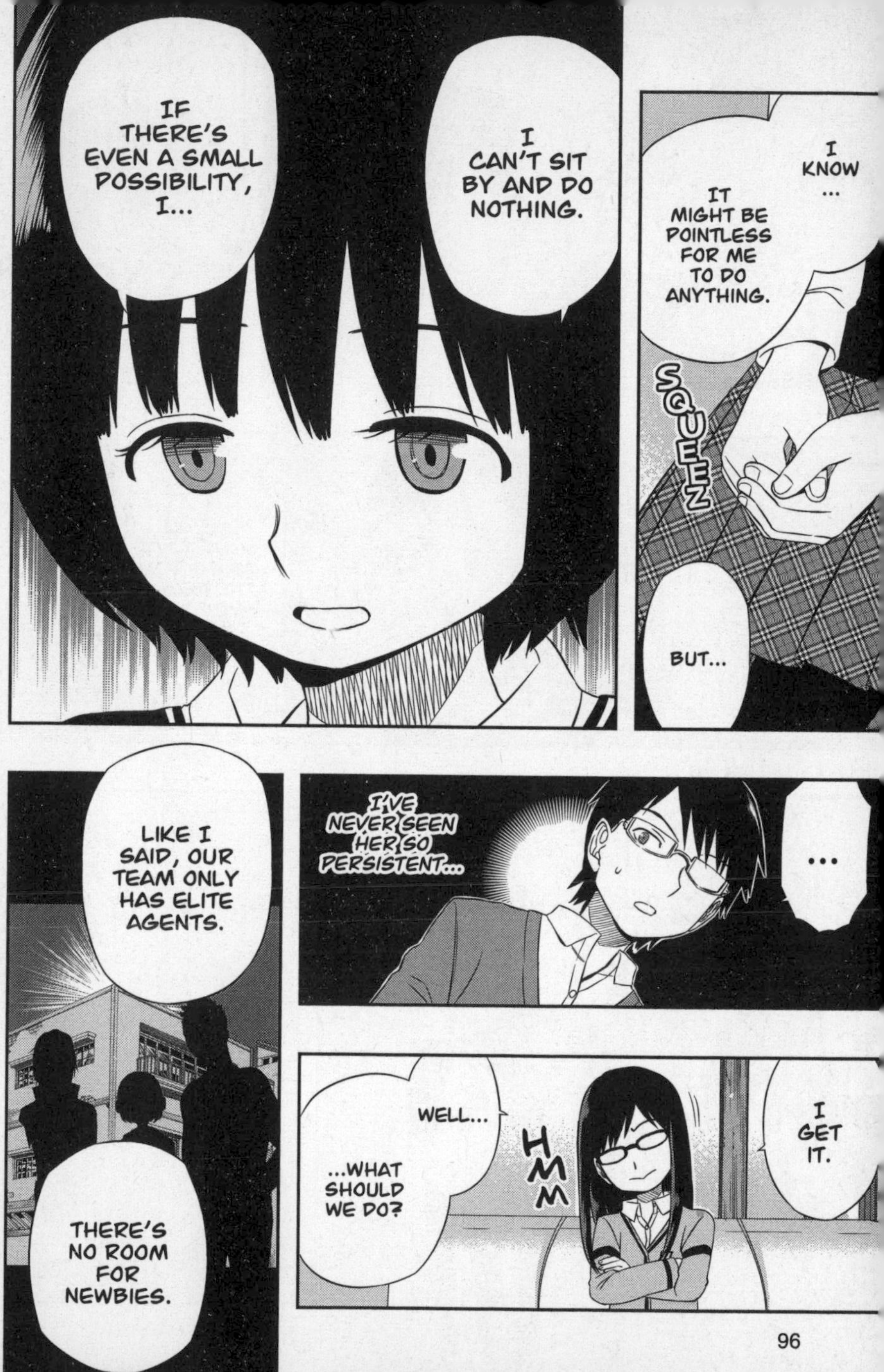
I KNOW ...
IT MIGHT BE POINTLESS FOR ME TO DO ANYTHING.
SQUEEZ
BUT...
I CAN'T SIT BY AND DO NOTHING.
IF THERE'S EVEN A SMALL POSSIBILITY, I...
...
I'VE NEVER SEEN HER SO PERSISTENT...
I GET IT.
HMM
WELL...
...WHAT SHOULD WE DO?
LIKE I SAID, OUR TEAM ONLY HAS ELITE AGENTS.
THERE'S NO ROOM FOR NEWBIES.

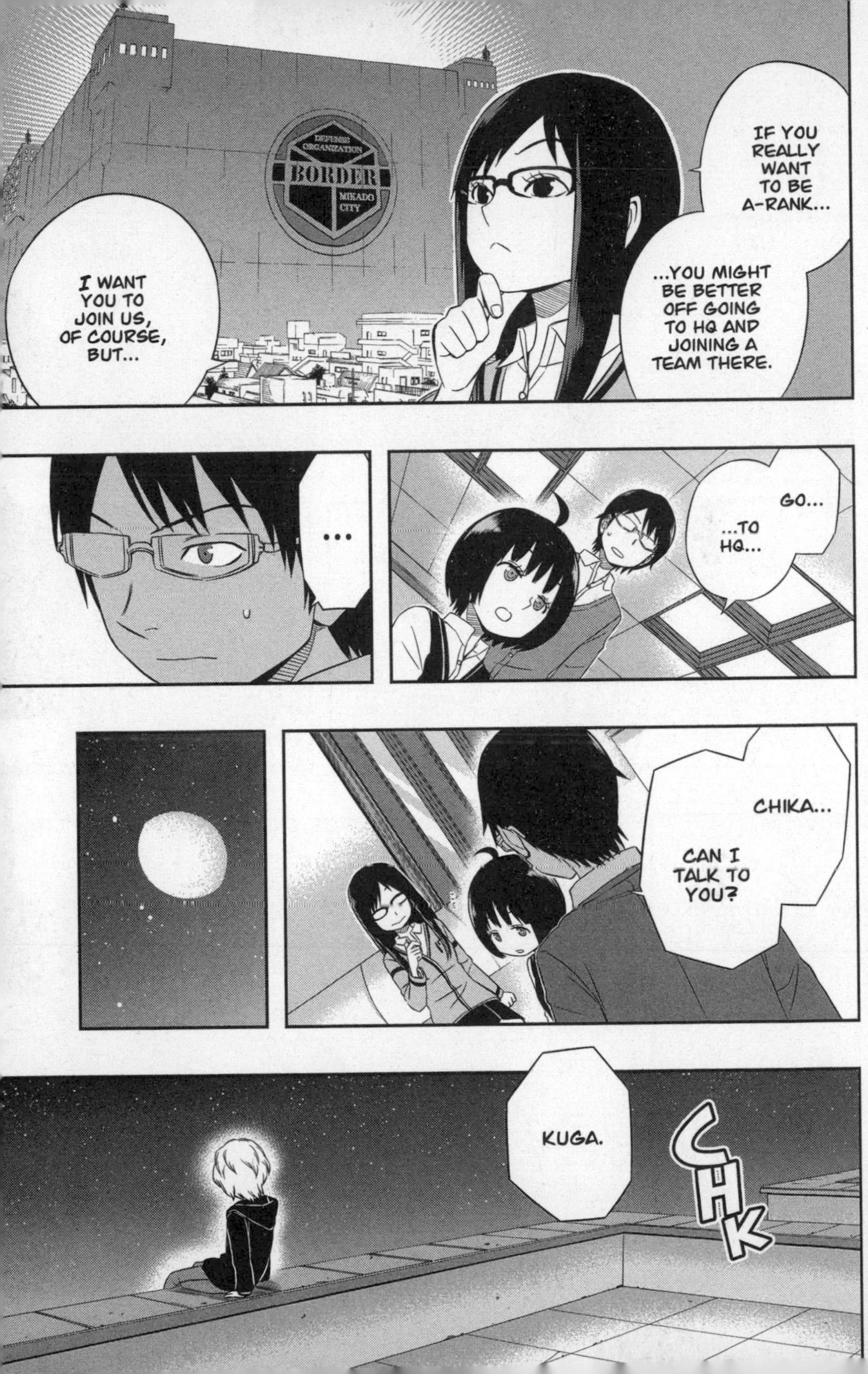
IF YOU REALLY WANT TO BE A-RANK...
...YOU MIGHT BE BETTER OFF GOING TO HQ AND JOINING A TEAM THERE.
I WANT YOU TO JOIN US, OF COURSE, BUT...
DEFENSE ORGANIZATION BORDER MIKADO CITY
GO...
...TO HQ...
...
CHIKA...
CAN I TALK TO YOU?
KUGA.
CHK

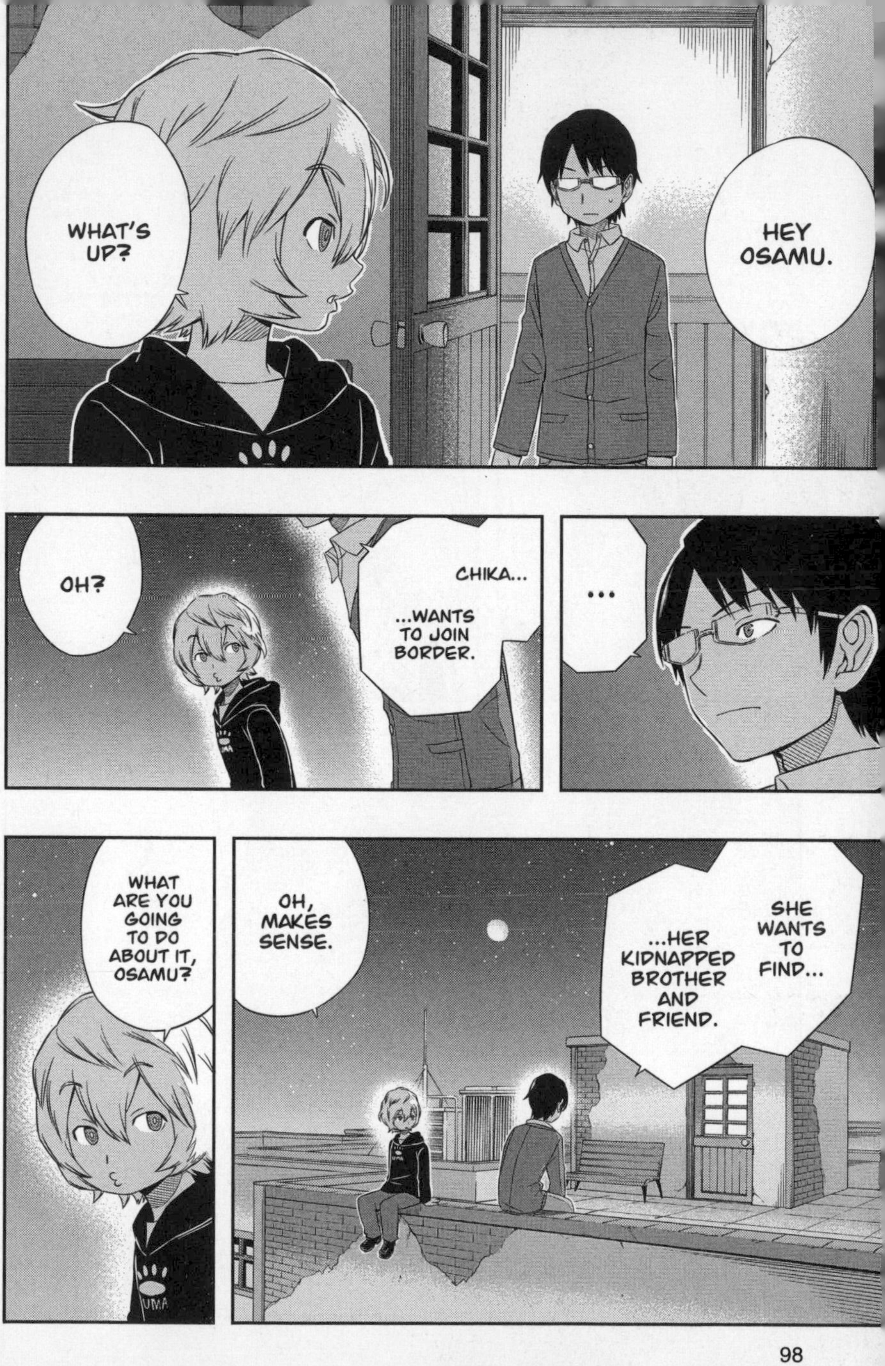
HEY OSAMU.
WHAT'S UP?
...
CHIKA...
...WANTS TO JOIN BORDER.
OH?
SHE WANTS TO FIND...
...HER KIDNAPPED BROTHER AND FRIEND.
OH, MAKES SENSE.
WHAT ARE YOU GOING TO DO ABOUT IT, OSAMU?

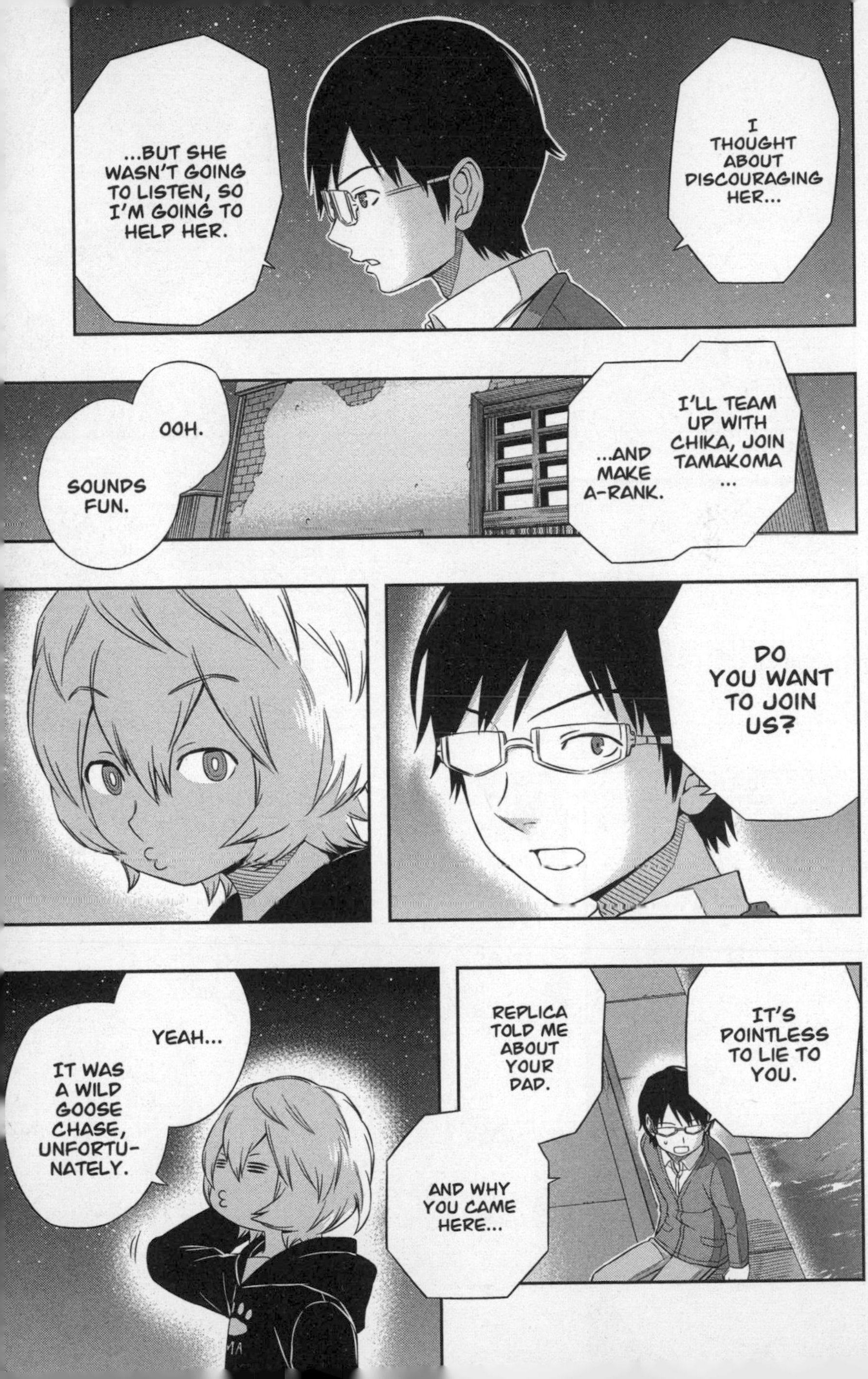
I THOUGHT ABOUT DISCOURAGING HER...
...BUT SHE WASN'T GOING TO LISTEN, SO I'M GOING TO HELP HER.
I'LL TEAM UP WITH CHIKA, JOIN TAMAKOMA ...
...AND MAKE A-RANK.
OOH.
SOUNDS FUN.
DO YOU WANT TO JOIN US?
IT'S POINTLESS TO LIE TO YOU.
REPLICA TOLD ME ABOUT YOUR DAD.
AND WHY YOU CAME HERE...
YEAH...
IT WAS A WILD GOOSE CHASE, UNFORTU-NATELY.

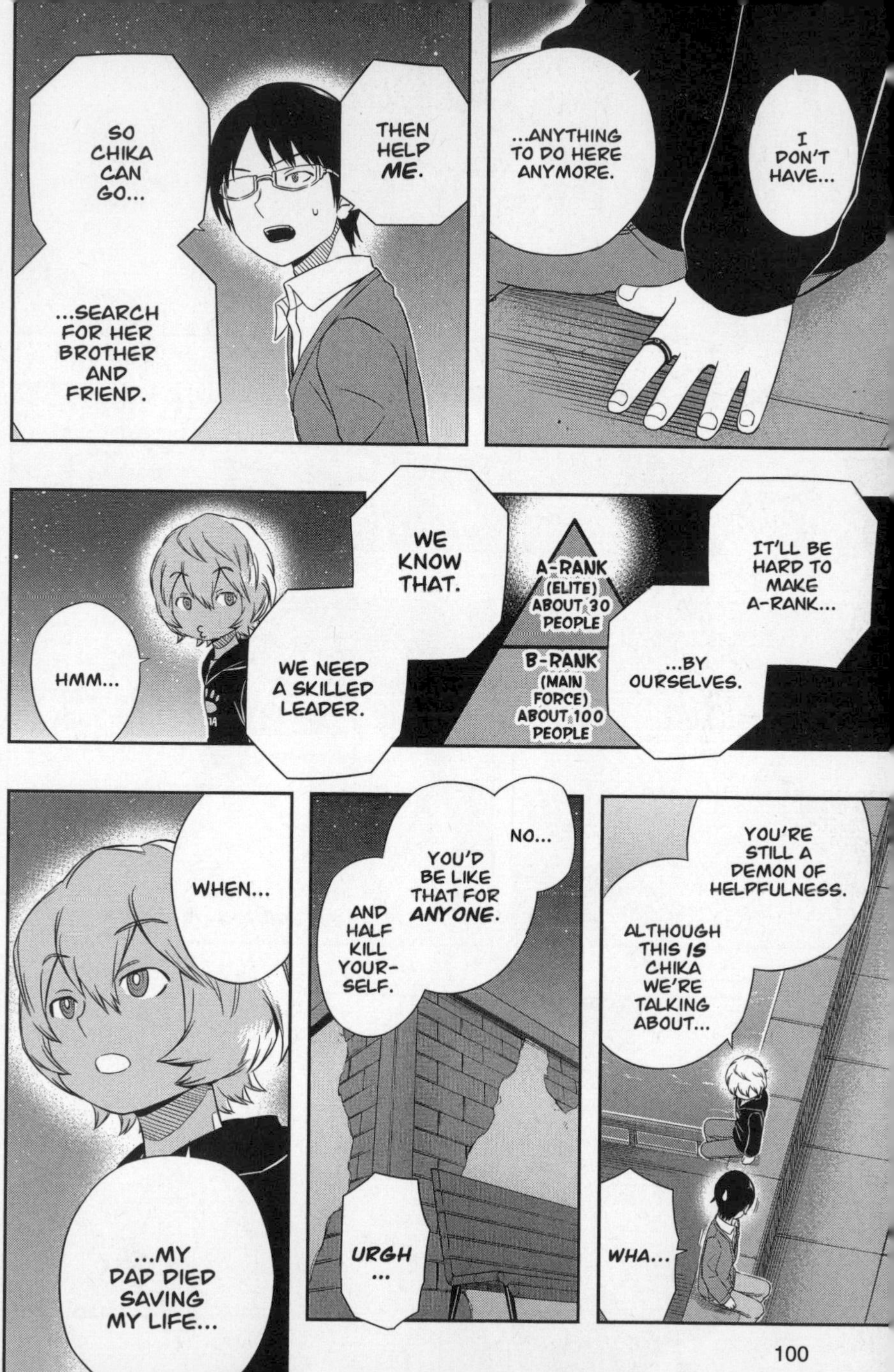
I DON'T HAVE...
...ANYTHING TO DO HERE ANYMORE.
THEN HELP ME.
SO CHIKA CAN GO...
...SEARCH FOR HER BROTHER AND FRIEND.
IT'LL BE HARD TO MAKE A-RANK...
...BY OURSELVES.
A-RANK (ELITE) ABOUT 30 PEOPLE
B-RANK (MAIN FORCE) ABOUT 100 PEOPLE
WE KNOW THAT.
WE NEED A SKILLED LEADER.
HMM...
YOU'RE STILL A DEMON OF HELPFULNESS.
ALTHOUGH THIS IS CHIKA WE'RE TALKING ABOUT...
WHA...
NO...
YOU'D BE LIKE THAT FOR ANYONE.
AND HALF KILL YOUR-SELF.
URGH ...
WHEN...
...MY DAD DIED SAVING MY LIFE...

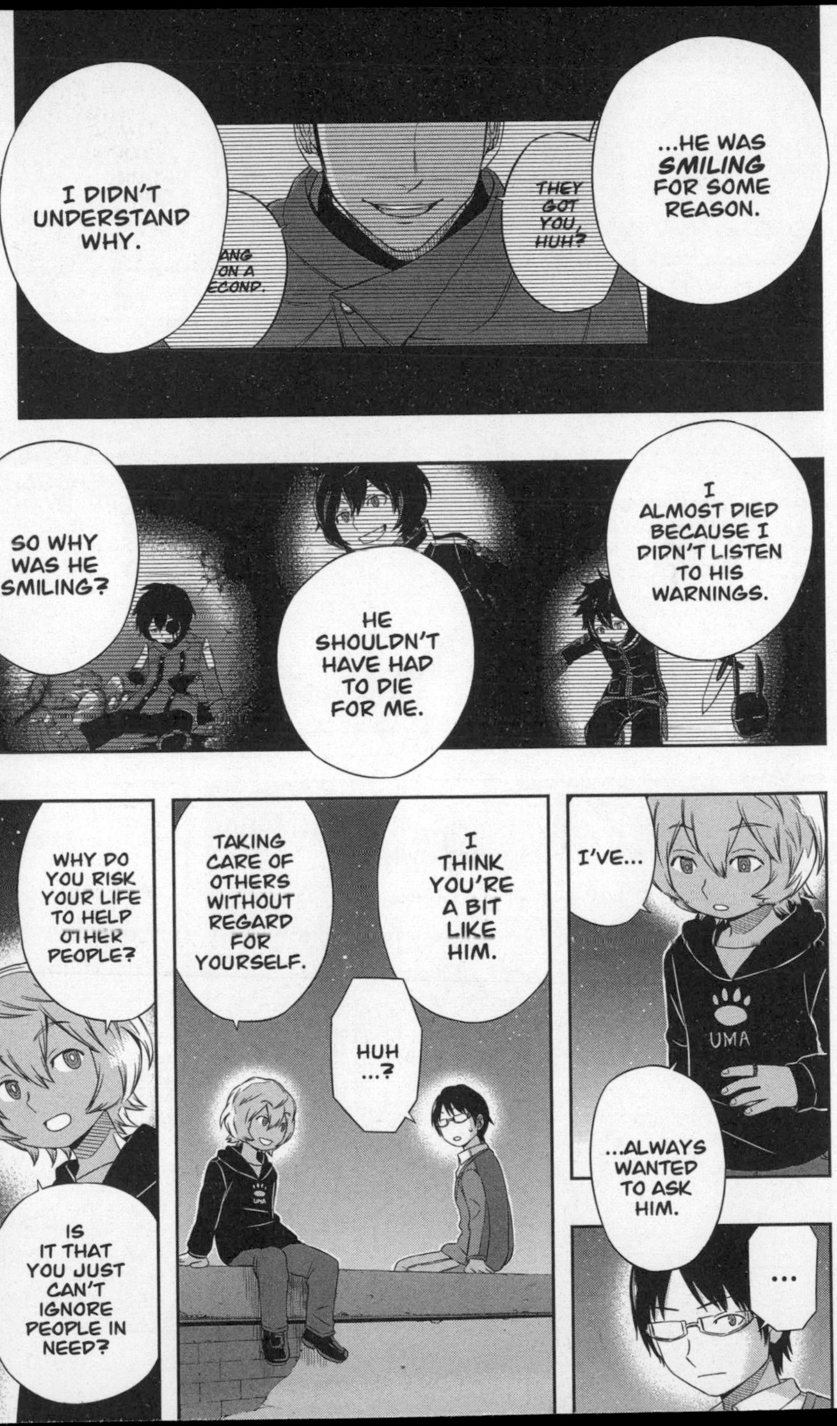
...HE WAS SMILING FOR SOME REASON.
THEY GOT YOU, HUH?
I DIDN'T UNDERSTAND WHY.
I ALMOST DIED BECAUSE I DIDN'T LISTEN TO HIS WARNINGS.
HE SHOULDN'T HAVE HAD TO DIE FOR ME.
SO WHY WAS HE SMILING?
I'VE...
...ALWAYS WANTED TO ASK HIM.
...
I THINK YOU'RE A BIT LIKE HIM.
TAKING CARE OF OTHERS WITHOUT REGARD FOR YOURSELF.
HUH ...?
WHY DO YOU RISK YOUR LIFE TO HELP OTHER PEOPLE?
IS IT THAT YOU JUST CAN'T IGNORE PEOPLE IN NEED?

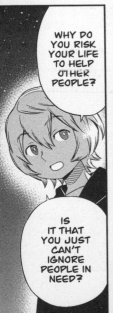

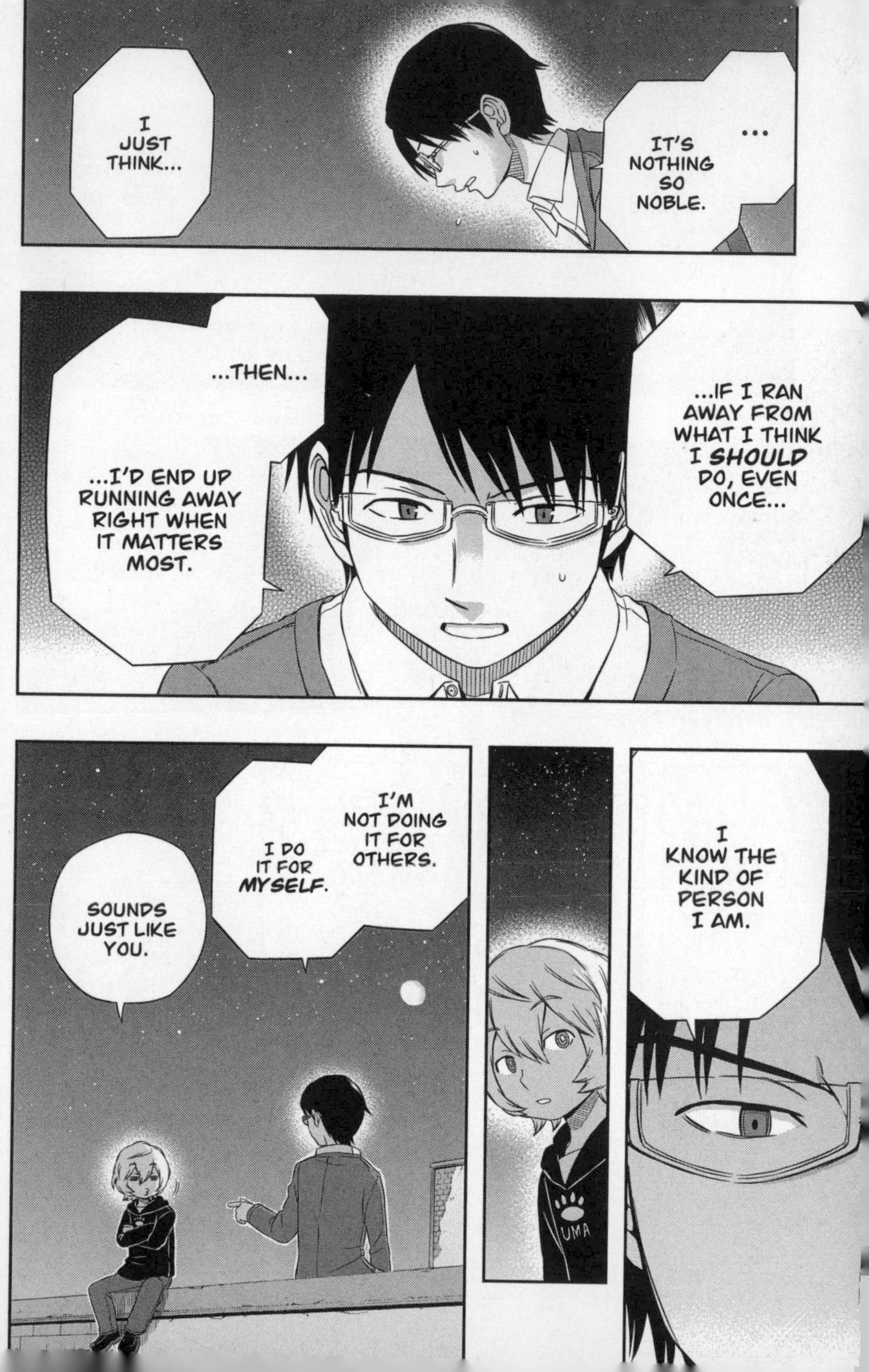
...
IT'S NOTHING SO NOBLE.
I JUST THINK...
...IF I RAN AWAY FROM WHAT I THINK I *SHOULD* DO, EVEN ONCE...
...THEN...
...I'D END UP RUNNING AWAY RIGHT WHEN IT MATTERS MOST.
I KNOW THE KIND OF PERSON I AM.
I'M NOT DOING IT FOR OTHERS.
I DO IT FOR *MYSELF*.
SOUNDS JUST LIKE YOU.

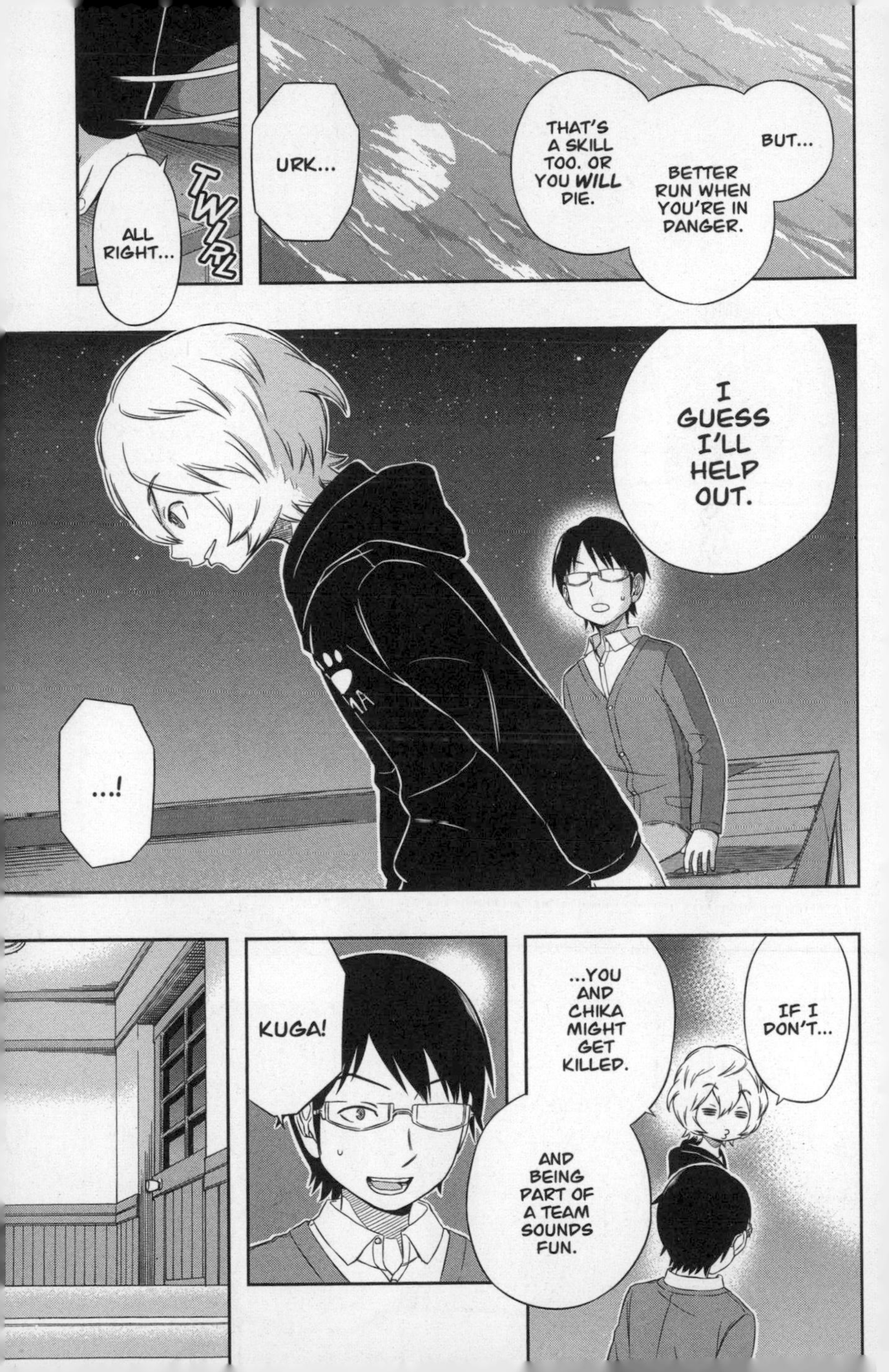
BUT...
BETTER RUN WHEN YOU'RE IN DANGER.
THAT'S A SKILL TOO. OR YOU WILL DIE.
URK...
TWIRL
ALL RIGHT...
I GUESS I'LL HELP OUT.
...!
IF I DON'T...
...YOU AND CHIKA MIGHT GET KILLED.
AND BEING PART OF A TEAM SOUNDS FUN.
KUGA!

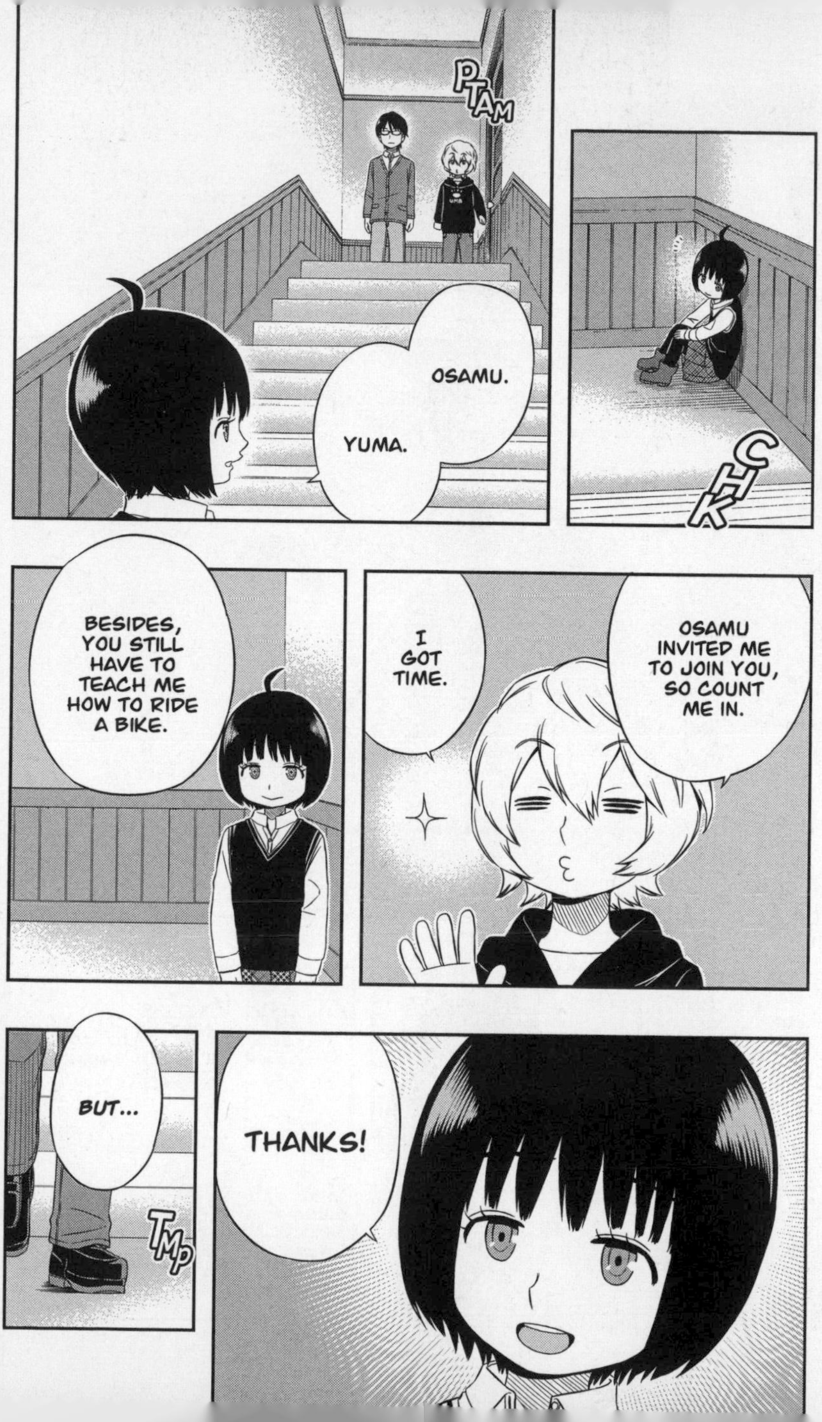
CHK
PTAM
OSAMU.
YUMA.
OSAMU INVITED ME TO JOIN YOU, SO COUNT ME IN.
I GOT TIME.
BESIDES, YOU STILL HAVE TO TEACH ME HOW TO RIDE A BIKE.
THANKS!
BUT...
TMP

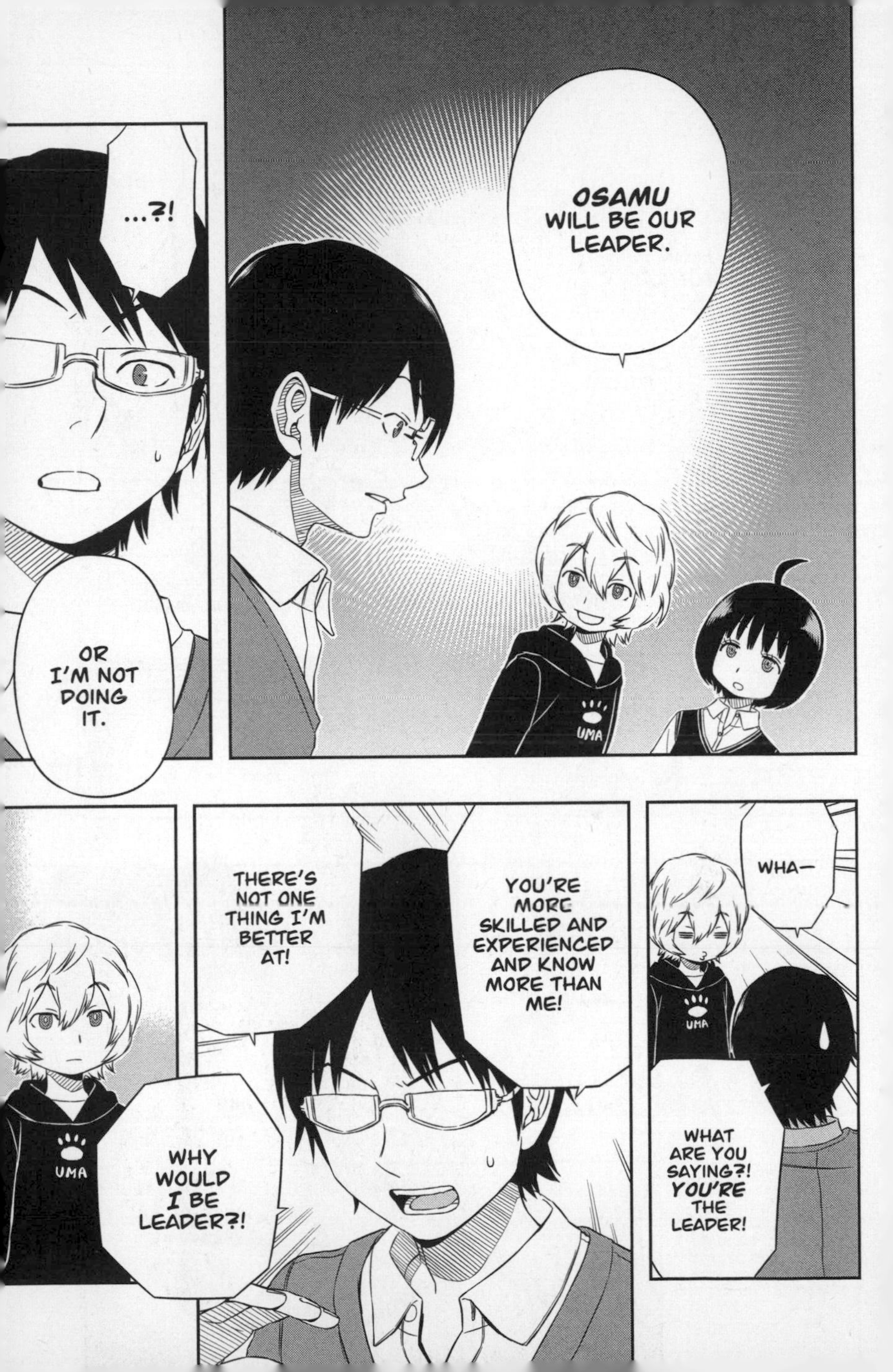
OSAMU WILL BE OUR LEADER.
...?!
OR I'M NOT DOING IT.
WHA—
WHAT ARE YOU SAYING?! YOU'RE THE LEADER!
YOU'RE MORE SKILLED AND EXPERIENCED AND KNOW MORE THAN ME!
THERE'S NOT ONE THING I'M BETTER AT!
WHY WOULD I BE LEADER?!

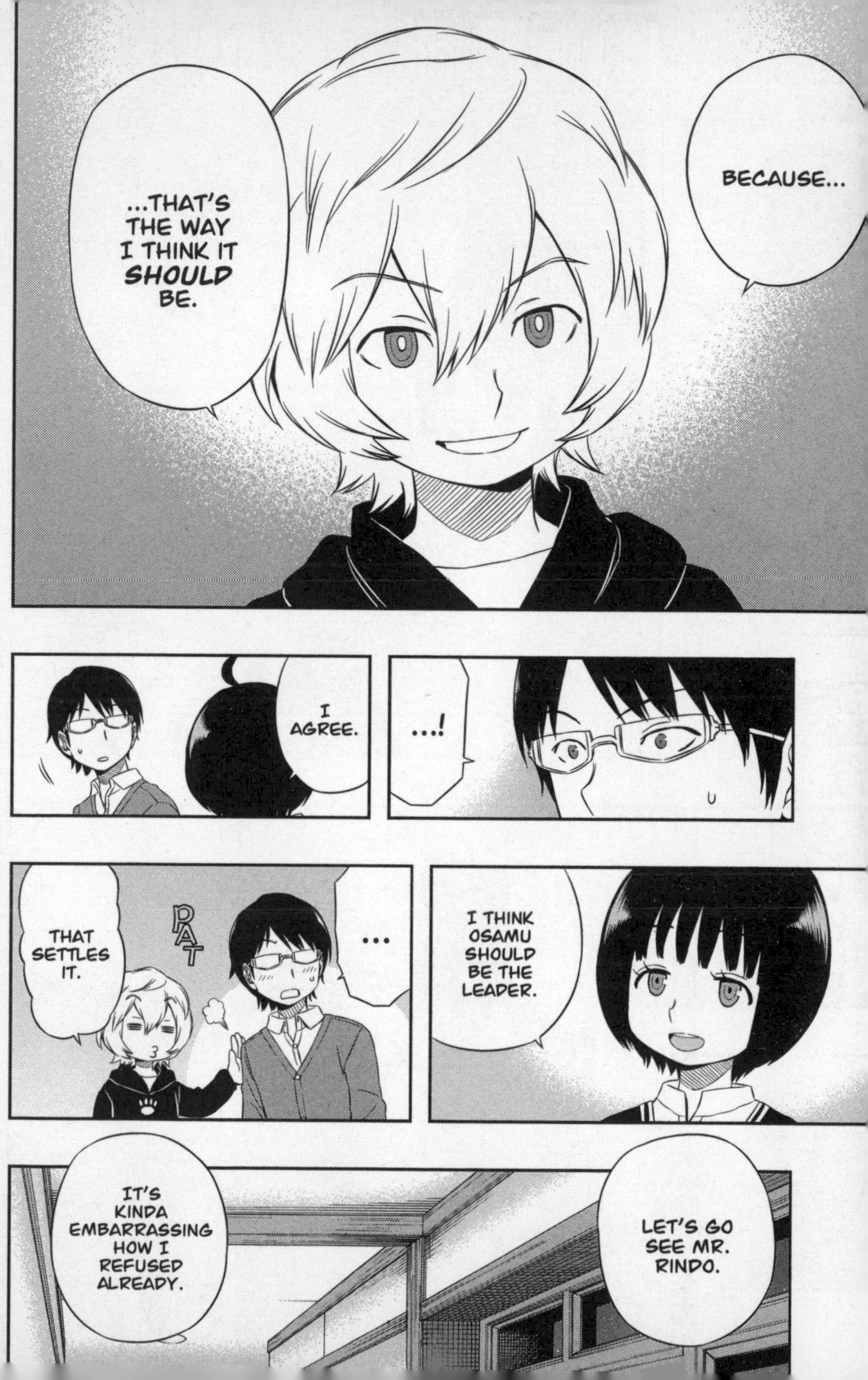
BECAUSE...
...THAT'S THE WAY I THINK IT SHOULD BE.
...!
I AGREE.
I THINK OSAMU SHOULD BE THE LEADER.
...
PAT
THAT SETTLES IT.
LET'S GO SEE MR. RINDO.
IT'S KINDA EMBARRASSING HOW I REFUSED ALREADY.

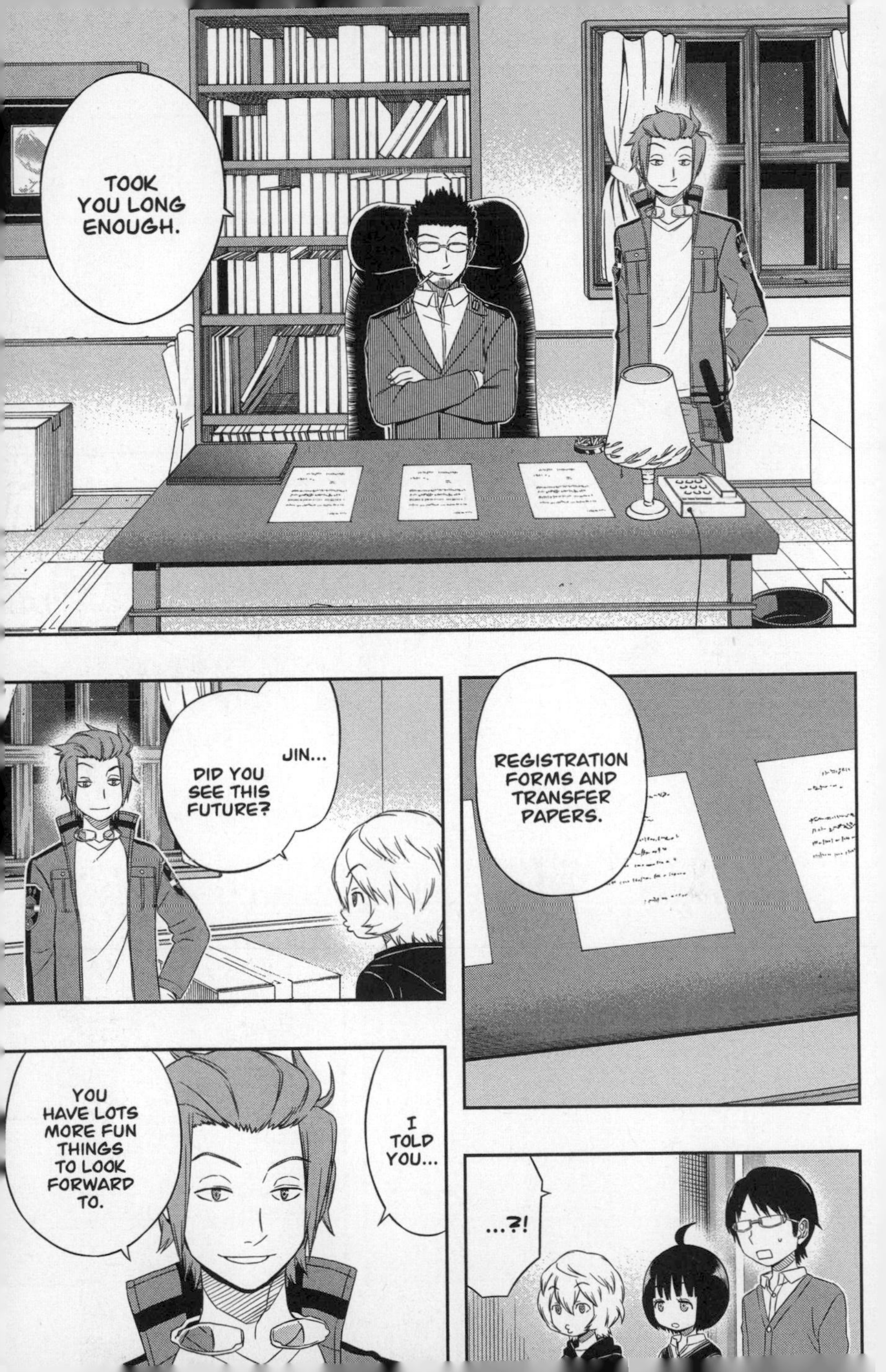
TOOK YOU LONG ENOUGH.
REGISTRATION FORMS AND TRANSFER PAPERS.
JIN... DID YOU SEE THIS FUTURE?
I TOLD YOU...
YOU HAVE LOTS MORE FUN THINGS TO LOOK FORWARD TO.
...?!

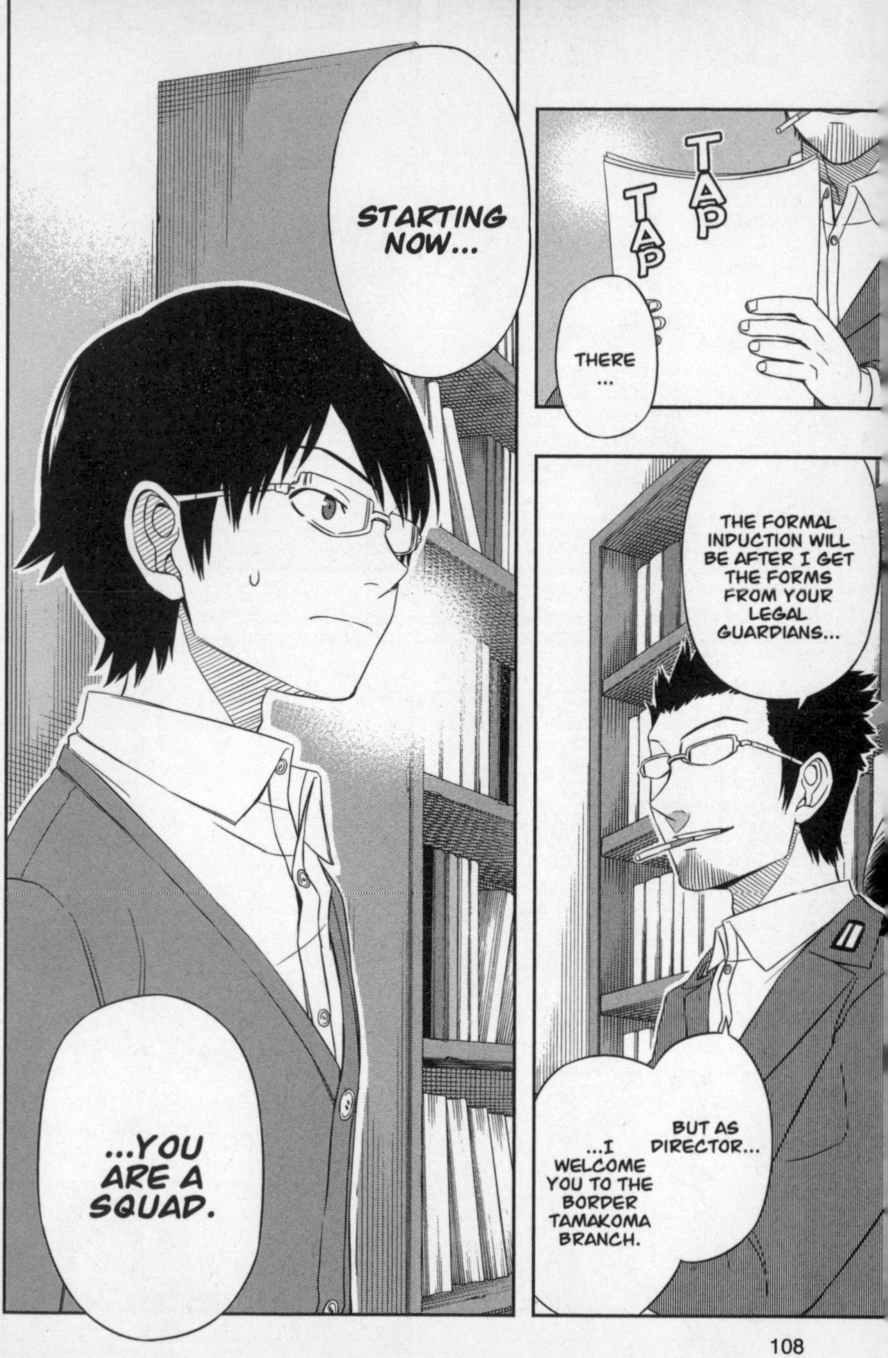
TAP
TAP
THERE ...
THE FORMAL INDUCTION WILL BE AFTER I GET THE FORMS FROM YOUR LEGAL GUARDIANS...
BUT AS DIRECTOR...
...I WELCOME YOU TO THE BORDER TAMAKOMA BRANCH.
STARTING NOW...
...YOU ARE A SQUAD.

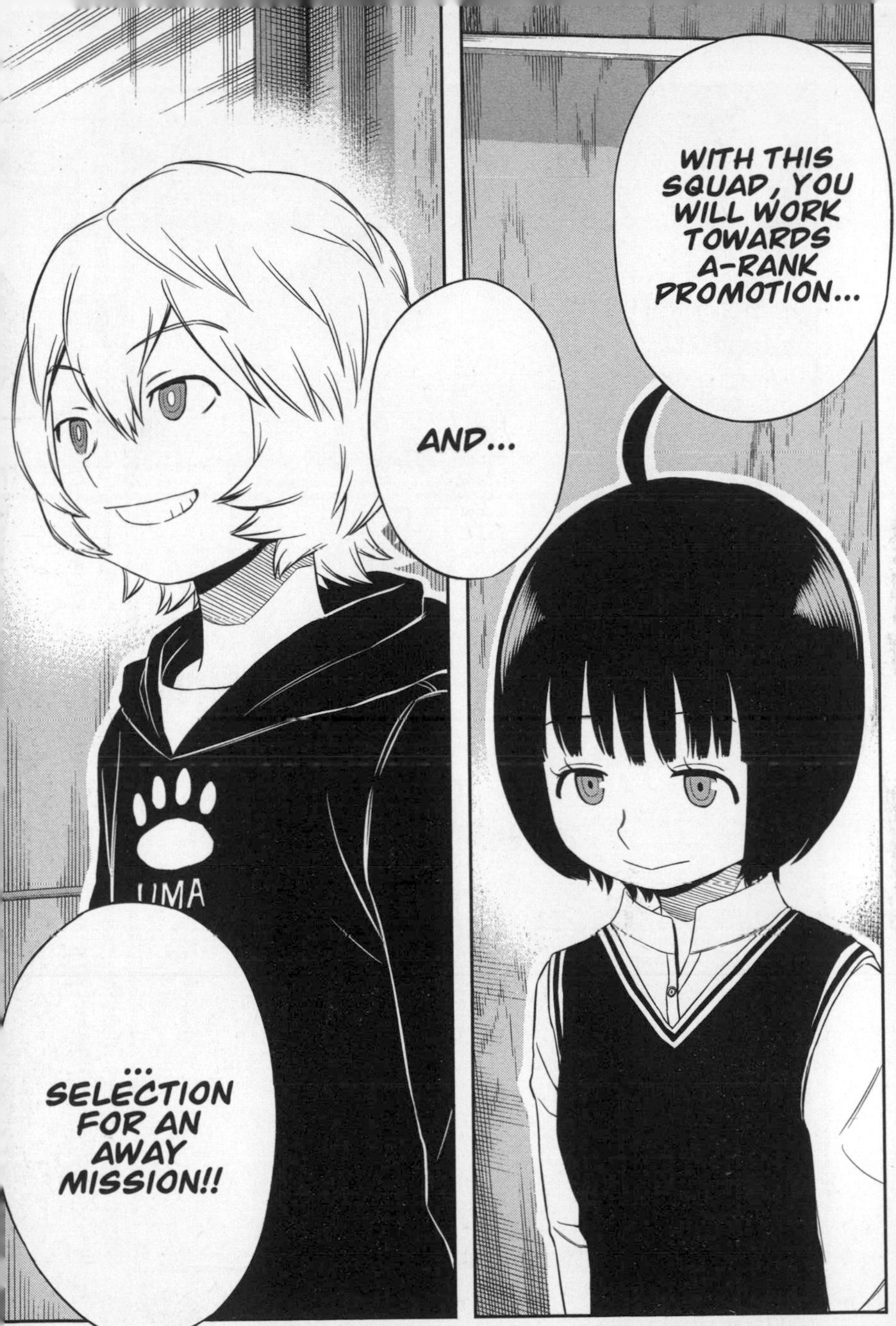
WITH THIS SQUAD, YOU WILL WORK TOWARDS A-RANK PROMOTION...
AND...
...SELECTION FOR AN AWAY MISSION!!

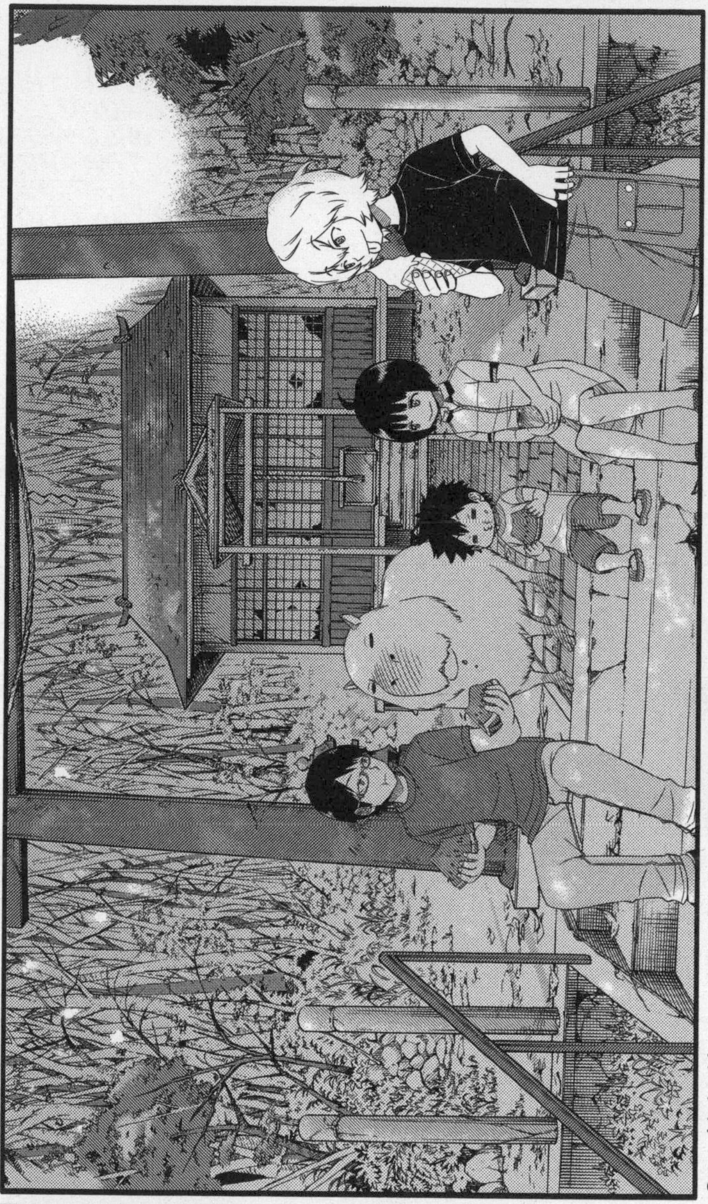

Sorry this is sideways. I drew this for a mobile app issue called *Jump LIVE*. The theme was summer. Besides the fact that I forgot Raijin-maru's collar, I think it came out pretty well. There's a blank space at the top right because the title logo was there.

■ Illustration for 2013 *Jump LIVE*

Jump LIVE Issue 1 (Aug. 2013)

Chapter 22 Tamakoma Branch: Part 2

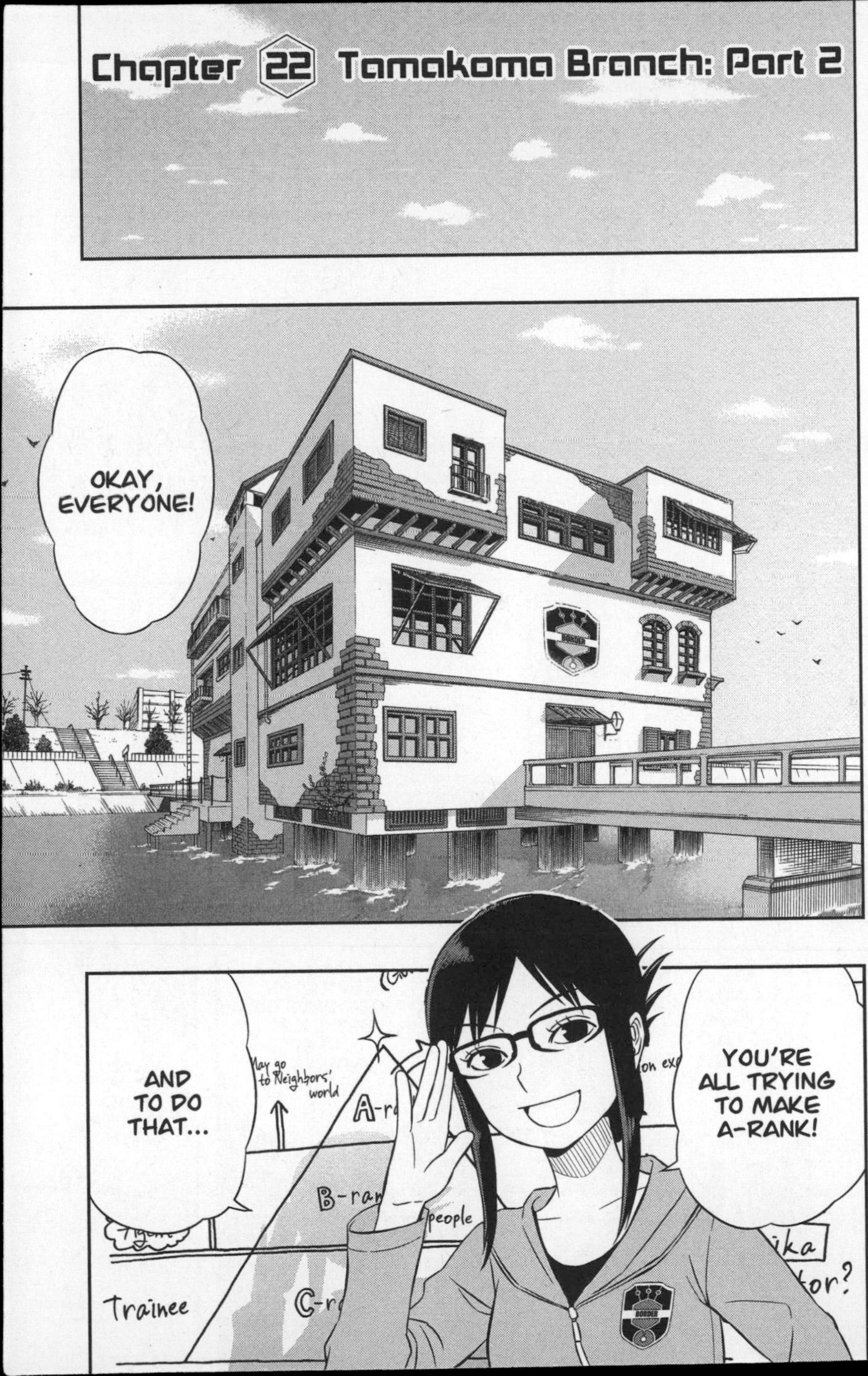
OKAY, EVERYONE!
YOU'RE ALL TRYING TO MAKE A-RANK!
May go to Neighbors' world
AND TO DO THAT...
Trainee

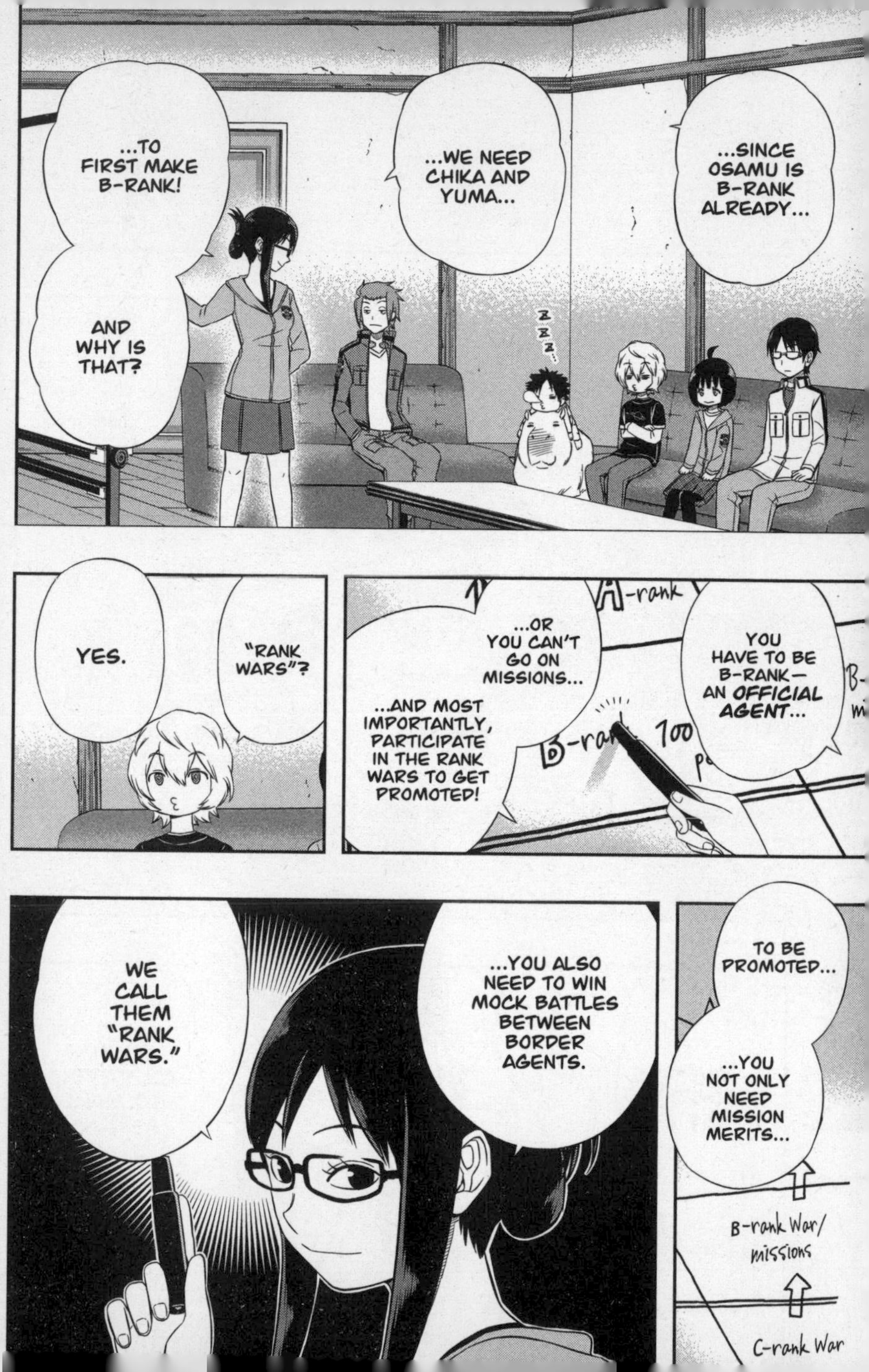
...SINCE OSAMU IS B-RANK ALREADY...
...WE NEED CHIKA AND YUMA...
...TO FIRST MAKE B-RANK!
AND WHY IS THAT?
Z Z Z...
YOU HAVE TO BE B-RANK— AN OFFICIAL AGENT...
A-rank
...OR YOU CAN'T GO ON MISSIONS...
...AND MOST IMPORTANTLY, PARTICIPATE IN THE RANK WARS TO GET PROMOTED!
"RANK WARS"?
YES.
TO BE PROMOTED...
...YOU NOT ONLY NEED MISSION MERITS...
B-rank War/ missions
C-rank War
...YOU ALSO NEED TO WIN MOCK BATTLES BETWEEN BORDER AGENTS.
WE CALL THEM "RANK WARS."

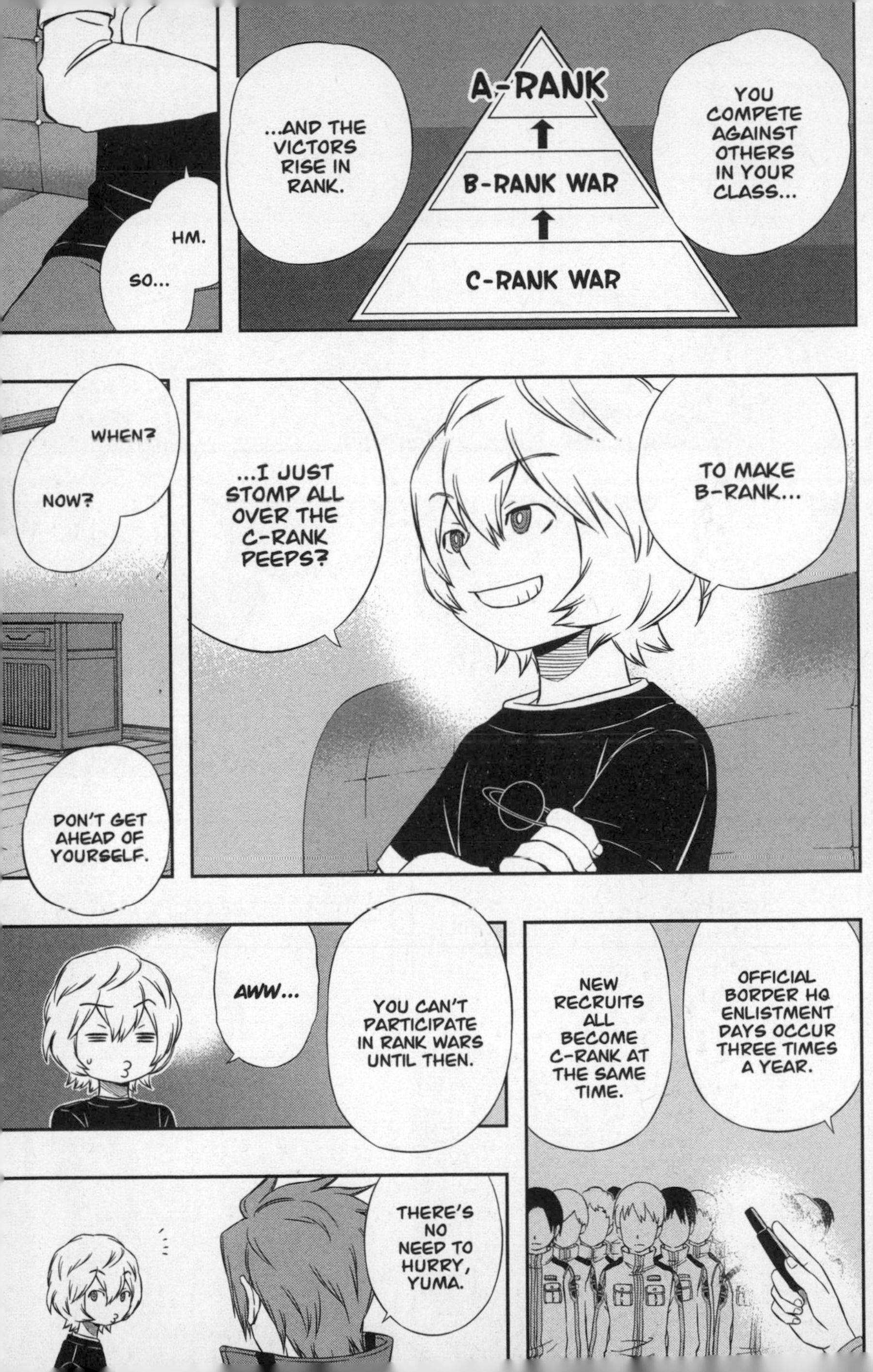
YOU COMPETE AGAINST OTHERS IN YOUR CLASS...
A-RANK
B-RANK WAR
C-RANK WAR
...AND THE VICTORS RISE IN RANK.
HM.
SO...
TO MAKE B-RANK...
...I JUST STOMP ALL OVER THE C-RANK PEEPS?
WHEN?
NOW?
DON'T GET AHEAD OF YOURSELF.
OFFICIAL BORDER HQ ENLISTMENT DAYS OCCUR THREE TIMES A YEAR.
NEW RECRUITS ALL BECOME C-RANK AT THE SAME TIME.
YOU CAN'T PARTICIPATE IN RANK WARS UNTIL THEN.
AWW...
THERE'S NO NEED TO HURRY, YUMA.

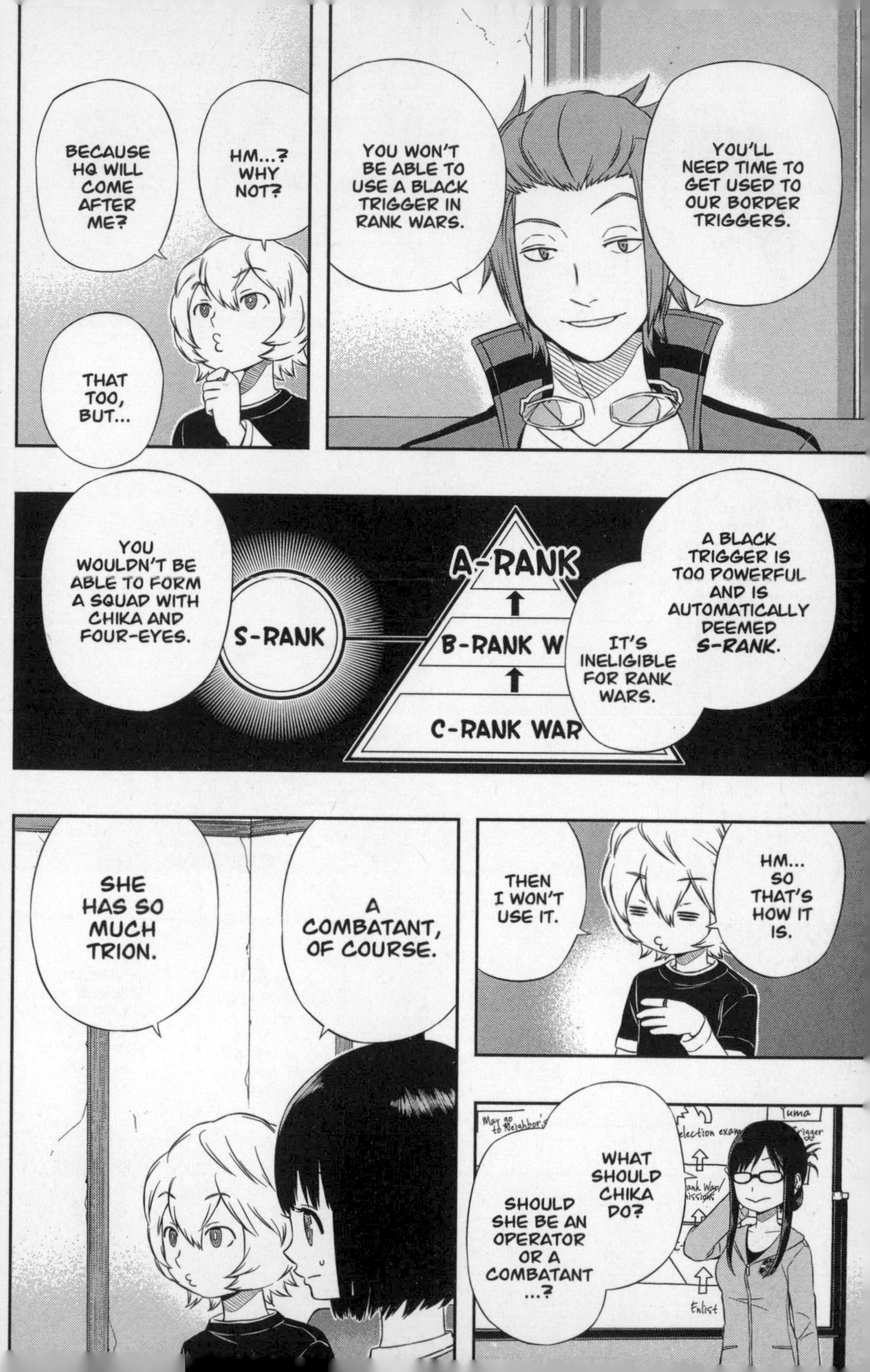
YOU'LL NEED TIME TO GET USED TO OUR BORDER TRIGGERS.
YOU WON'T BE ABLE TO USE A BLACK TRIGGER IN RANK WARS.
HM...? WHY NOT?
BECAUSE HQ WILL COME AFTER ME?
THAT TOO, BUT...
A BLACK TRIGGER IS TOO POWERFUL AND IS AUTOMATICALLY DEEMED S-RANK.
IT'S INELIGIBLE FOR RANK WARS.
A-RANK
B-RANK W
C-RANK WAR
S-RANK
YOU WOULDN'T BE ABLE TO FORM A SQUAD WITH CHIKA AND FOUR-EYES.
HM... SO THAT'S HOW IT IS.
THEN I WON'T USE IT.
May go to Neighbor's
Yuma
Enlist
WHAT SHOULD CHIKA DO?
SHOULD SHE BE AN OPERATOR OR A COMBATANT ...?
A COMBATANT, OF COURSE.
SHE HAS SO MUCH TRION.

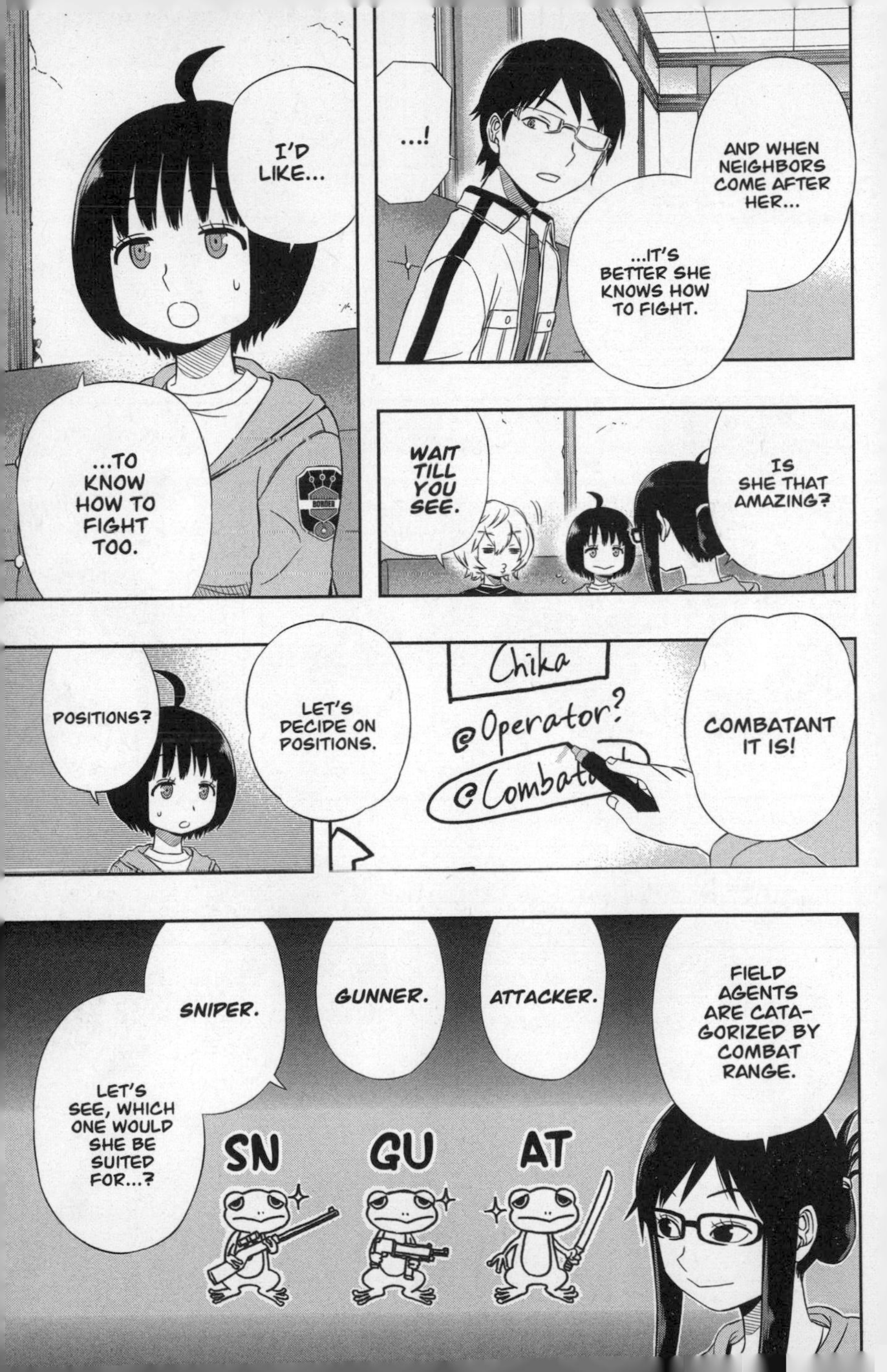
AND WHEN NEIGHBORS COME AFTER HER...
...IT'S BETTER SHE KNOWS HOW TO FIGHT.
...!
IS SHE THAT AMAZING?
WAIT TILL YOU SEE.
I'D LIKE...
...TO KNOW HOW TO FIGHT TOO.
BORDER
COMBATANT IT IS!
Chika
@Operator?
@Combata
LET'S DECIDE ON POSITIONS.
POSITIONS?
FIELD AGENTS ARE CATA-GORIZED BY COMBAT RANGE.
ATTACKER.
GUNNER.
SNIPER.
LET'S SEE, WHICH ONE WOULD SHE BE SUITED FOR...?
AT
GU
SN

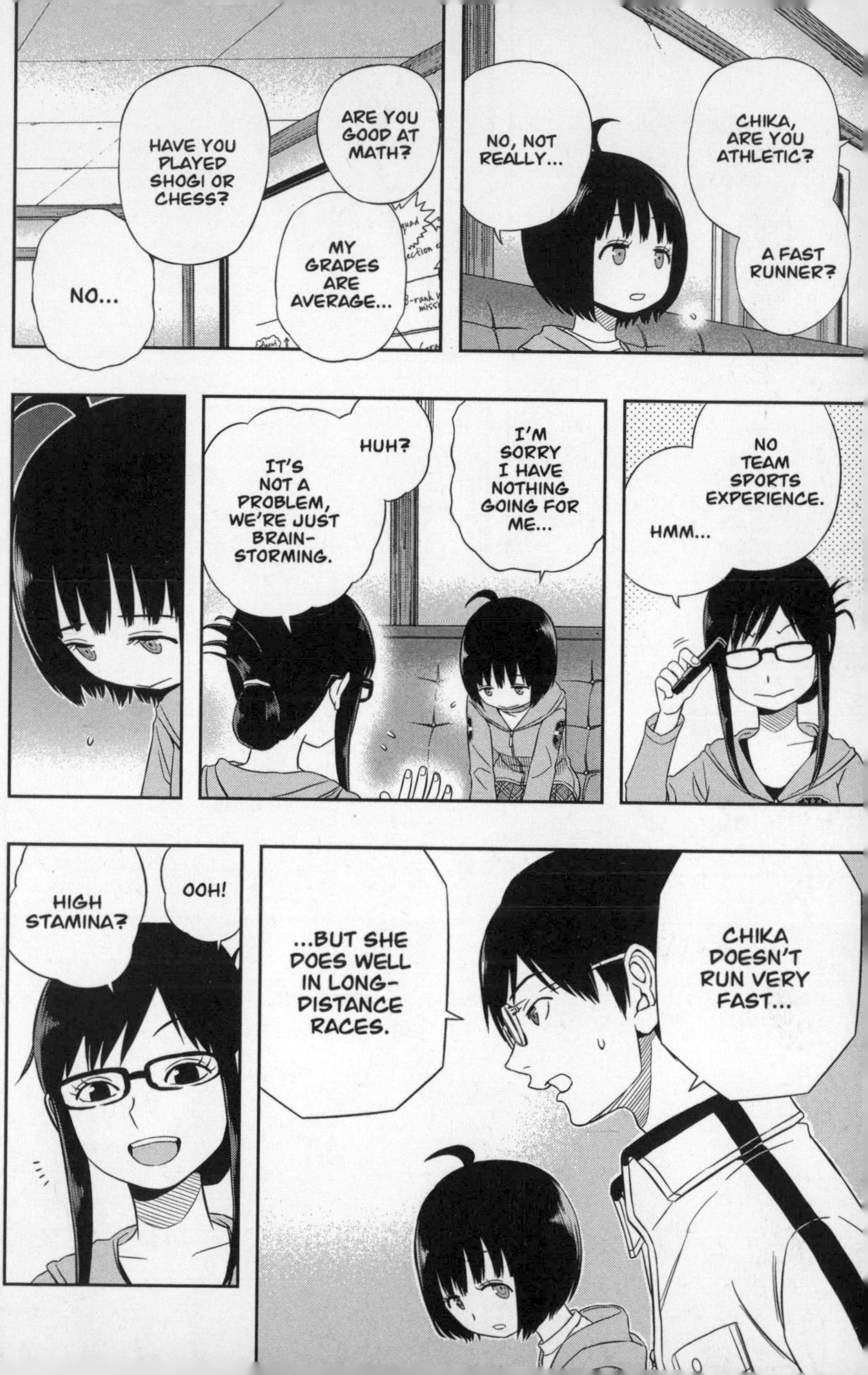
CHIKA, ARE YOU ATHLETIC?
A FAST RUNNER?
NO, NOT REALLY...
ARE YOU GOOD AT MATH?
MY GRADES ARE AVERAGE...
HAVE YOU PLAYED SHOGI OR CHESS?
NO...
NO TEAM SPORTS EXPERIENCE.
HMM...
I'M SORRY I HAVE NOTHING GOING FOR ME...
HUH?
IT'S NOT A PROBLEM, WE'RE JUST BRAIN-STORMING.
CHIKA DOESN'T RUN VERY FAST...
...BUT SHE DOES WELL IN LONG-DISTANCE RACES.
OOH!
HIGH STAMINA?

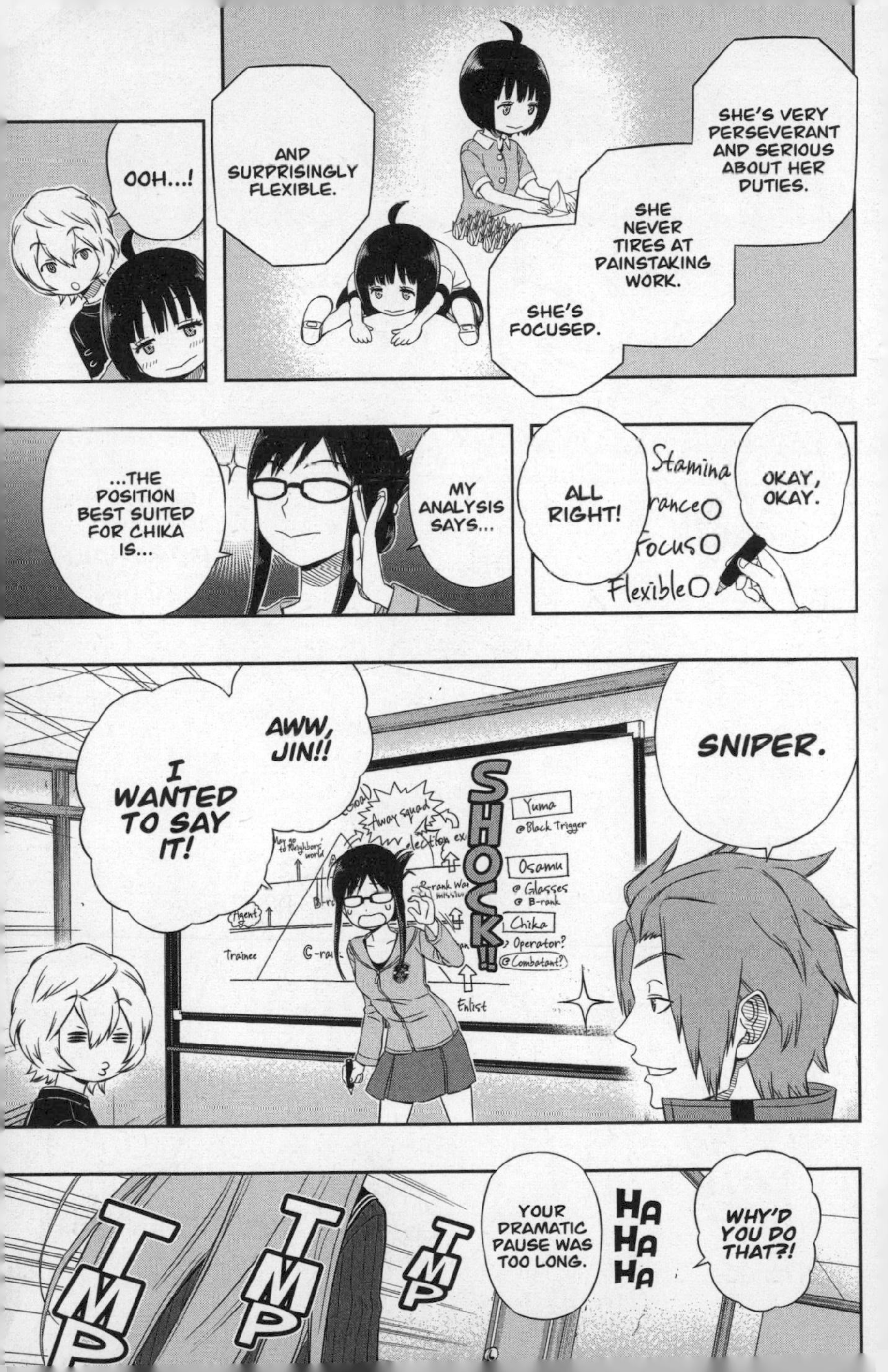
SHE'S VERY PERSEVERANT AND SERIOUS ABOUT HER DUTIES.
SHE NEVER TIRES AT PAINSTAKING WORK.
SHE'S FOCUSED.
AND SURPRISINGLY FLEXIBLE.
OOH...!
OKAY, OKAY.
ALL RIGHT!
Stamina
Focus○
Flexible○
MY ANALYSIS SAYS...
...THE POSITION BEST SUITED FOR CHIKA IS...
SNIPER.
SHOCK!!
Yuma
@Black Trigger
Osamu
@Glasses
@B-rank
Chika
Operator?
@Combatant?
Away squad
Agent
Trainee
Enlist
AWW, JIN!!
I WANTED TO SAY IT!
WHY'D YOU DO THAT?!
HA HA HA
YOUR DRAMATIC PAUSE WAS TOO LONG.
TMP
TMP
TMP

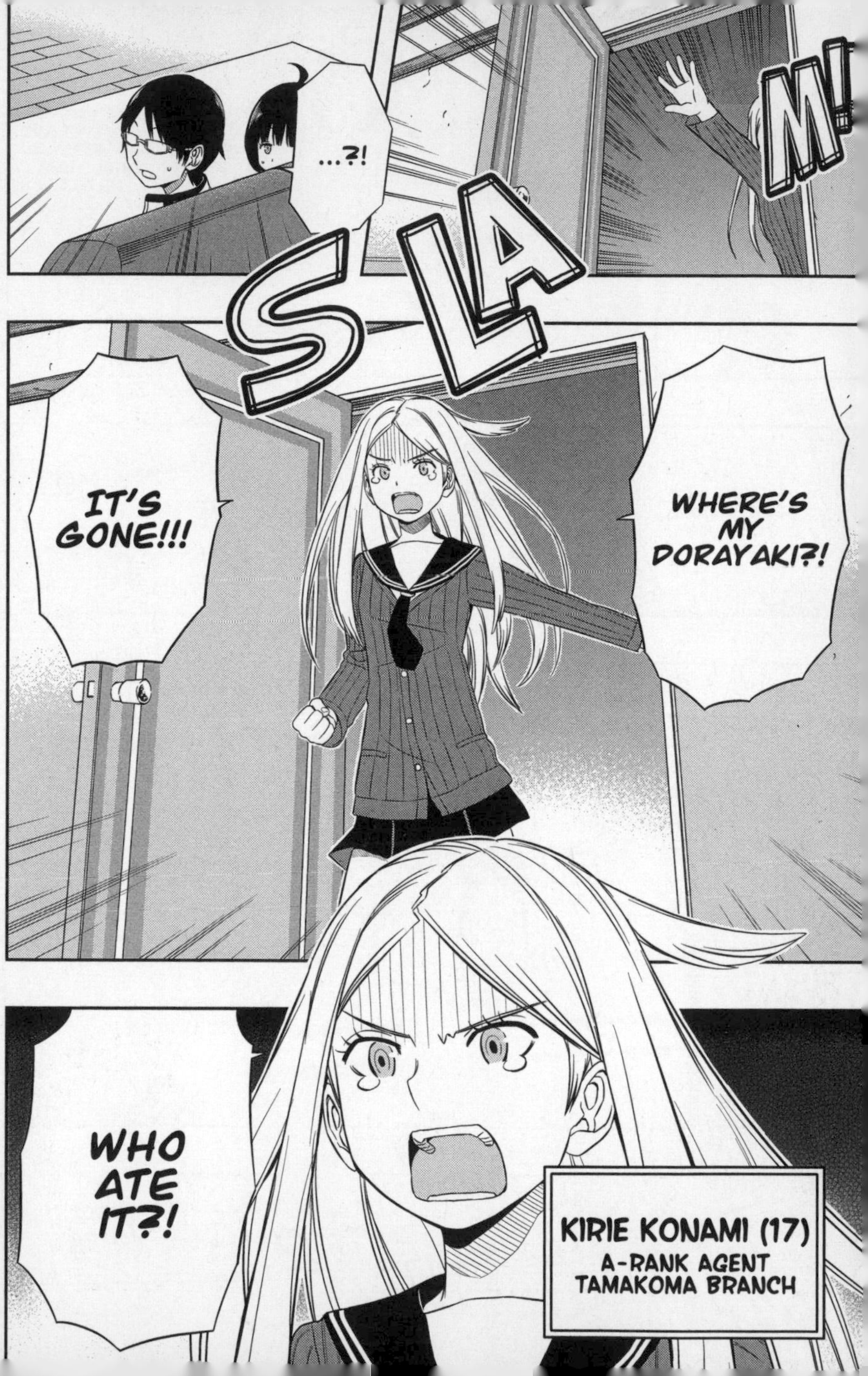
SLAM!
...?!
WHERE'S MY DORAYAKI?!
IT'S GONE!!!
WHO ATE IT?!
KIRIE KONAMI (17)
A-RANK AGENT
TAMAKOMA BRANCH

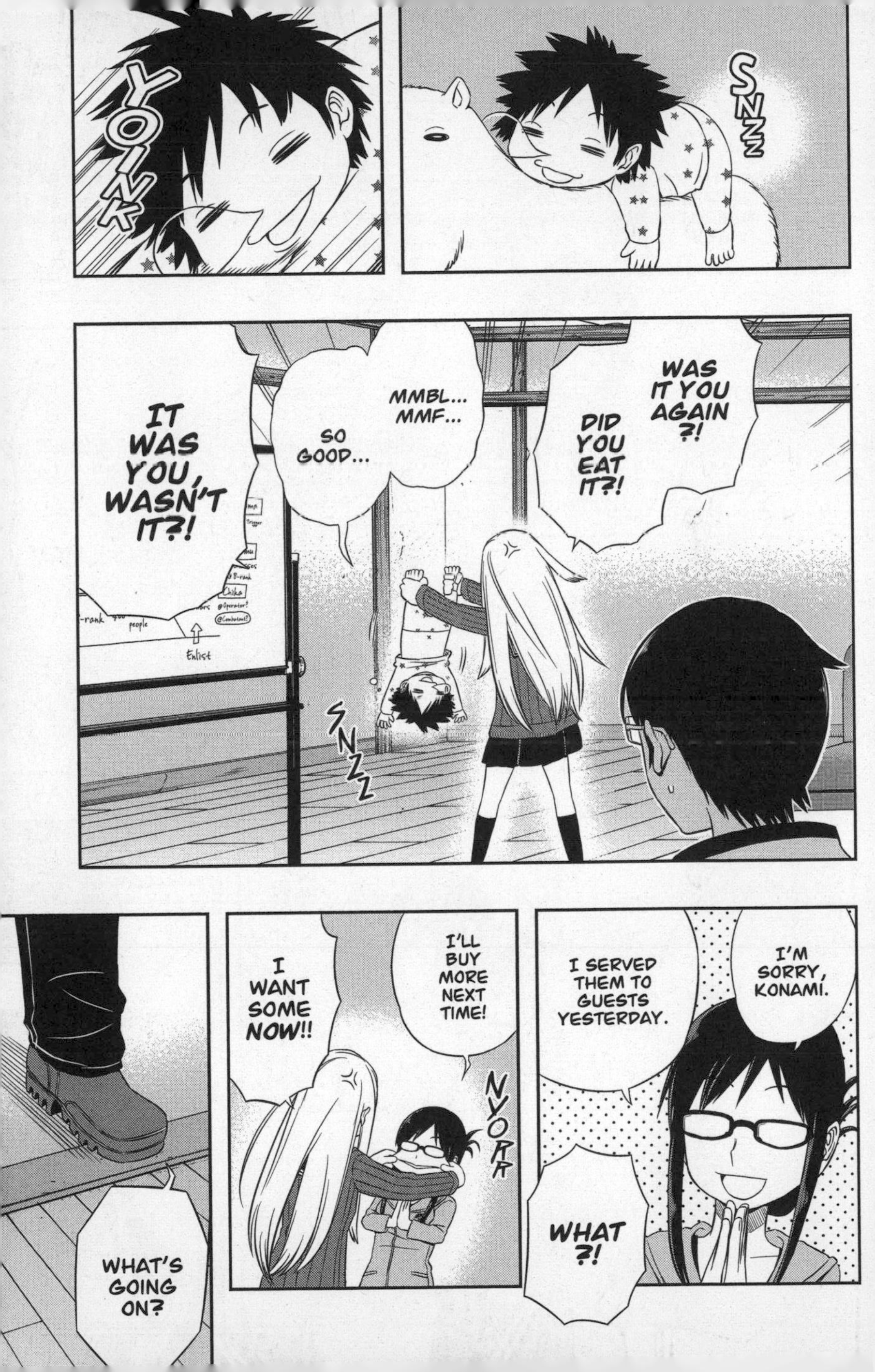
SNZZ
YOINK
WAS IT YOU AGAIN?!
DID YOU EAT IT?!
MMBL... MMF...
SO GOOD...
IT WAS YOU, WASN'T IT?!
Chika
people
Enlist
SNZZ
I'M SORRY, KONAMI.
I SERVED THEM TO GUESTS YESTERDAY.
WHAT?!
I'LL BUY MORE NEXT TIME!
I WANT SOME NOW!!
NYORR
WHAT'S GOING ON?

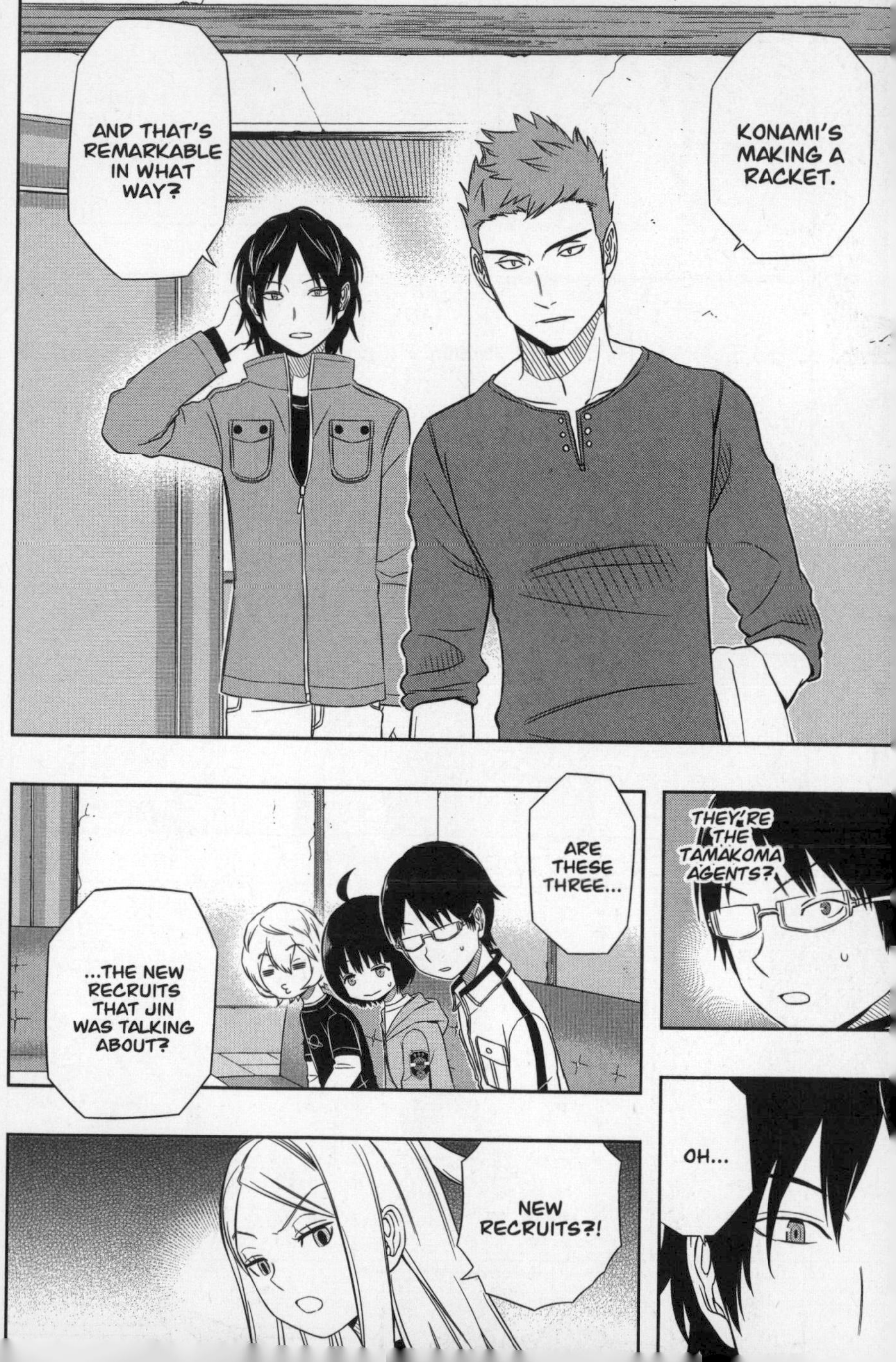
KONAMI'S MAKING A RACKET.
AND THAT'S REMARKABLE IN WHAT WAY?
THEY'RE THE TAMAKOMA AGENTS?
ARE THESE THREE...
...THE NEW RECRUITS THAT JIN WAS TALKING ABOUT?
OH...
NEW RECRUITS?!

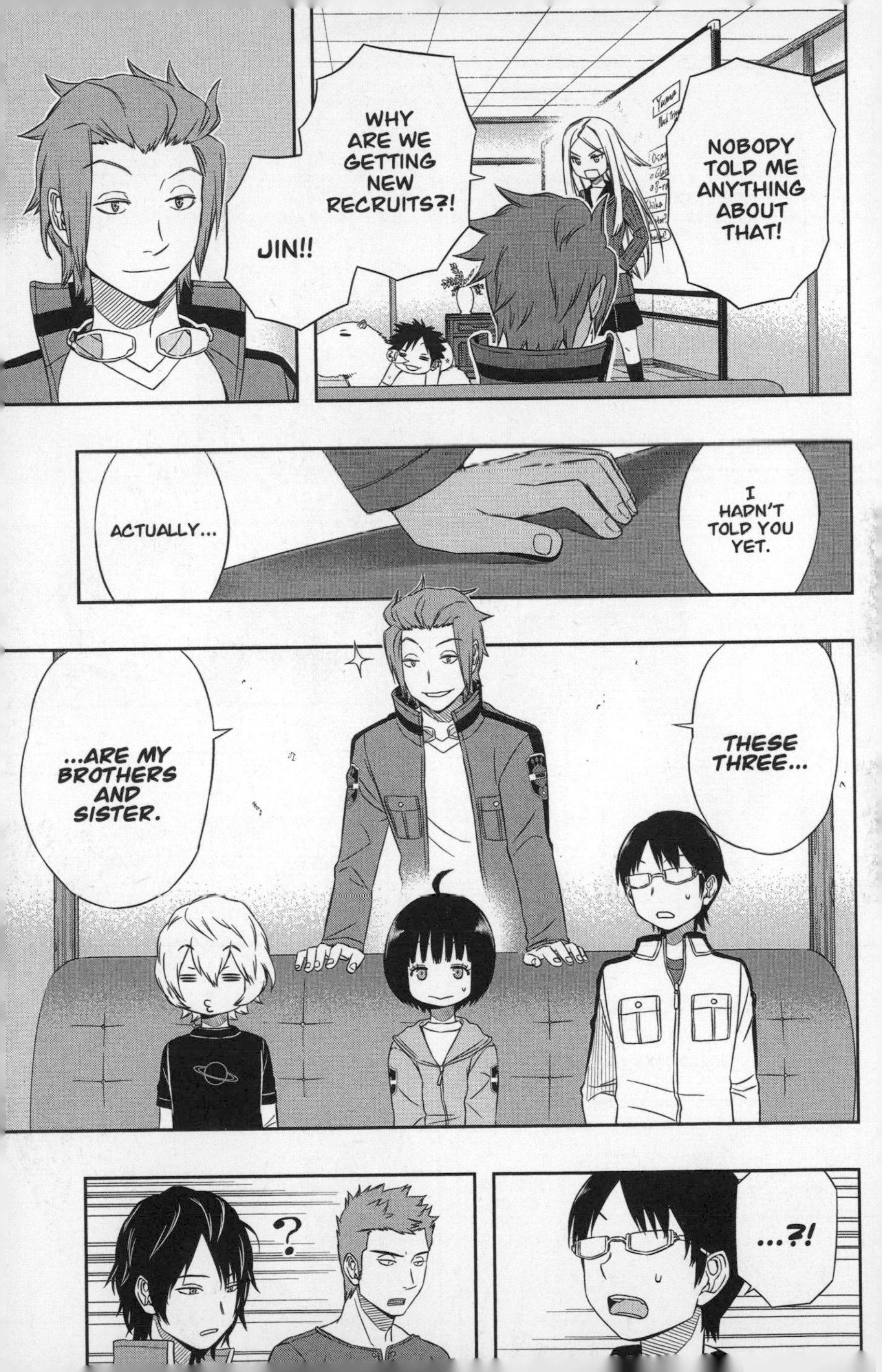
NOBODY TOLD ME ANYTHING ABOUT THAT!
WHY ARE WE GETTING NEW RECRUITS?!
JIN!!
I HADN'T TOLD YOU YET.
ACTUALLY...
THESE THREE...
...ARE MY BROTHERS AND SISTER.
...?!
?

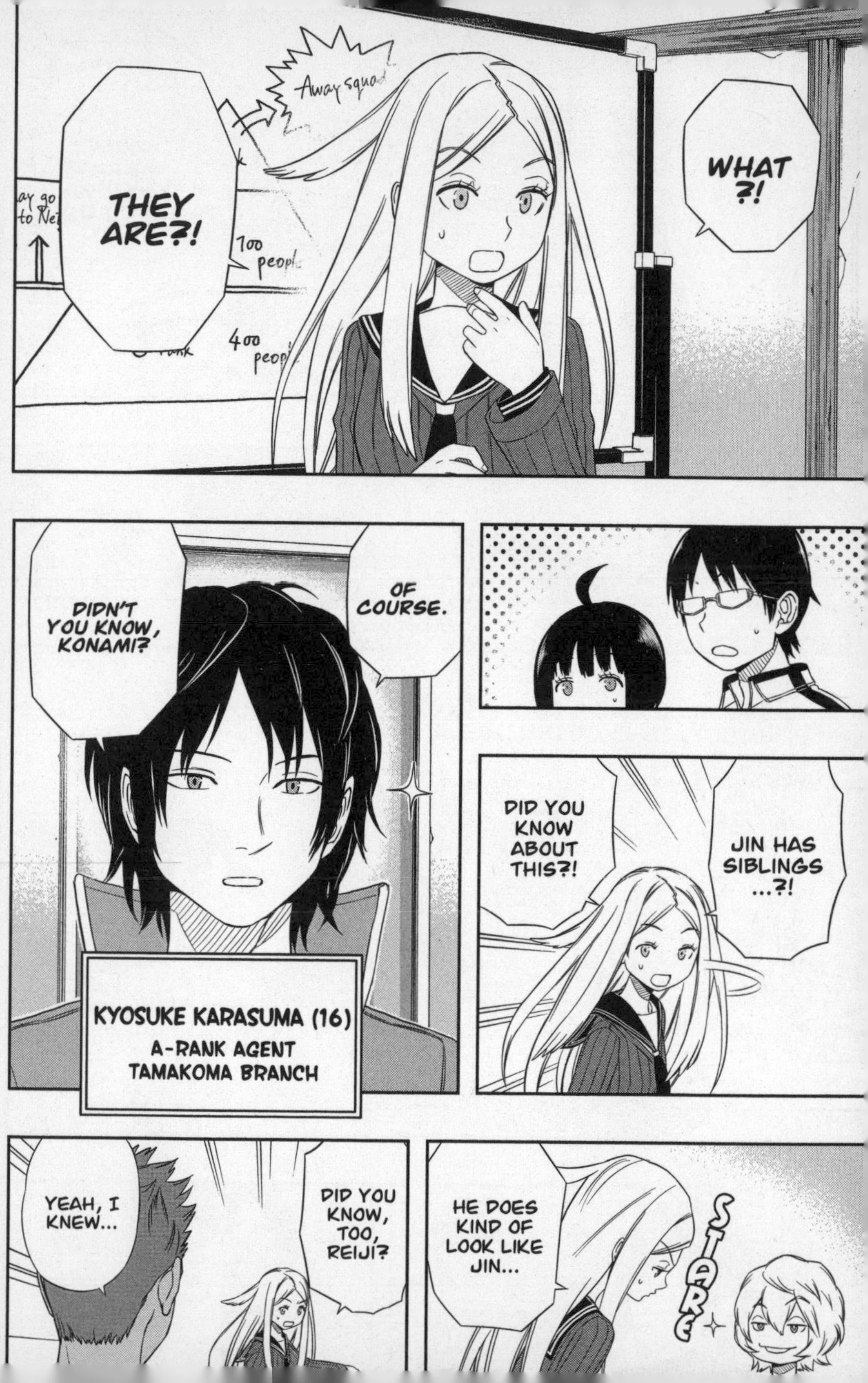
WHAT?!
THEY ARE?!
JIN HAS SIBLINGS...?!
DID YOU KNOW ABOUT THIS?!
OF COURSE.
DIDN'T YOU KNOW, KONAMI?
KYOSUKE KARASUMA (16)
A-RANK AGENT
TAMAKOMA BRANCH
STARE
HE DOES KIND OF LOOK LIKE JIN...
DID YOU KNOW, TOO, REIJI?
YEAH, I KNEW...

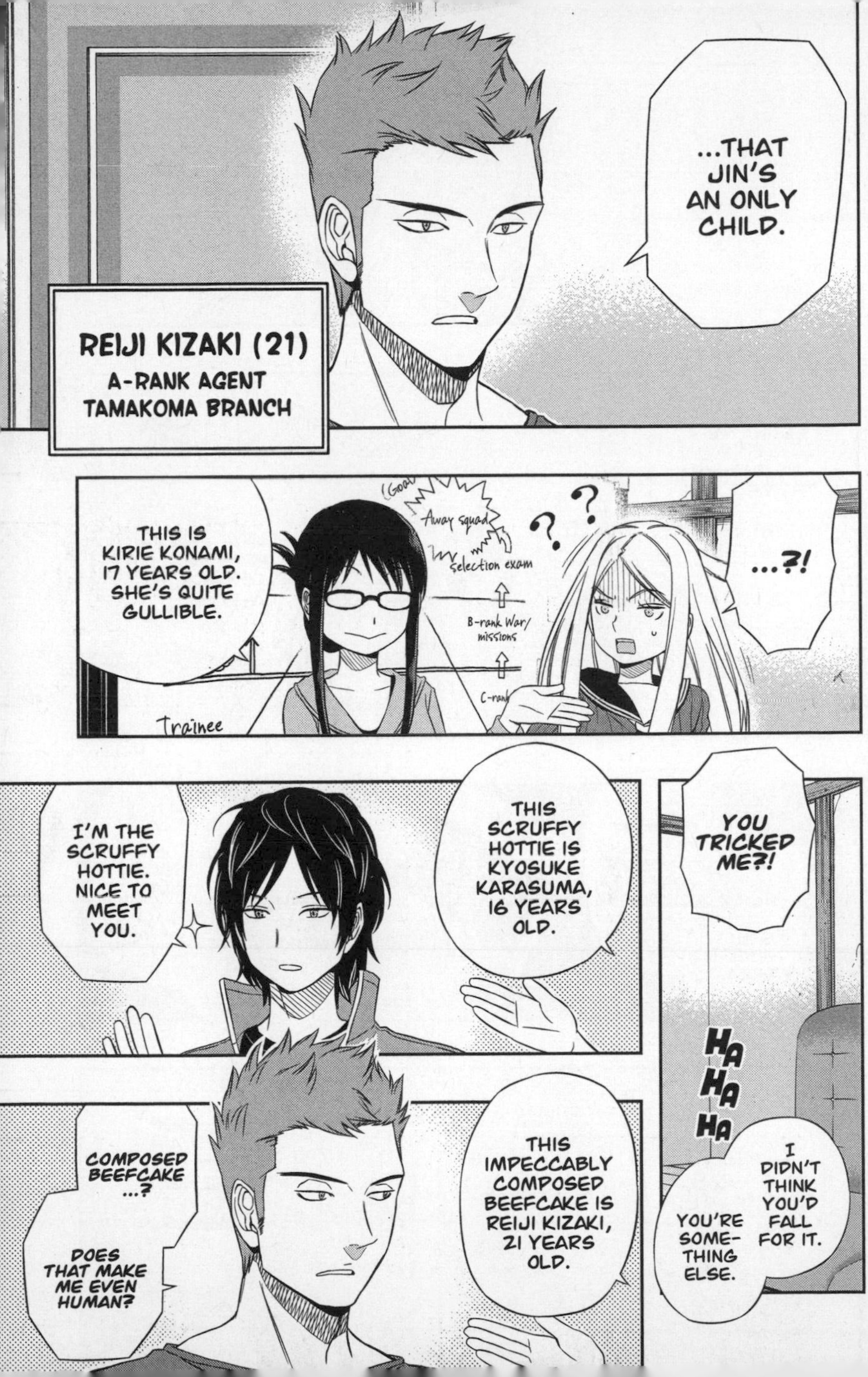
...THAT JIN'S AN ONLY CHILD.
REIJI KIZAKI (21)
A-RANK AGENT
TAMAKOMA BRANCH
...?!
(Goal)
Away squad
Selection exam
B-rank War/ missions
C-rank
Trainee
THIS IS KIRIE KONAMI, 17 YEARS OLD. SHE'S QUITE GULLIBLE.
YOU TRICKED ME?!
HA HA HA
I DIDN'T THINK YOU'D FALL FOR IT.
YOU'RE SOME-THING ELSE.
THIS SCRUFFY HOTTIE IS KYOSUKE KARASUMA, 16 YEARS OLD.
I'M THE SCRUFFY HOTTIE. NICE TO MEET YOU.
THIS IMPECCABLY COMPOSED BEEFCAKE IS REIJI KIZAKI, 21 YEARS OLD.
COMPOSED BEEFCAKE ...?
DOES THAT MAKE ME EVEN HUMAN?

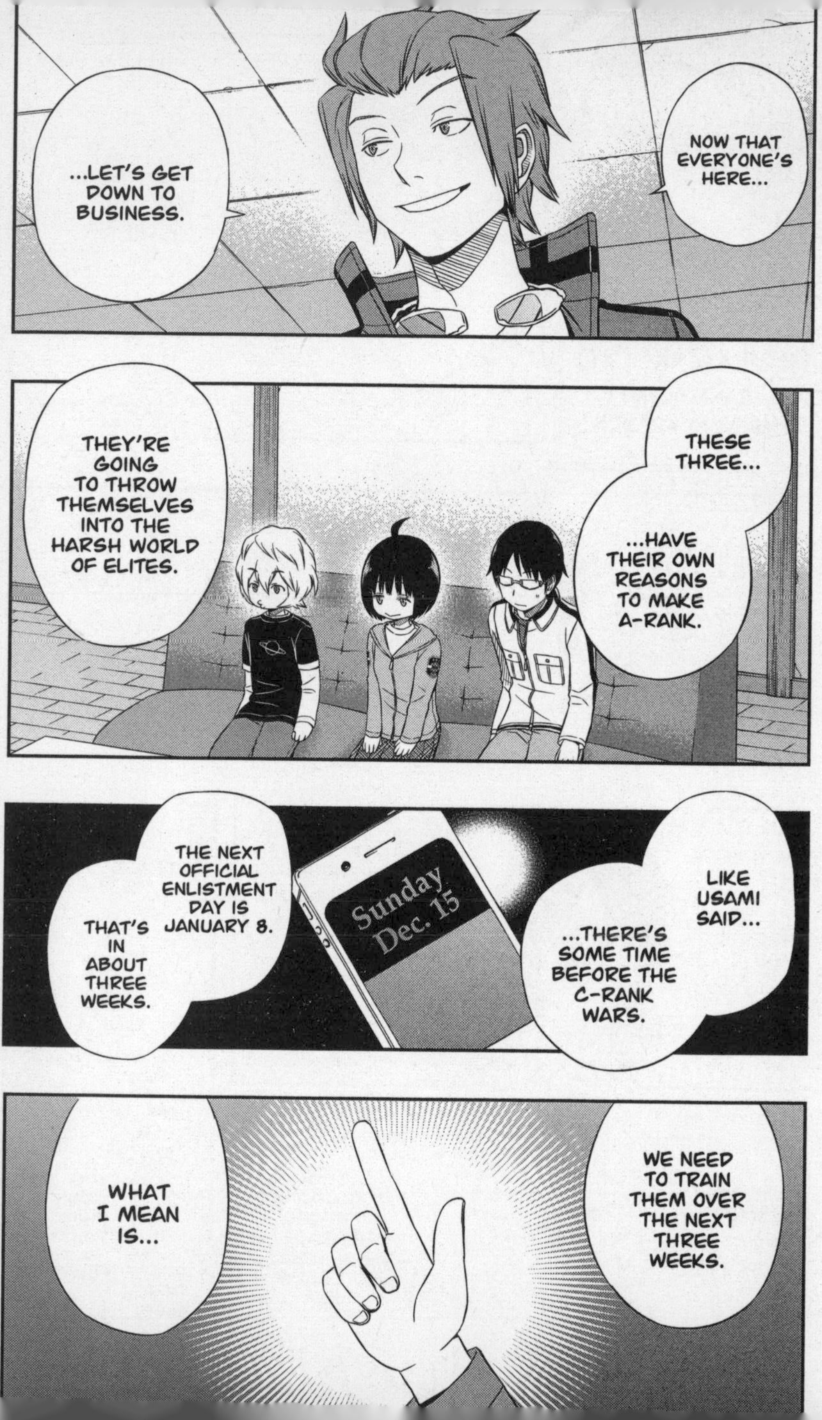
NOW THAT EVERYONE'S HERE...
...LET'S GET DOWN TO BUSINESS.
THESE THREE...
...HAVE THEIR OWN REASONS TO MAKE A-RANK.
THEY'RE GOING TO THROW THEMSELVES INTO THE HARSH WORLD OF ELITES.
LIKE USAMI SAID...
...THERE'S SOME TIME BEFORE THE C-RANK WARS.
Sunday Dec. 15
THE NEXT OFFICIAL ENLISTMENT DAY IS JANUARY 8.
THAT'S IN ABOUT THREE WEEKS.
WHAT I MEAN IS...
WE NEED TO TRAIN THEM OVER THE NEXT THREE WEEKS.

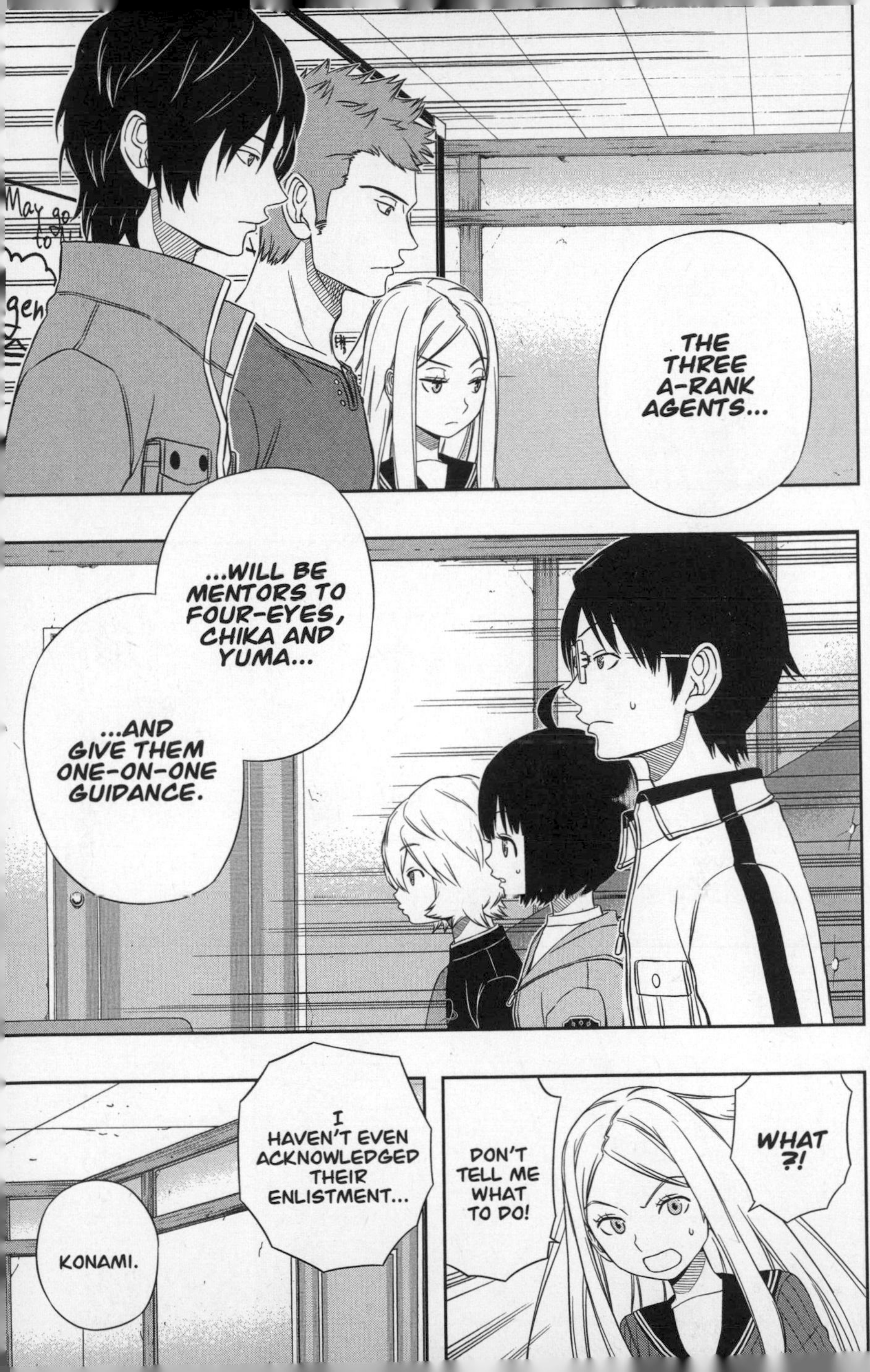
THE THREE A-RANK AGENTS...
...WILL BE MENTORS TO FOUR-EYES, CHIKA AND YUMA...
...AND GIVE THEM ONE-ON-ONE GUIDANCE.
WHAT ?!
DON'T TELL ME WHAT TO DO!
I HAVEN'T EVEN ACKNOWLEDGED THEIR ENLISTMENT...
KONAMI.

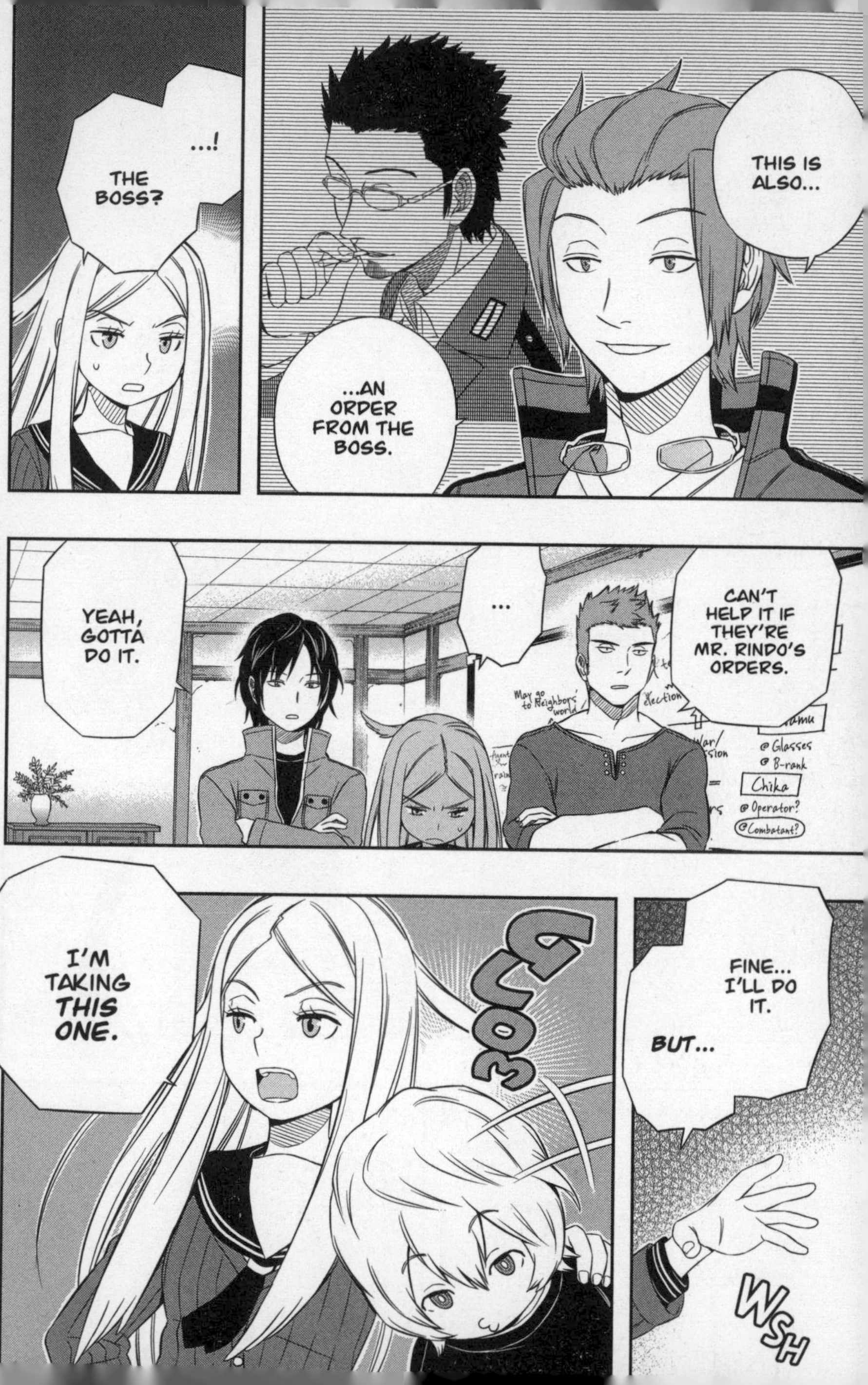
THIS IS ALSO...
...AN ORDER FROM THE BOSS.
...!
THE BOSS?
CAN'T HELP IT IF THEY'RE MR. RINDO'S ORDERS.
...
YEAH, GOTTA DO IT.
May go to Neighbors' world
Election
@ Glasses
@ B-rank
Chika
@ Operator?
@ Combatant?
FINE... I'LL DO IT.
BUT...
WSH
I'M TAKING THIS ONE.

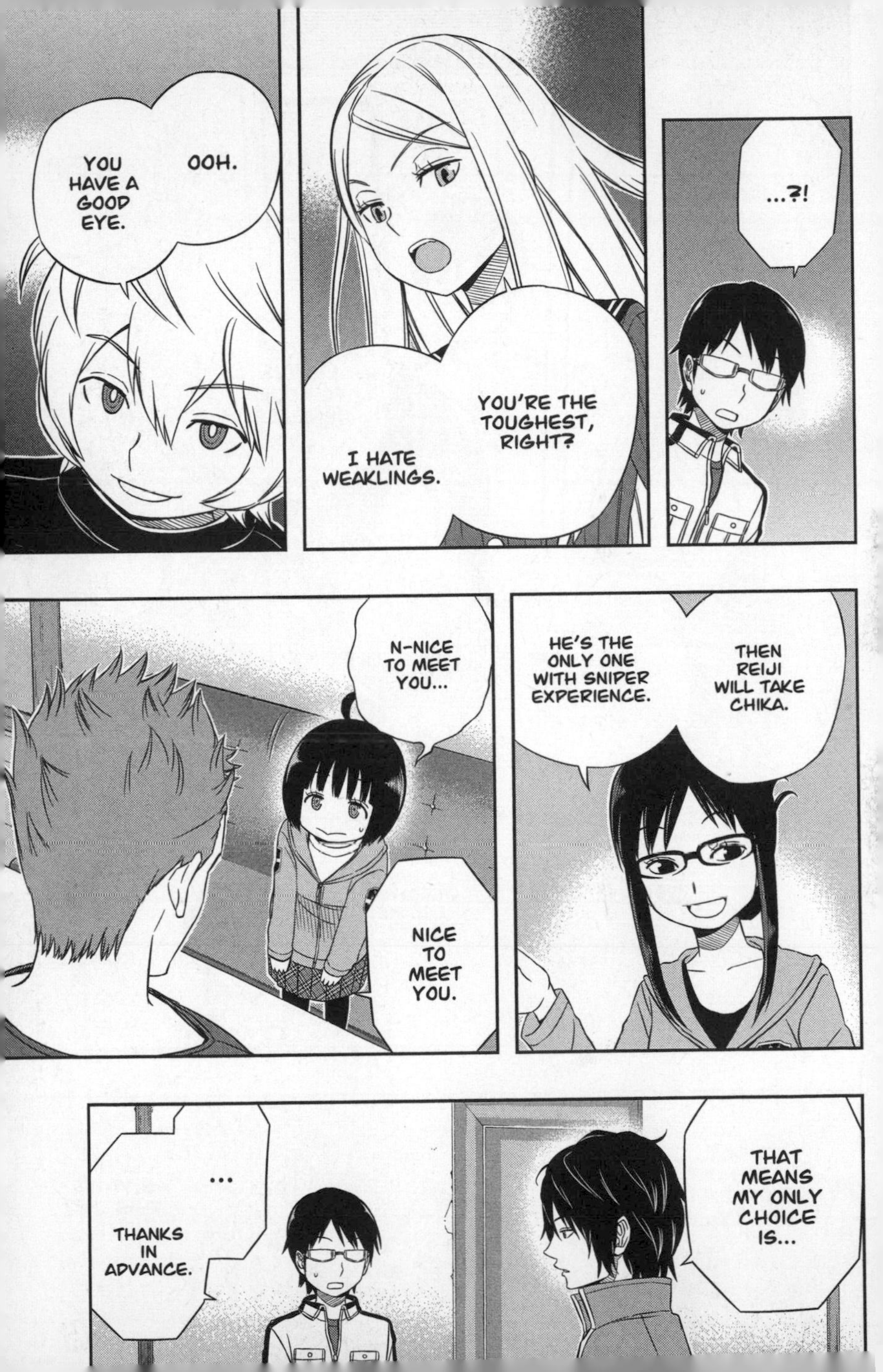
...?!
YOU'RE THE TOUGHEST, RIGHT?
I HATE WEAKLINGS.
OOH.
YOU HAVE A GOOD EYE.
THEN REIJI WILL TAKE CHIKA.
HE'S THE ONLY ONE WITH SNIPER EXPERIENCE.
N-NICE TO MEET YOU...
NICE TO MEET YOU.
THAT MEANS MY ONLY CHOICE IS...
...
THANKS IN ADVANCE.

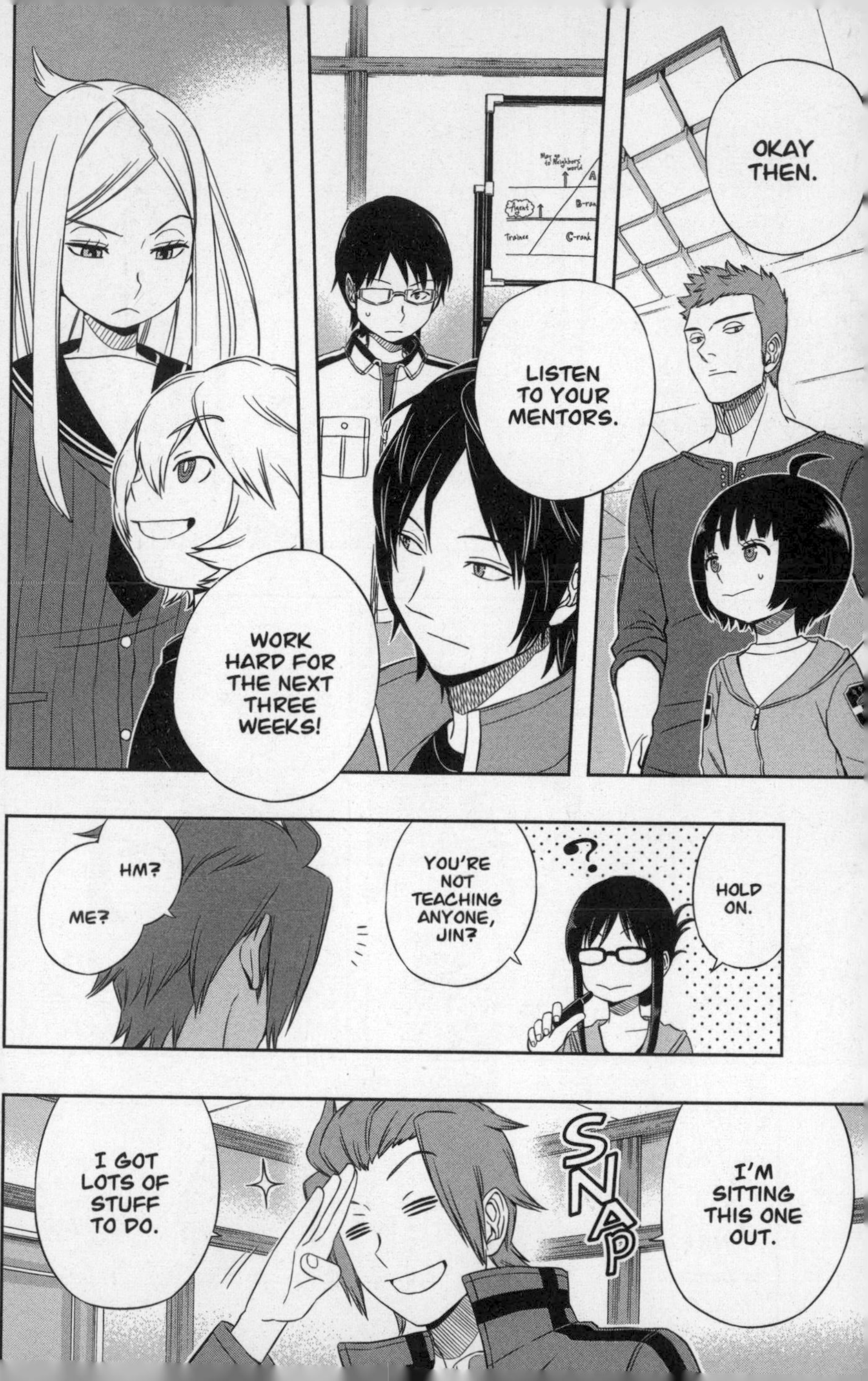
OKAY THEN.
LISTEN TO YOUR MENTORS.
WORK HARD FOR THE NEXT THREE WEEKS!
HOLD ON.
YOU'RE NOT TEACHING ANYONE, JIN?
HM?
ME?
I'M SITTING THIS ONE OUT.
SNAP
I GOT LOTS OF STUFF TO DO.

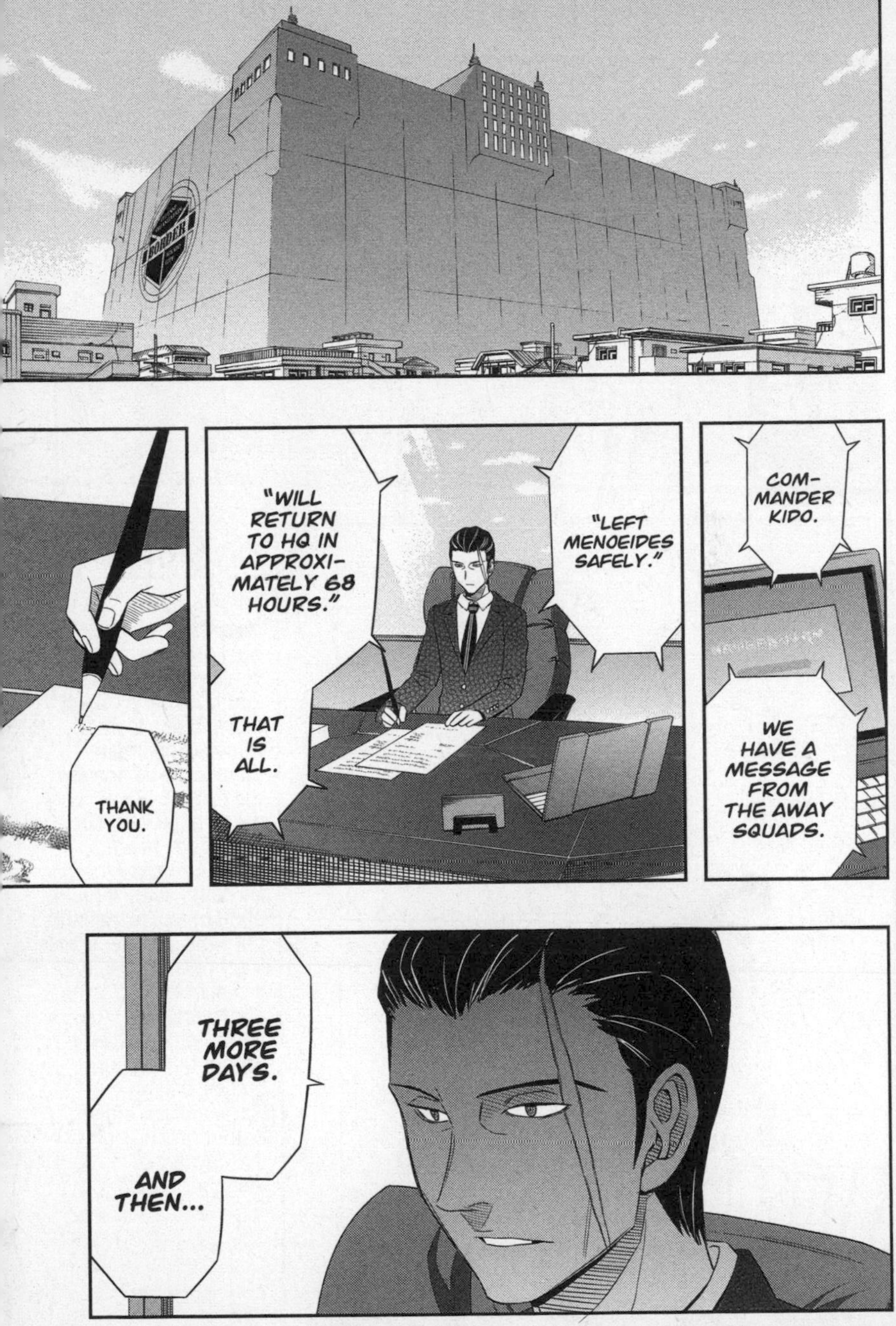
COM-MANDER KIDO.
WE HAVE A MESSAGE FROM THE AWAY SQUADS.
"LEFT MENOEIDES SAFELY."
"WILL RETURN TO HQ IN APPROXI-MATELY 68 HOURS."
THAT IS ALL.
THANK YOU.
THREE MORE DAYS.
AND THEN...

Rejected Storyboard

I unearthed a rejected storyboard

Chapter 2 Reject

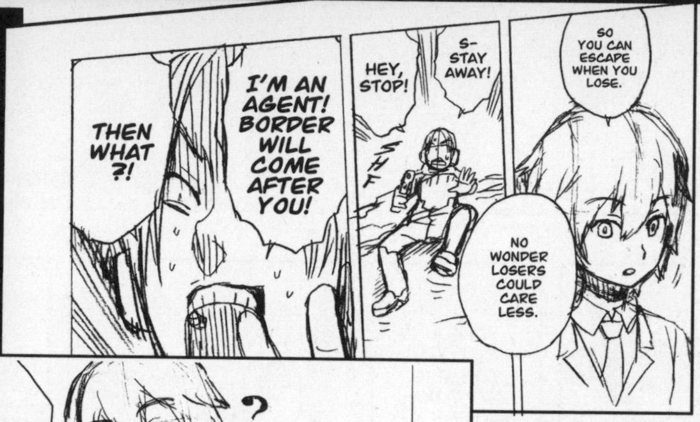
SO YOU CAN ESCAPE WHEN YOU LOSE.
NO WONDER LOSERS COULD CARE LESS.
S-STAY AWAY!
HEY, STOP!
SHF
I'M AN AGENT! BORDER WILL COME AFTER YOU!
THEN WHAT?!

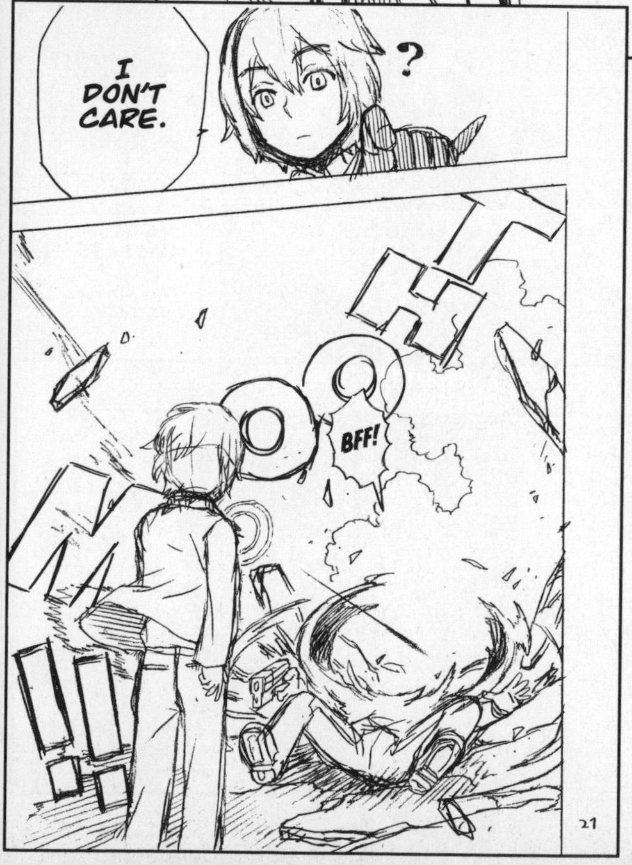
?
I DON'T CARE.
BFF!

I didn't revise chapter 1 much, but I drew several versions of chapters 2 and 3. This is one of them. Since C-Rank Osamu fighting in chapter 1 was against the rules, B-Rank idiots came to pick on him. Since they're jerks, Yuma punished them. My editor said, "It feels good because the jerks get what they deserve." It got rejected because it was clearly information overload, introducing all the Border ranks, Trion bodies, bailing out, Yuma's Black Trigger, Border finding out that Yuma's a Neighbor, etc.

Chapter 23 Tamakoma Branch: Part 3

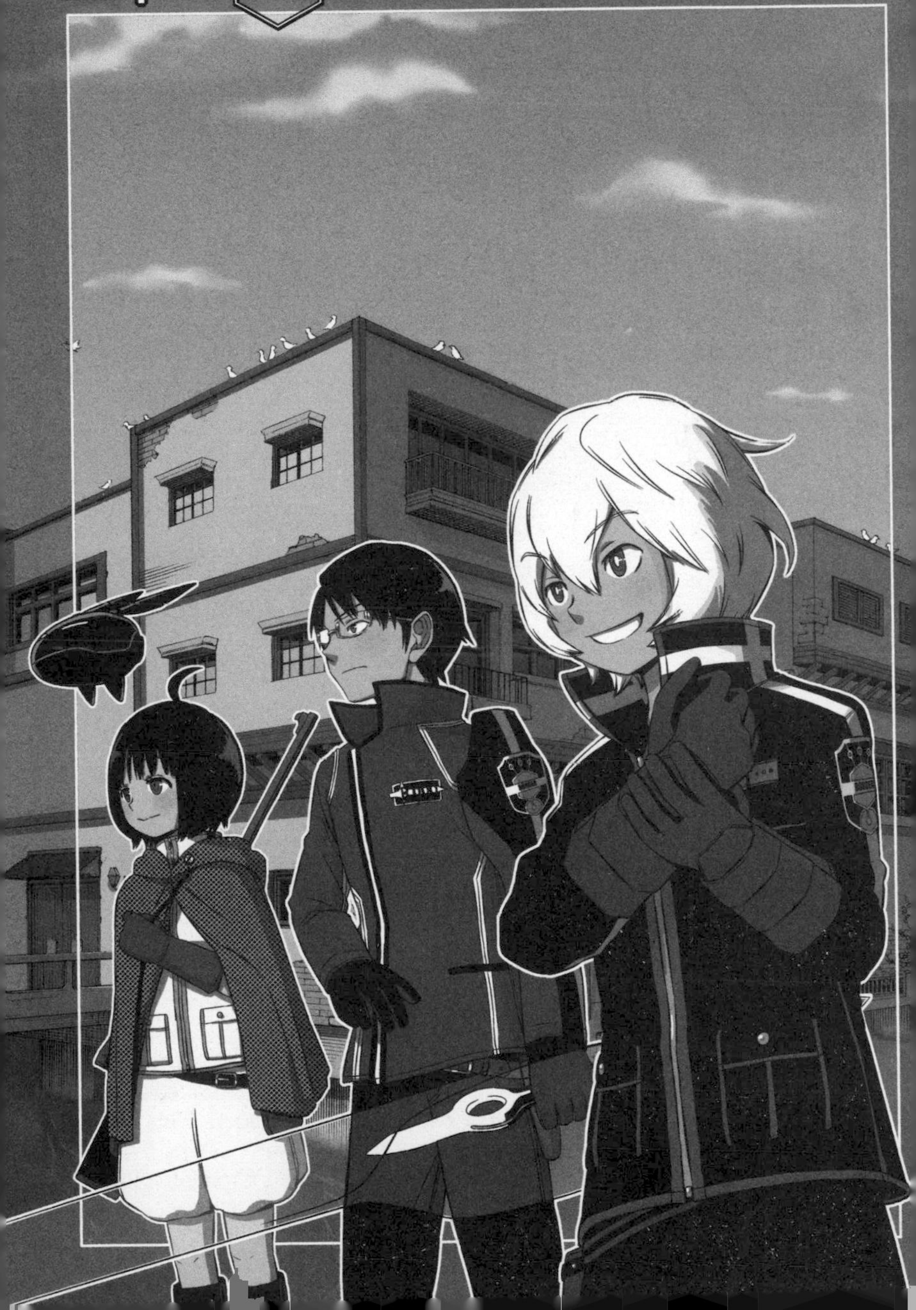

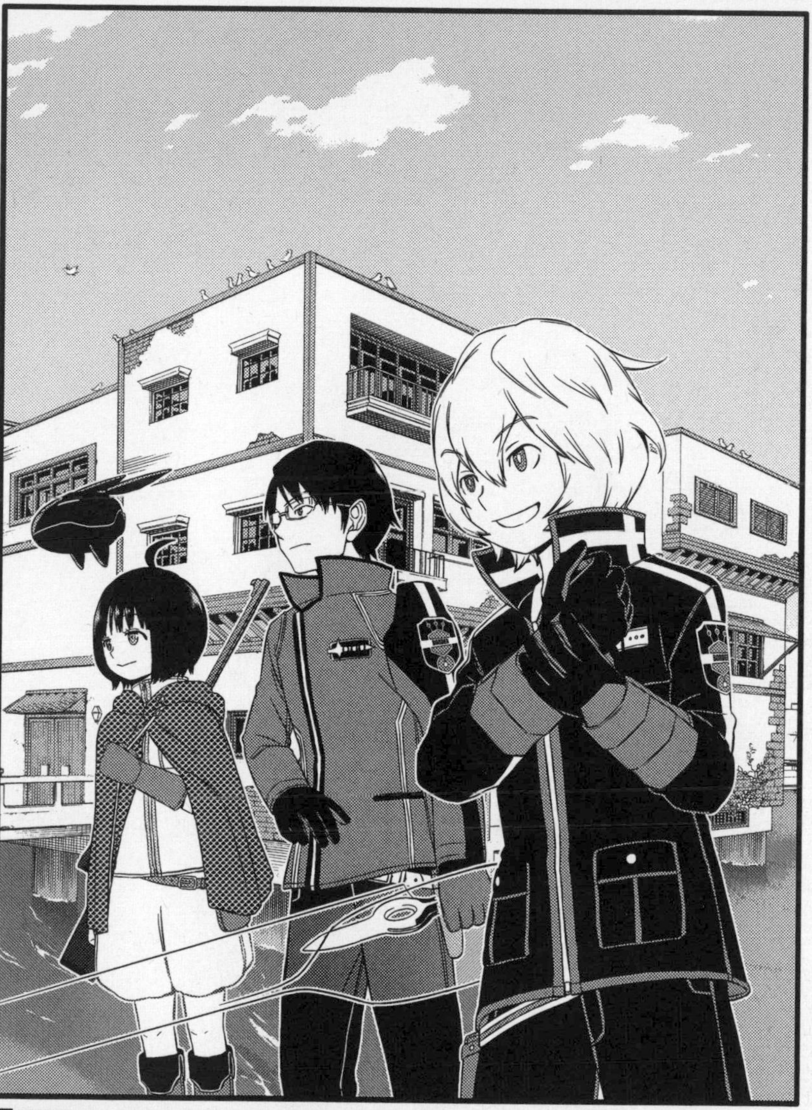

■ 2013 *Weekly Shonen Jump* issue 34, center color page (fifth one)
The clothes and accessories are subtly different. I don't remember why. But things are still changing now, so don't worry about it. I'm glad Yuma looks like he's having fun.

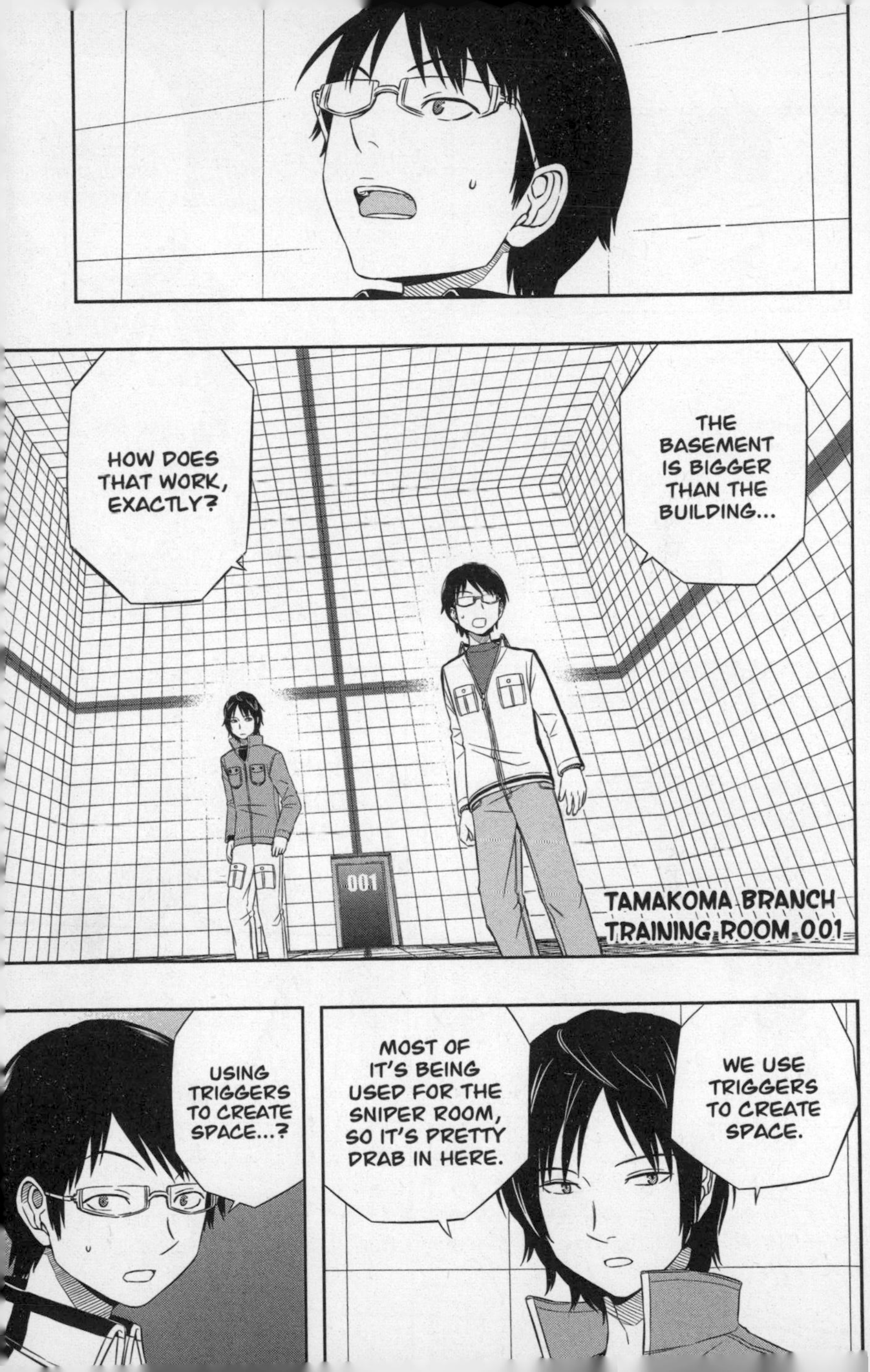
THE BASEMENT IS BIGGER THAN THE BUILDING...
HOW DOES THAT WORK, EXACTLY?
001
TAMAKOMA BRANCH TRAINING ROOM 001
WE USE TRIGGERS TO CREATE SPACE.
MOST OF IT'S BEING USED FOR THE SNIPER ROOM, SO IT'S PRETTY DRAB IN HERE.
USING TRIGGERS TO CREATE SPACE...?

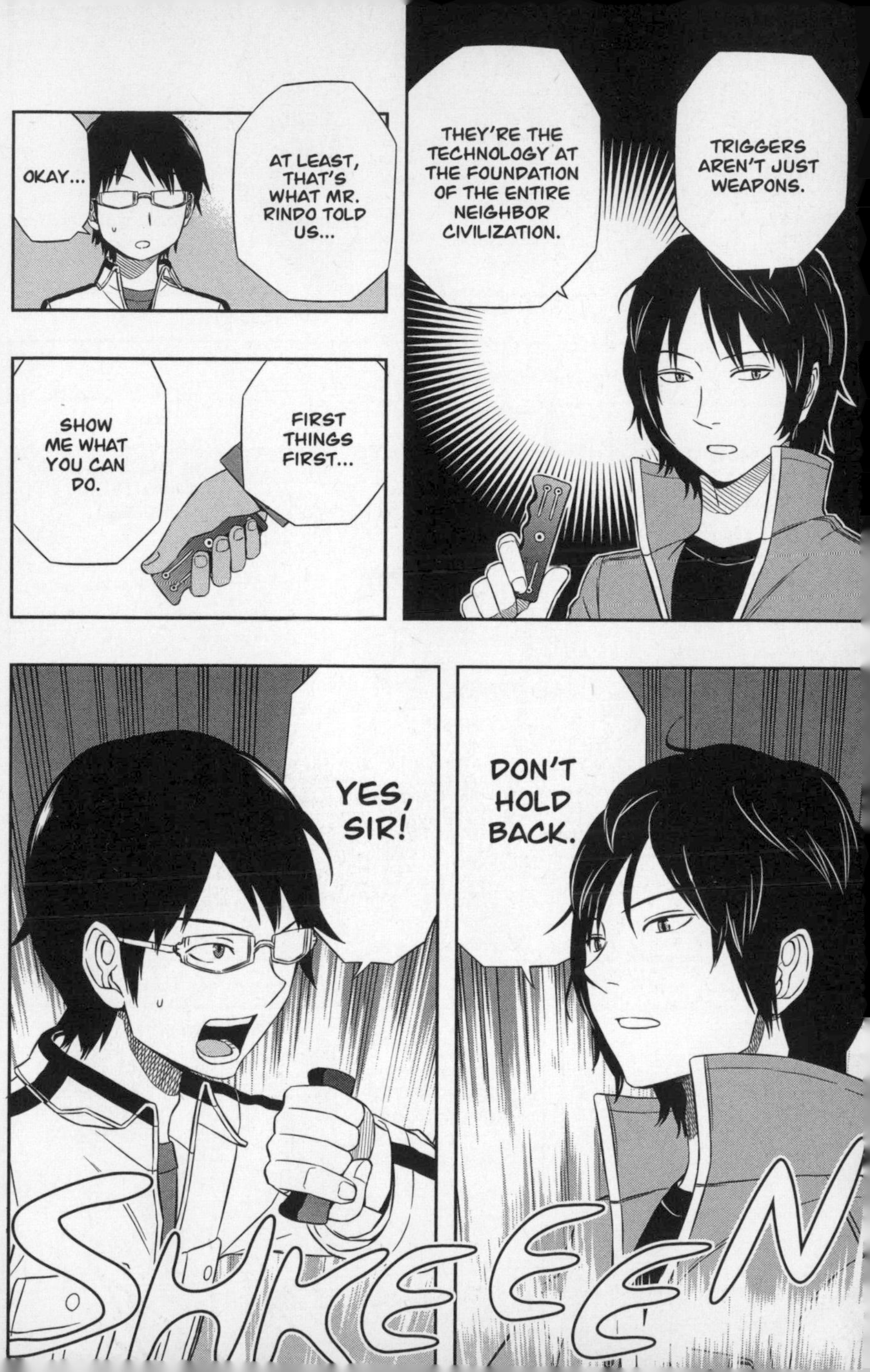
TRIGGERS AREN'T JUST WEAPONS.
THEY'RE THE TECHNOLOGY AT THE FOUNDATION OF THE ENTIRE NEIGHBOR CIVILIZATION.
AT LEAST, THAT'S WHAT MR. RINDO TOLD US...
OKAY...
FIRST THINGS FIRST...
SHOW ME WHAT YOU CAN DO.
DON'T HOLD BACK.
YES, SIR!
SHKEEEN

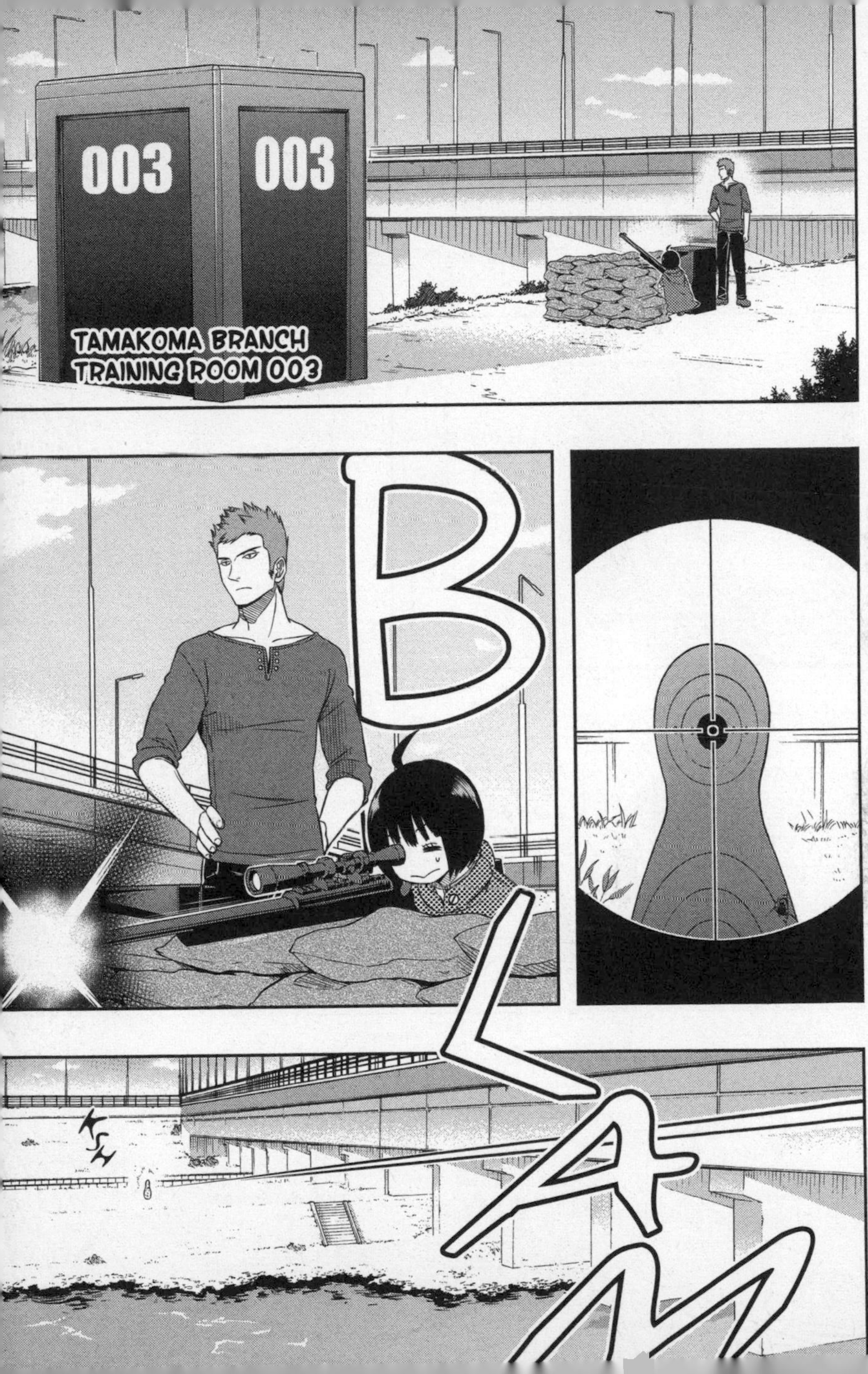
003
003
TAMAKOMA BRANCH
TRAINING ROOM 003
BLAM
KSH

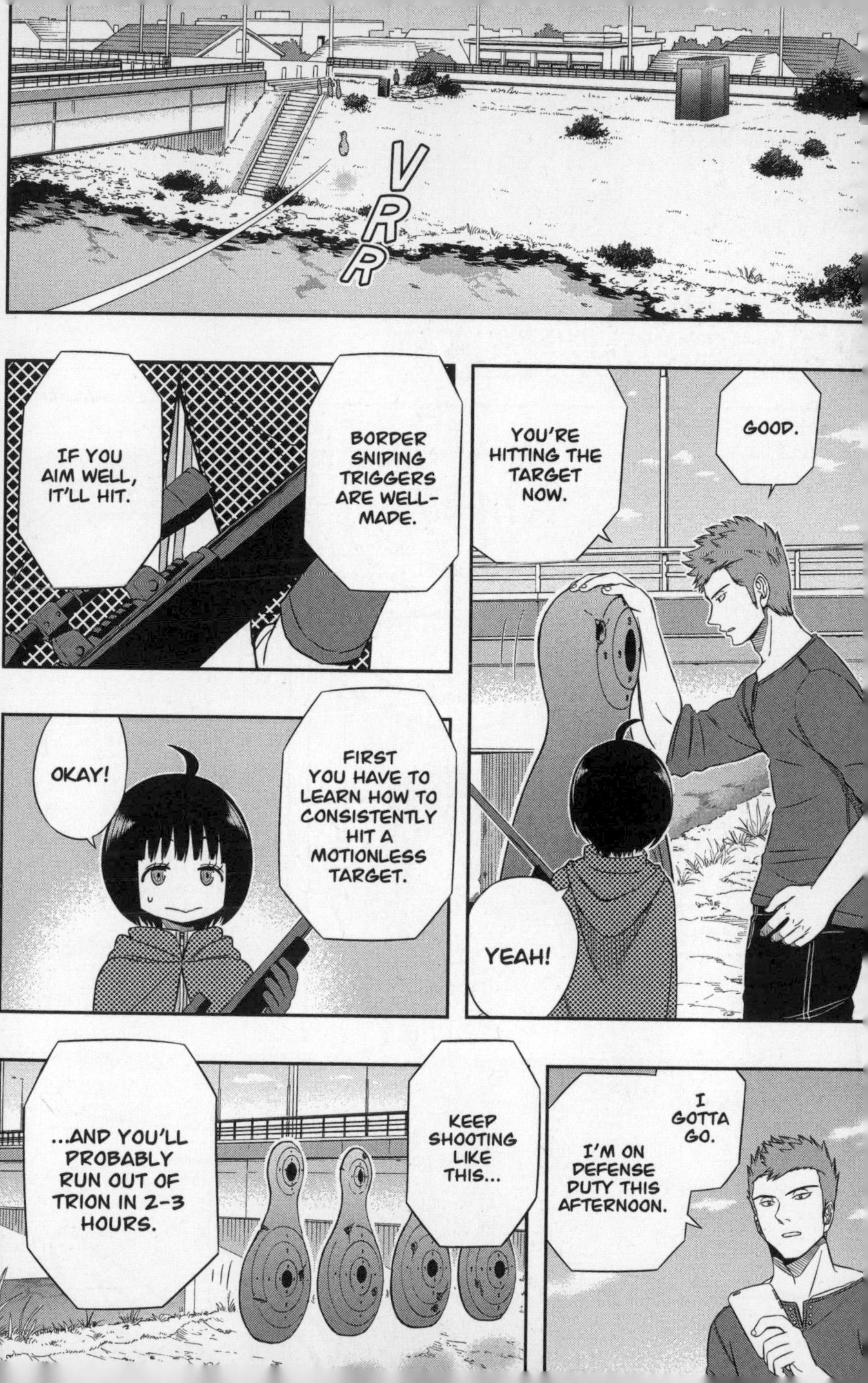
VRR
GOOD.
YOU'RE HITTING THE TARGET NOW.
YEAH!
BORDER SNIPING TRIGGERS ARE WELL-MADE.
IF YOU AIM WELL, IT'LL HIT.
FIRST YOU HAVE TO LEARN HOW TO CONSISTENTLY HIT A MOTIONLESS TARGET.
OKAY!
I GOTTA GO.
I'M ON DEFENSE DUTY THIS AFTERNOON.
KEEP SHOOTING LIKE THIS...
...AND YOU'LL PROBABLY RUN OUT OF TRION IN 2-3 HOURS.

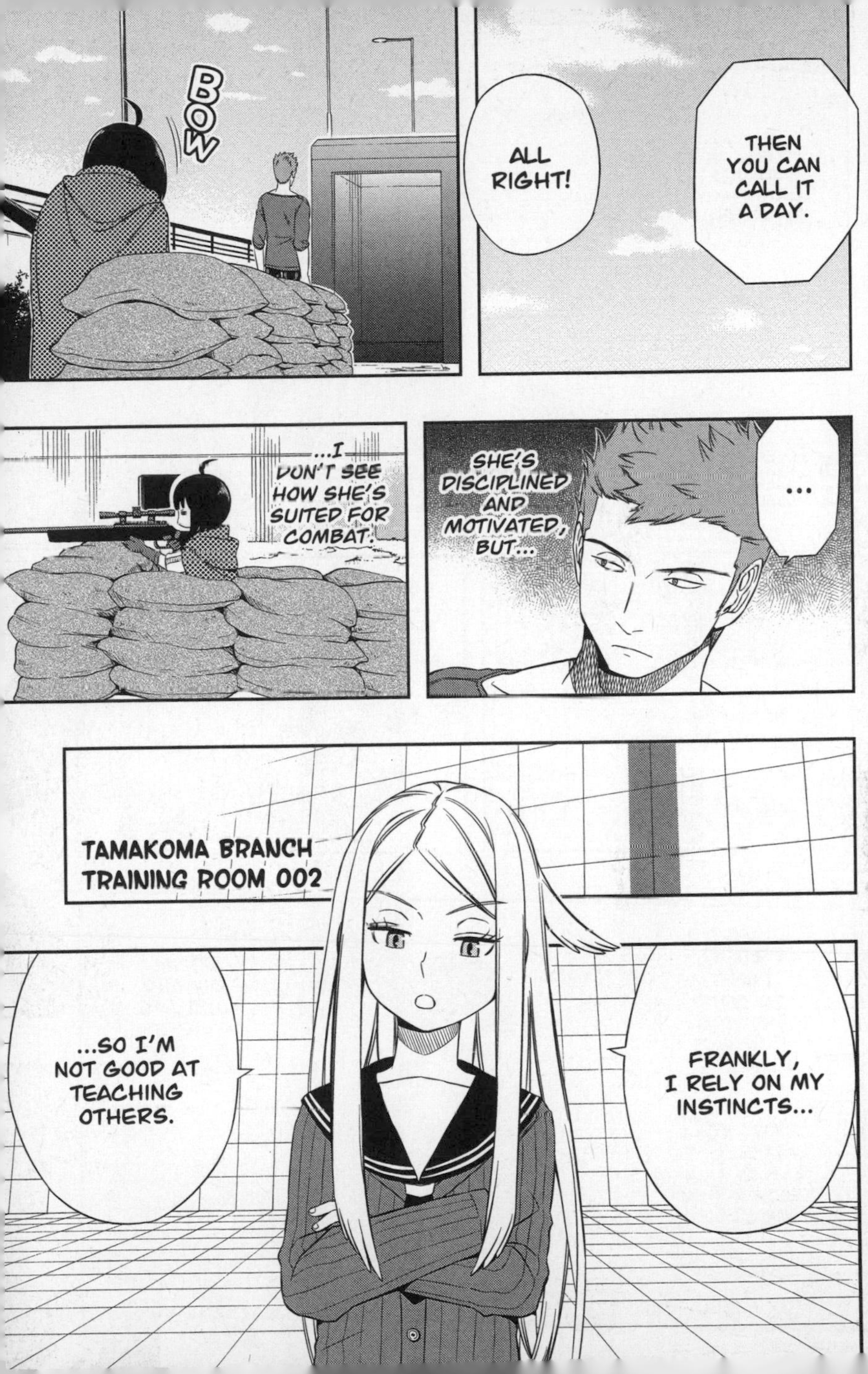
THEN YOU CAN CALL IT A DAY.
ALL RIGHT!
BOW
...
SHE'S DISCIPLINED AND MOTIVATED, BUT...
...I DON'T SEE HOW SHE'S SUITED FOR COMBAT.
TAMAKOMA BRANCH TRAINING ROOM 002
FRANKLY, I RELY ON MY INSTINCTS...
...SO I'M NOT GOOD AT TEACHING OTHERS.

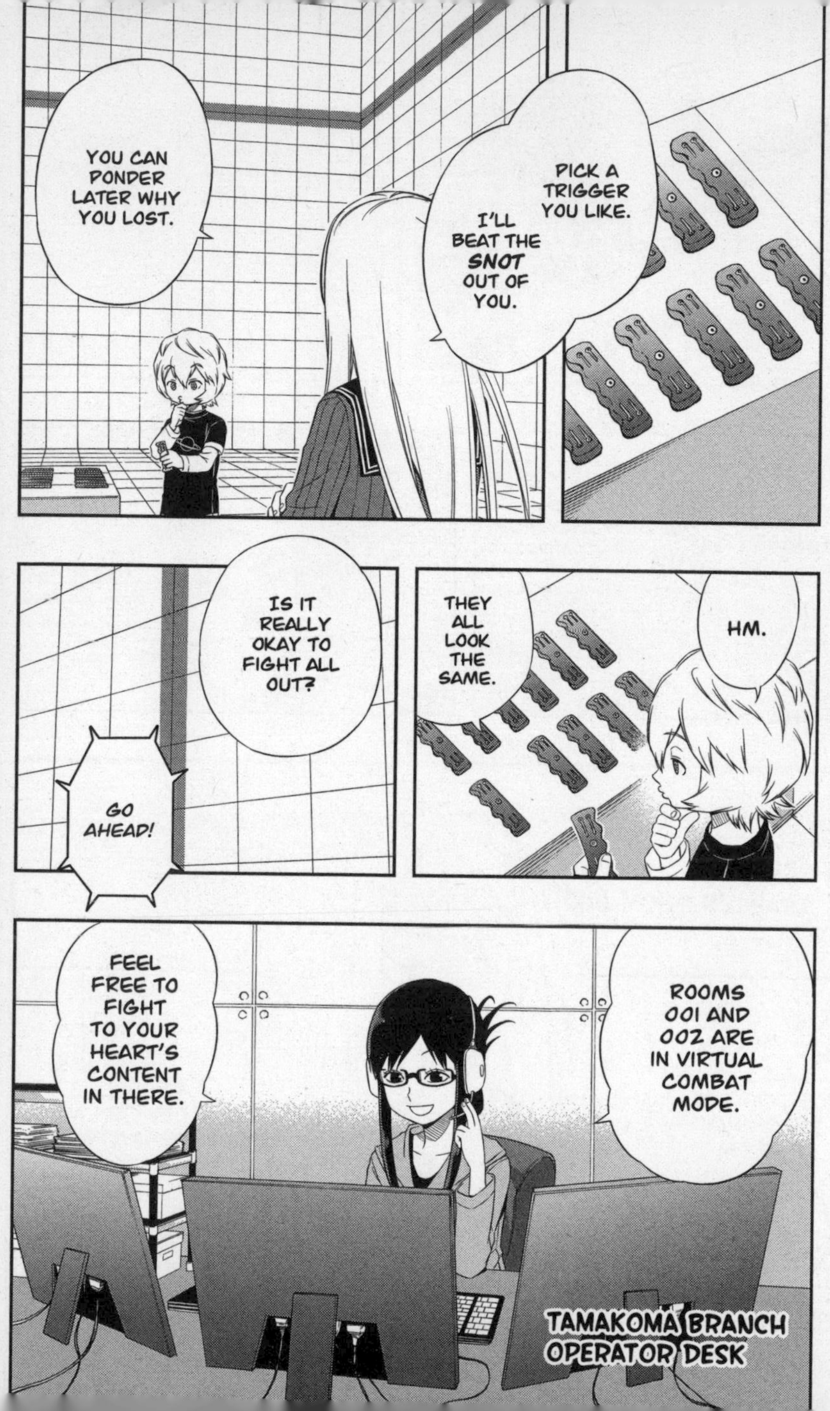
PICK A TRIGGER YOU LIKE.
I'LL BEAT THE SNOT OUT OF YOU.
YOU CAN PONDER LATER WHY YOU LOST.
HM.
THEY ALL LOOK THE SAME.
IS IT REALLY OKAY TO FIGHT ALL OUT?
GO AHEAD!
ROOMS 001 AND 002 ARE IN VIRTUAL COMBAT MODE.
FEEL FREE TO FIGHT TO YOUR HEART'S CONTENT IN THERE.
TAMAKOMA BRANCH OPERATOR DESK

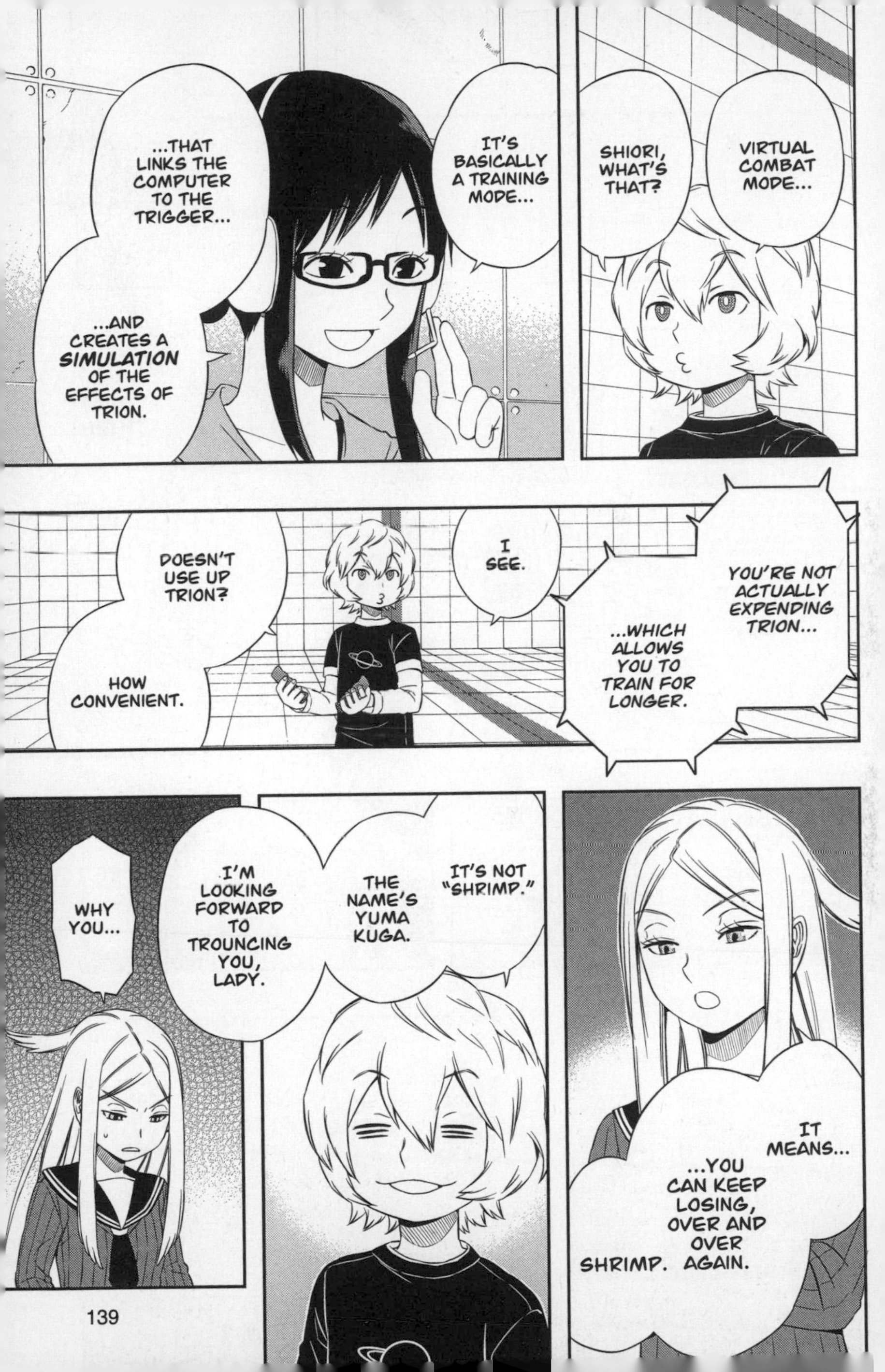
VIRTUAL COMBAT MODE...
SHIORI, WHAT'S THAT?
IT'S BASICALLY A TRAINING MODE...
...THAT LINKS THE COMPUTER TO THE TRIGGER...
...AND CREATES A SIMULATION OF THE EFFECTS OF TRION.
YOU'RE NOT ACTUALLY EXPENDING TRION...
...WHICH ALLOWS YOU TO TRAIN FOR LONGER.
I SEE.
DOESN'T USE UP TRION?
HOW CONVENIENT.
IT MEANS...
...YOU CAN KEEP LOSING, OVER AND OVER AGAIN.
SHRIMP.
IT'S NOT "SHRIMP."
THE NAME'S YUMA KUGA.
I'M LOOKING FORWARD TO TROUNCING YOU, LADY.
WHY YOU...

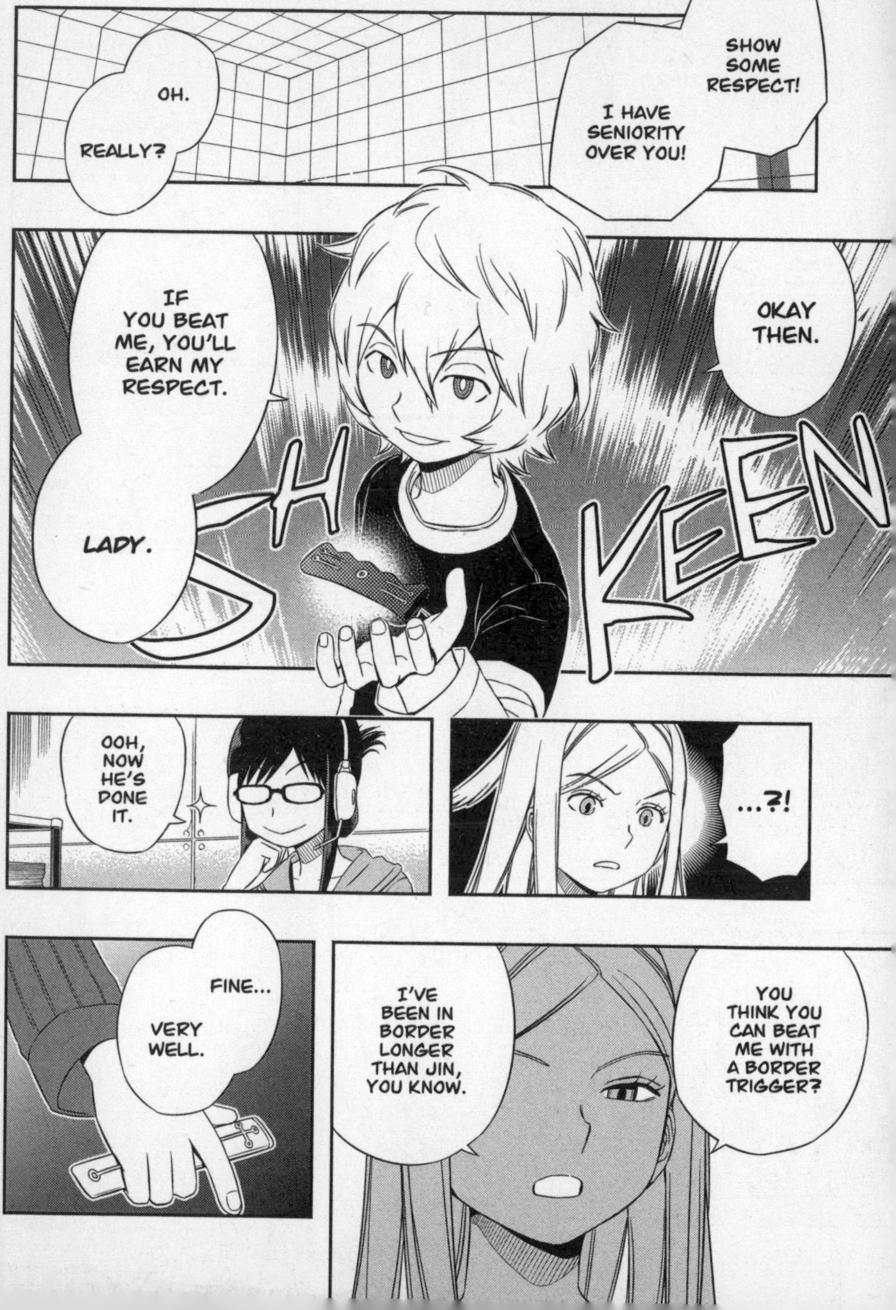
SHOW SOME RESPECT! I HAVE SENIORITY OVER YOU!
OH. REALLY?
OKAY THEN.
IF YOU BEAT ME, YOU'LL EARN MY RESPECT.
SHKEEN
LADY.
...?!
OOH, NOW HE'S DONE IT.
YOU THINK YOU CAN BEAT ME WITH A BORDER TRIGGER?
I'VE BEEN IN BORDER LONGER THAN JIN, YOU KNOW.
FINE... VERY WELL.

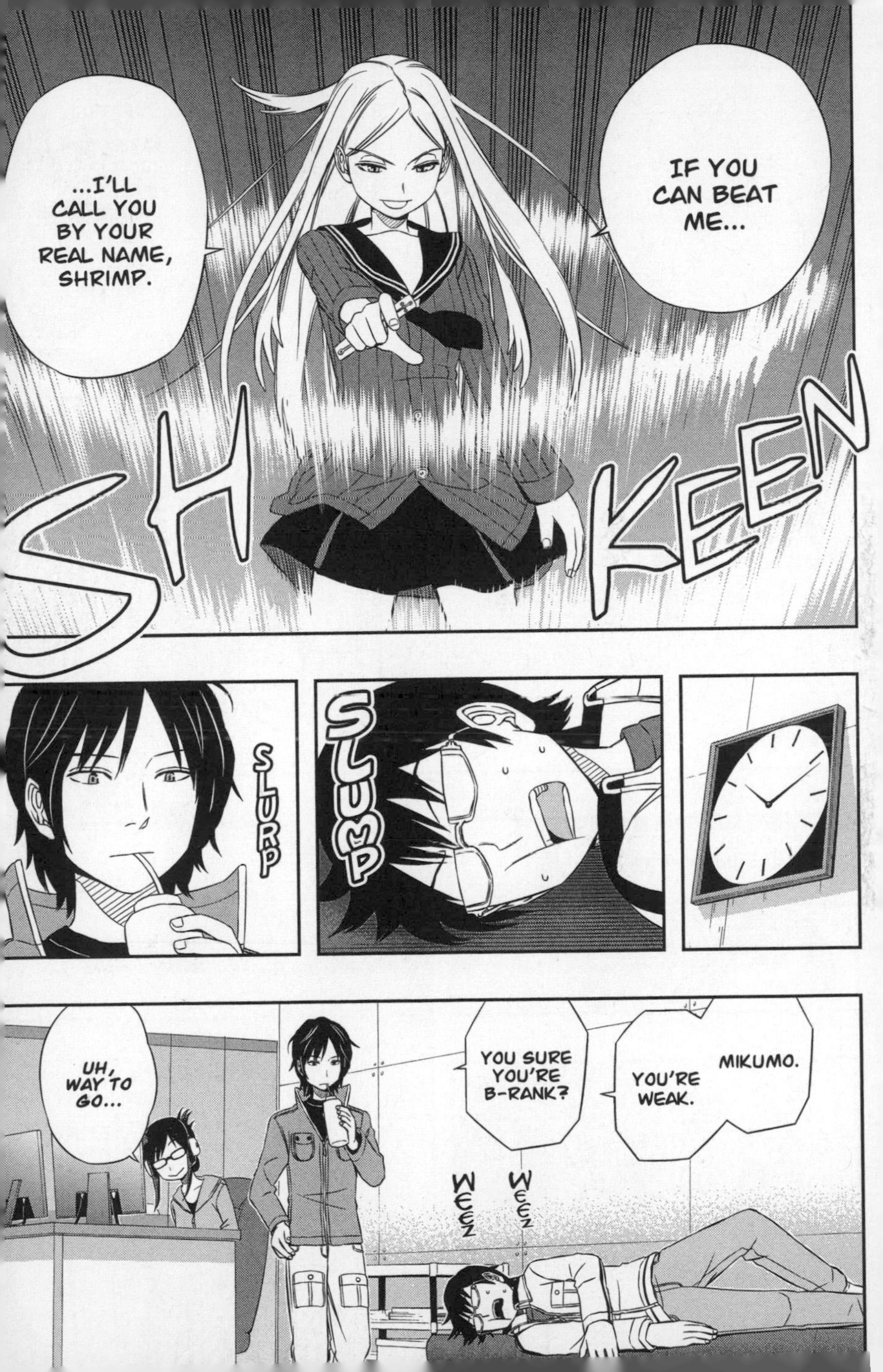
IF YOU CAN BEAT ME...
...I'LL CALL YOU BY YOUR REAL NAME, SHRIMP.
SHKEEN
SLUMP
SLURP
MIKUMO. YOU'RE WEAK.
YOU SURE YOU'RE B-RANK?
UH, WAY TO GO...
WEEZ
WEEZ

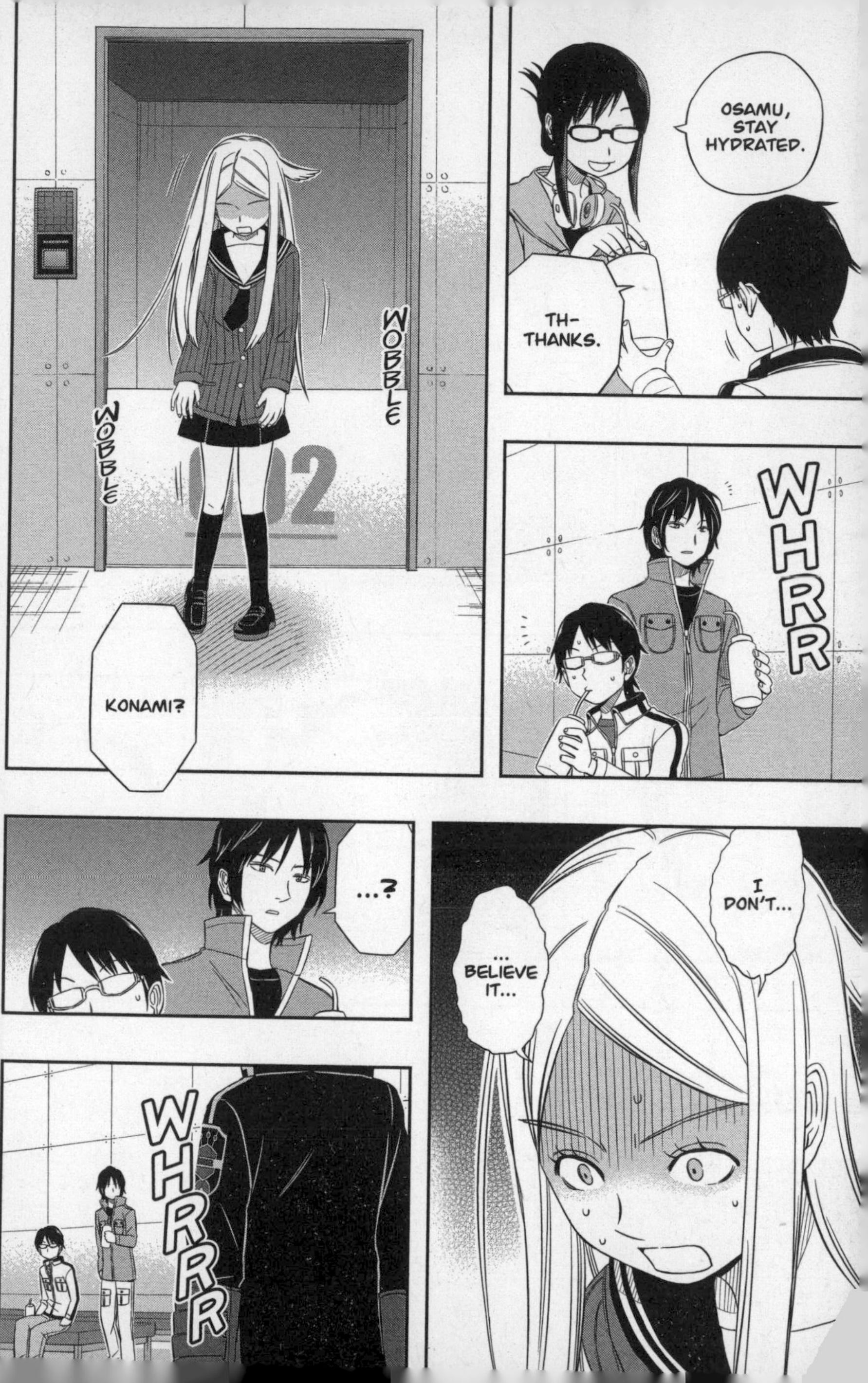
OSAMU, STAY HYDRATED.
TH- THANKS.
WHRR
WOBBLE
WOBBLE
KONAMI?
I DON'T...
...BELIEVE IT...
...?
WHRRR

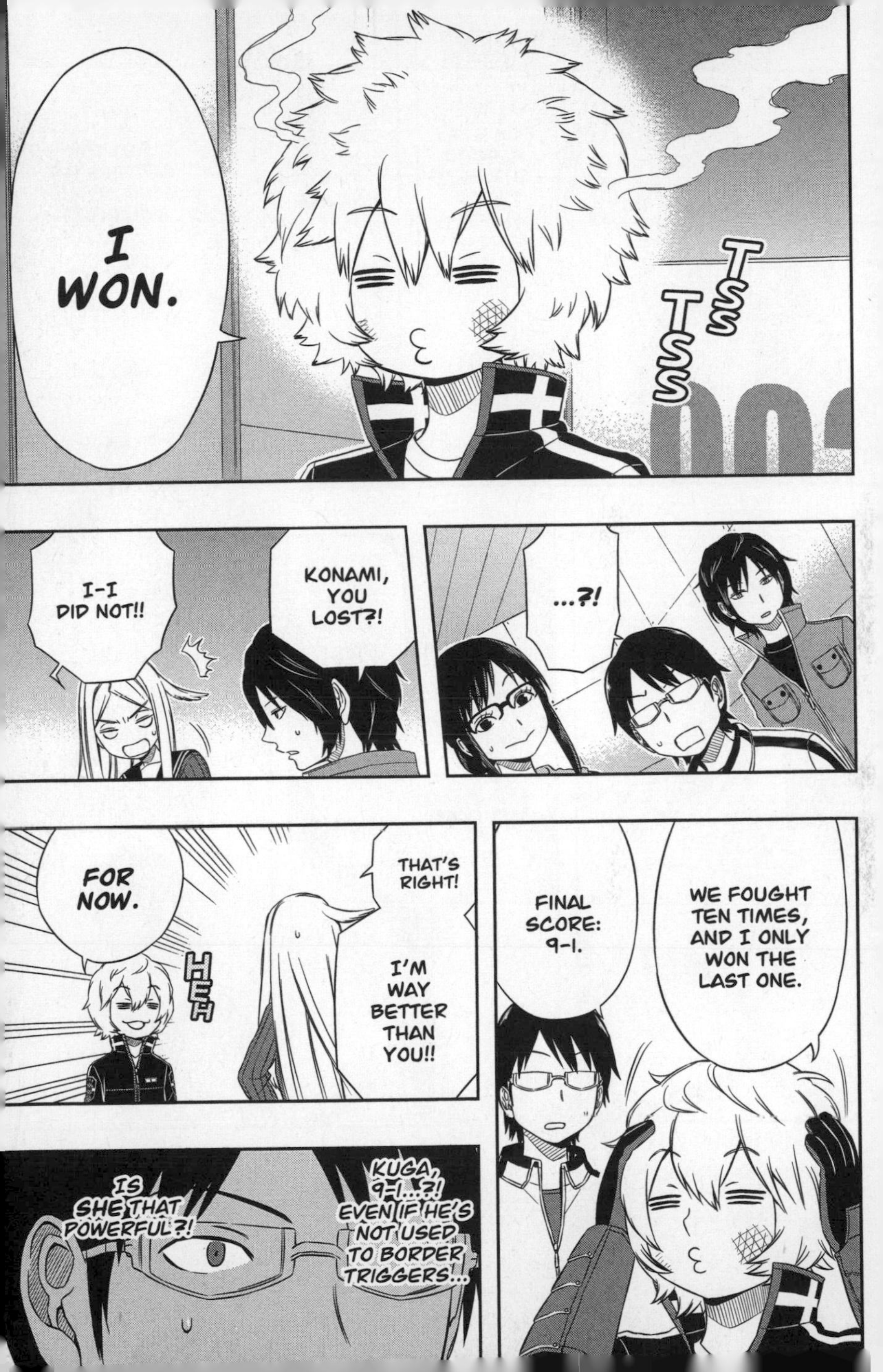
TSS TSS
I WON.
...?!
KONAMI, YOU LOST?!
I-I DID NOT!!
WE FOUGHT TEN TIMES, AND I ONLY WON THE LAST ONE.
FINAL SCORE: 9-1.
THAT'S RIGHT!
I'M WAY BETTER THAN YOU!!
FOR NOW.
HEH
KUGA, 9-1...?! EVEN IF HE'S NOT USED TO BORDER TRIGGERS...
IS SHE THAT POWERFUL?!

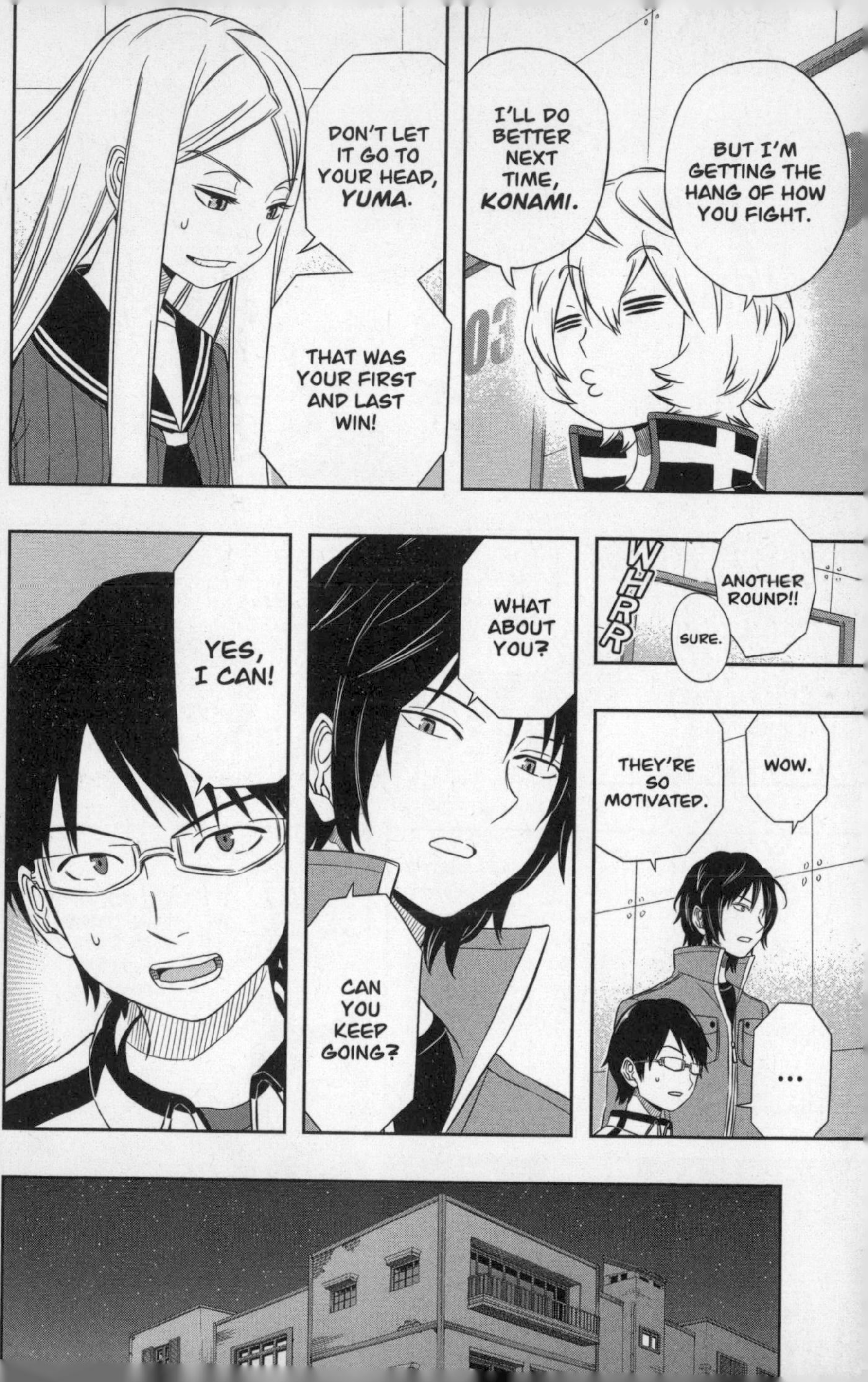
I'LL DO BETTER NEXT TIME, KONAMI.
BUT I'M GETTING THE HANG OF HOW YOU FIGHT.
DON'T LET IT GO TO YOUR HEAD, YUMA.
THAT WAS YOUR FIRST AND LAST WIN!
WHRR
ANOTHER ROUND!!
SURE.
WOW.
THEY'RE SO MOTIVATED.
...
WHAT ABOUT YOU?
CAN YOU KEEP GOING?
YES, I CAN!

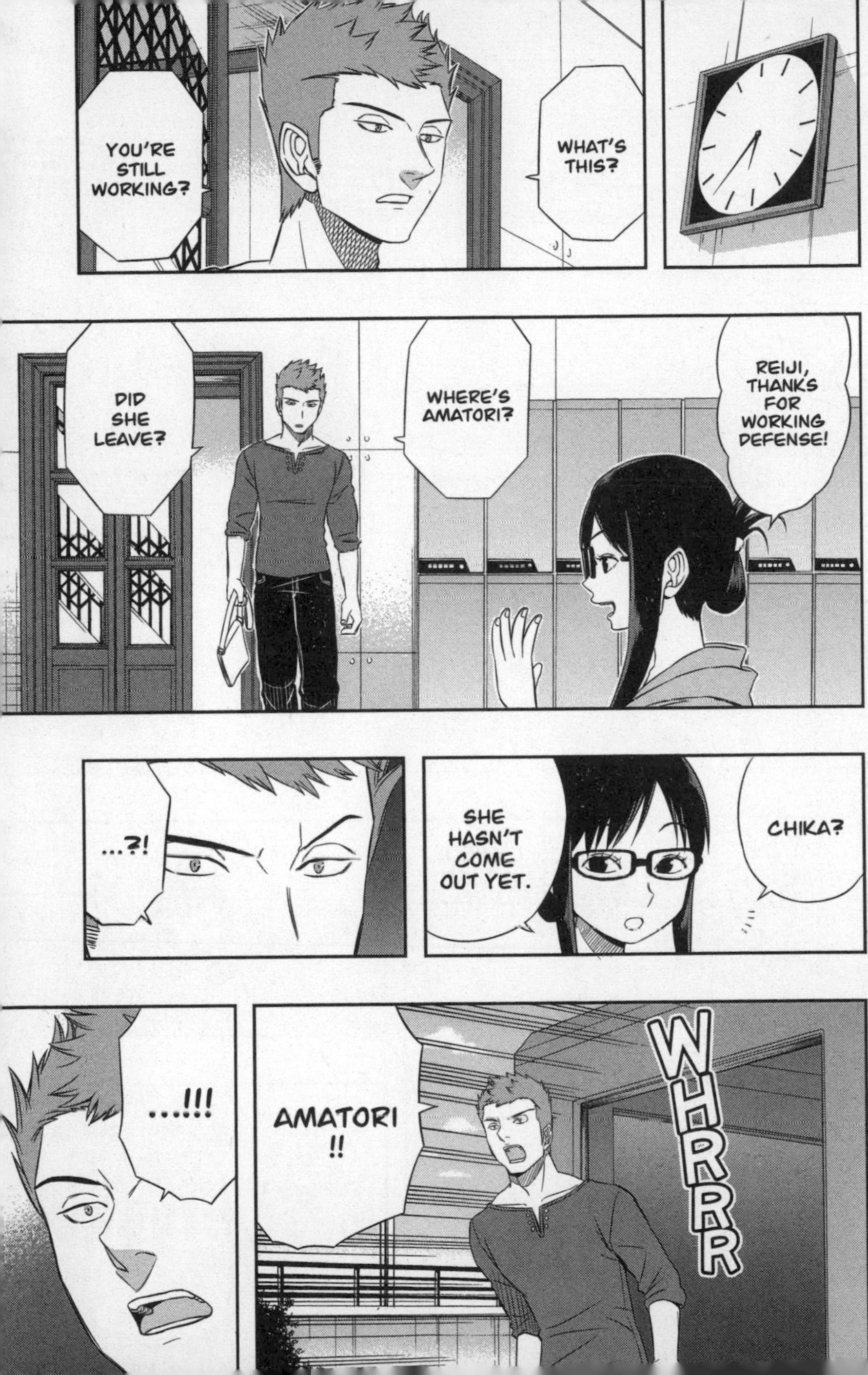
WHAT'S THIS?
YOU'RE STILL WORKING?
REIJI, THANKS FOR WORKING DEFENSE!
WHERE'S AMATORI?
DID SHE LEAVE?
CHIKA?
SHE HASN'T COME OUT YET.
...?!
WHRRR
AMATORI !!
...!!!

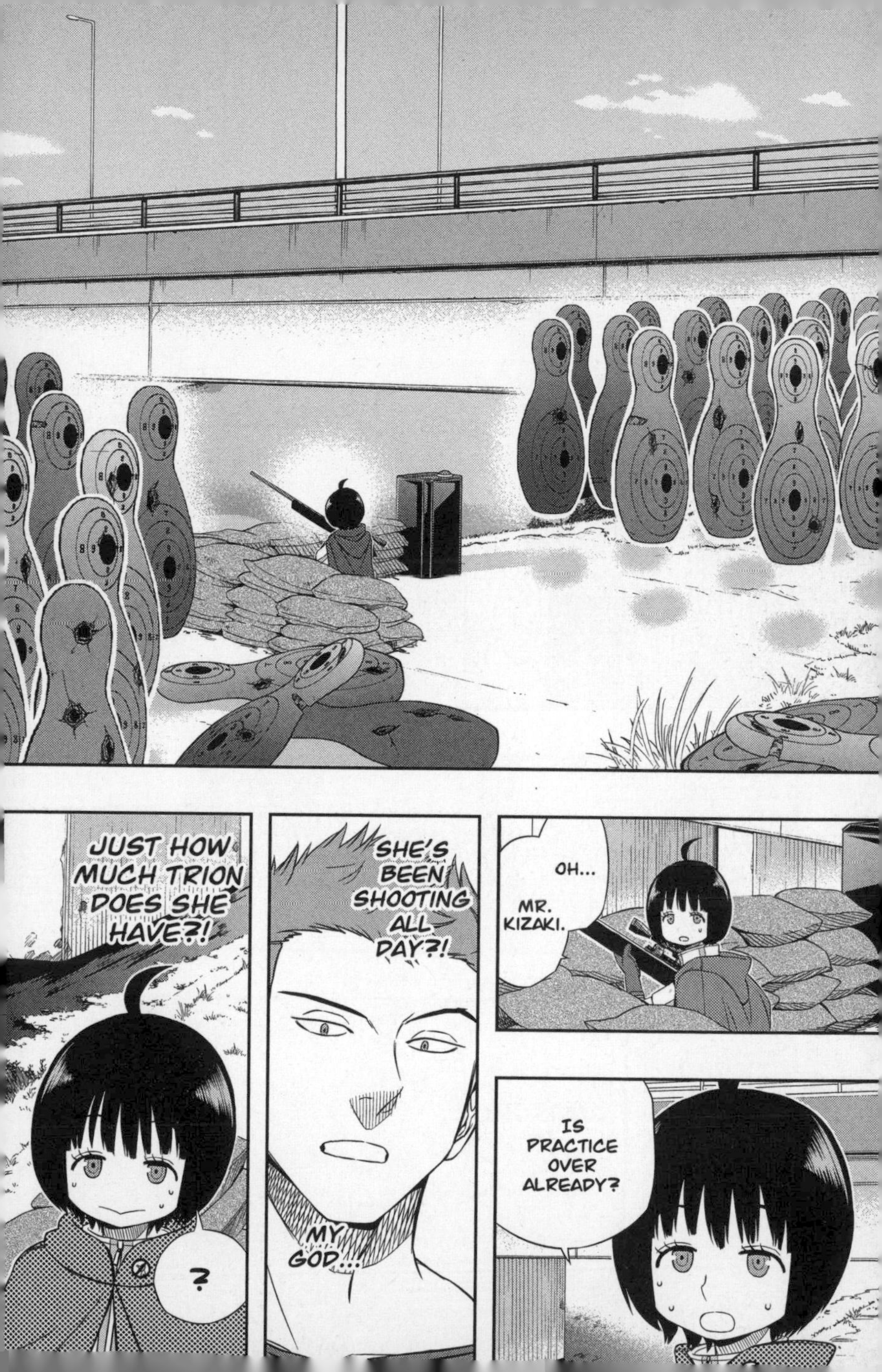
OH... MR. KIZAKI.
IS PRACTICE OVER ALREADY?
SHE'S BEEN SHOOTING ALL DAY?!
MY GOD...
JUST HOW MUCH TRION DOES SHE HAVE?!
?

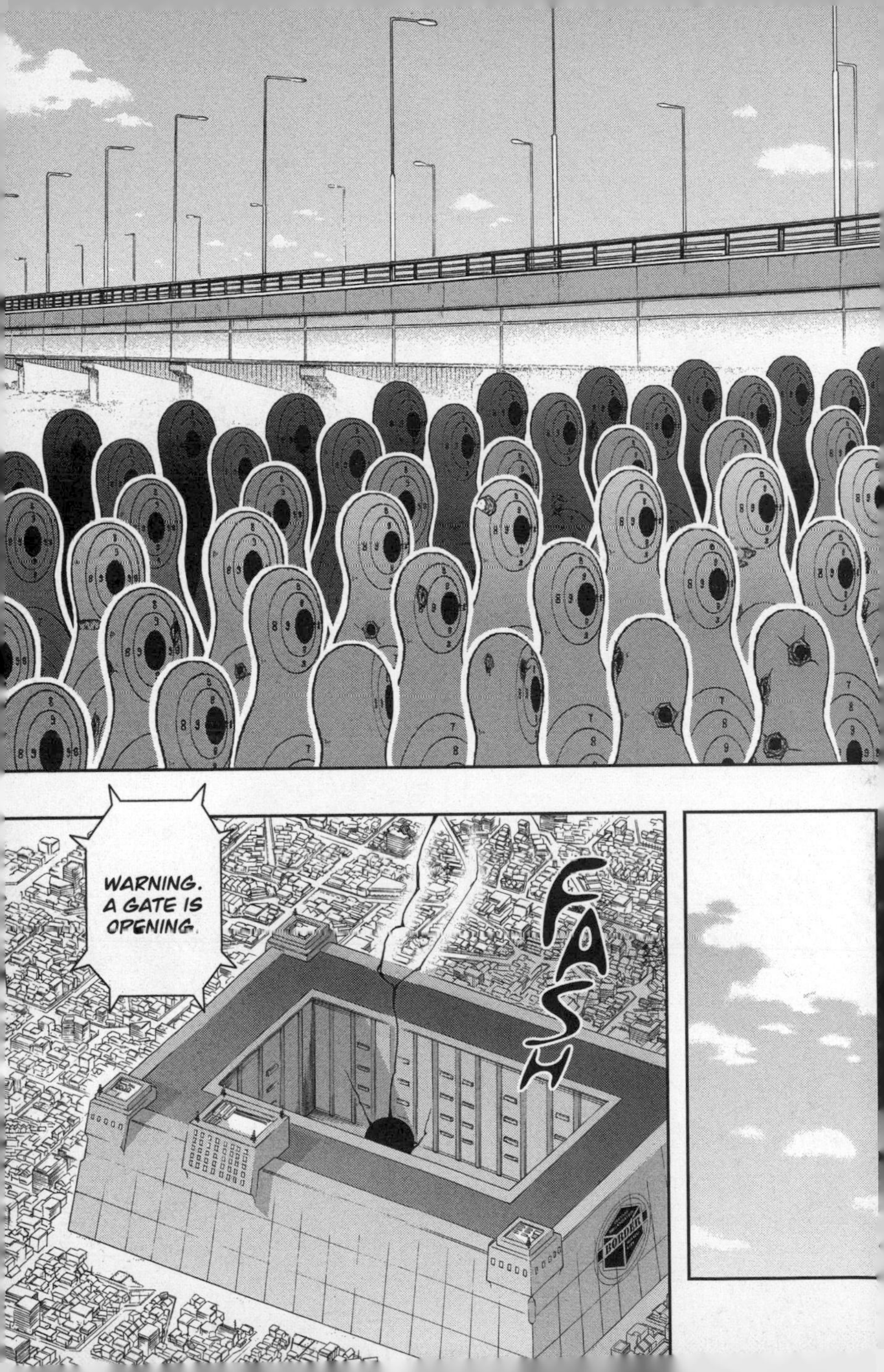
WARNING. A GATE IS OPENING.
FASH

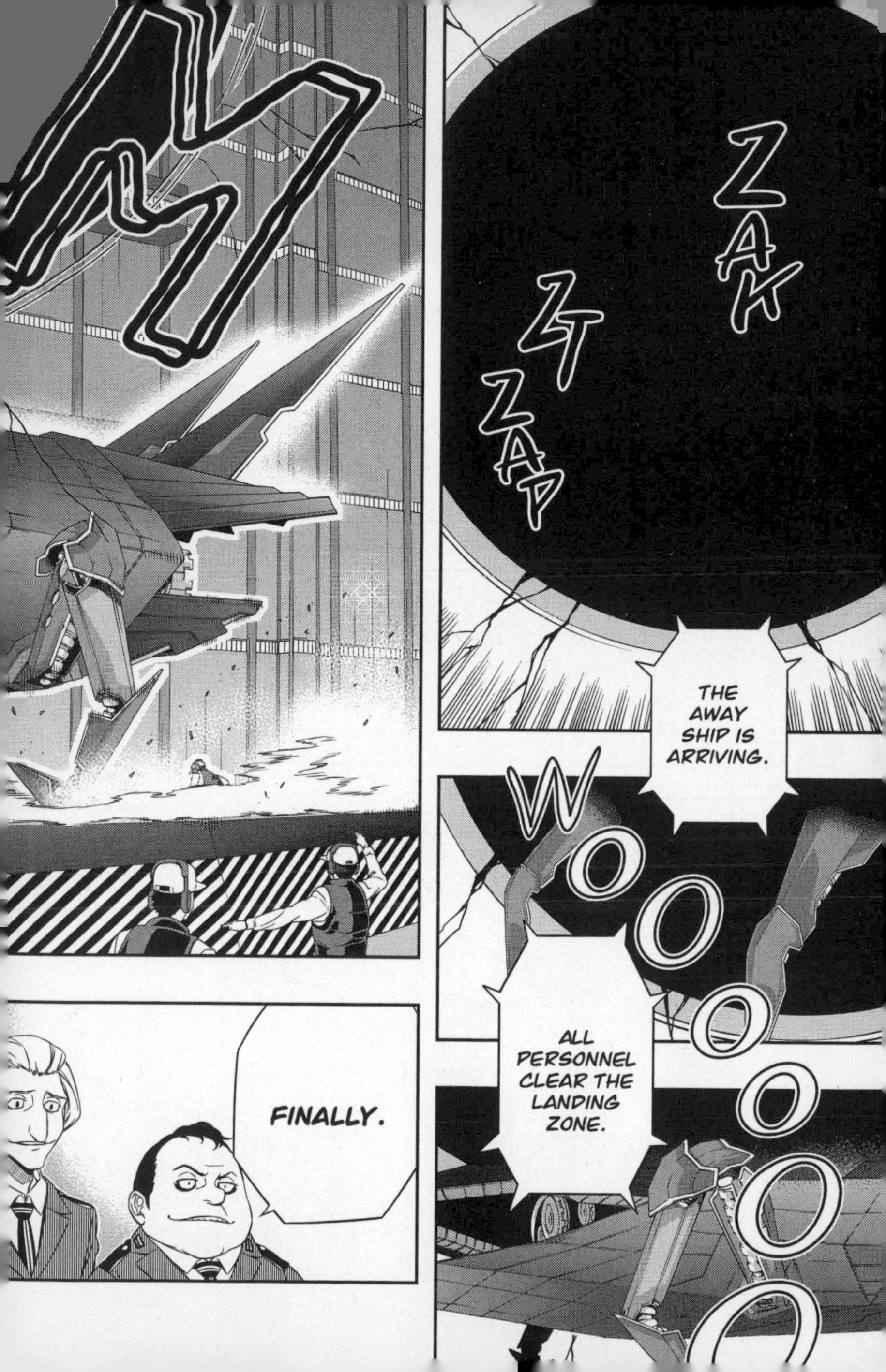

ZAK
ZT
ZAP
THE AWAY SHIP IS ARRIVING.
WOOOOOO
ALL PERSONNEL CLEAR THE LANDING ZONE.
FINALLY.

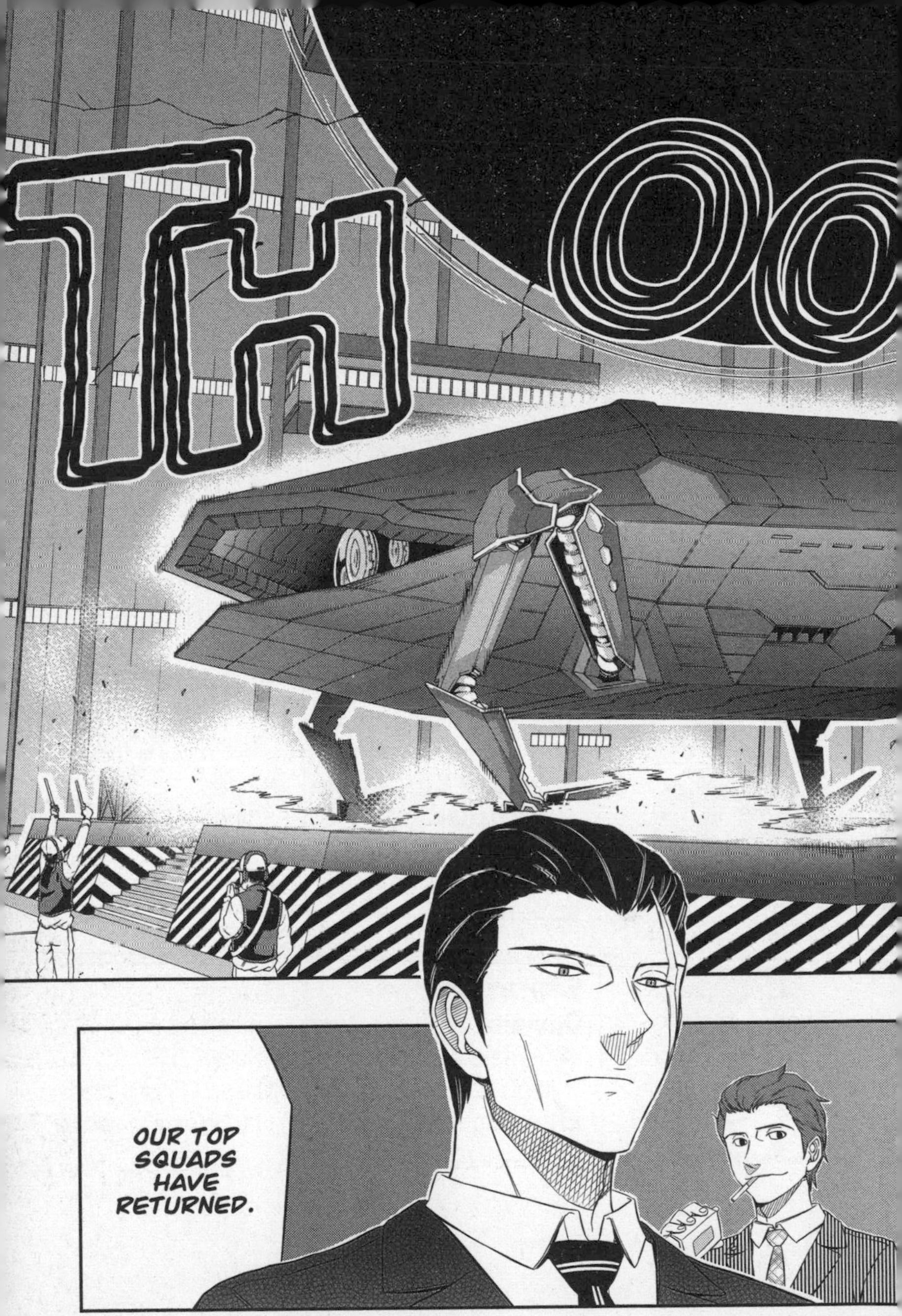
THOO
OUR TOP SQUADS HAVE RETURNED.

Tamakoma-1 Squad
Border Tamakoma Branch

Reiji Kizaki
Captain, All-Rounder
- 21 years old (college student)
- Born July 2

- Gladius, Blood type A
- Height: 6'3"
- Likes: Discipline, cooking

Kirie Konami
Attacker
- 17 years old (high school student)
- Born July 28

- Aptenodytes, Blood type B
- Height: 5'2"
- Likes: Snacks, fruit, red things

Kyosuke Karasuma
All-Rounder
- 16 years old (high school student)
- Born May 9

- Felis, Blood type O
- Height: 5'10"
- Likes: Pork cutlet

Shiori Usami
Operator
- 17 years old (high school student)
- Born April 27

- Lepus, Blood type O
- Height: 5'3"
- Likes: Glasses, reading, taking care of people

Chapter 24 HQ's Top Squads

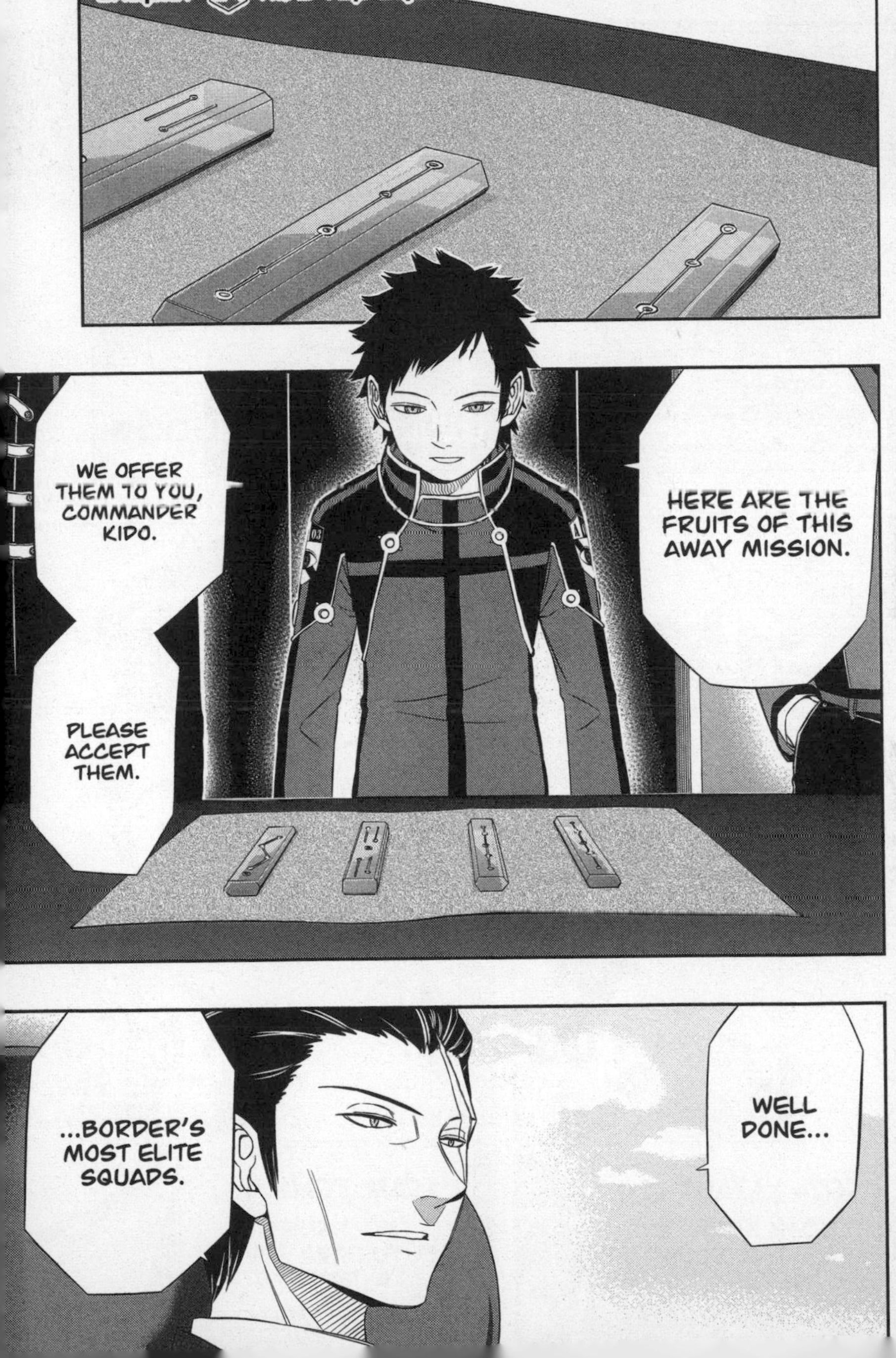
HERE ARE THE FRUITS OF THIS AWAY MISSION.
WE OFFER THEM TO YOU, COMMANDER KIDO.
PLEASE ACCEPT THEM.
WELL DONE...
...BORDER'S MOST ELITE SQUADS.

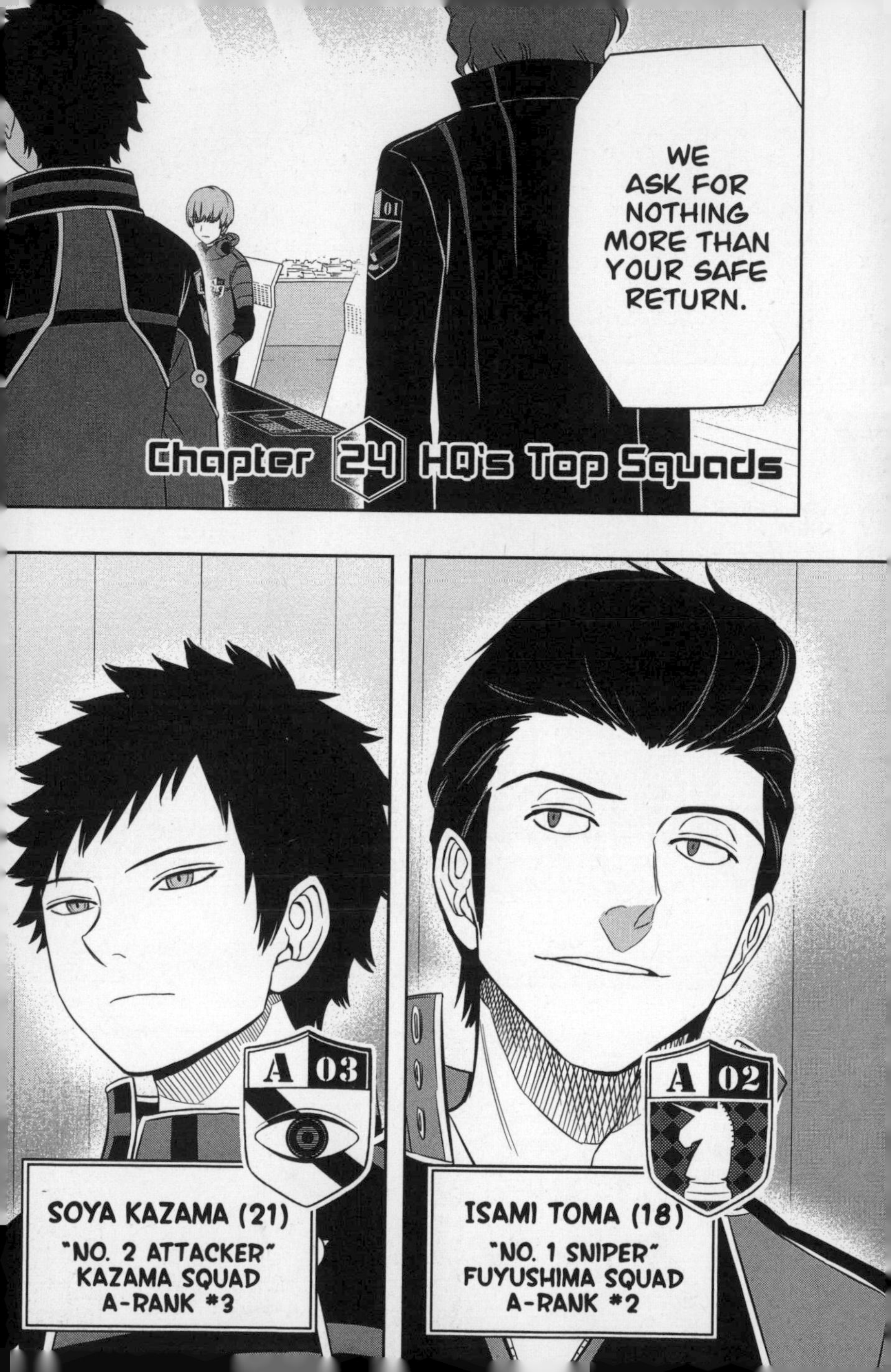
WE ASK FOR NOTHING MORE THAN YOUR SAFE RETURN.
Chapter 24 HQ's Top Squads
A 02
ISAMI TOMA (18)
"NO. 1 SNIPER"
FUYUSHIMA SQUAD
A-RANK #2
A 03
SOYA KAZAMA (21)
"NO. 2 ATTACKER"
KAZAMA SQUAD
A-RANK #3

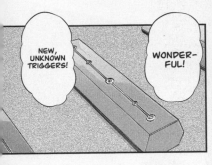

ORGANIZATION
BORDER
MIKADO CITY
A 02
WONDERFUL!
NEW, UNKNOWN TRIGGERS!
NOW BORDER'S TRIGGER TECHNOLOGY WILL ADVANCE BY LEAPS AND BOUNDS!
A 01
KEI TACHIKAWA (20)
"NO. 1 ATTACKER" TACHIKAWA SQUAD A-RANK #1
C'MON, MR. KINUTA.
CAN'T YOU BUILD US A BIGGER EXPEDITION SHIP?
MY LEGS ARE SO LONG I FEEL LIKE THEY'RE IN MY ARMPITS ON THIS SHIP.

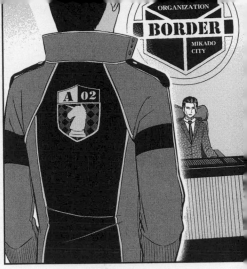

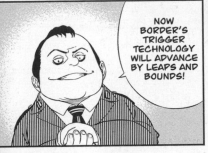

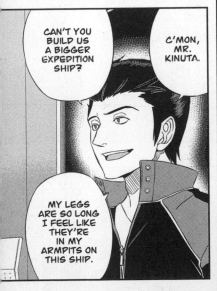

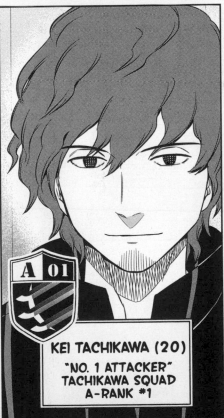

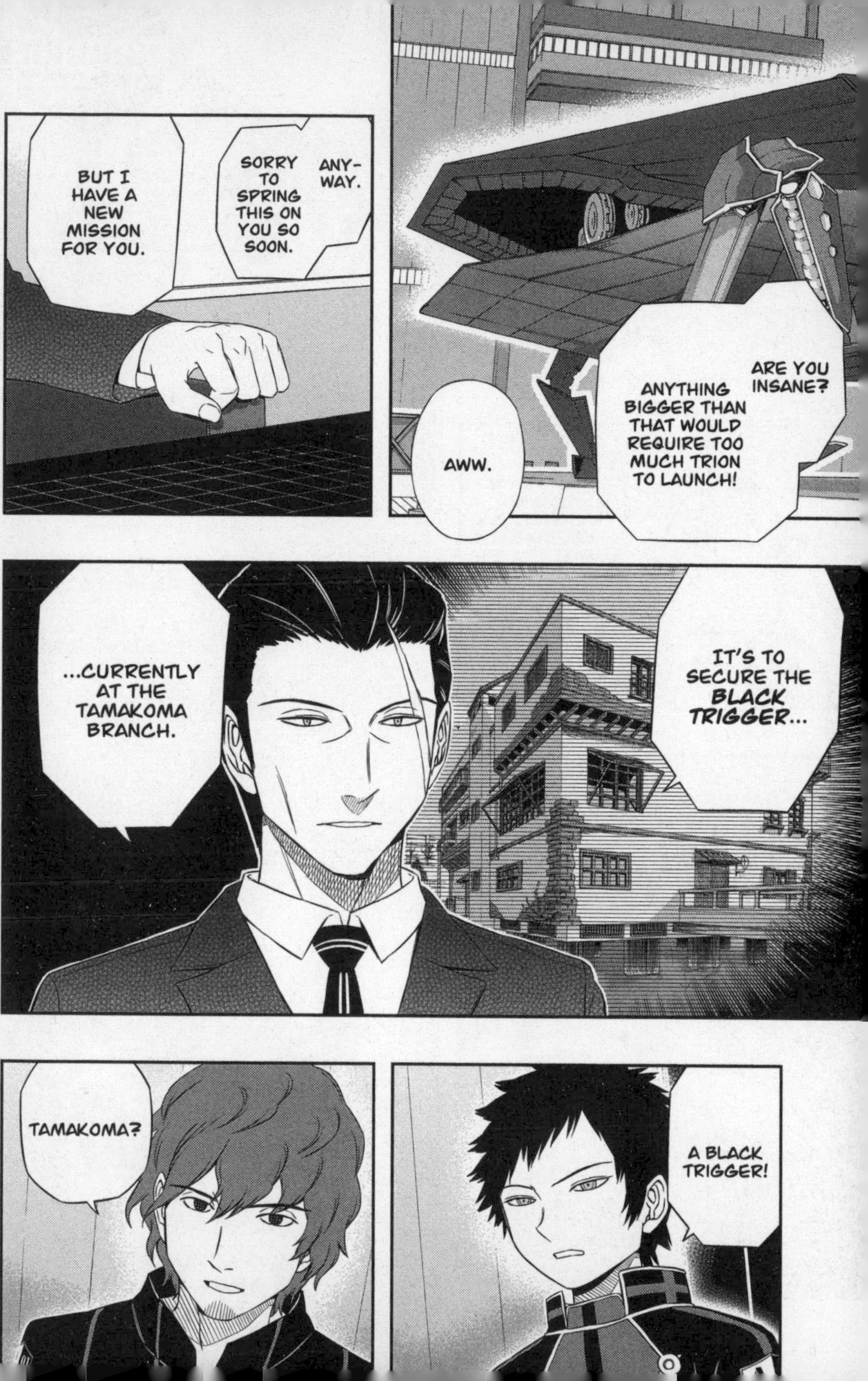
ARE YOU INSANE?
ANYTHING BIGGER THAN THAT WOULD REQUIRE TOO MUCH TRION TO LAUNCH!
AWW.
ANY-WAY.
SORRY TO SPRING THIS ON YOU SO SOON.
BUT I HAVE A NEW MISSION FOR YOU.
IT'S TO SECURE THE BLACK TRIGGER...
...CURRENTLY AT THE TAMAKOMA BRANCH.
A BLACK TRIGGER!
TAMAKOMA?

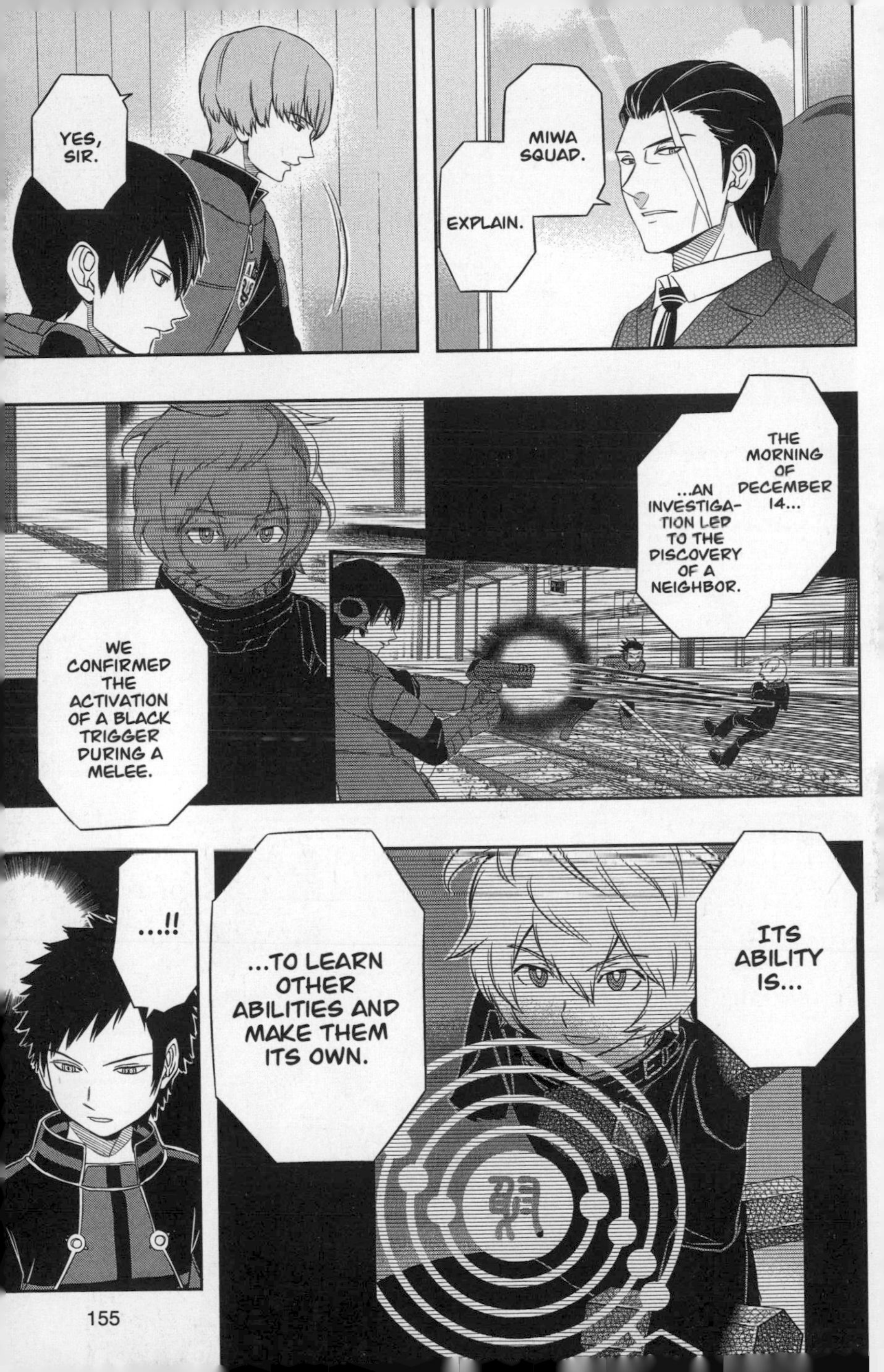
MIWA SQUAD.
EXPLAIN.
YES, SIR.
THE MORNING OF DECEMBER 14...
...AN INVESTIGATION LED TO THE DISCOVERY OF A NEIGHBOR.
WE CONFIRMED THE ACTIVATION OF A BLACK TRIGGER DURING A MELEE.
ITS ABILITY IS...
...TO LEARN OTHER ABILITIES AND MAKE THEM ITS OWN.
...!!

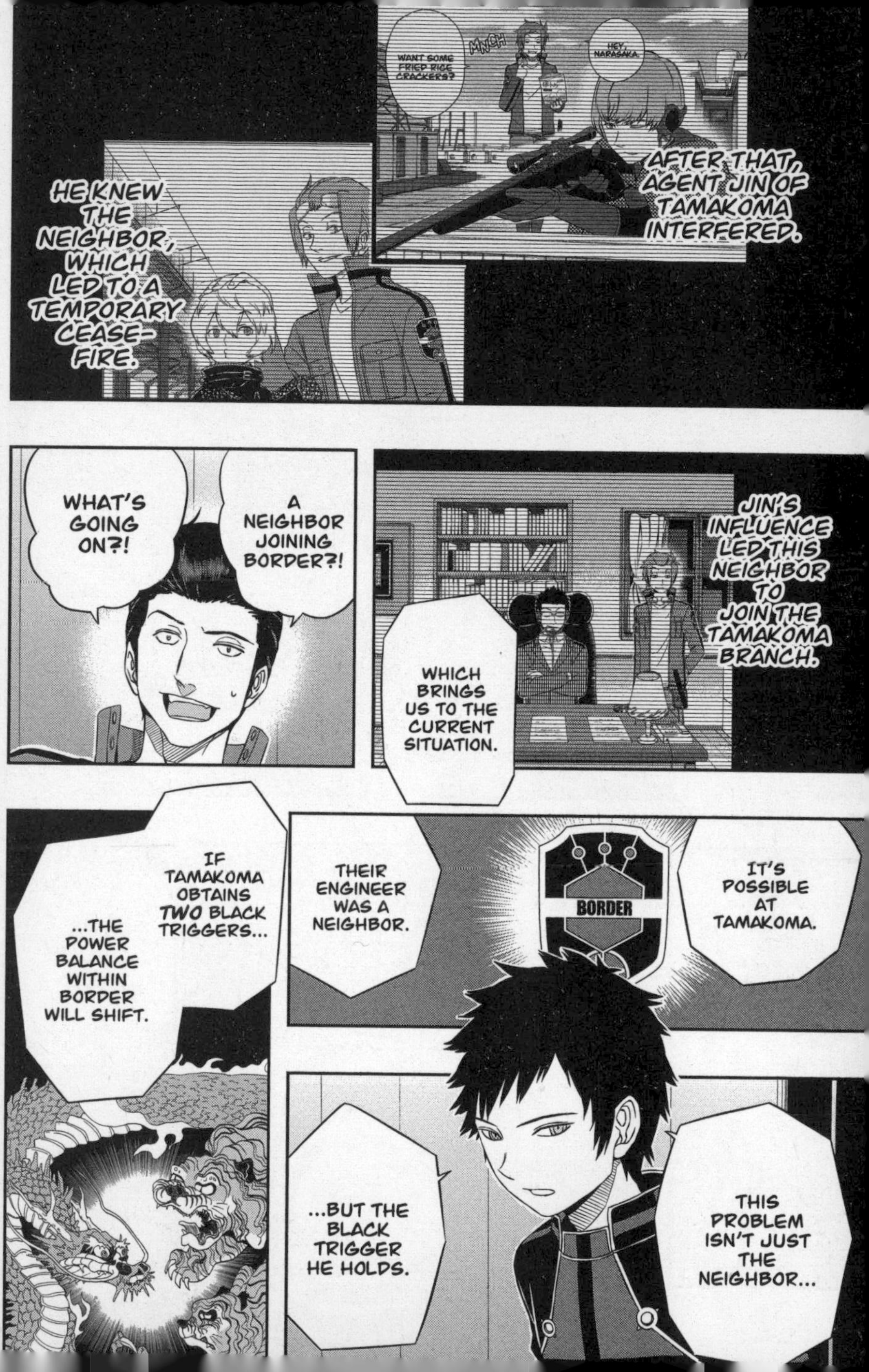
AFTER THAT, AGENT JIN OF TAMAKOMA INTERFERED.
HEY, NARASAKA.
MNCH
WANT SOME FRIED RICE CRACKERS?
HE KNEW THE NEIGHBOR, WHICH LED TO A TEMPORARY CEASE-FIRE.
JIN'S INFLUENCE LED THIS NEIGHBOR TO JOIN THE TAMAKOMA BRANCH.
WHICH BRINGS US TO THE CURRENT SITUATION.
A NEIGHBOR JOINING BORDER?!
WHAT'S GOING ON?!
IT'S POSSIBLE AT TAMAKOMA.
BORDER
THEIR ENGINEER WAS A NEIGHBOR.
THIS PROBLEM ISN'T JUST THE NEIGHBOR...
...BUT THE BLACK TRIGGER HE HOLDS.
IF TAMAKOMA OBTAINS TWO BLACK TRIGGERS...
...THE POWER BALANCE WITHIN BORDER WILL SHIFT.

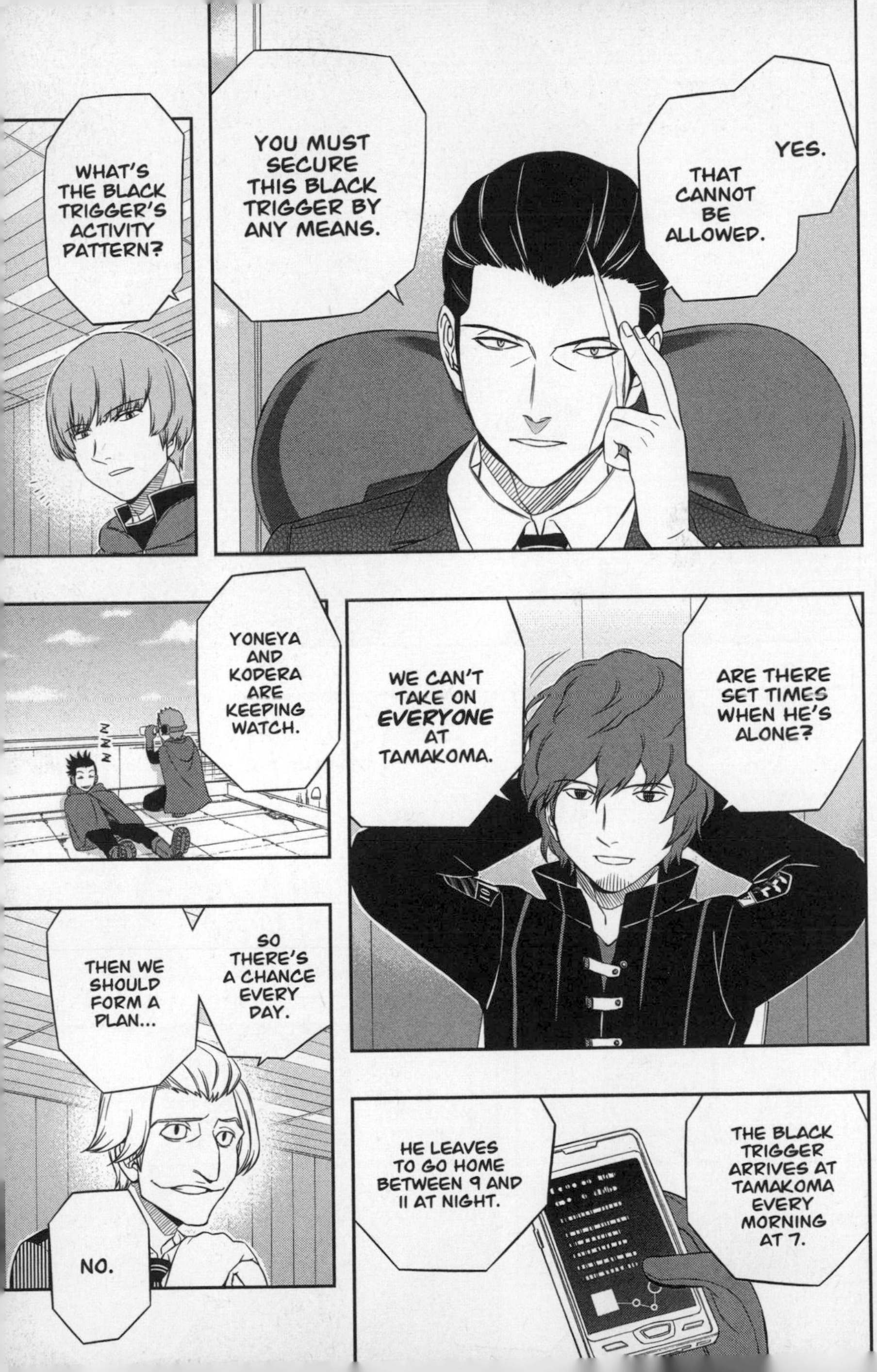
YES.
THAT CANNOT BE ALLOWED.
YOU MUST SECURE THIS BLACK TRIGGER BY ANY MEANS.
WHAT'S THE BLACK TRIGGER'S ACTIVITY PATTERN?
ARE THERE SET TIMES WHEN HE'S ALONE?
WE CAN'T TAKE ON EVERYONE AT TAMAKOMA.
YONEYA AND KODERA ARE KEEPING WATCH.
ZZZ
THE BLACK TRIGGER ARRIVES AT TAMAKOMA EVERY MORNING AT 7.
HE LEAVES TO GO HOME BETWEEN 9 AND 11 AT NIGHT.
SO THERE'S A CHANCE EVERY DAY.
THEN WE SHOULD FORM A PLAN...
NO.

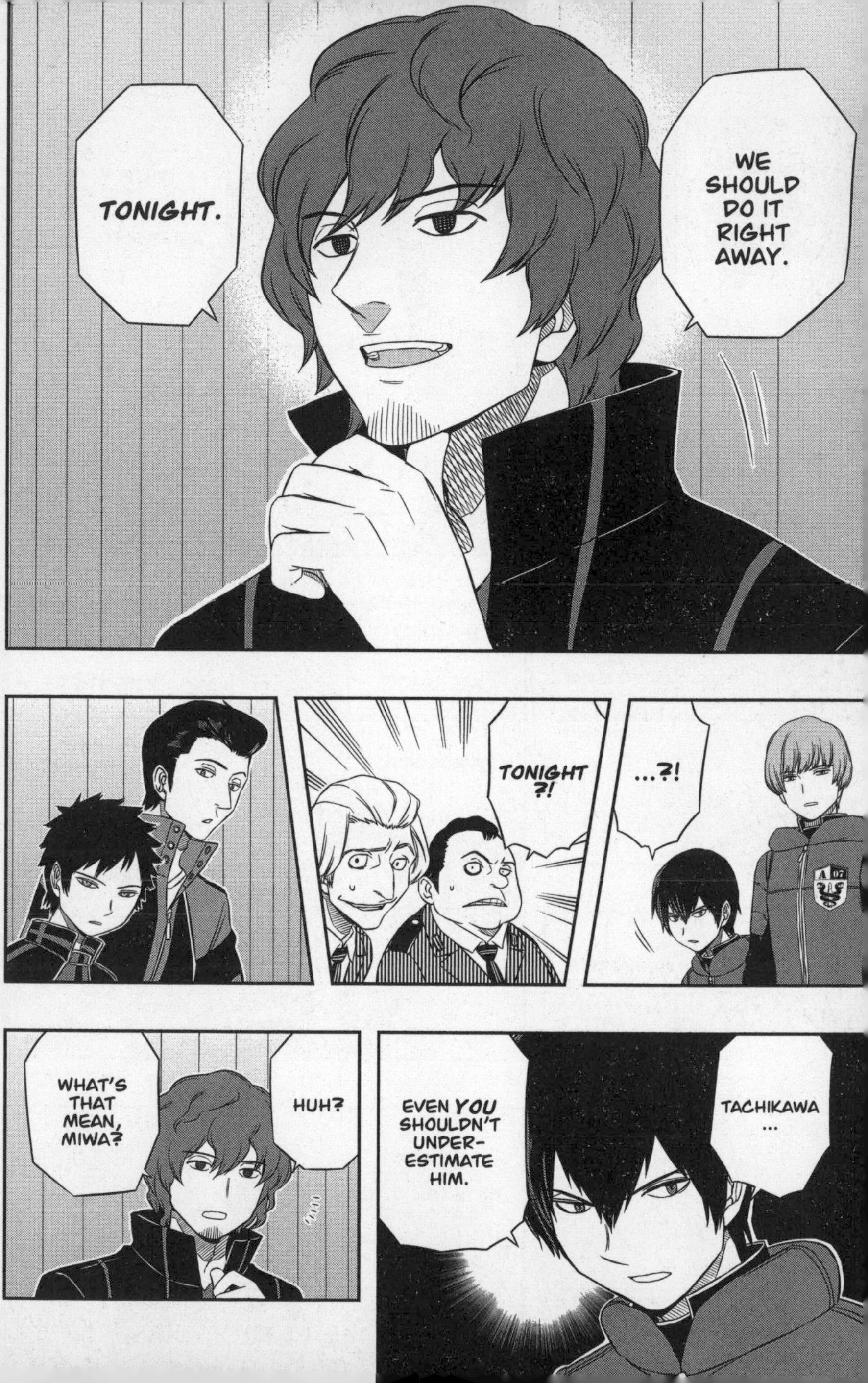
WE SHOULD DO IT RIGHT AWAY.
TONIGHT.
...?!
TONIGHT ?!
TACHIKAWA ...
EVEN YOU SHOULDN'T UNDER-ESTIMATE HIM.
HUH?
WHAT'S THAT MEAN, MIWA?

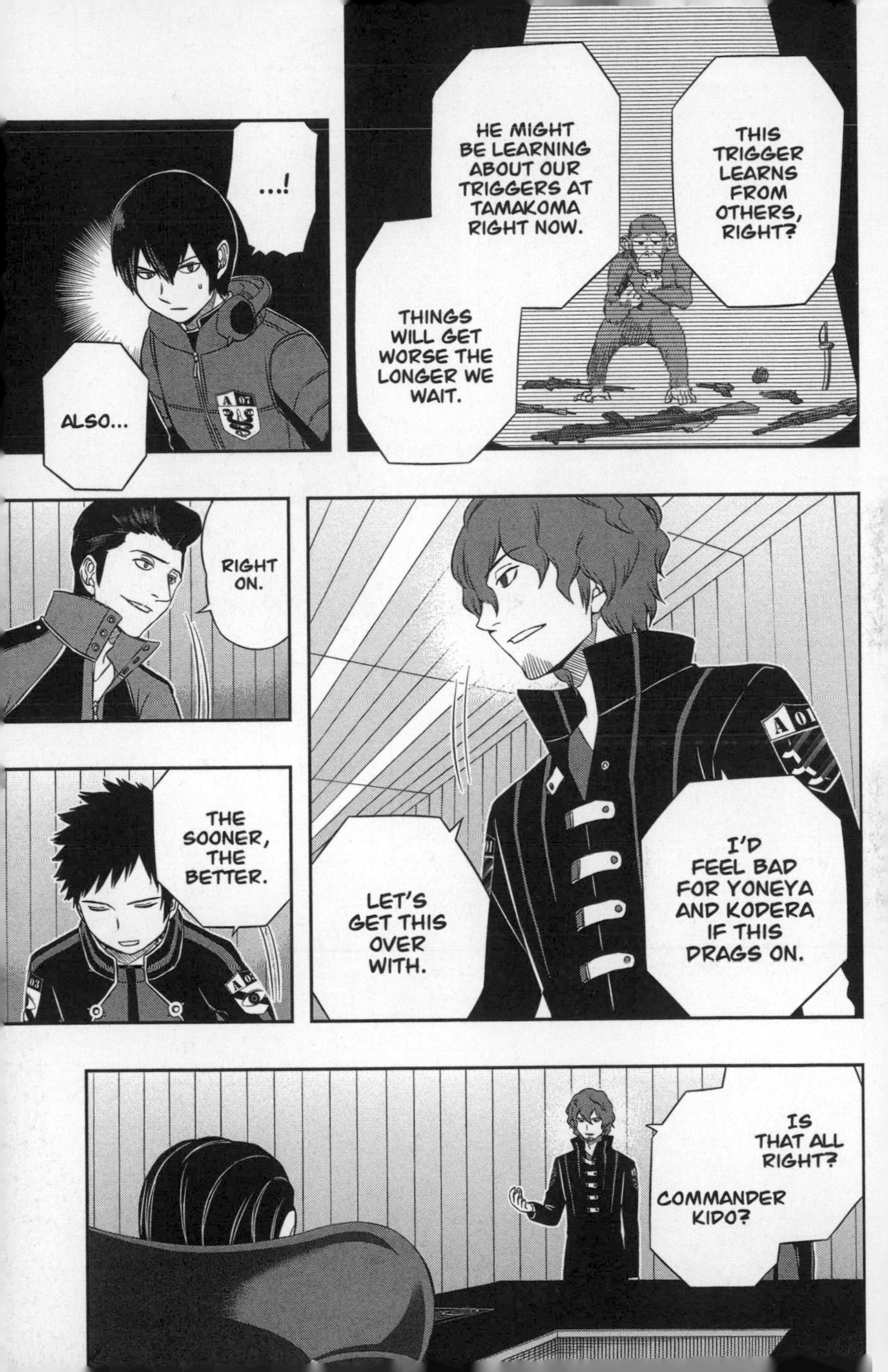
THIS TRIGGER LEARNS FROM OTHERS, RIGHT?
HE MIGHT BE LEARNING ABOUT OUR TRIGGERS AT TAMAKOMA RIGHT NOW.
THINGS WILL GET WORSE THE LONGER WE WAIT.
...!
ALSO...
I'D FEEL BAD FOR YONEYA AND KODERA IF THIS DRAGS ON.
LET'S GET THIS OVER WITH.
RIGHT ON.
THE SOONER, THE BETTER.
IS THAT ALL RIGHT?
COMMANDER KIDO?

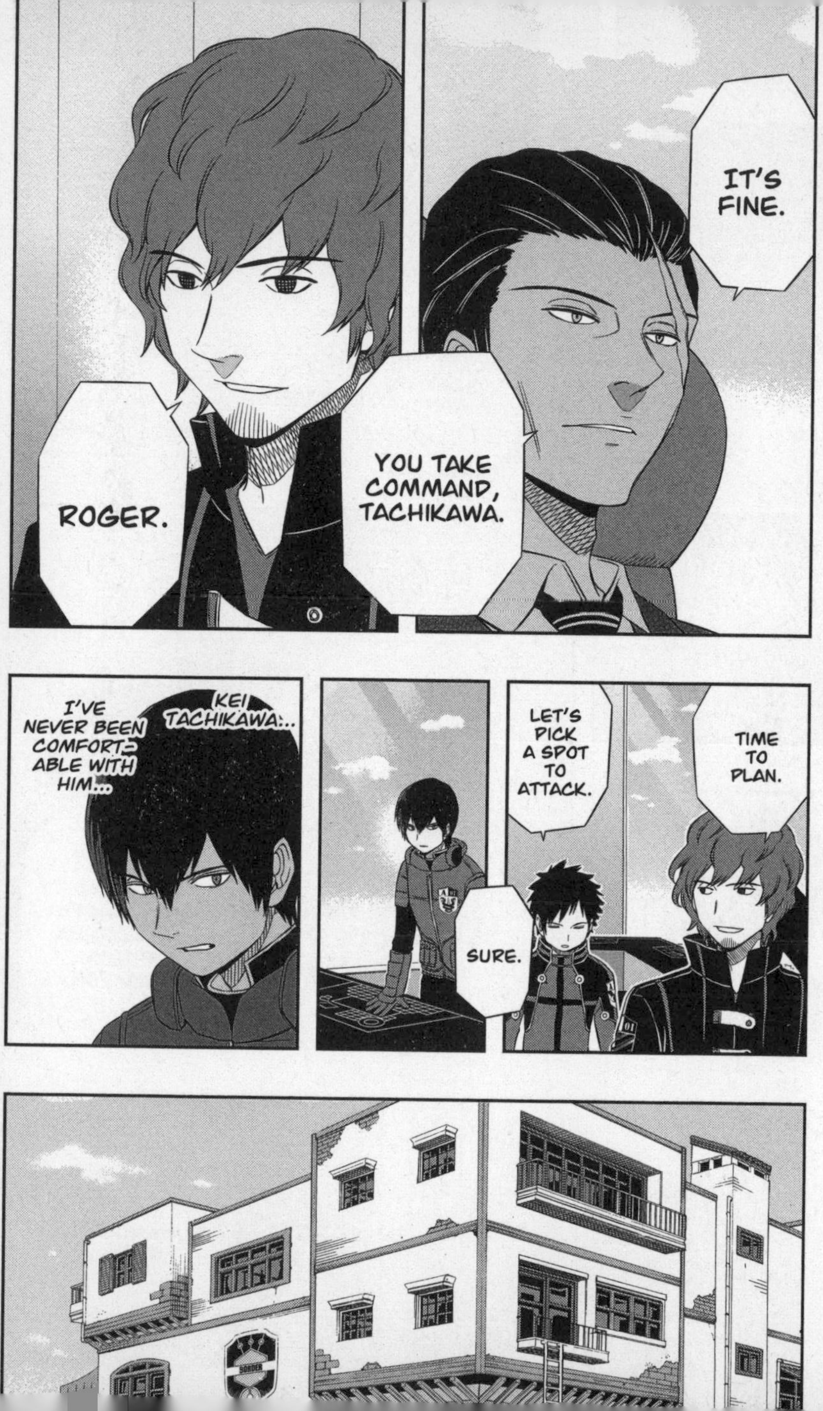
IT'S FINE.
YOU TAKE COMMAND, TACHIKAWA.
ROGER.
TIME TO PLAN.
LET'S PICK A SPOT TO ATTACK.
SURE.
KEI TACHIKAWA...
I'VE NEVER BEEN COMFORT-ABLE WITH HIM...

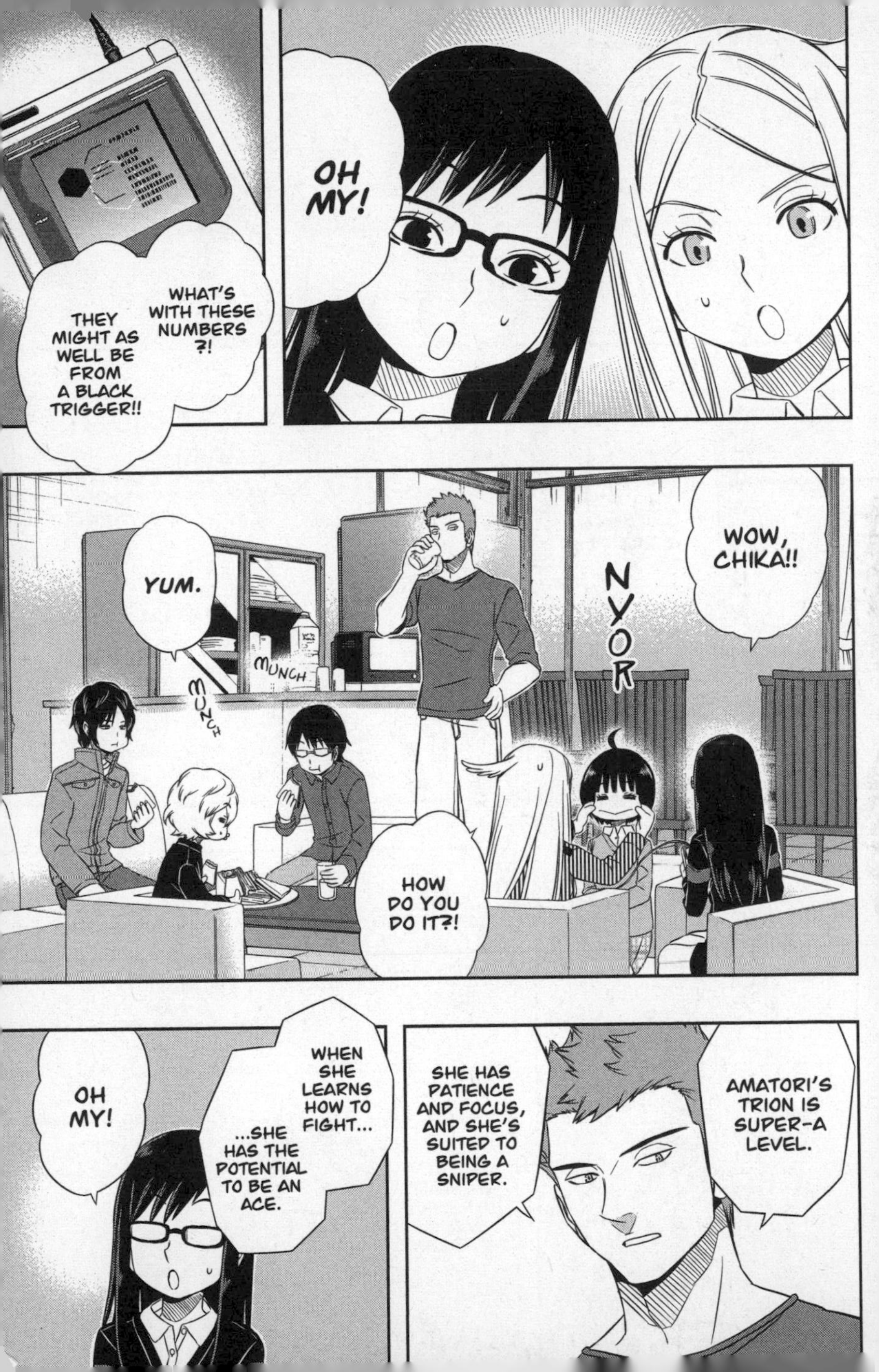
OH MY!
WHAT'S WITH THESE NUMBERS ?!
THEY MIGHT AS WELL BE FROM A BLACK TRIGGER!!
WOW, CHIKA!!
NYOR
HOW DO YOU DO IT?!
YUM.
MUNCH
MUNCH
AMATORI'S TRION IS SUPER-A LEVEL.
SHE HAS PATIENCE AND FOCUS, AND SHE'S SUITED TO BEING A SNIPER.
WHEN SHE LEARNS HOW TO FIGHT...
...SHE HAS THE POTENTIAL TO BE AN ACE.
OH MY!

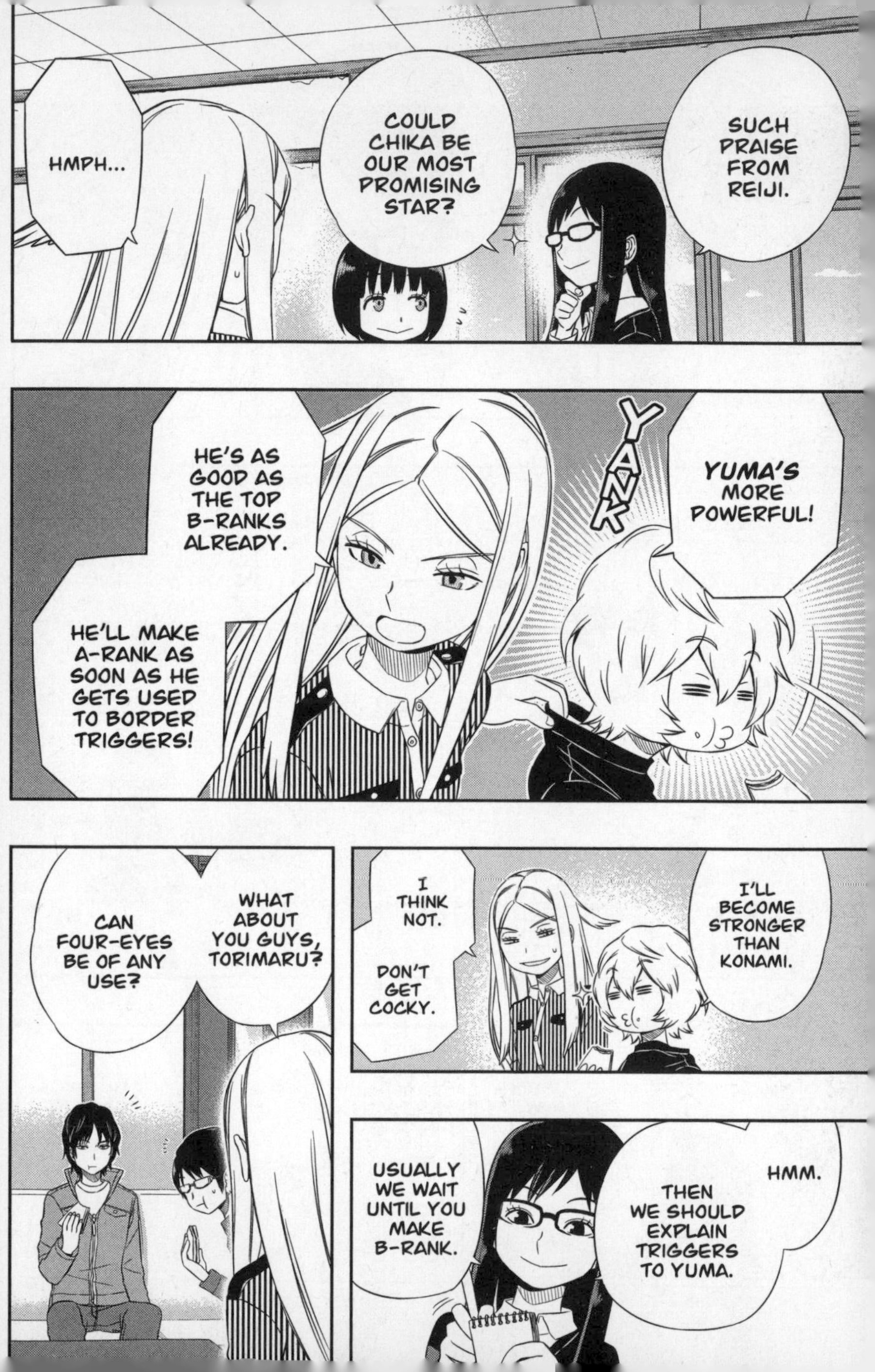
SUCH PRAISE FROM REIJI.
COULD CHIKA BE OUR MOST PROMISING STAR?
HMPH...
YUMA'S MORE POWERFUL!
YANK
HE'S AS GOOD AS THE TOP B-RANKS ALREADY.
HE'LL MAKE A-RANK AS SOON AS HE GETS USED TO BORDER TRIGGERS!
I'LL BECOME STRONGER THAN KONAMI.
I THINK NOT.
DON'T GET COCKY.
HMM.
THEN WE SHOULD EXPLAIN TRIGGERS TO YUMA.
USUALLY WE WAIT UNTIL YOU MAKE B-RANK.
WHAT ABOUT YOU GUYS, TORIMARU?
CAN FOUR-EYES BE OF ANY USE?

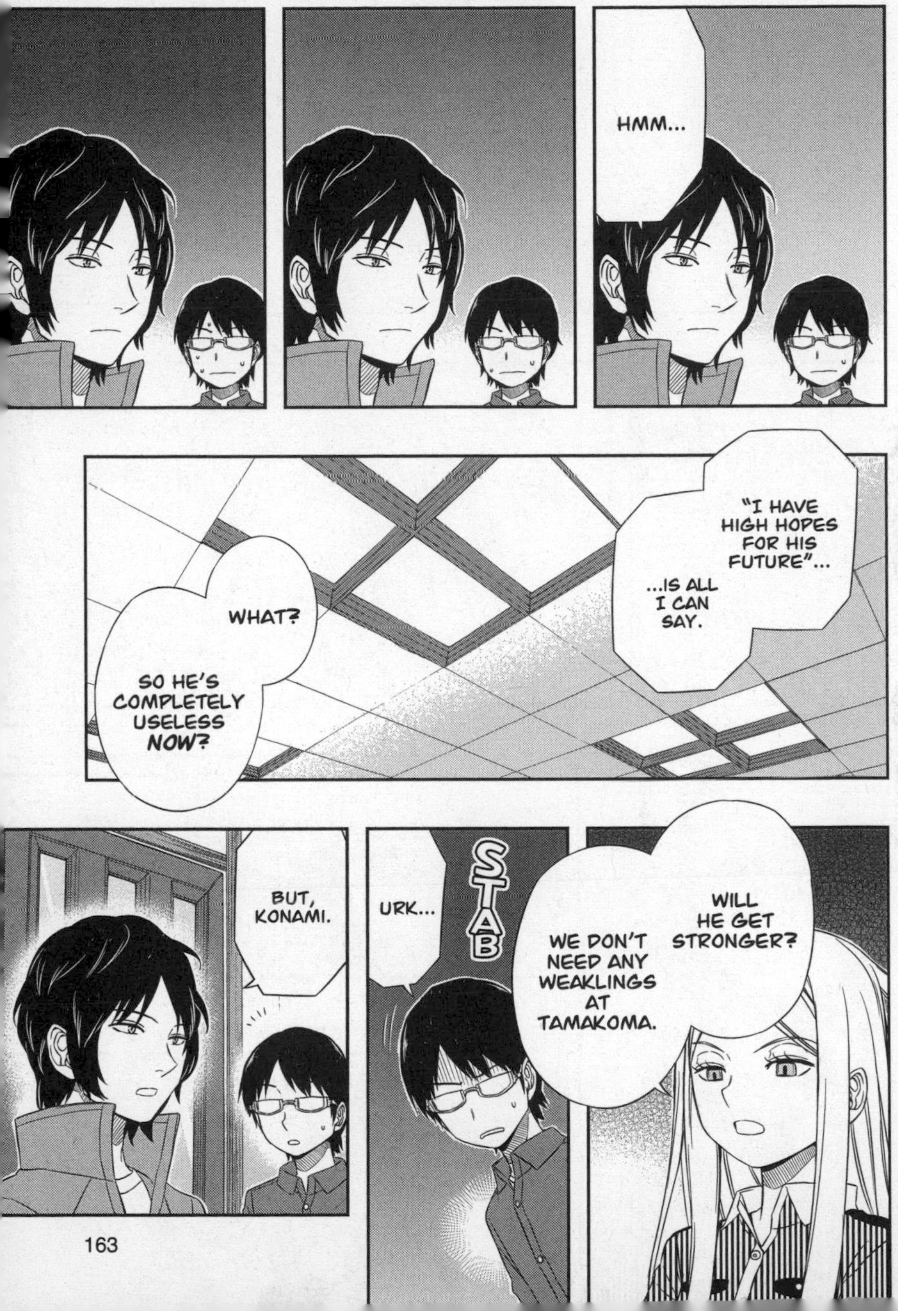
HMM...
"I HAVE HIGH HOPES FOR HIS FUTURE"...
...IS ALL I CAN SAY.
WHAT?
SO HE'S COMPLETELY USELESS NOW?
WILL HE GET STRONGER?
WE DON'T NEED ANY WEAKLINGS AT TAMAKOMA.
STAB
URK...
BUT, KONAMI.

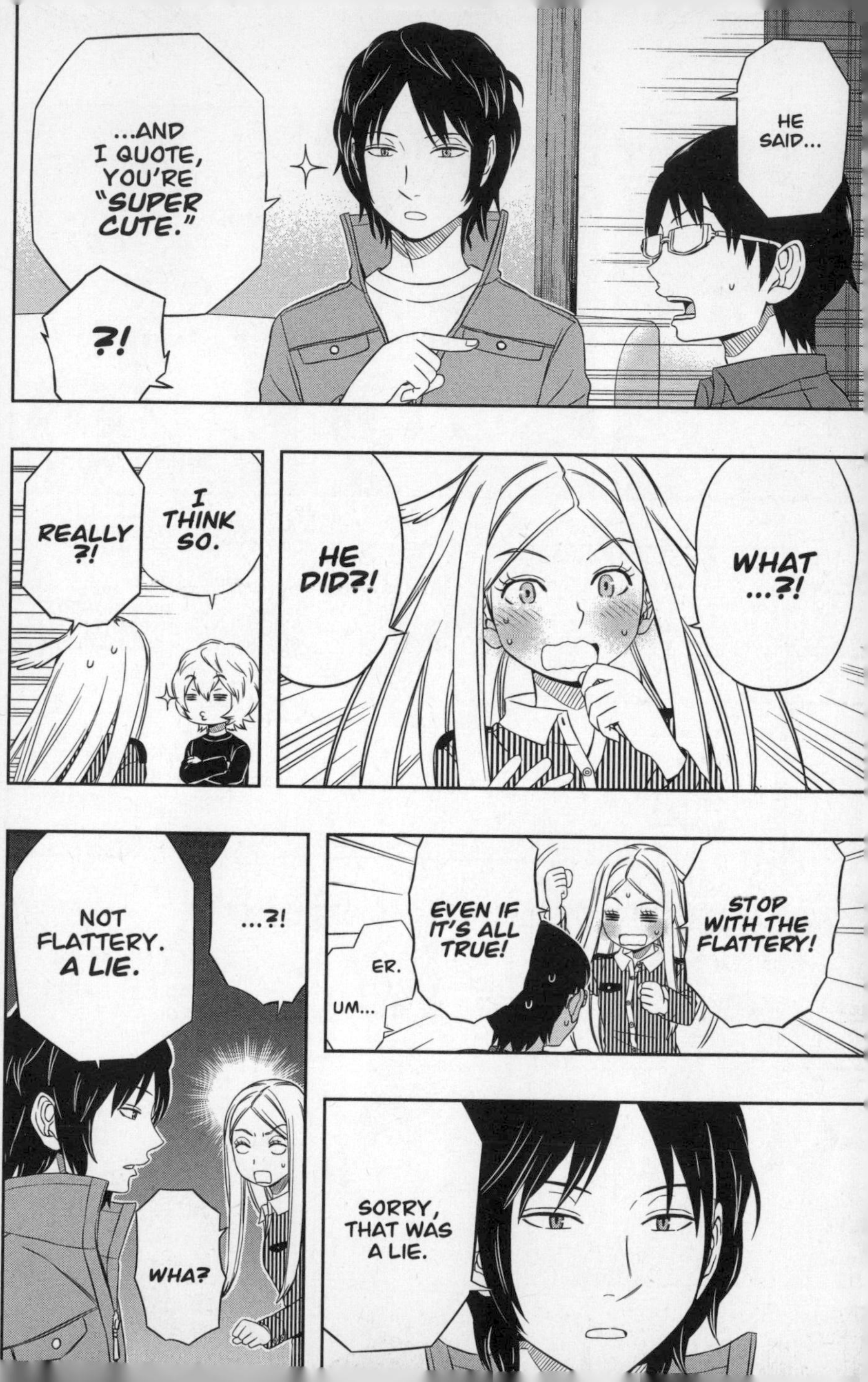
HE SAID...
...AND I QUOTE, YOU'RE "SUPER CUTE."
?!
WHAT ...?!
HE DID?!
I THINK SO.
REALLY ?!
STOP WITH THE FLATTERY!
EVEN IF IT'S ALL TRUE!
ER.
UM...
SORRY, THAT WAS A LIE.
...?!
NOT FLATTERY. A LIE.
WHA?

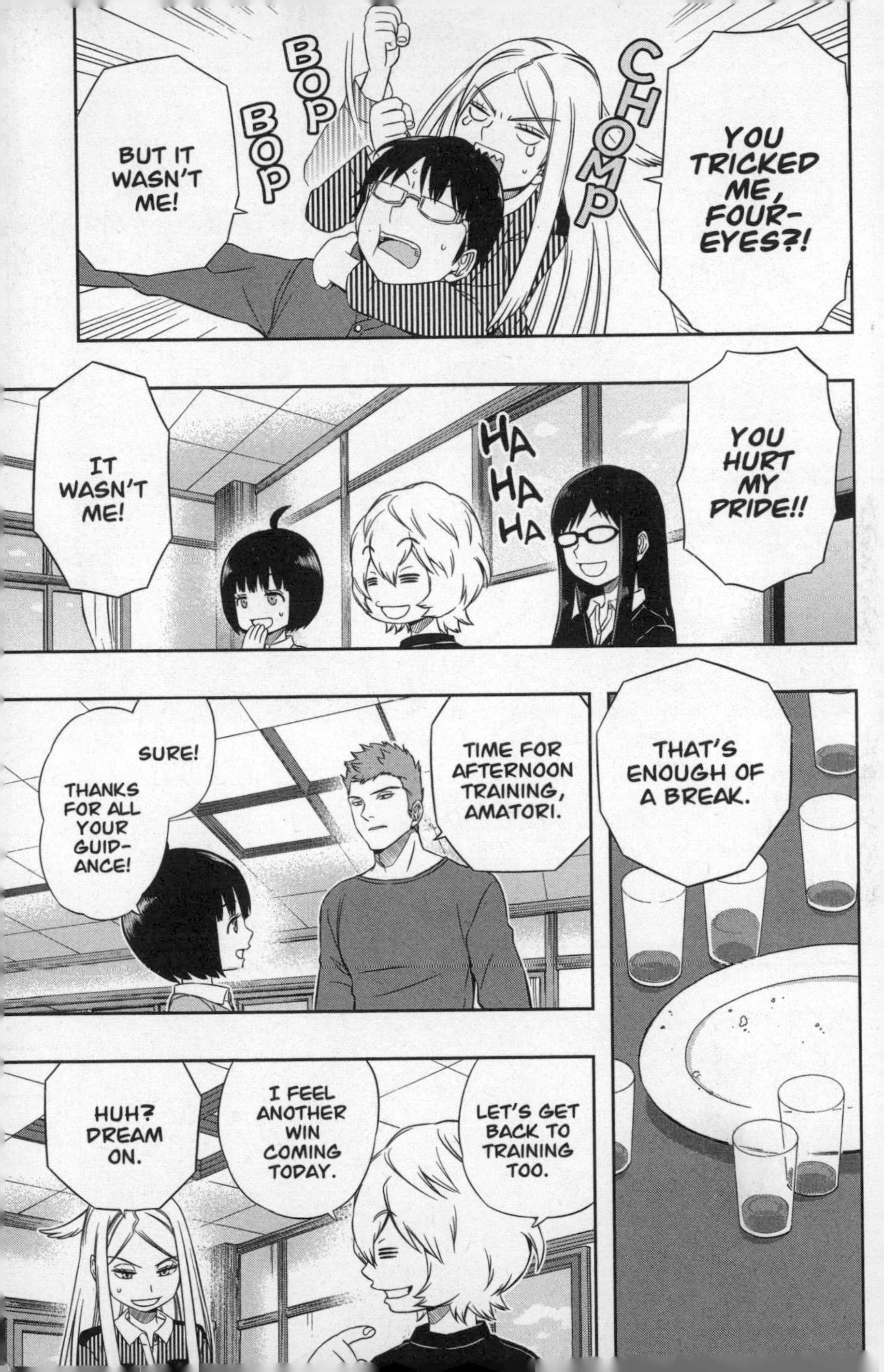
YOU TRICKED ME, FOUR-EYES?!
CHOMP
BOP
BOP
BUT IT WASN'T ME!
YOU HURT MY PRIDE!!
HA HA HA
IT WASN'T ME!
THAT'S ENOUGH OF A BREAK.
TIME FOR AFTERNOON TRAINING, AMATORI.
SURE!
THANKS FOR ALL YOUR GUID-ANCE!
LET'S GET BACK TO TRAINING TOO.
I FEEL ANOTHER WIN COMING TODAY.
HUH? DREAM ON.

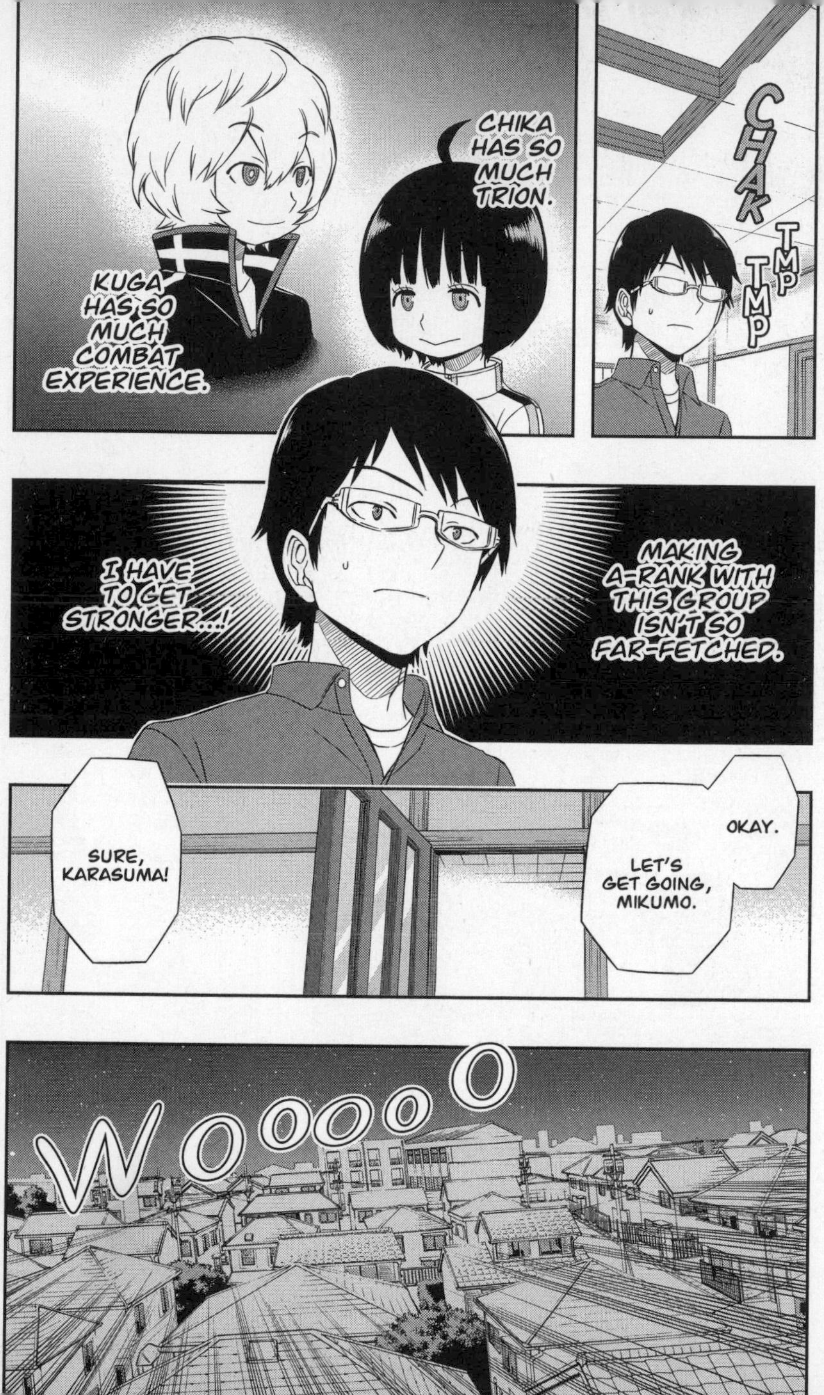
CHAK
TMP TMP
CHIKA HAS SO MUCH TRION.
KUGA HAS SO MUCH COMBAT EXPERIENCE.
MAKING A-RANK WITH THIS GROUP ISN'T SO FAR-FETCHED.
I HAVE TO GET STRONGER...!
OKAY.
LET'S GET GOING, MIKUMO.
SURE, KARASUMA!
WOOOOO

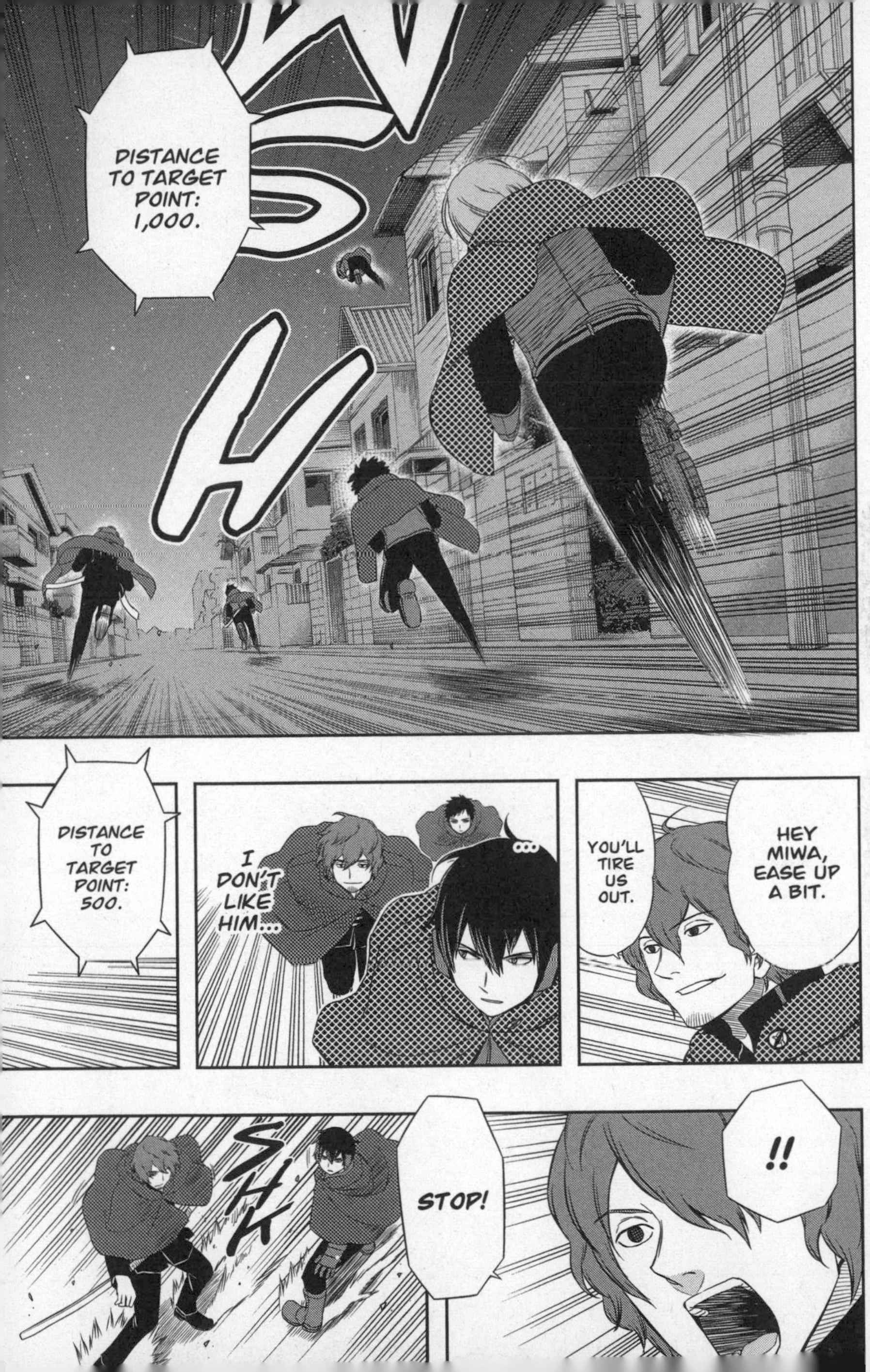
DISTANCE TO TARGET POINT: 1,000.
HEY MIWA, EASE UP A BIT.
YOU'LL TIRE US OUT.
...
I DON'T LIKE HIM...
DISTANCE TO TARGET POINT: 500.
!!
STOP!
SHK

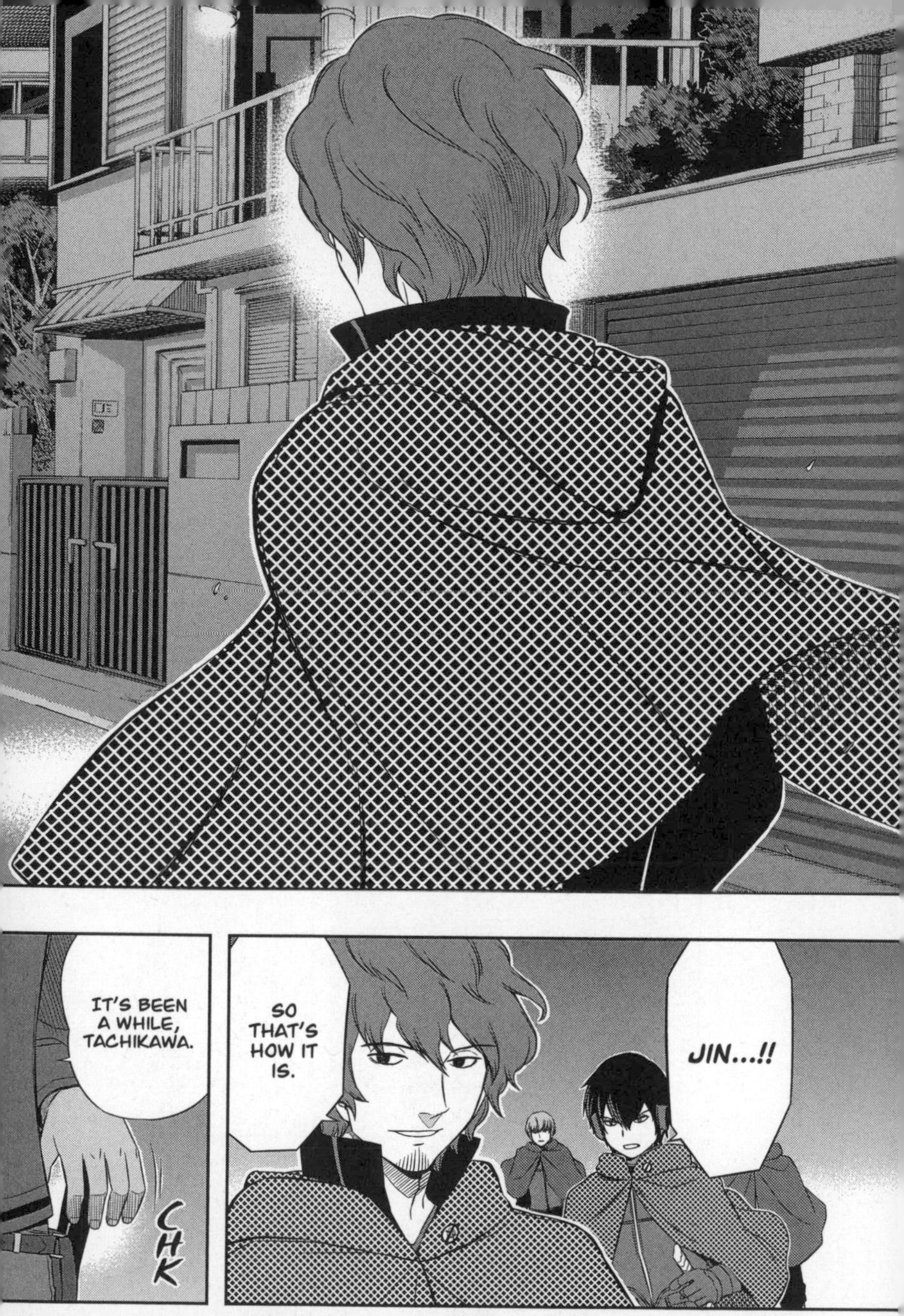
JIN...!!
SO THAT'S HOW IT IS.
IT'S BEEN A WHILE, TACHIKAWA.
CHK

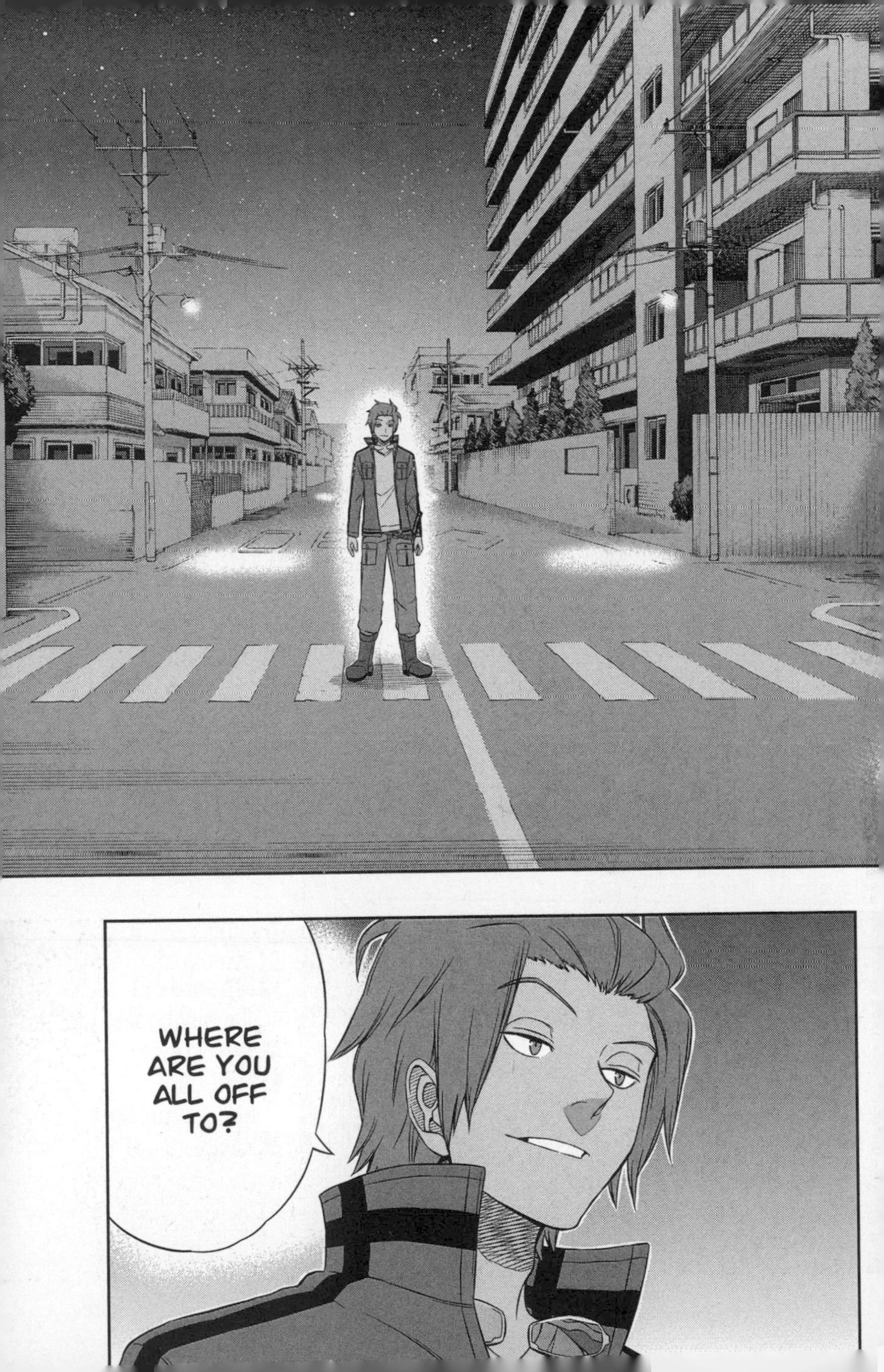
WHERE ARE YOU ALL OFF TO?

HQ A-Rank Top 3
Away Squads

DEFENSE ORGANIZATION
BORDER
MIKADO CITY

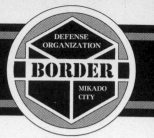

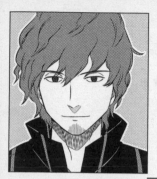

Kei Tachikawa
Tachikawa Squad (A-Rank #1)
Captain
Attacker

■Solo comprehensive rank #1
■Solo Attacker rank #1

■20 years old (college student)
■Born Aug. 29
■Lupus, Blood type A
■Height: 5'11"

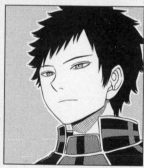

Soya Kazama
Kazama Squad (A-Rank #3)
Captain
Attacker

■Solo comprehensive rank #3
■Solo Attacker rank #3

■21 years old (college student)
■Born Sept. 24
■Luna Falcata, Blood type A
■Height: 5'2"

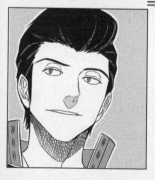

Isami Toma
Fuyushima Squad (A-Rank #2)
Sniper

■Solo comprehensive rank #4
■Solo Sniper rank #1

■18 years old (high school student)
■Born July 7
■Gladius, Blood type AB
■Height: 6'

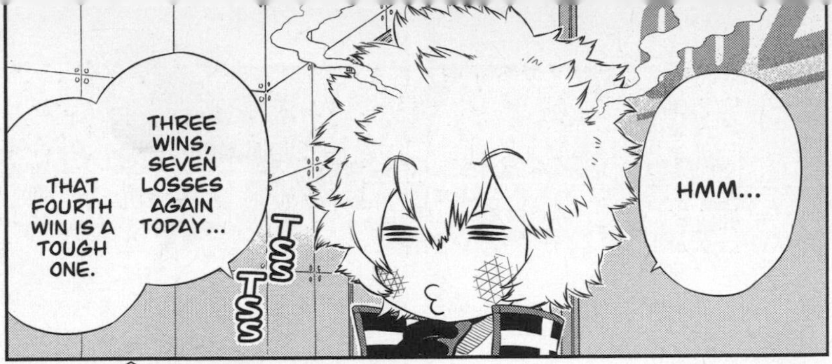
HMM...
THREE WINS, SEVEN LOSSES AGAIN TODAY...
TSS TSS
THAT FOURTH WIN IS A TOUGH ONE.

Chapter 25 Yuichi Jin: Part 3

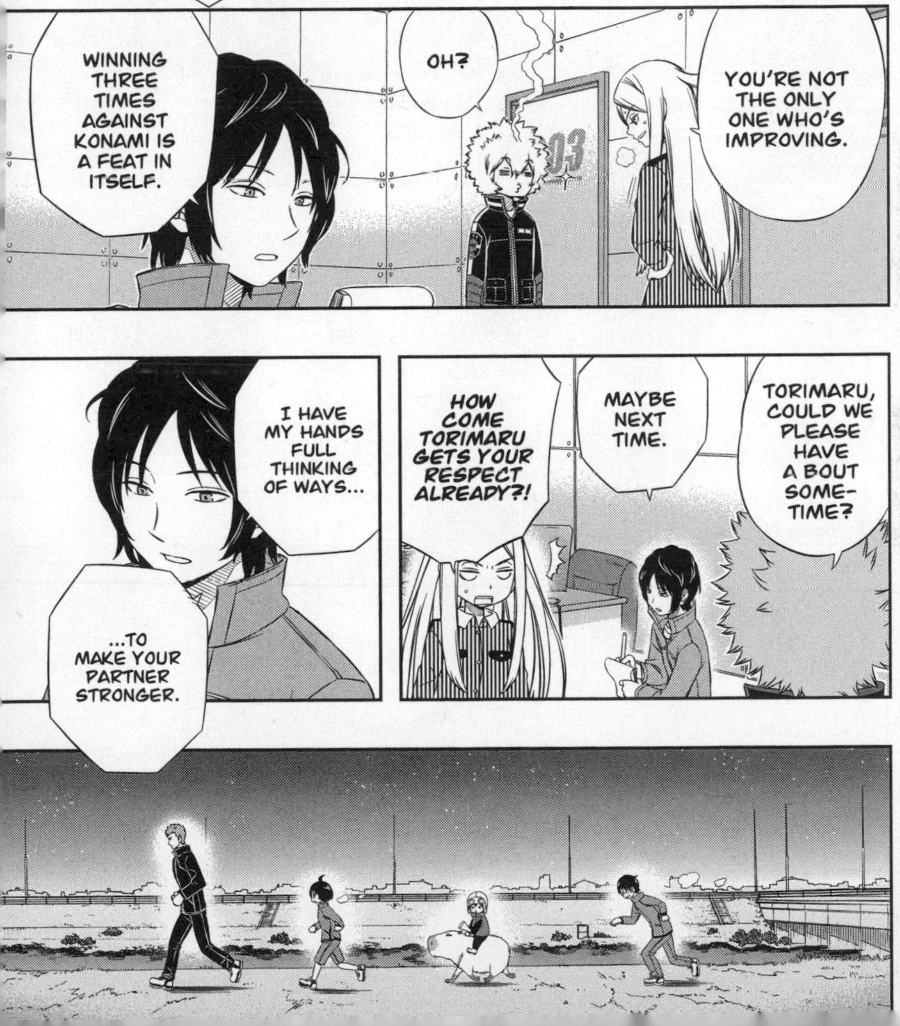
YOU'RE NOT THE ONLY ONE WHO'S IMPROVING.
OH?
WINNING THREE TIMES AGAINST KONAMI IS A FEAT IN ITSELF.
TORIMARU, COULD WE PLEASE HAVE A BOUT SOME-TIME?
MAYBE NEXT TIME.
HOW COME TORIMARU GETS YOUR RESPECT ALREADY?!
I HAVE MY HANDS FULL THINKING OF WAYS...
...TO MAKE YOUR PARTNER STRONGER.

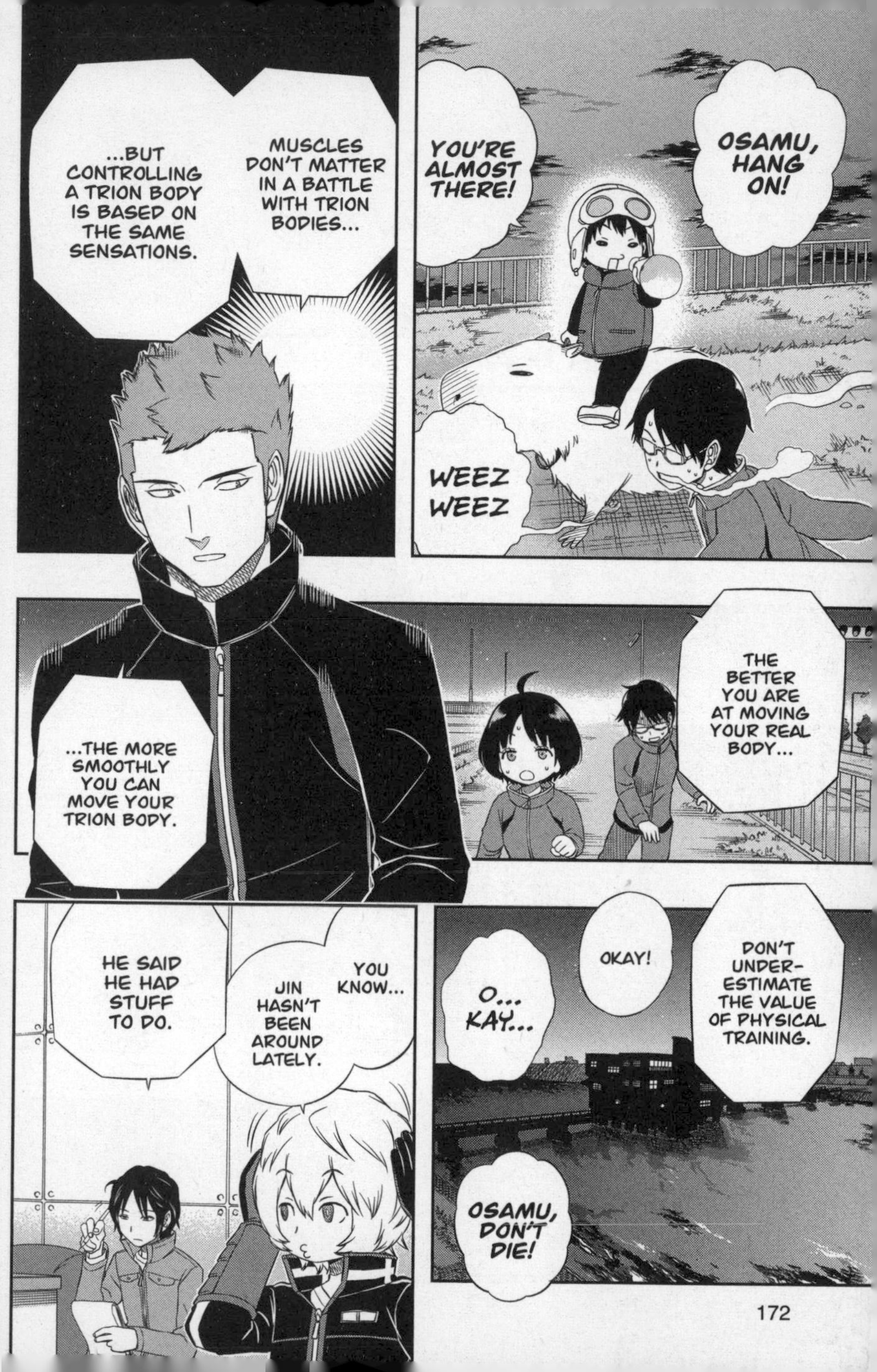
OSAMU, HANG ON!
YOU'RE ALMOST THERE!
WEEZ WEEZ
MUSCLES DON'T MATTER IN A BATTLE WITH TRION BODIES...
...BUT CONTROLLING A TRION BODY IS BASED ON THE SAME SENSATIONS.
THE BETTER YOU ARE AT MOVING YOUR REAL BODY...
...THE MORE SMOOTHLY YOU CAN MOVE YOUR TRION BODY.
DON'T UNDER-ESTIMATE THE VALUE OF PHYSICAL TRAINING.
OKAY!
O... KAY...
OSAMU, DON'T DIE!
YOU KNOW...
JIN HASN'T BEEN AROUND LATELY.
HE SAID HE HAD STUFF TO DO.

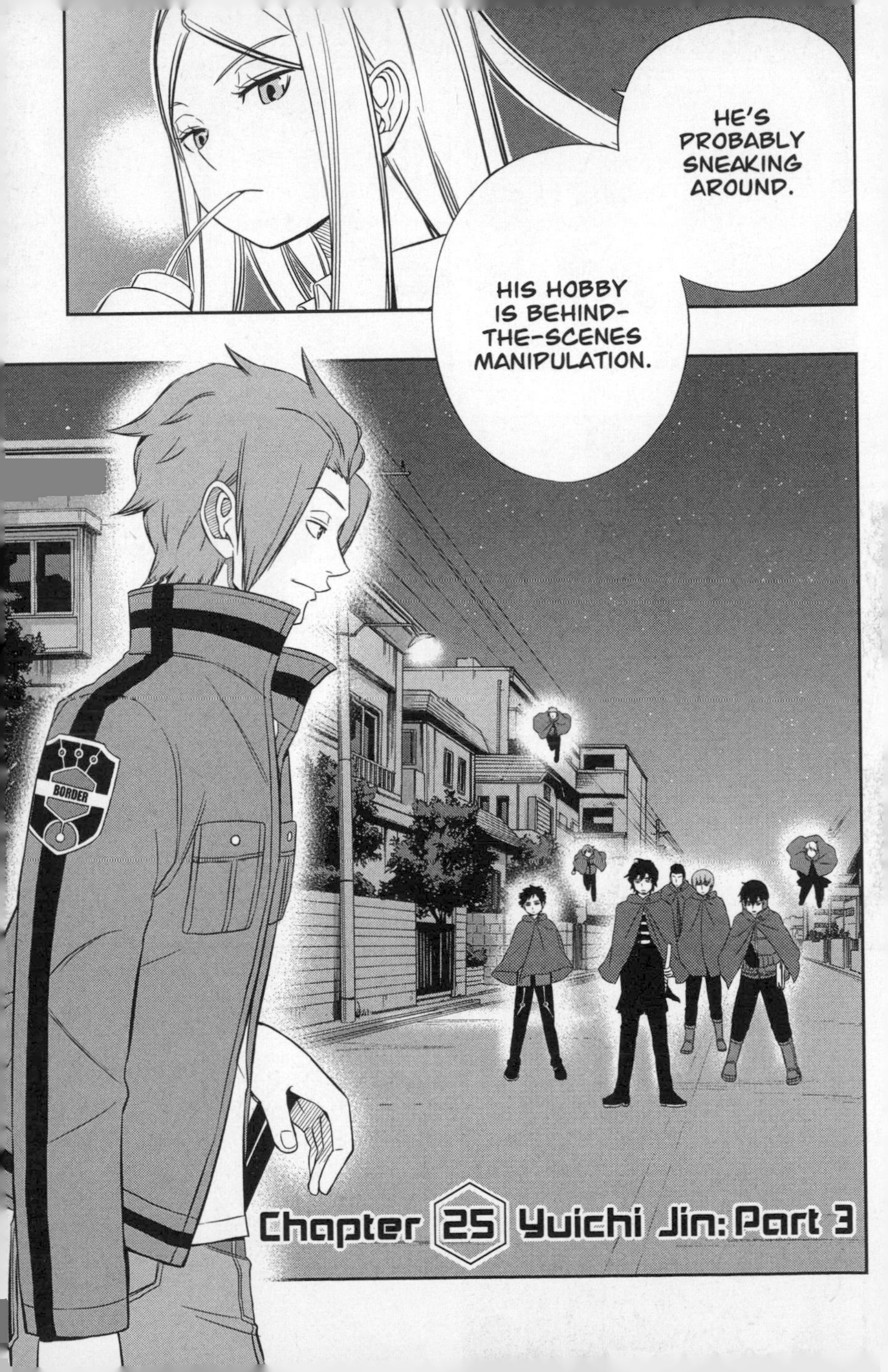
HE'S PROBABLY SNEAKING AROUND.
HIS HOBBY IS BEHIND-THE-SCENES MANIPULATION.
BORDER
Chapter 25 Yuichi Jin: Part 3

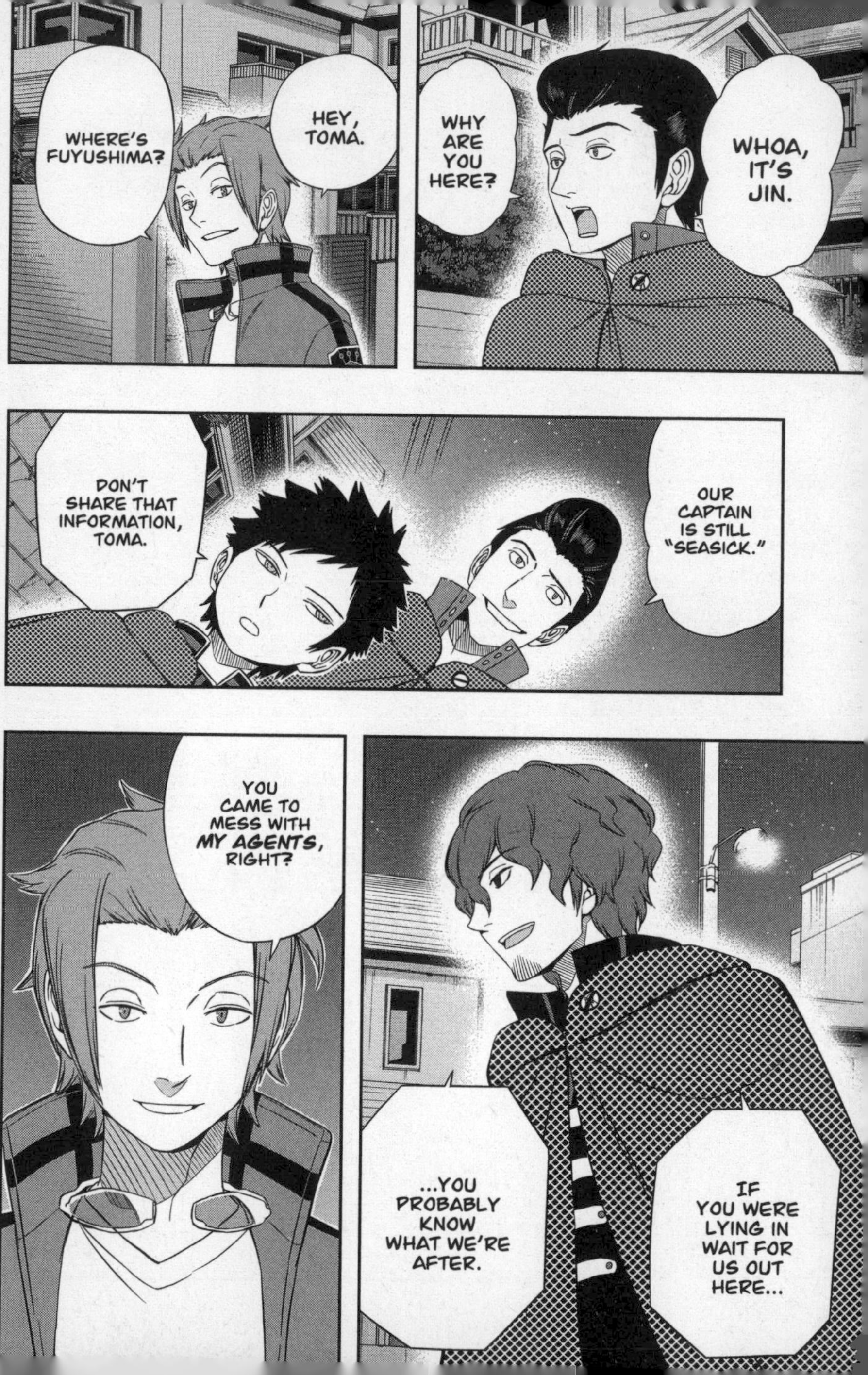
WHOA, IT'S JIN.
WHY ARE YOU HERE?
HEY, TOMA.
WHERE'S FUYUSHIMA?
OUR CAPTAIN IS STILL "SEASICK."
DON'T SHARE THAT INFORMATION, TOMA.
IF YOU WERE LYING IN WAIT FOR US OUT HERE...
...YOU PROBABLY KNOW WHAT WE'RE AFTER.
YOU CAME TO MESS WITH *MY AGENTS*, RIGHT?

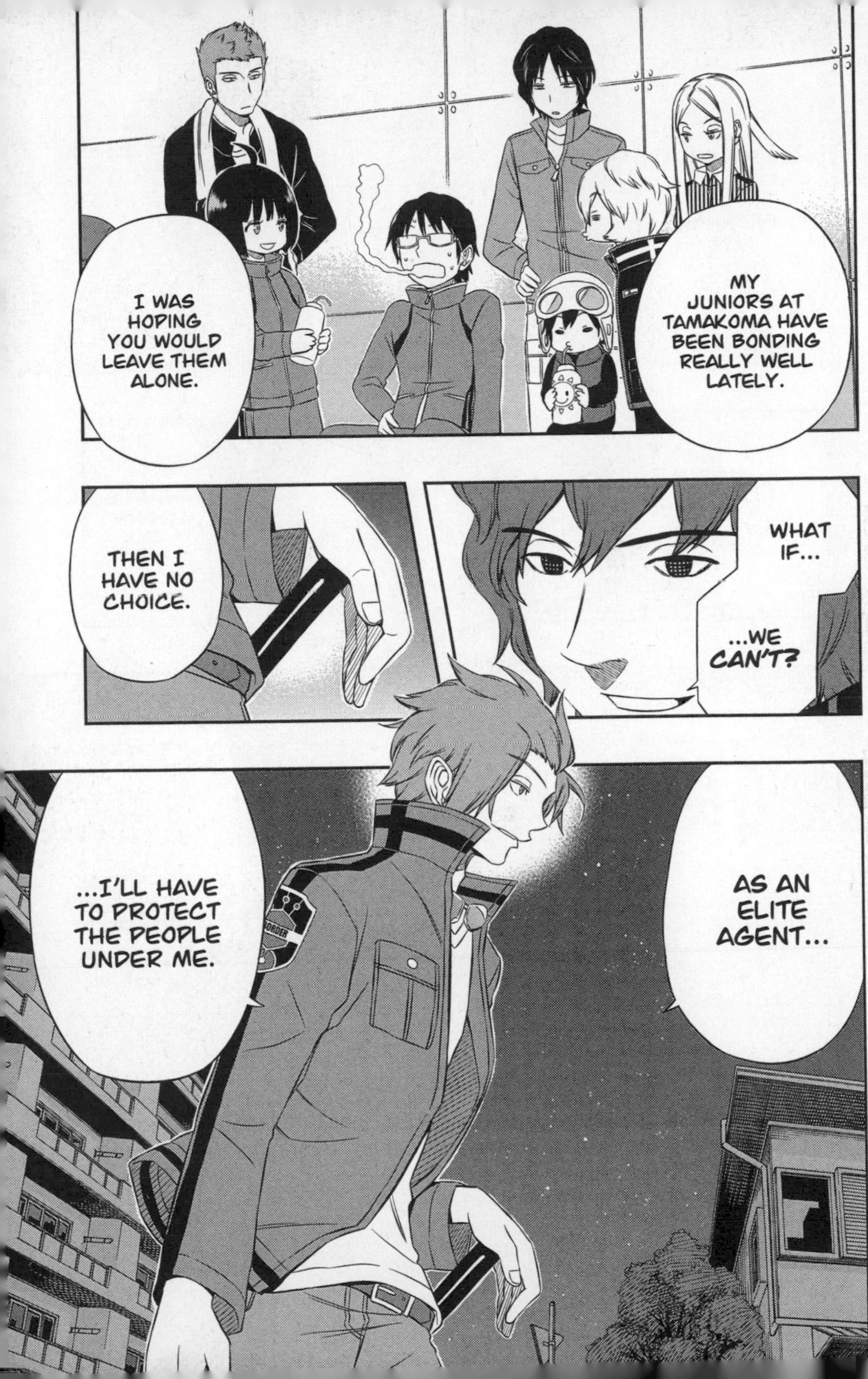
MY JUNIORS AT TAMAKOMA HAVE BEEN BONDING REALLY WELL LATELY.
I WAS HOPING YOU WOULD LEAVE THEM ALONE.
WHAT IF...
...WE CAN'T?
THEN I HAVE NO CHOICE.
AS AN ELITE AGENT...
...I'LL HAVE TO PROTECT THE PEOPLE UNDER ME.

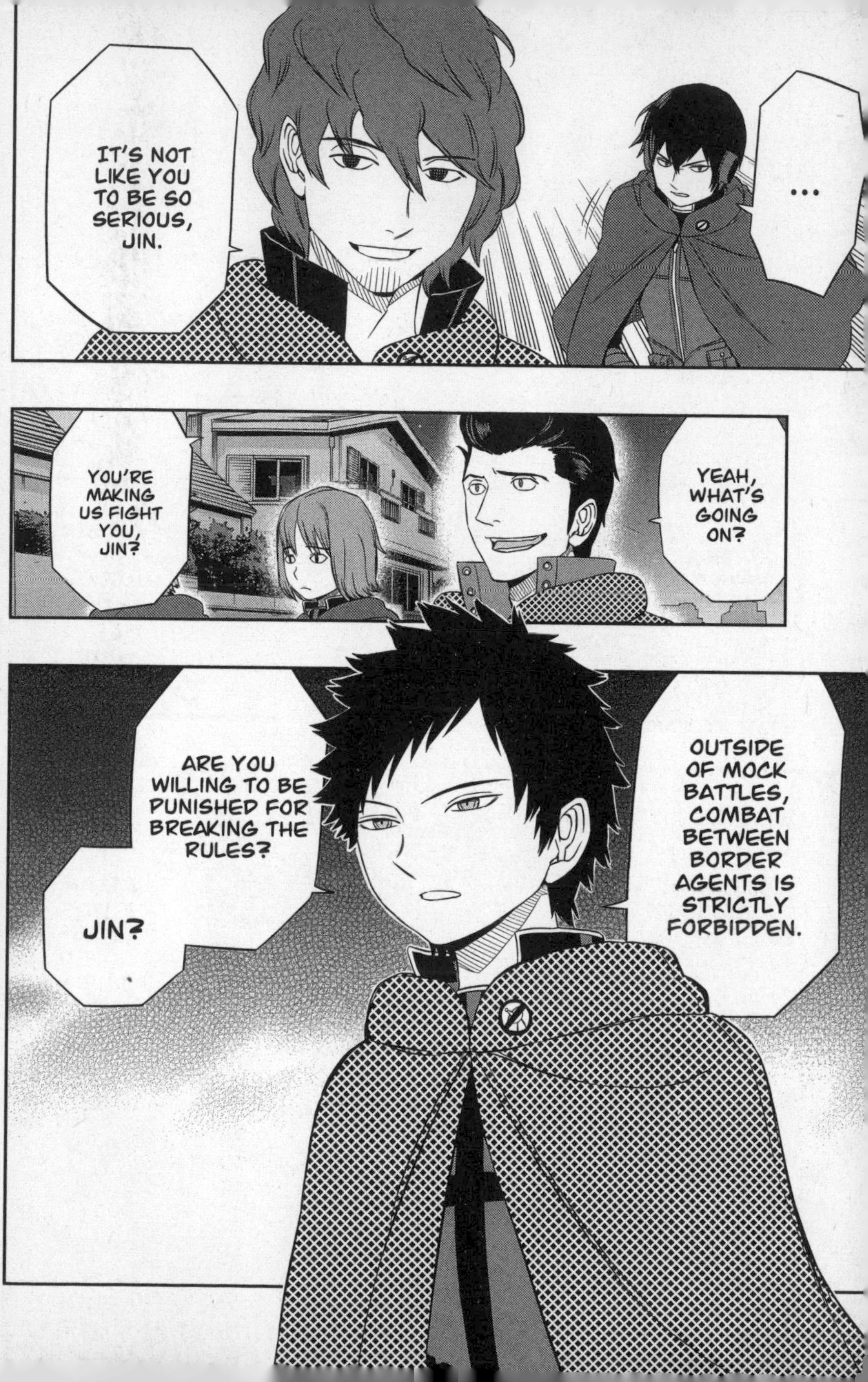
...
IT'S NOT LIKE YOU TO BE SO SERIOUS, JIN.
YEAH, WHAT'S GOING ON?
YOU'RE MAKING US FIGHT YOU, JIN?
OUTSIDE OF MOCK BATTLES, COMBAT BETWEEN BORDER AGENTS IS STRICTLY FORBIDDEN.
ARE YOU WILLING TO BE PUNISHED FOR BREAKING THE RULES?
JIN?

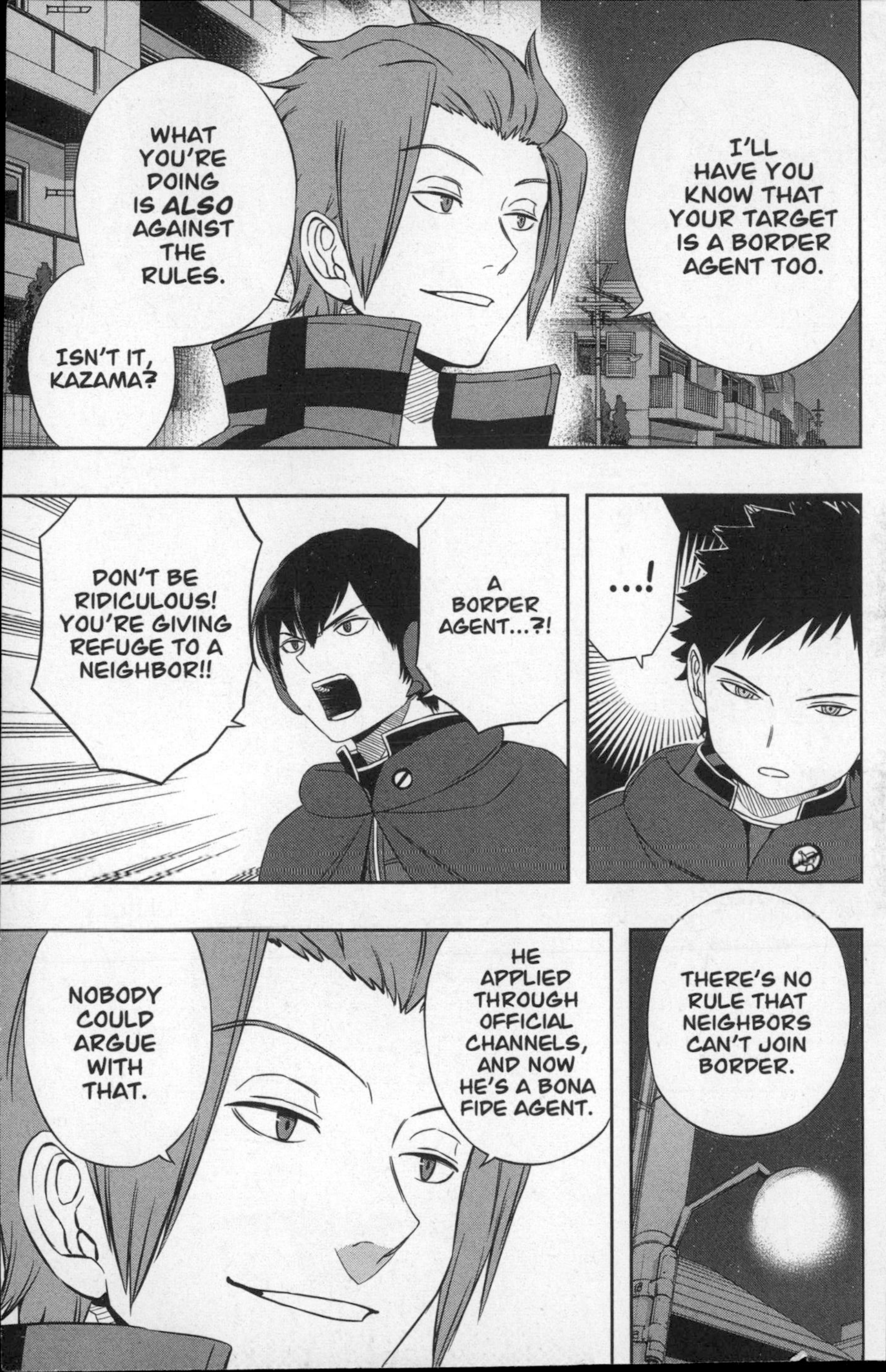
I'LL HAVE YOU KNOW THAT YOUR TARGET IS A BORDER AGENT TOO.
WHAT YOU'RE DOING IS ALSO AGAINST THE RULES.
ISN'T IT, KAZAMA?
...!
A BORDER AGENT...?!
DON'T BE RIDICULOUS! YOU'RE GIVING REFUGE TO A NEIGHBOR!!
THERE'S NO RULE THAT NEIGHBORS CAN'T JOIN BORDER.
HE APPLIED THROUGH OFFICIAL CHANNELS, AND NOW HE'S A BONA FIDE AGENT.
NOBODY COULD ARGUE WITH THAT.

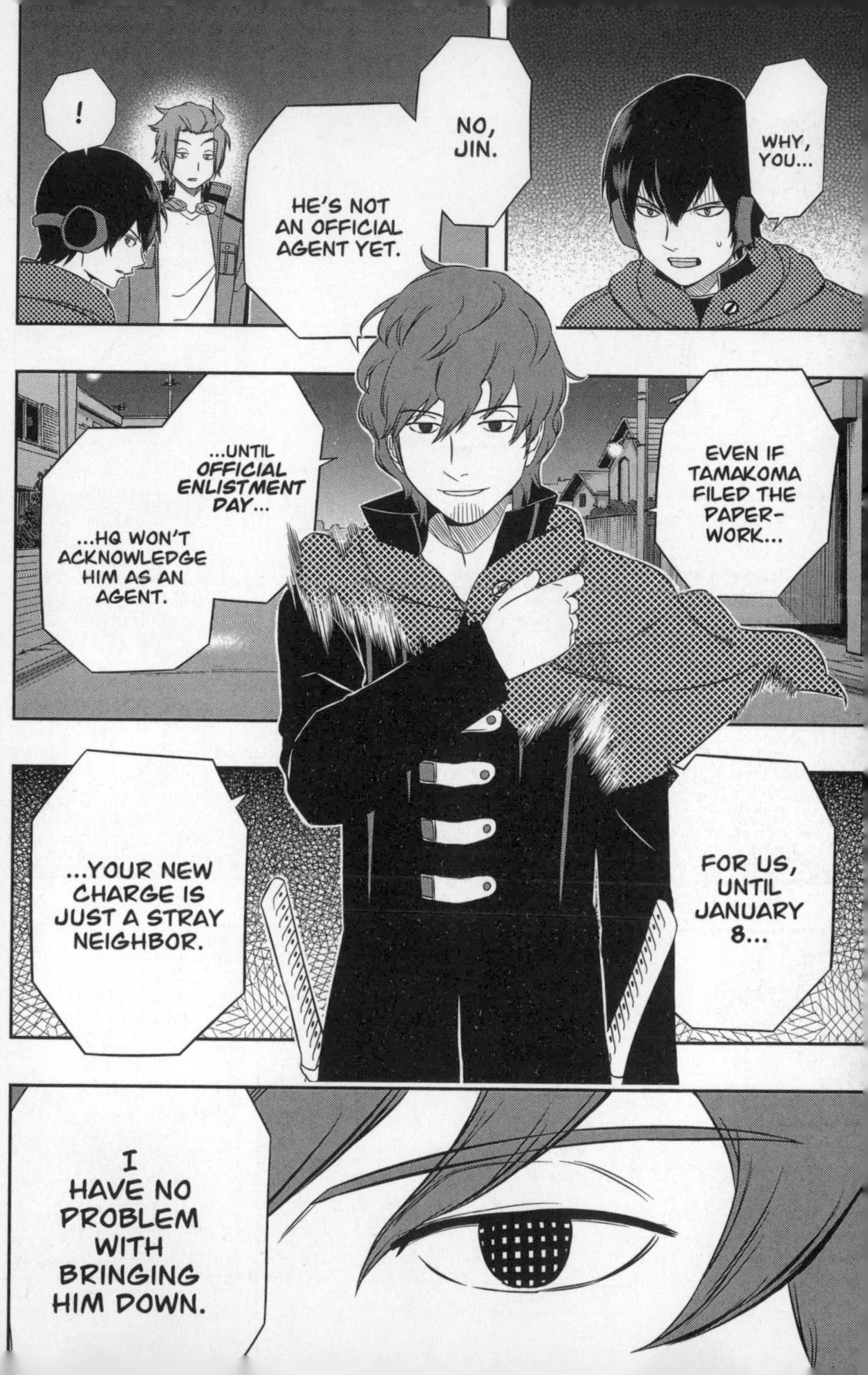
WHY, YOU...
NO, JIN.
!
HE'S NOT AN OFFICIAL AGENT YET.
EVEN IF TAMAKOMA FILED THE PAPER-WORK...
...UNTIL OFFICIAL ENLISTMENT DAY...
...HQ WON'T ACKNOWLEDGE HIM AS AN AGENT.
FOR US, UNTIL JANUARY 8...
...YOUR NEW CHARGE IS JUST A STRAY NEIGHBOR.
I HAVE NO PROBLEM WITH BRINGING HIM DOWN.

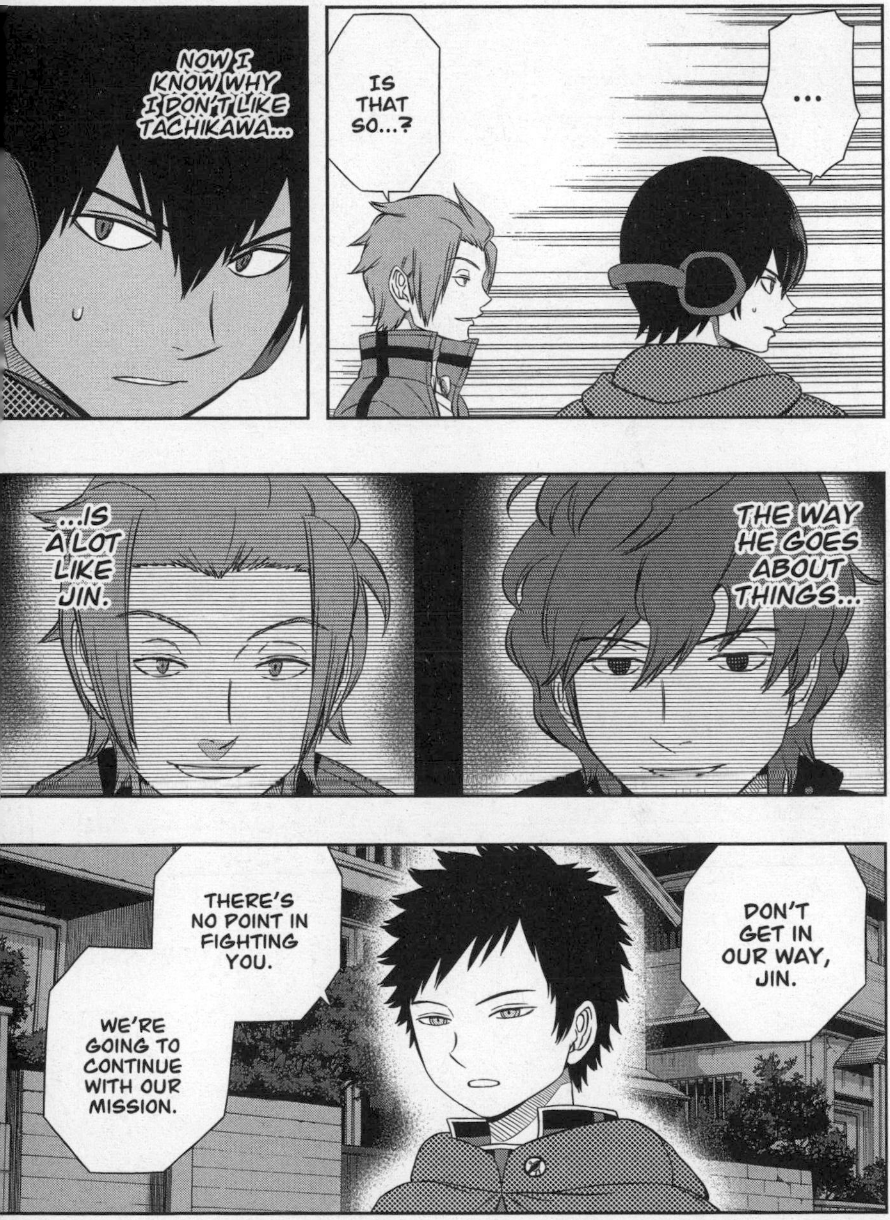
...
IS THAT SO...?
NOW I KNOW WHY I DON'T LIKE TACHIKAWA...
THE WAY HE GOES ABOUT THINGS...
...IS A LOT LIKE JIN.
DON'T GET IN OUR WAY, JIN.
THERE'S NO POINT IN FIGHTING YOU.
WE'RE GOING TO CONTINUE WITH OUR MISSION.

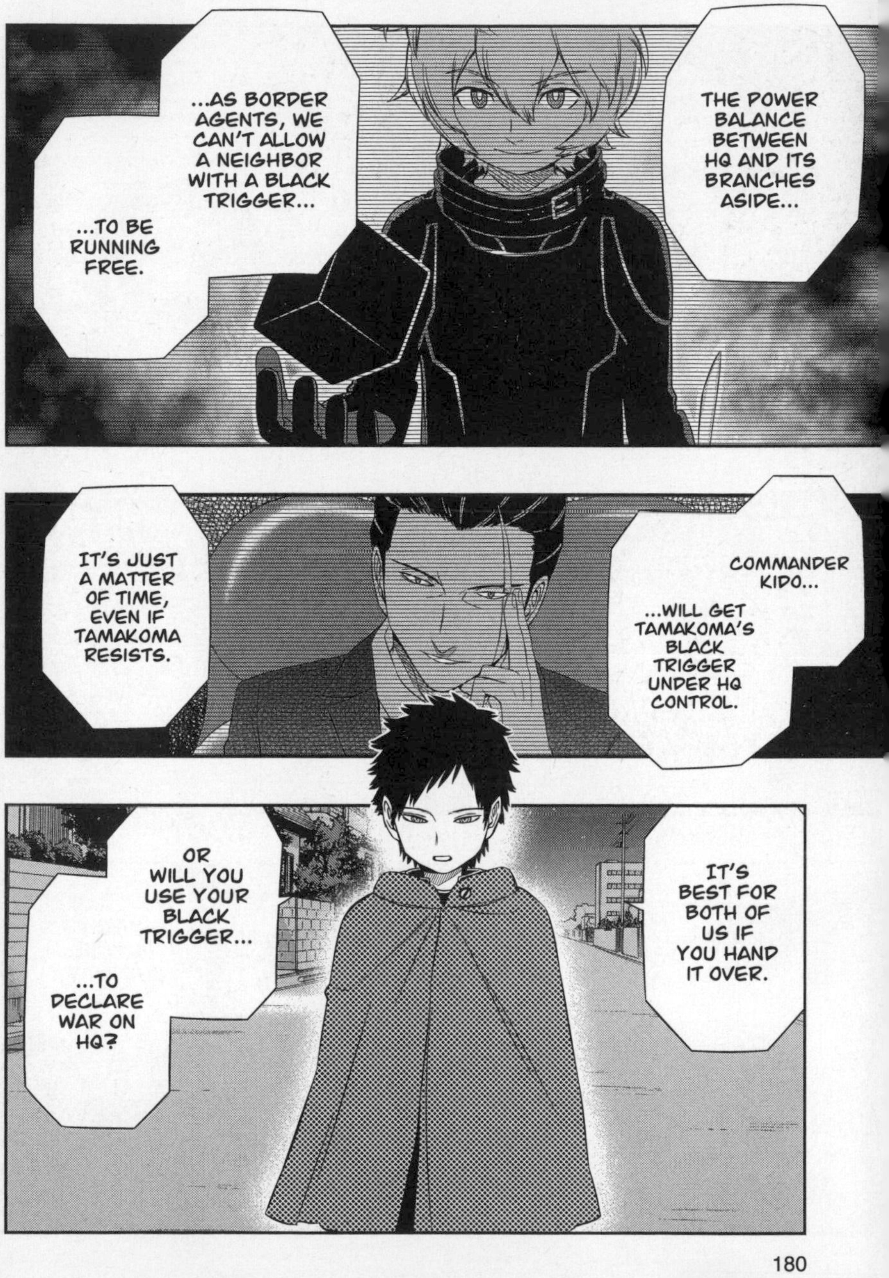
THE POWER BALANCE BETWEEN HQ AND ITS BRANCHES ASIDE...
...AS BORDER AGENTS, WE CAN'T ALLOW A NEIGHBOR WITH A BLACK TRIGGER...
...TO BE RUNNING FREE.
COMMANDER KIDO...
...WILL GET TAMAKOMA'S BLACK TRIGGER UNDER HQ CONTROL.
IT'S JUST A MATTER OF TIME, EVEN IF TAMAKOMA RESISTS.
IT'S BEST FOR BOTH OF US IF YOU HAND IT OVER.
OR WILL YOU USE YOUR BLACK TRIGGER...
...TO DECLARE WAR ON HQ?

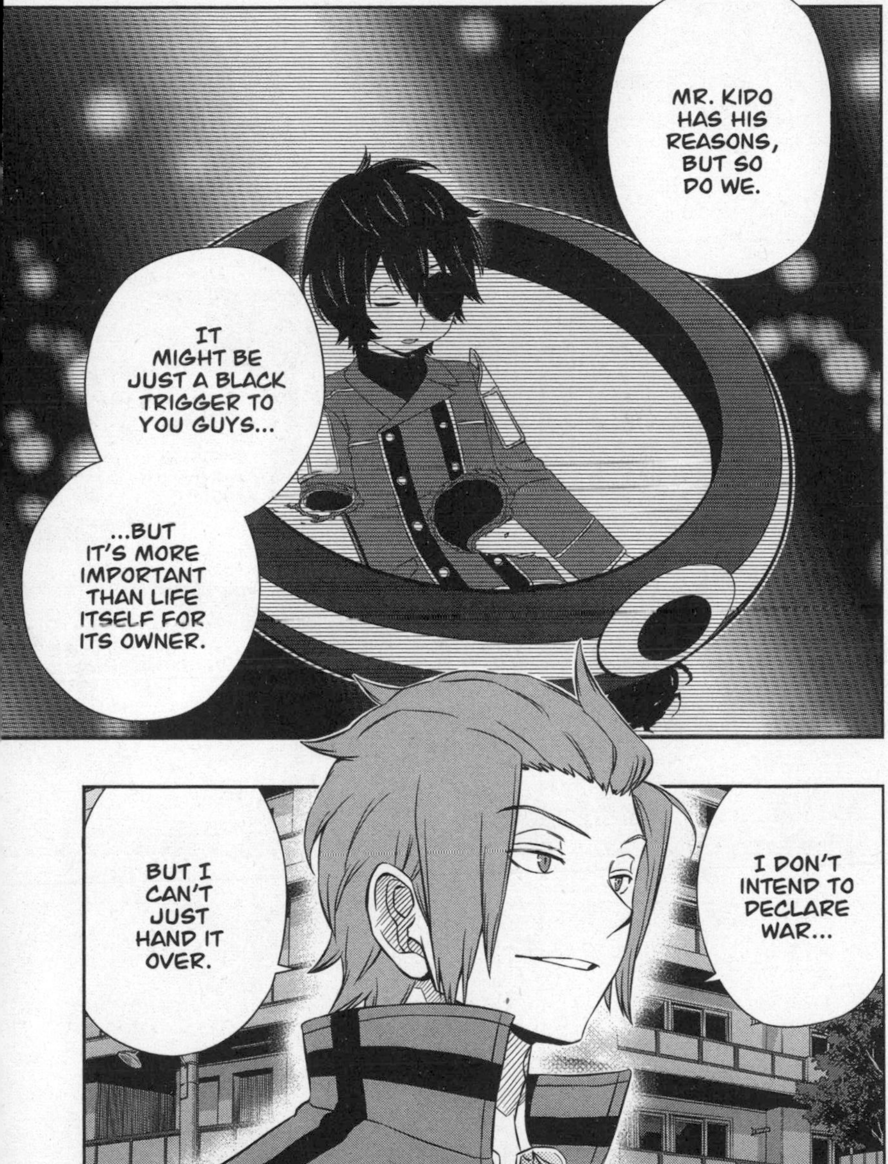
MR. KIDO HAS HIS REASONS, BUT SO DO WE.
IT MIGHT BE JUST A BLACK TRIGGER TO YOU GUYS...
...BUT IT'S MORE IMPORTANT THAN LIFE ITSELF FOR ITS OWNER.
I DON'T INTEND TO DECLARE WAR...
BUT I CAN'T JUST HAND IT OVER.

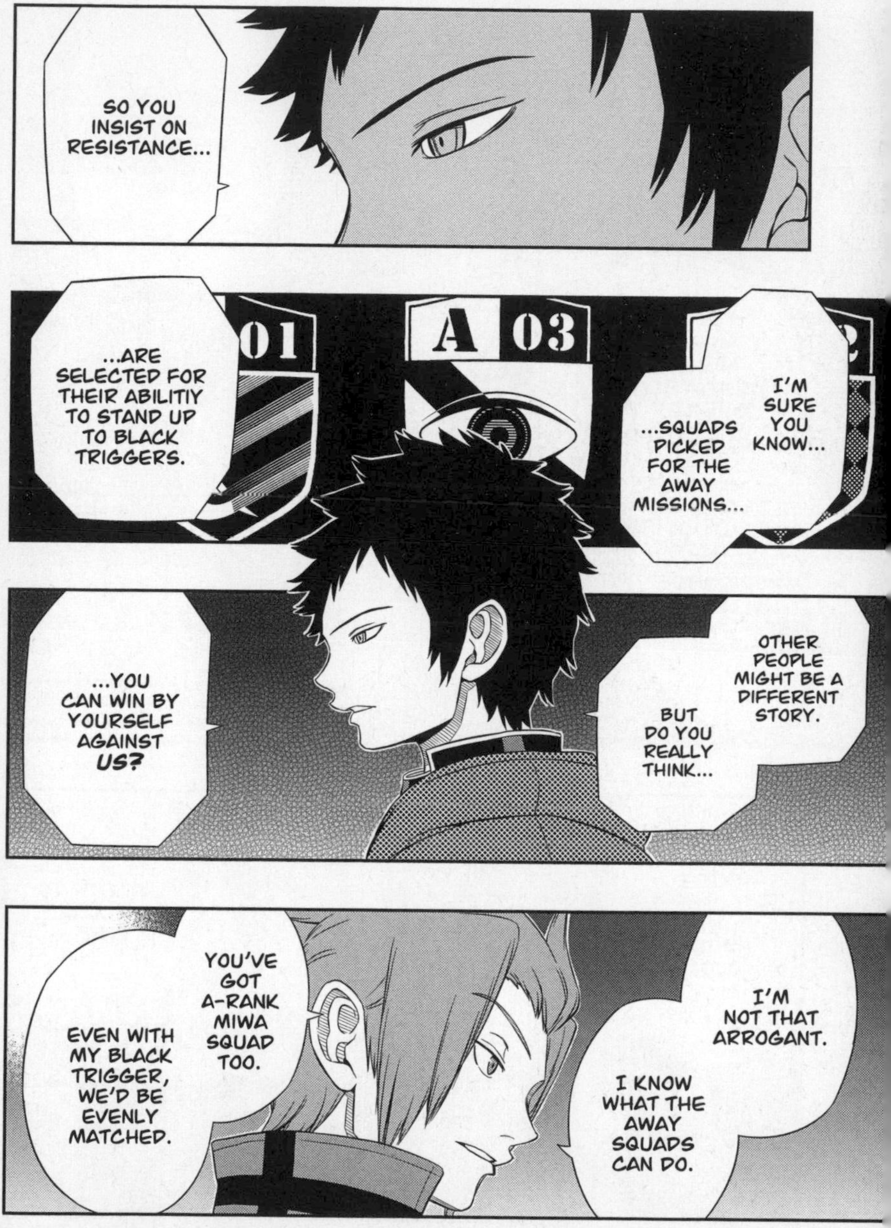
SO YOU INSIST ON RESISTANCE...
A 03
01
I'M SURE YOU KNOW...
...SQUADS PICKED FOR THE AWAY MISSIONS...
...ARE SELECTED FOR THEIR ABILITIY TO STAND UP TO BLACK TRIGGERS.
OTHER PEOPLE MIGHT BE A DIFFERENT STORY.
BUT DO YOU REALLY THINK...
...YOU CAN WIN BY YOURSELF AGAINST *US?*
I'M NOT THAT ARROGANT.
I KNOW WHAT THE AWAY SQUADS CAN DO.
YOU'VE GOT A-RANK MIWA SQUAD TOO.
EVEN WITH MY BLACK TRIGGER, WE'D BE EVENLY MATCHED.

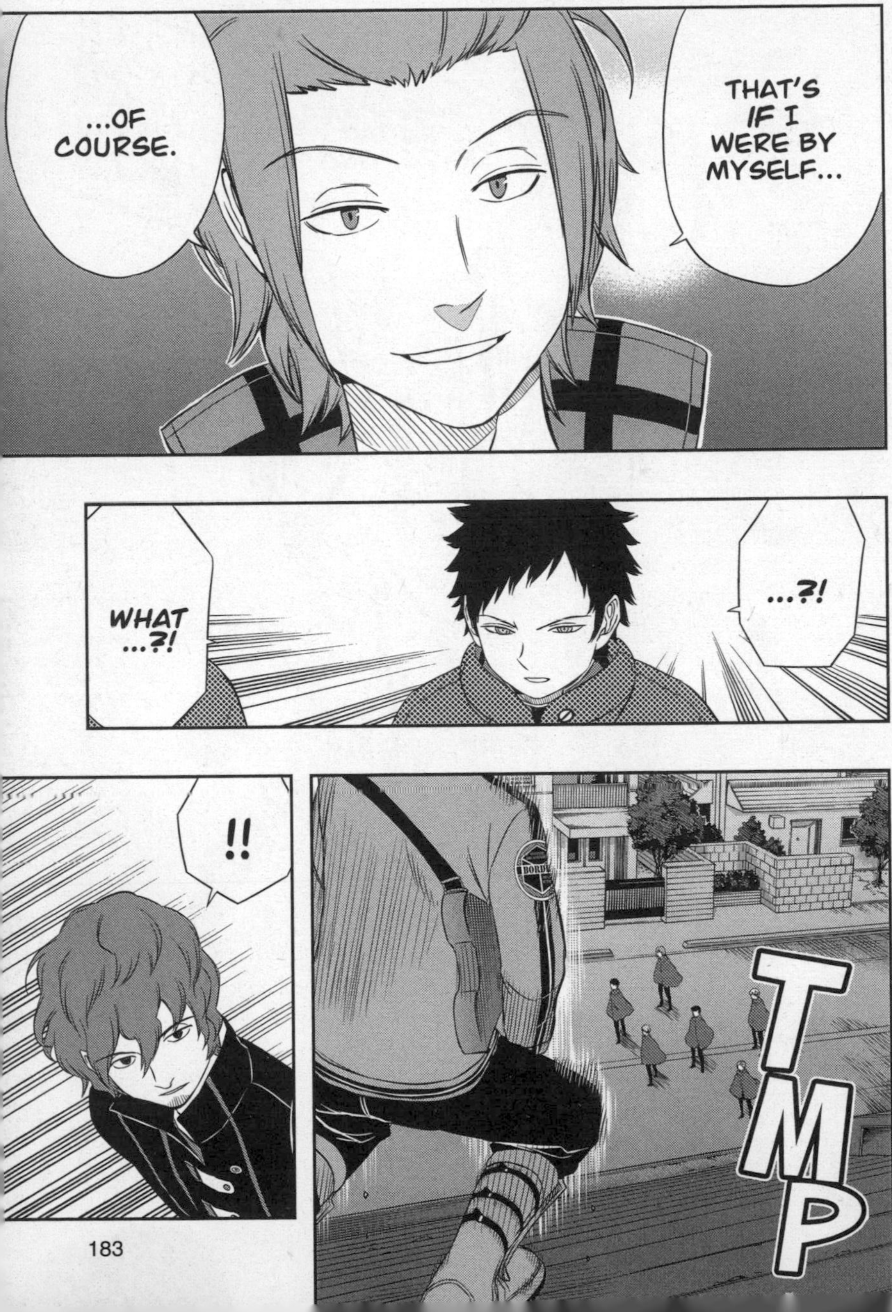
THAT'S IF I WERE BY MYSELF...
...OF COURSE.
...?!
WHAT ...?!
TMP
!!

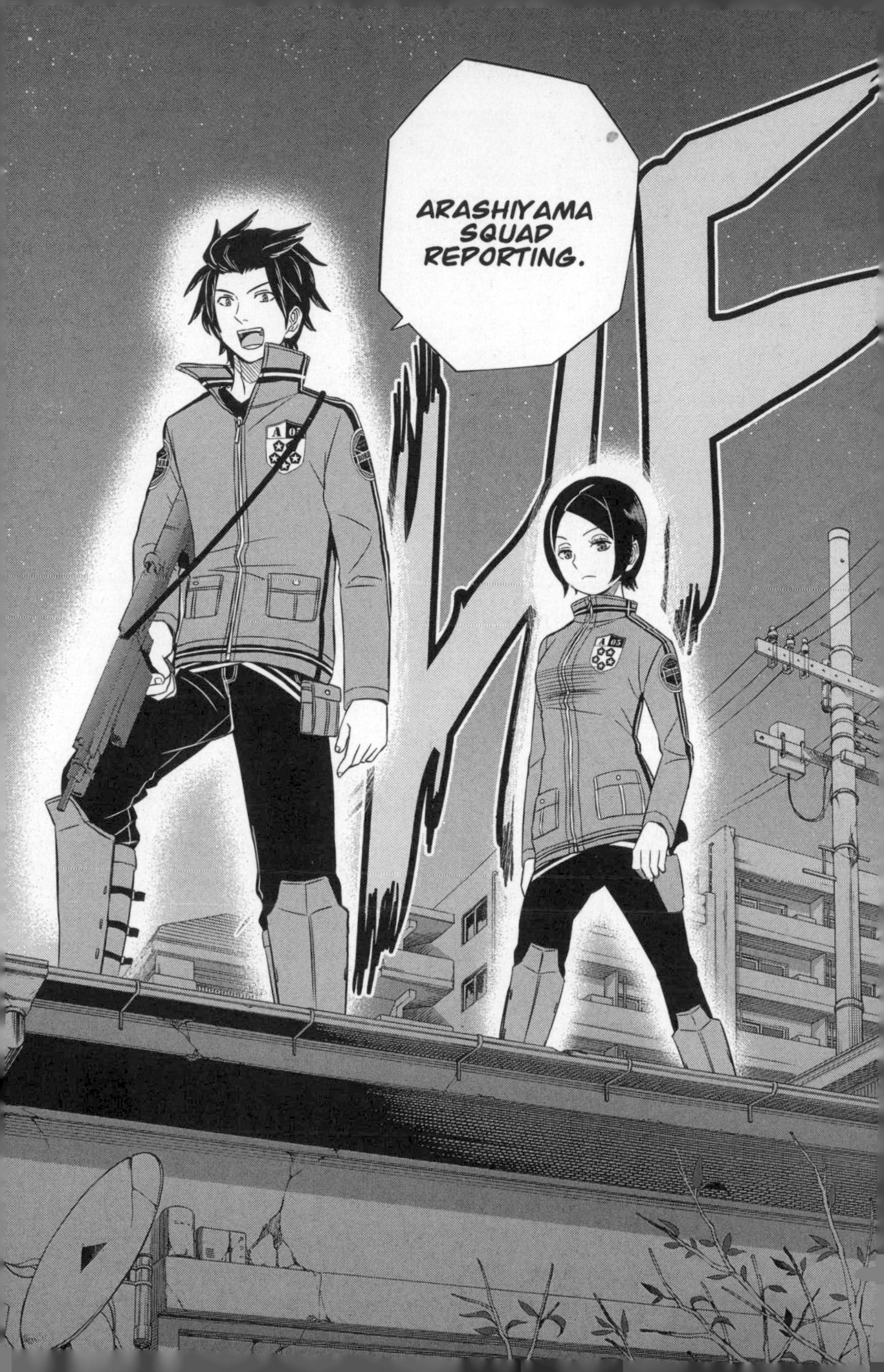
ARASHIYAMA SQUAD REPORTING.

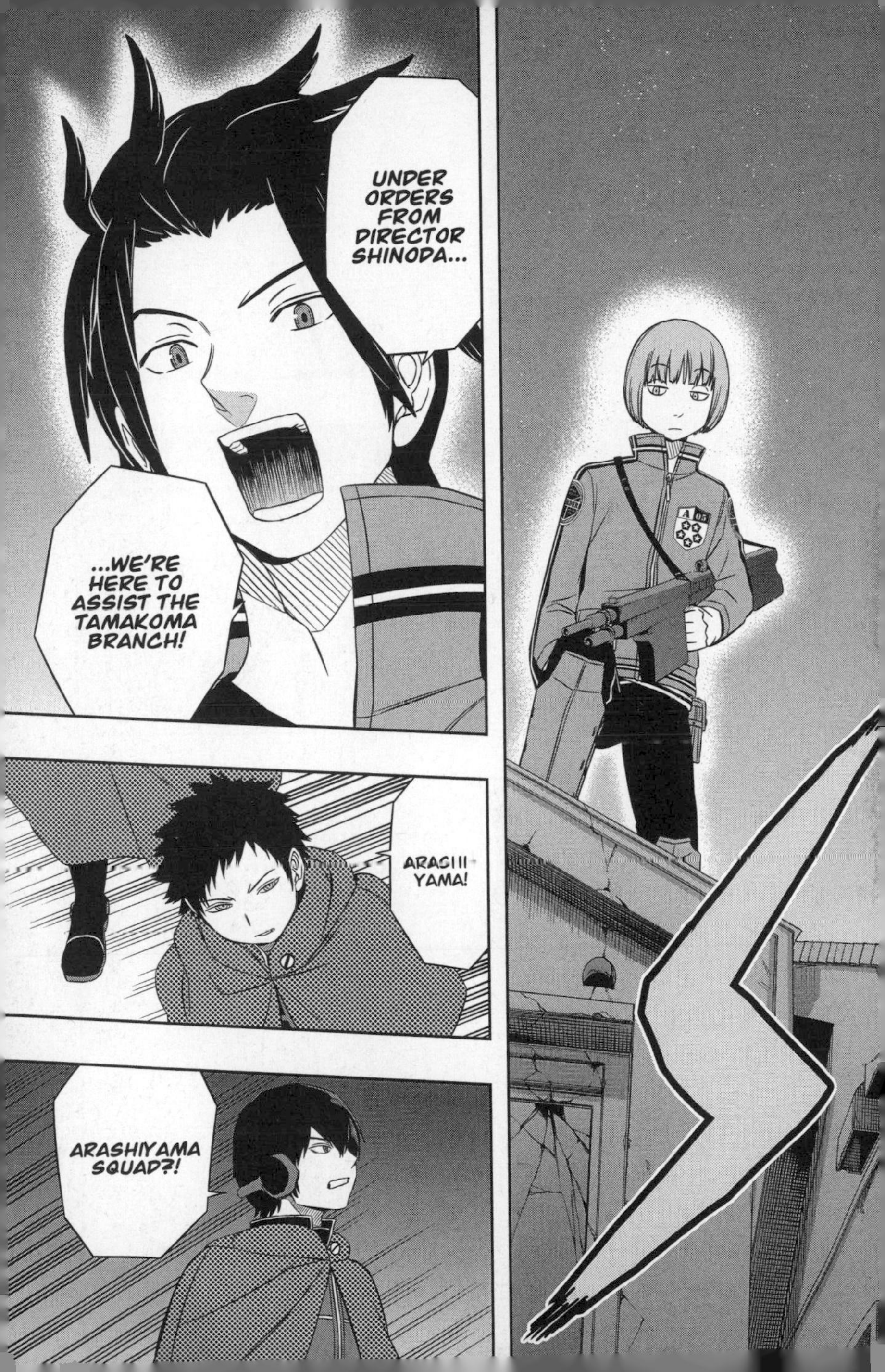
UNDER ORDERS FROM DIRECTOR SHINODA...
...WE'RE HERE TO ASSIST THE TAMAKOMA BRANCH!
ARASHI-YAMA!
ARASHIYAMA SQUAD?!

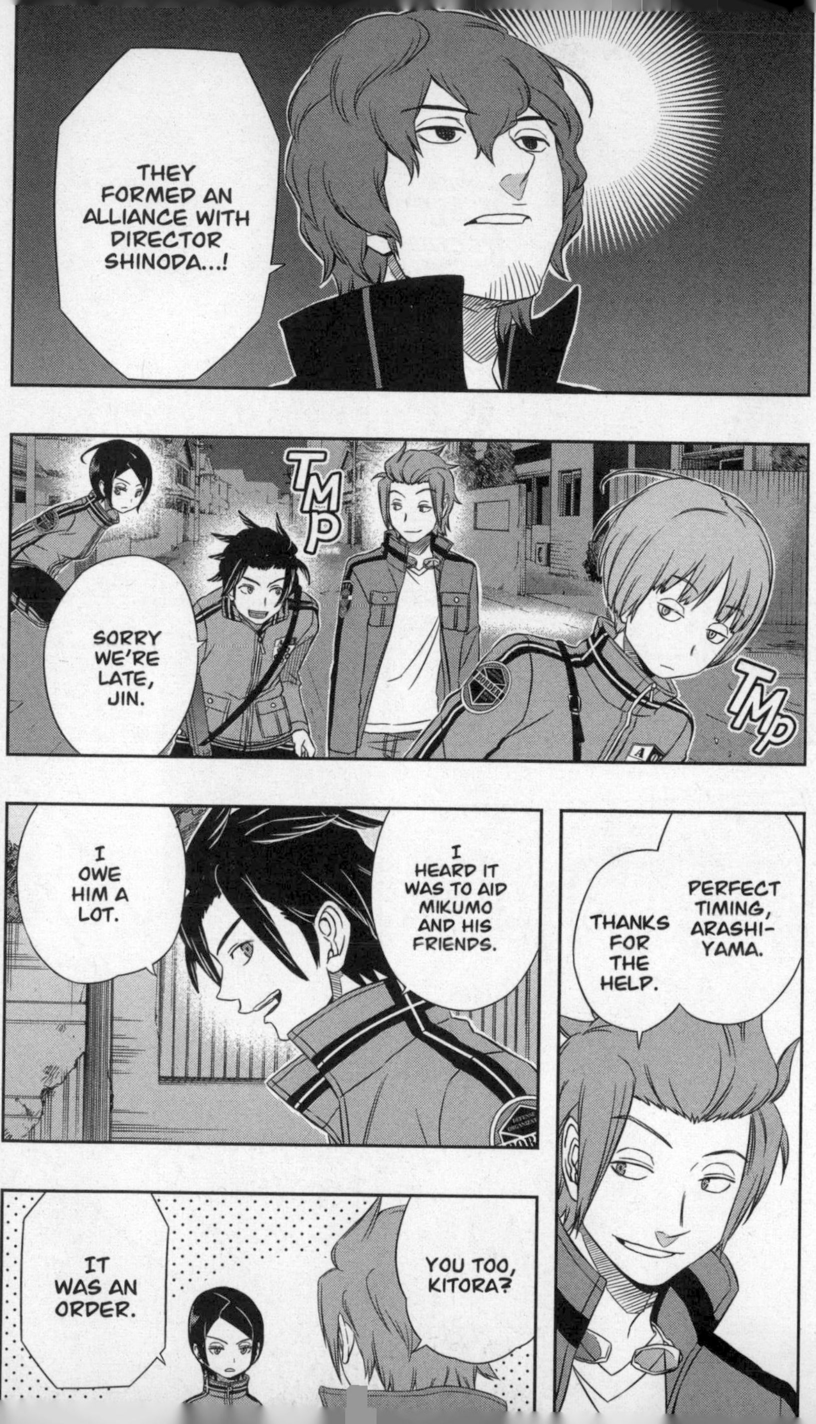
THEY FORMED AN ALLIANCE WITH DIRECTOR SHINODA...!
TMP
TMP
SORRY WE'RE LATE, JIN.
PERFECT TIMING, ARASHI-YAMA.
THANKS FOR THE HELP.
I HEARD IT WAS TO AID MIKUMO AND HIS FRIENDS.
I OWE HIM A LOT.
YOU TOO, KITORA?
IT WAS AN ORDER.

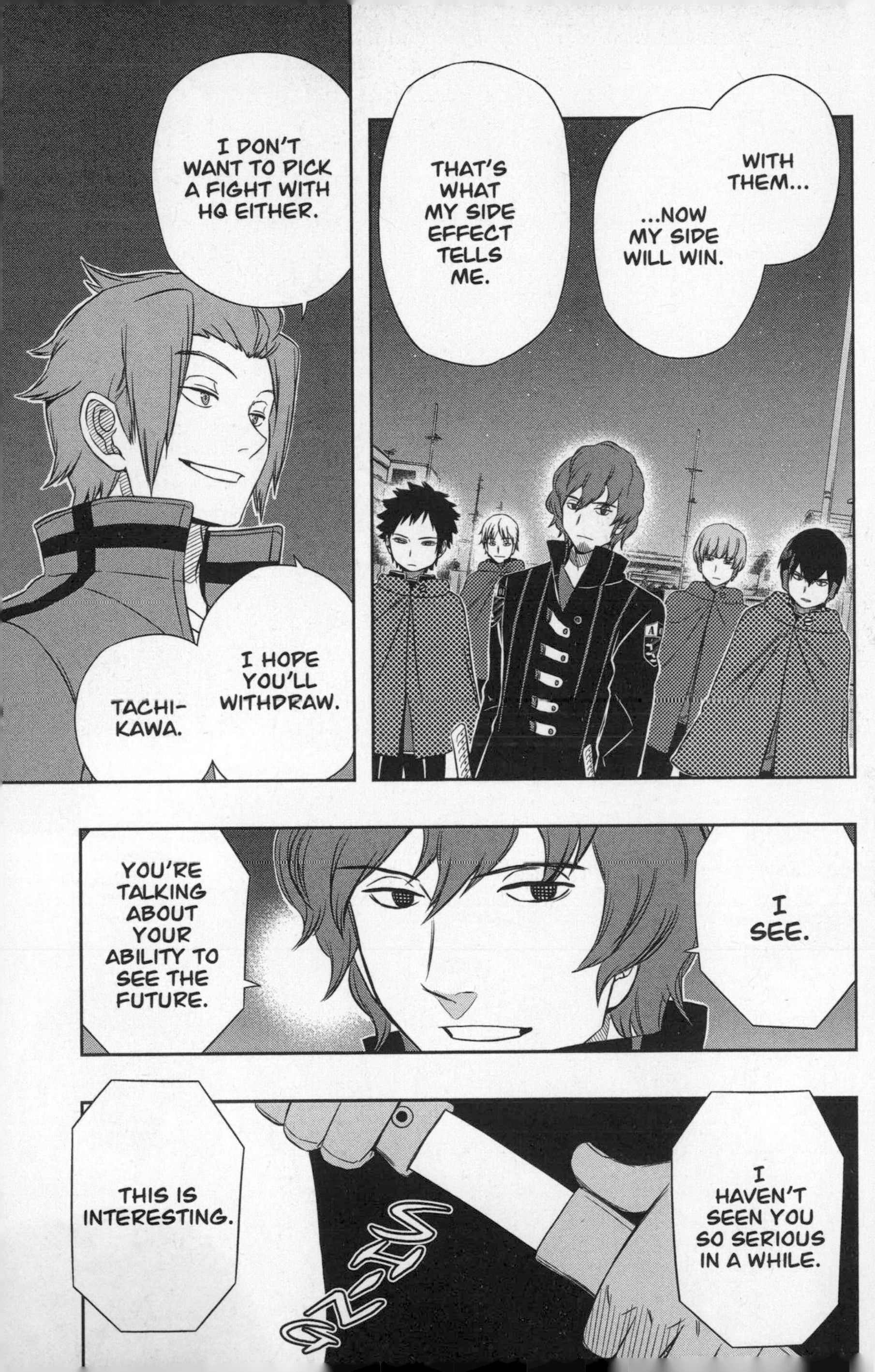
WITH THEM...
...NOW MY SIDE WILL WIN.
THAT'S WHAT MY SIDE EFFECT TELLS ME.
I DON'T WANT TO PICK A FIGHT WITH HQ EITHER.
I HOPE YOU'LL WITHDRAW.
TACHI-KAWA.
I SEE.
YOU'RE TALKING ABOUT YOUR ABILITY TO SEE THE FUTURE.
I HAVEN'T SEEN YOU SO SERIOUS IN A WHILE.
SHING
THIS IS INTERESTING.

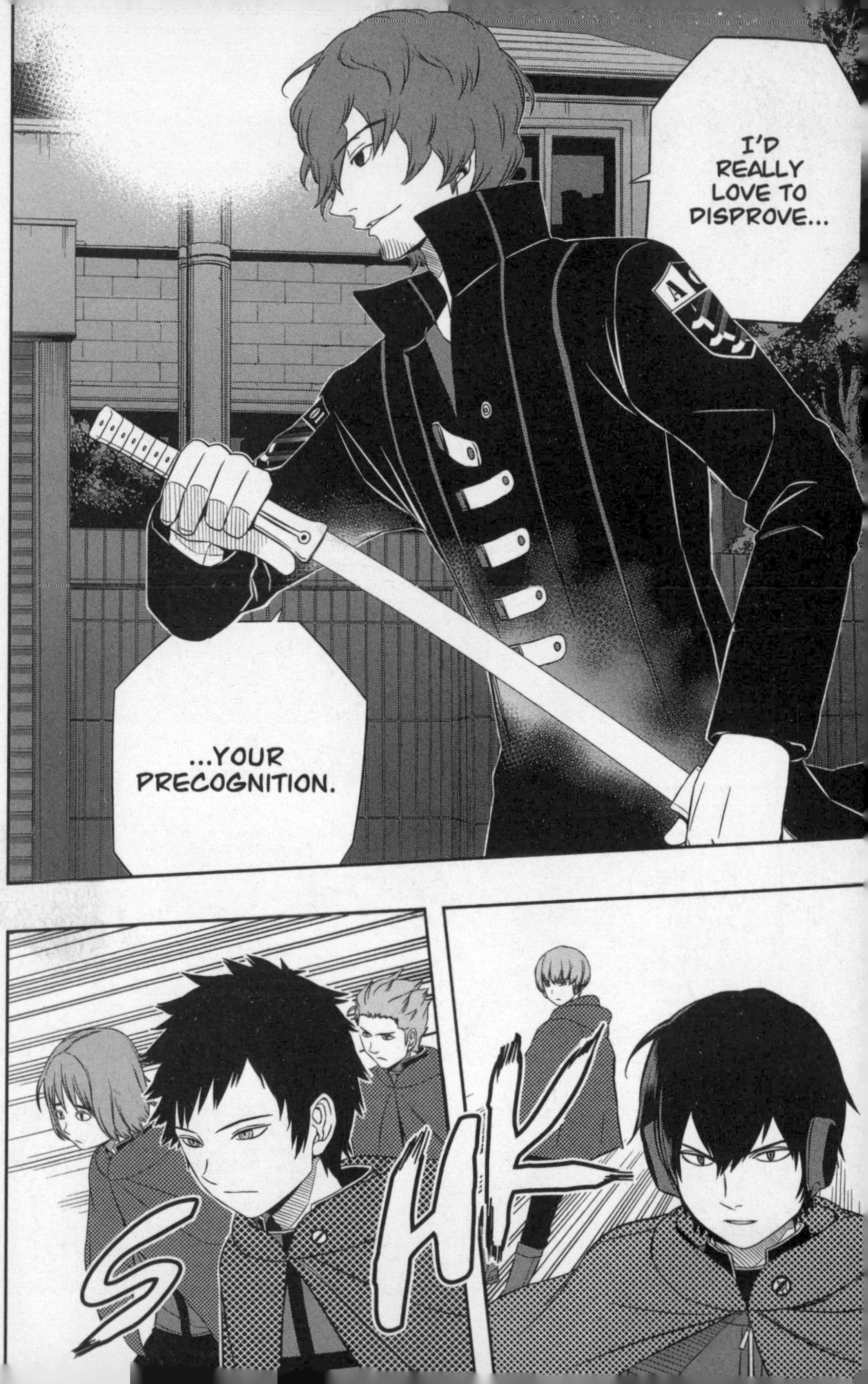
I'D REALLY LOVE TO DISPROVE...
...YOUR PRECOGNITION.
SHK

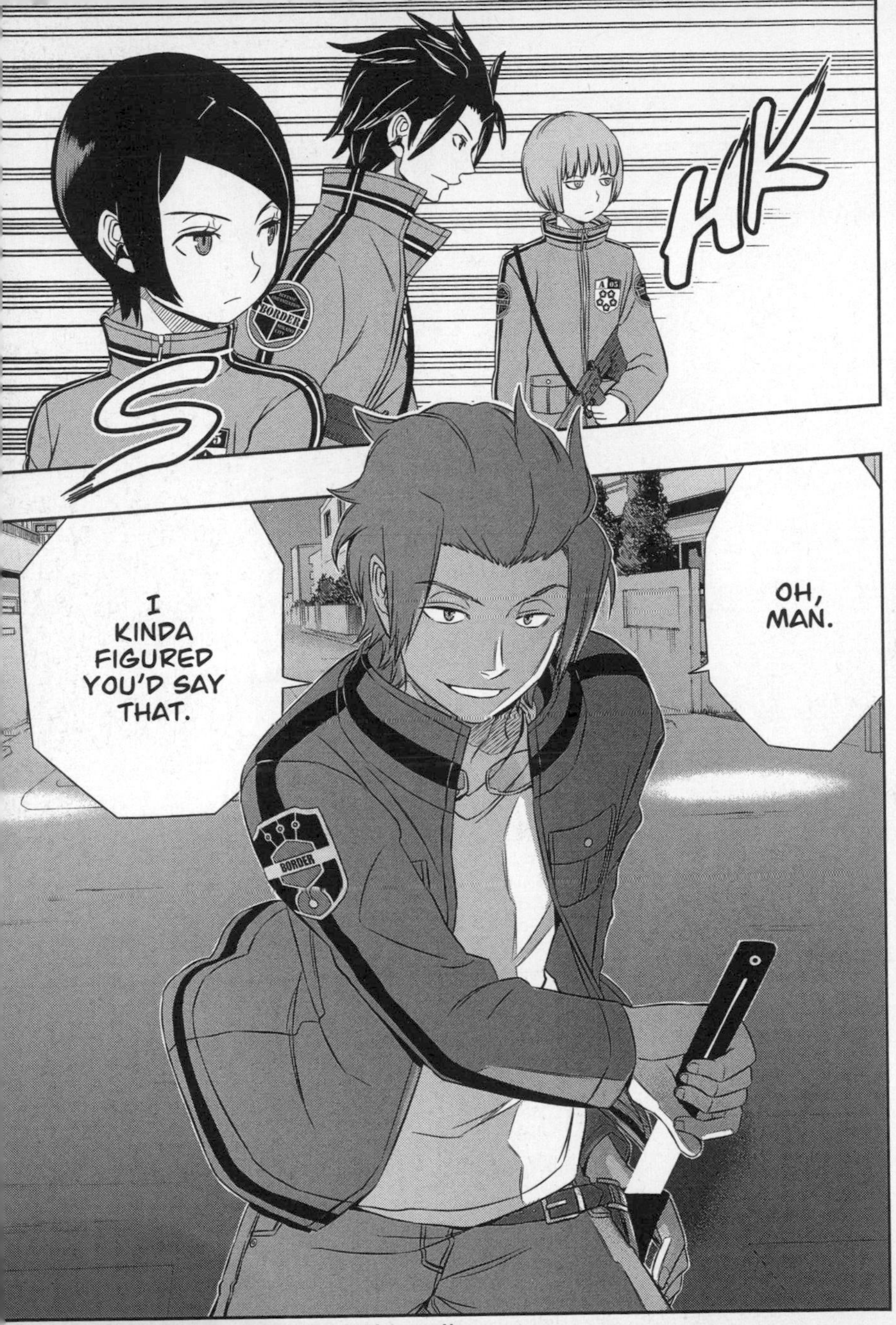
HK
S
OH, MAN.
I KINDA FIGURED YOU'D SAY THAT.

To Be Continued In **World Trigger** 4!

WORLD TRIGGER

Bonus Character Pages

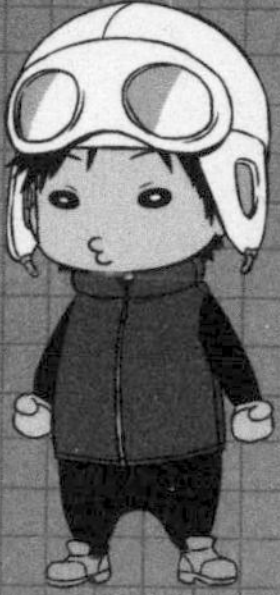

YOTARO

Capybara Cowboy

A Border lifer who sort of has respect for Jin and Reiji, but not Konami. Everyone else he considers beneath him. He has a Side Effect that lets him talk to animals, but it only allows them to understand each other, and the animals don't necessarily do what he says. He believes Raijin-maru is a dog.

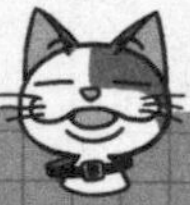

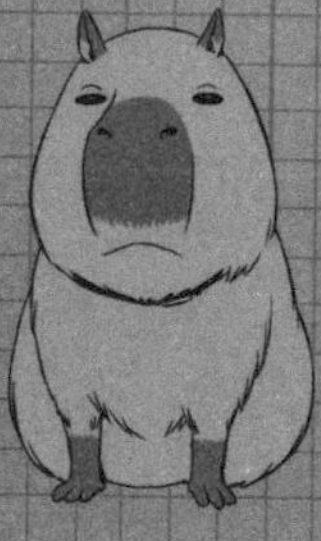

RAIJIN-MARU

Tamakoma's Dark Beast

One of the Three Mascots of World Trigger, along with Replica and Mr. Kinuta. He's Yotaro's companion but has no respect for him. The name Raijin-maru comes from Yotaro's favorite TV hero's dog.

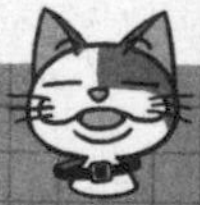

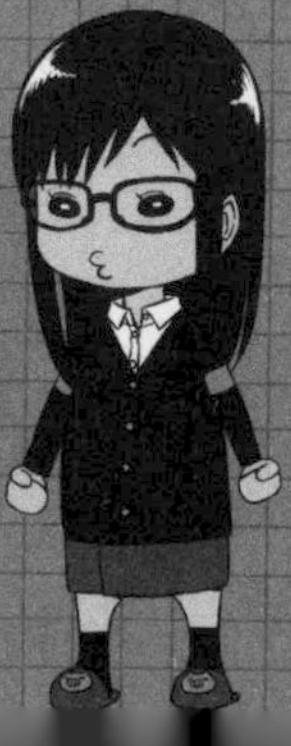

SHIORI

Glasses for All

Honorary president of the Border Glasses Association. Nice to everyone on principle, but secretly even nicer to people with glasses. Along with Kitora, she's the female character I have the most fun drawing. It's said her family runs a bookstore, and she has a little sister who's good at cooking.

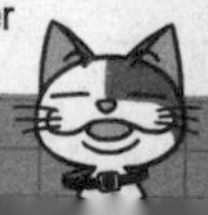

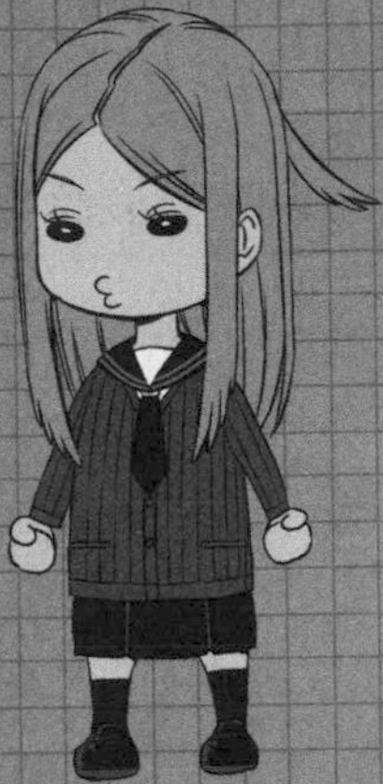

KONAMI

So Cute Yet So Gullible

Her tenure is second only to Director Rindo's. She believes anything she's told, so everyone toys with her. The better friends she is with someone, the more willing she is to believe them. She believes in ghosts, E.S.P., aliens, and even Torimaru when he says Raijin-maru is a dog. But she's very book smart. Not that it matters, but she's Arashiyama's cousin.

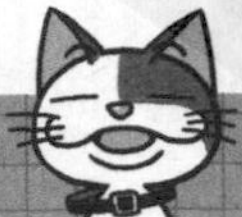

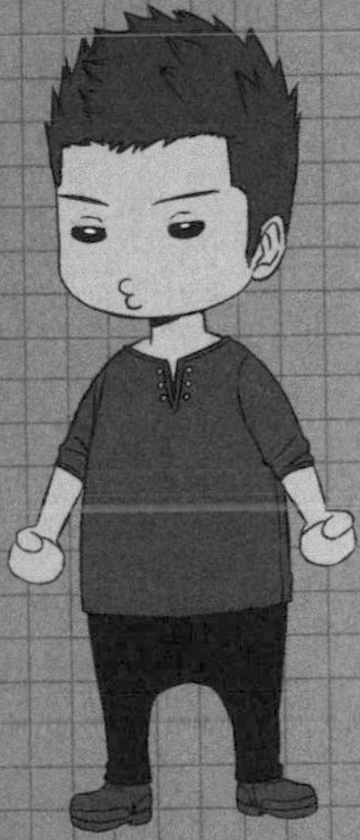

REIJI

The Almighty Beefcake

Skilled beefcake who's good at everything from sniping to making sandwiches. Believer in "muscles are for being used," and at odds with believers of "muscles are for showing off." He's all about muscles, but he doesn't look down upon the physically weak. Instead, he believes in using his physical strength to help those who are less muscularly endowed.

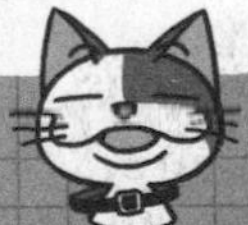

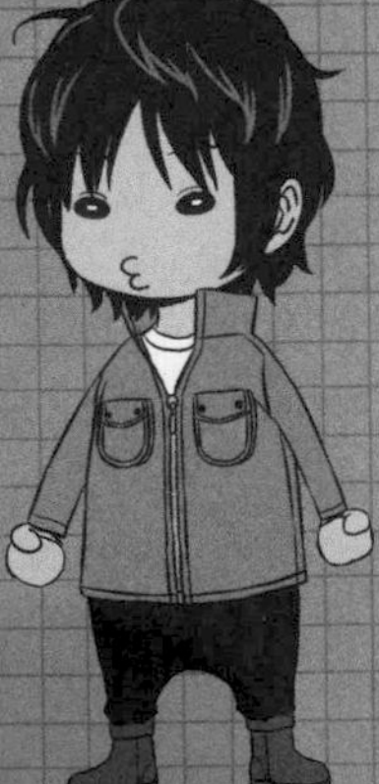

TORIMARU

Gets By on His Good Looks

One of the few characters officially recognized as good-looking within the story. He inherited his sullen look from his teacher Reiji, which makes him look even cooler. His family is poor, but I missed the timing to bring it up, so I may not be able to. The jacket he's wearing is a hand-me-down from Jin.

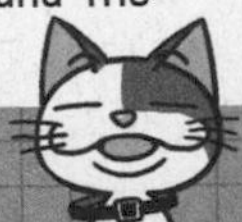

YOU'RE READING THE WRONG WAY!

World Trigger reads from right to left, starting in the upper-right corner. Japanese is read from right to left, meaning that action, sound effects, and word-balloon order are completely reversed from the English order.

142